Studio Visual Steps

iPhone® with iOS 8 for SENIORS

Get Started Quickly with the iPhone

This book has been written using the Visual Steps™ method.
Cover design by Studio Willemien Haagsma bNO

Author: Studio Visual Steps

Second printing: November 2014
ISBN 978 90 5905 380 9

Resources used: A number of definitions and explanations of computer terminology are taken over from the *iPhone User Guide.*

Do you have any questions or suggestions?
Email: info@visualsteps.com

Would you like more information?
www.visualsteps.com

Website for this book:
www.visualsteps.com/iphone8

Subscribe to the free Visual Steps Newsletter:
www.visualsteps.com/newsletter

Table of Contents

Foreword

The iPhone from Apple is a type of smartphone that not only functions as a regular cellular telephone but also includes many other advanced multimedia features. It is extolled and adored by an ever increasing number of people.

In this comprehensive book you will get acquainted with the core features of the iPhone as well as many of the additional options that are available. You work in your own tempo, step by step through each task. The clear and concise instructions and fullcolor screenshots will tell you exactly what to do. The extra tips, notes and help sections will help you even further to get the most out of your iPhone.

Along with making and receiving calls, the iPhone allows you to read your email, surf the Internet and even make video calls. There are also a number of built-in apps (programs) that will allow you to take pictures, shoot video, listen to music and even maintain a calendar. And if you're heading out the door and going to someplace new, you can use your iPhone to look up the directions on how to get there! That makes the iPhone a very handy device.

Once you have mastered the standard built-in apps, you can take a look at the *App Store* where many additional apps are available for free or for a small charge. There are apps for recipes, horoscopes, popular card games, photo editing and much more. No matter what you are interested in, there is bound to be an app for it. This book will help you learn how to find, download and install these apps.

On the website for this book **www.visualsteps.com/iphone8** you will find news and additional information as well as supplemental chapters. Be sure to check back often!

I hope you have a lot of fun getting to know your iPhone!

Studio Visual Steps

PS After you have worked through this book, you will know how to send an email. We welcome your comments and suggestions. Our email address is: info@visualsteps.com

Introduction to Visual Steps™

The Visual Steps handbooks and manuals are the best instructional materials available for learning how to work with the iPhone, iPad, computers and software applications. Nowhere else can you find better support for getting to know an iPhone, iPad, computer, the Internet, *Windows*, *Mac OS X* and other computer topics.

Properties of the Visual Steps books:

- **Comprehensible contents**
  Addresses the needs of the beginner or intermediate user for a manual written in simple, straight-forward English.
- **Clear structure**
  Precise, easy to follow instructions. The material is broken down into small enough segments to allow for easy absorption.
- **Screenshots of every step**
  Quickly compare what you see on your iPhone screen with the screenshots in the book. Pointers and tips guide you when new windows or alert boxes are opened so you always know what to do next.
- **Get started right away**
  All you have to do is have your iPhone and your book at hand. Sit some where's comfortable, begin reading and perform the operations as indicated on your own iPhone.
- **Layout**
  The text is printed in a large size font and is clearly legible.

In short, I believe these manuals will be excellent guides for you.

dr. H. van der Meij
Faculty of Applied Education, Department of Instruction Technology, University of Twente, the Netherlands

Newsletter

All Visual Steps books follow the same methodology: clear and concise step-by-step instructions with screenshots to demonstrate each task. A complete list of all our books can be found on our website **www.visualsteps.com**. You can also sign up to receive our **free Visual Steps Newsletter**.
In this Newsletter you will receive periodic information by email regarding:
- the latest titles and previously released books;
- special offers, supplemental chapters, tips and free informative booklets.
Our Newsletter subscribers may also download any of the documents listed on the web pages **www.visualsteps.com/info_downloads**

When you subscribe to our Newsletter you can be assured that we will never use your email address for any purpose other than sending you the information as previously described. We will not share this address with any third-party. Each Newsletter also contains a one-click link to unsubscribe.

What You Will Need

In order to work through this book, you will need to have a number of things:

An iPhone 6, 6 Plus, 5S, 5C, 5 or 4S with *iOS 8*.

A computer, laptop or notebook computer with the *iTunes* program installed. In *Bonus Chapter Download and Install iTunes* you can read how to install *iTunes*. In *Appendix B Opening Bonus Chapters* you can read how to open this bonus chapter.

If you do not own a computer, you may be able to perform certain exercises by using the computer of a friend or family member or just read through the section.

You will need a printer with the *Airprint* option for the exercises about printing. If you do not have a printer, you can skip the printing exercises.

How to Use This Book

This book has been written using the Visual Steps™ method. The method is simple: you put the book next to your iPhone and execute all the tasks step by step, directly on your iPhone. Because of the clear instructions and the multitude of screenshots, you will know exactly what to do. By executing all the tasks at once, you will learn how to use the iPhone in the quickest possible way.
In this Visual Steps™ book, you will see various icons. This is what they mean:

Techniques
These icons indicate an action to be carried out:

 The index finger indicates you need to do something on the iPhone's screen, for instance, tap something.

 The keyboard icon means you should type something using the onscreen keyboard of your iPhone or the one from your computer.

 The mouse icon means you should do something on your computer with the mouse.

 The hand icon means you should do something else, for example rotate the iPhone or turn it off. The hand can also be used for a series of operations which you have learned at an earlier stage.

Apart from these operations, in some parts of this book extra assistance is provided to help you successfully work through this book.

Help
These icons indicate that extra help is available:

 The arrow icon warns you about something.

 The bandage icon will help you if something has gone wrong.

 The hand icon is also used for the exercises. These exercises at the end of each chapter will help you repeat the operations independently.

 Have you forgotten how to do something? The number next to the footsteps tells you where to look it up at the end of the book in the appendix *How Do I Do That Again?*

In separate boxes you will find general information or tips concerning the iPhone.

Extra information
Information boxes are denoted by these icons:

The book icon gives you extra background information that you can read at your convenience. This extra information is not necessary for working through the book.

The light bulb icon indicates an extra tip for using the iPhone.

Website

This book has its own website: **www.visualsteps.com/iphone8**
Visit this website regularly and check if there are any recent updates or additions to this book, or possible errata.

Test Your Knowledge

After you have worked through this book, you can test your knowledge online, at the **www.ccforseniors.com** website.
By answering a number of multiple choice questions you will be able to test your knowledge. After you have finished the test, your *Computer Certificate* will be sent to the email address you have entered.
Participating in the test is **free of charge**. The computer certificate website is a free Visual Steps service.

For Teachers

The Visual Steps books have been written as self-study guides for individual use. These books are also well suited for use in a group or a classroom setting. For this purpose, some of our books come with a free teacher's manual. You can download the available teacher's manuals and additional materials from this webpage:
www.visualsteps.com/instructor

The Screenshots

The screenshots in this book indicate which button, file or hyperlink you need to tap on your iPhone screen or click on your computer. In the instruction text (in **bold** letters) you will see a small image of the item you need to tap or click. The line will point you to the right place on your iPhone screen, onscreen keyboard or your computer screen.

Here you see an example of an instruction text and a screenshot of the item you need to tap or click. The line indicates where to find this item on the iPhone screen:

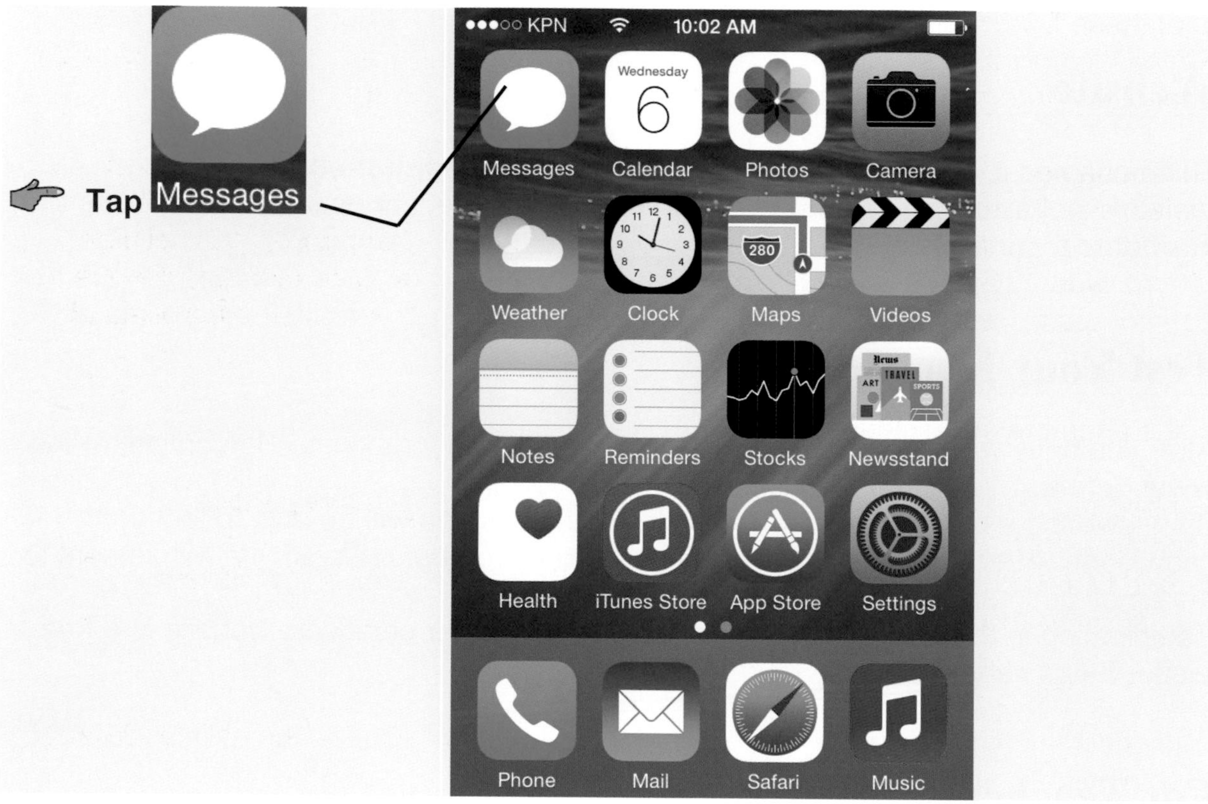

In some cases, the screenshot only displays part of the screen. Below you see an example of this:

At the bottom of the screen:

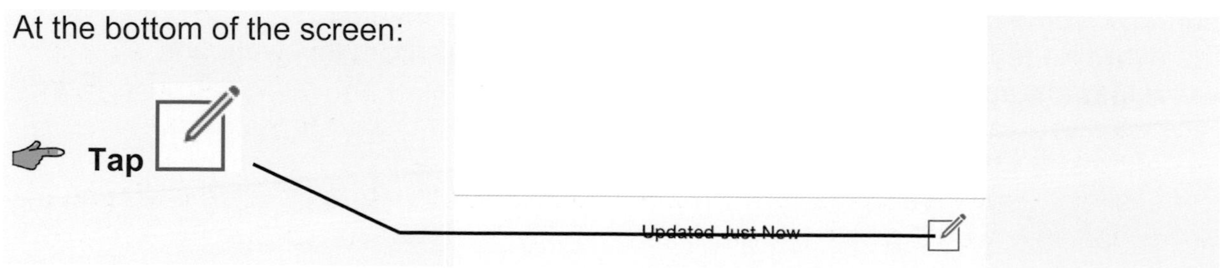

1. The iPhone

The iPhone is one of the most popular *smartphones* in the world. Given the design and appearance of the device, it is no wonder that the iPhone has become so popular. The phone is easy to use, and not just for making phone calls. You can use it to send text messages as well as many other things, like surfing the Internet, sending email, listening to music, maintaining appointments or playing games. The phone can even be used to take pictures, and create and view videos. You can do all of these things by using *apps*. These are the programs that are installed on the iPhone. Apart from the standard apps already installed on your iPhone, you can add other apps (free or paid) by going to Apple's web shop: the *App Store*.

In this chapter you will get to know the iPhone, its onscreen keyboard and learn some of the basic operations needed to use your phone. You will learn how to connect to the Internet through a wireless network (Wi-Fi), or through the cellular data network (3G or 4G). Further on, we will show you how to connect the iPhone to your computer, where you can use the *iTunes* program to manage the contents of your iPhone.

In this chapter you will learn how to:

- insert the SIM card, turn on the iPhone, or wake it up from sleep mode;
- enter the PIN code for the simlock;
- modify the iPhone's settings and use the main components of the iPhone;
- update the iPhone;
- use the basic functions on the iPhone;
- work with the onscreen keyboard;
- connect to the Internet through a wireless network (Wi-Fi) and the cellular data network (3G or 4G);
- connect the iPhone to the computer;
- turn off the iPhone, or put it into sleep mode.

Please note:

This book has been written for iPhones that use the *iOS 8* operating system. As this operating system is only compatible with the iPhone models 4S, 5, 5S, 5C, 6, 6 Plus and newer models, we will not be discussing the earlier editions of the iPhone or operating system with this book.
If necessary, you can update your iPhone as described in *1.6 Updating the iPhone* before you start working through this book.

1.1 Inserting the SIM Card

Before you can start using the iPhone, you will need to insert the SIM card that your mobile phone service provider has given you. The iPhone 6, 6 Plus, 5S, 5C and 5 use a nano SIM card, the iPhone 4S uses a micro SIM card. This is how you insert the SIM card into these models:

Remove the SIM card tray with the SIM eject tool :

If you have lost this tool, you can also use a bent paperclip.

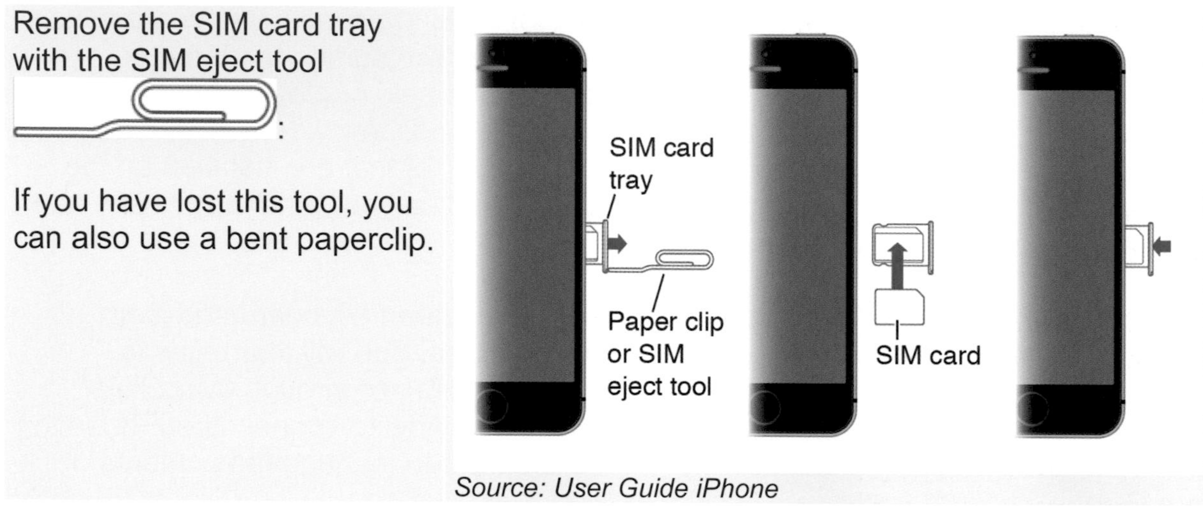

Source: User Guide iPhone

☞ **Insert the nano or micro SIM card into the SIM card tray**

☞ **Gently push the SIM card tray back into the iPhone**

1.2 Turn On the iPhone or Wake It Up From Sleep Mode

The iPhone may be turned off or it can be locked. If your iPhone has been turned off, this is how you can turn it on again:

☞ **Press and hold the on/off button pressed in, until the Apple logo appears on the screen**

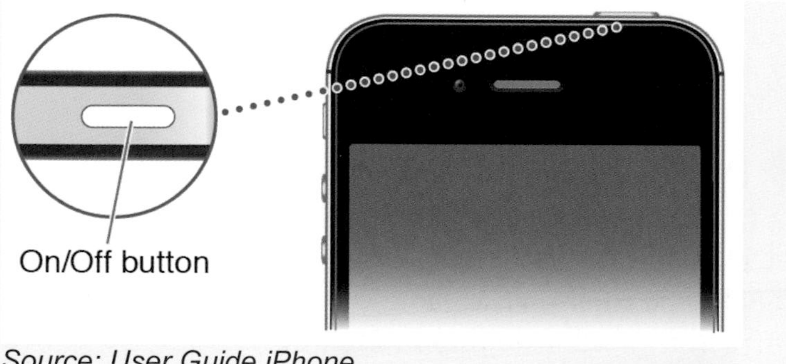

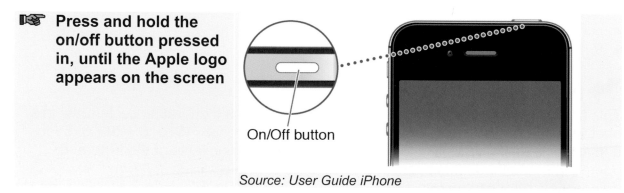

Source: User Guide iPhone

The iPhone will start up:

Afterwards, you will see the home screen.

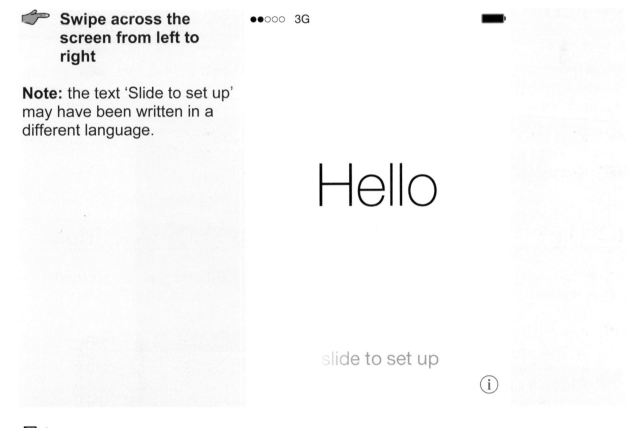

The iPhone may also be locked. This is called the sleep mode. If this is the case with your iPhone, then you can unlock your phone (wake it up) like this:

Press the Home button 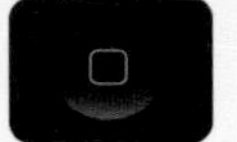

Now you will see the locked screen of the iPhone. Here is how you unlock the iPhone:

 **Swipe across the screen from left to right**

Note: the text 'Slide to set up' may have been written in a different language.

●●○○○ 3G

slide to set up

 **Please note:**

In this book we will always use the iPhone in an upright position. If you use the iPhone in a horizontal (landscape) position, you may see slightly different screenshots every now and then.

1.3 SIM Lock Active

When you turn on the iPhone, the SIM lock will be active. You need to enter the PIN code of your SIM card in order to be able to use the phone:

Tap **Unlock**

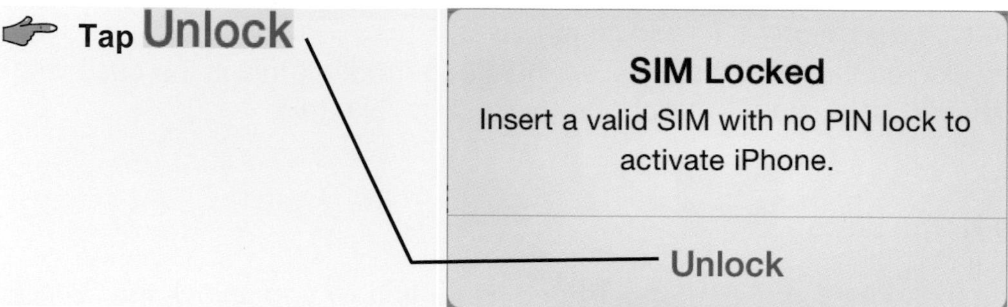

HELP! I do not see this window.

If you do not see this window, please continue with *section 1.4 Set Up the iPhone.*

If you have not yet used the phone, you can enter 0000 as a default PIN code, which is used by most providers.

Enter the PIN code

Tap **OK**

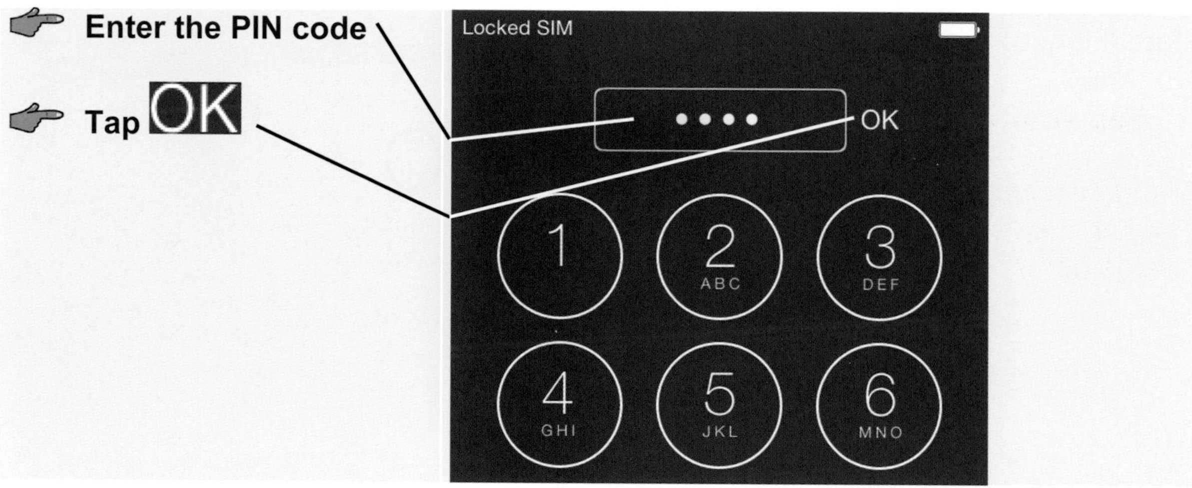

Please note:

It could also be that you will see this screen at a different moment, while using the iPhone.

1.4 Set Up the iPhone

When you start up the iPhone for the very first time, you will see a number of screens where you can enter information and configure several settings. If you have previously used your iPhone, you can skip this set up section and continue reading on page 32. The first thing to do is to set the language for your iPhone:

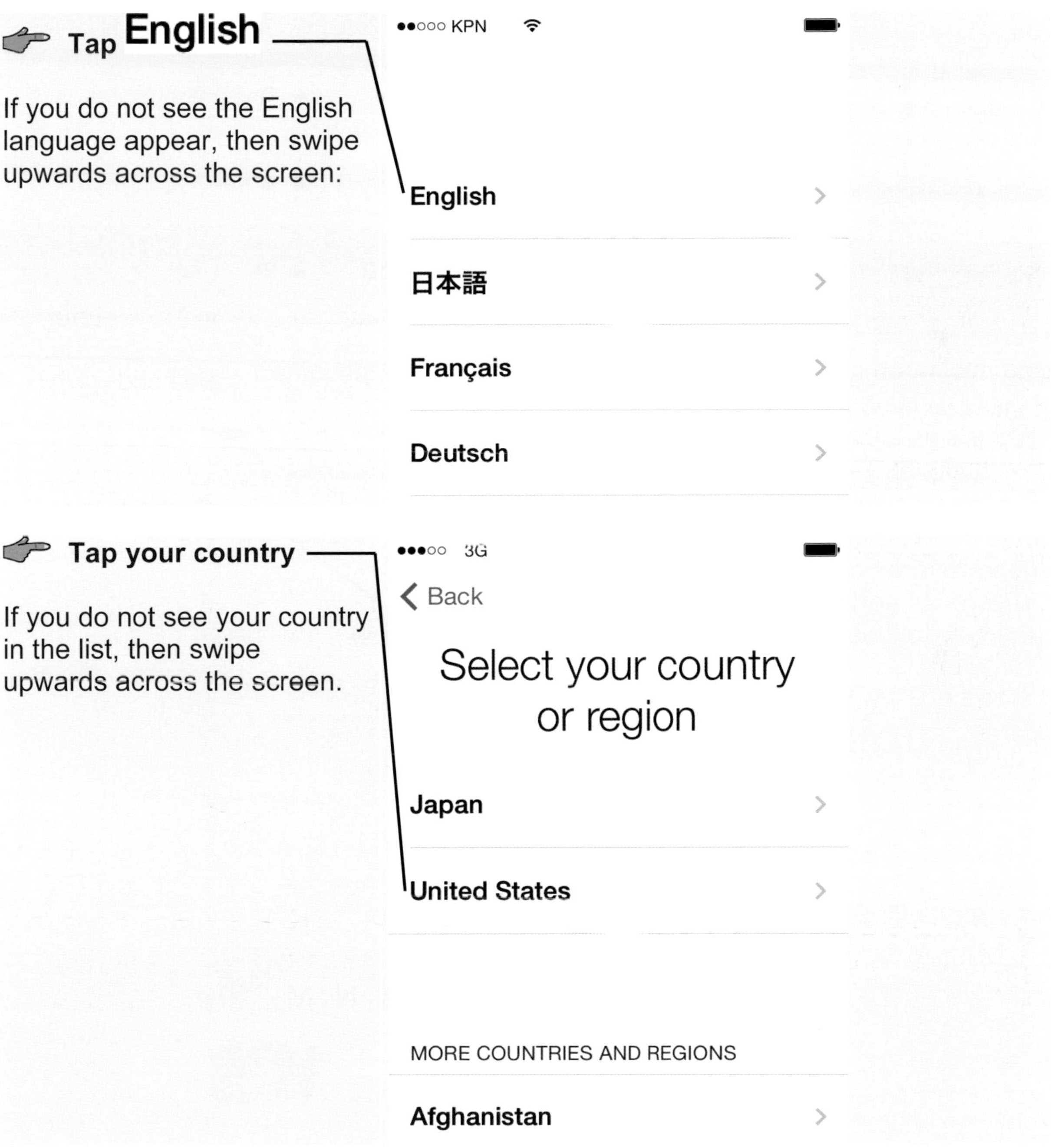

Tap **English**

If you do not see the English language appear, then swipe upwards across the screen:

Tap your country

If you do not see your country in the list, then swipe upwards across the screen.

In the next screen you can select the Wi-Fi network you want to use:

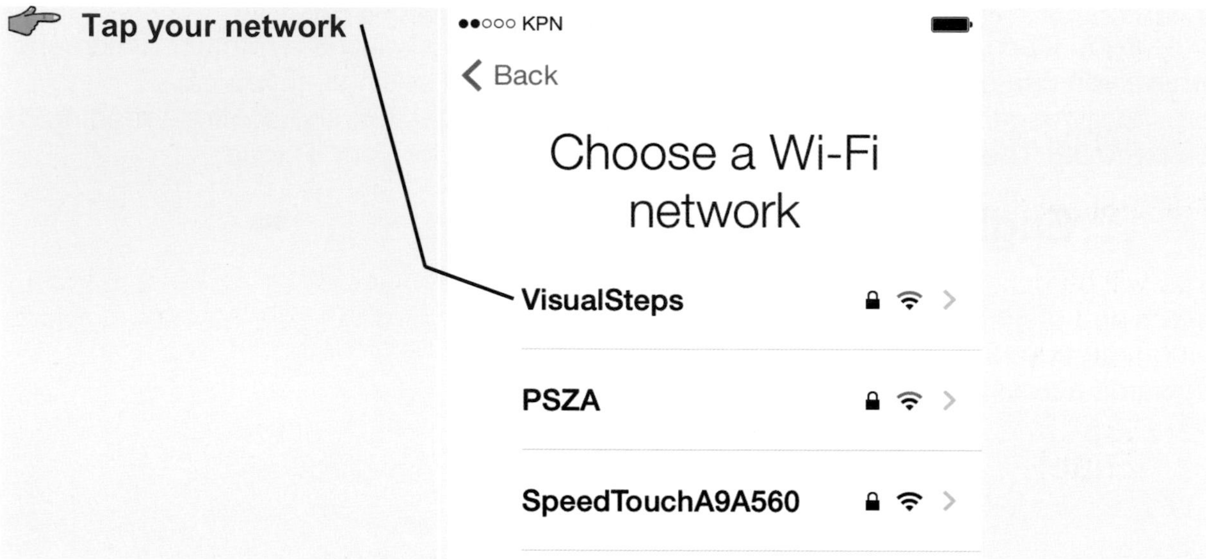

Tap your network

You may need to enter a password in order to use the network:

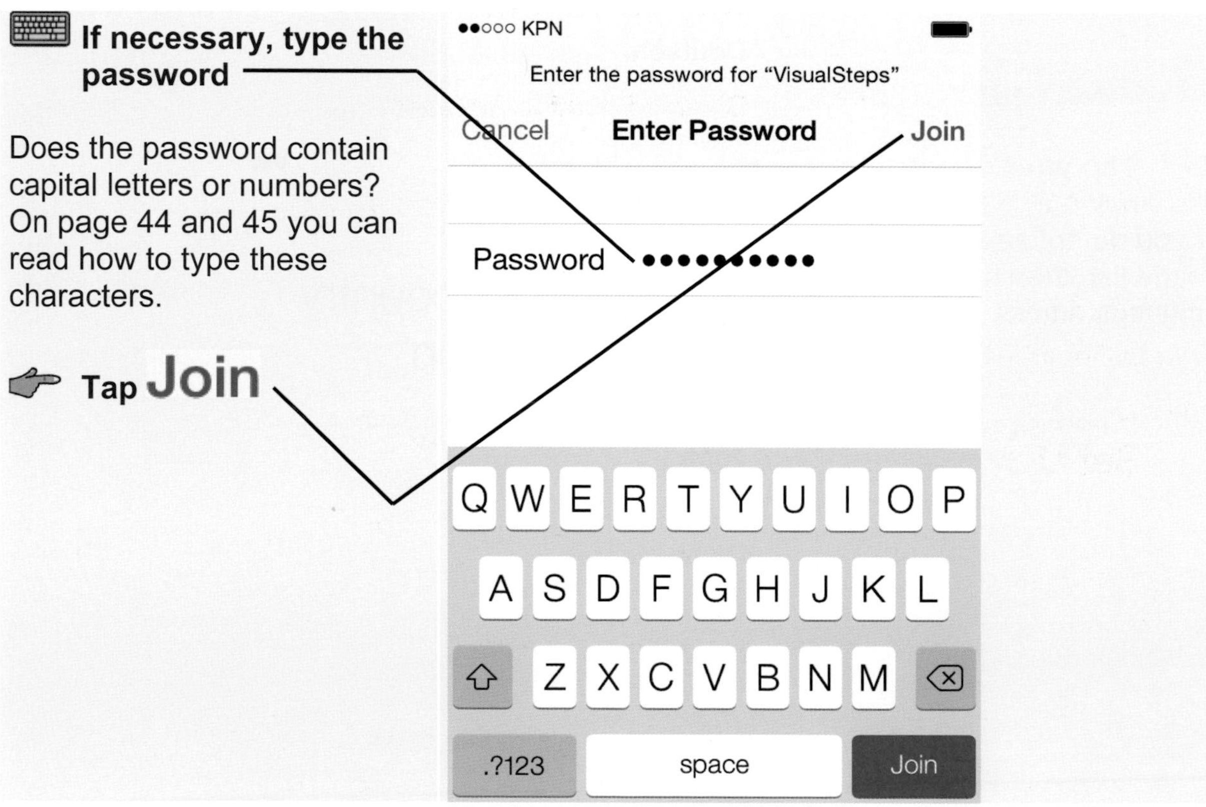

If necessary, type the password

Does the password contain capital letters or numbers? On page 44 and 45 you can read how to type these characters.

Tap Join

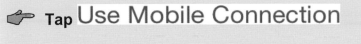

HELP! I do not have a Wi-Fi network.

If you do not have a Wi-Fi network, or do not wish to use this network, you can connect to the Internet through *iTunes*. In the *Wi-Fi networks* window:

Tap Use Mobile Connection

Follow the onscreen instructions

You will be asked if you want to turn on the Location Services. With this option, the *Maps* app can collect and use data that will enable it to pinpoint your location. To turn on Location Services:

Tap
Enable Location Sei

●●○○○ KPN 6:00 AM

Back

Location Services

Enable Location Services

Disable Location Services

You may now see this screen:

In this example, the iPhone is configured as a new iPhone:

If necessary, tap
Set Up as New iPh

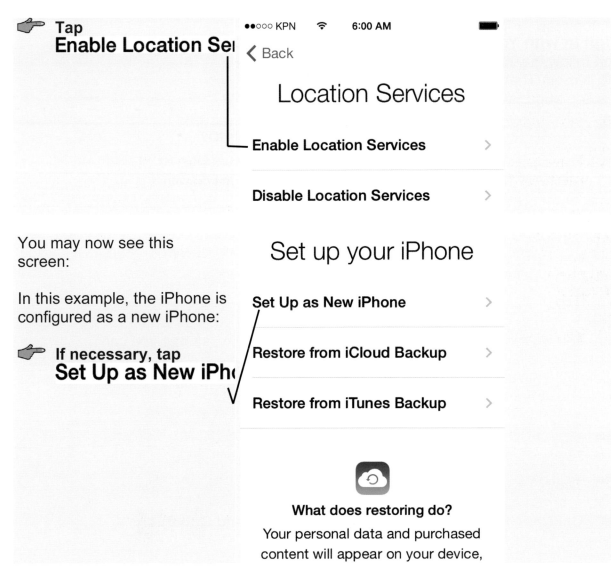

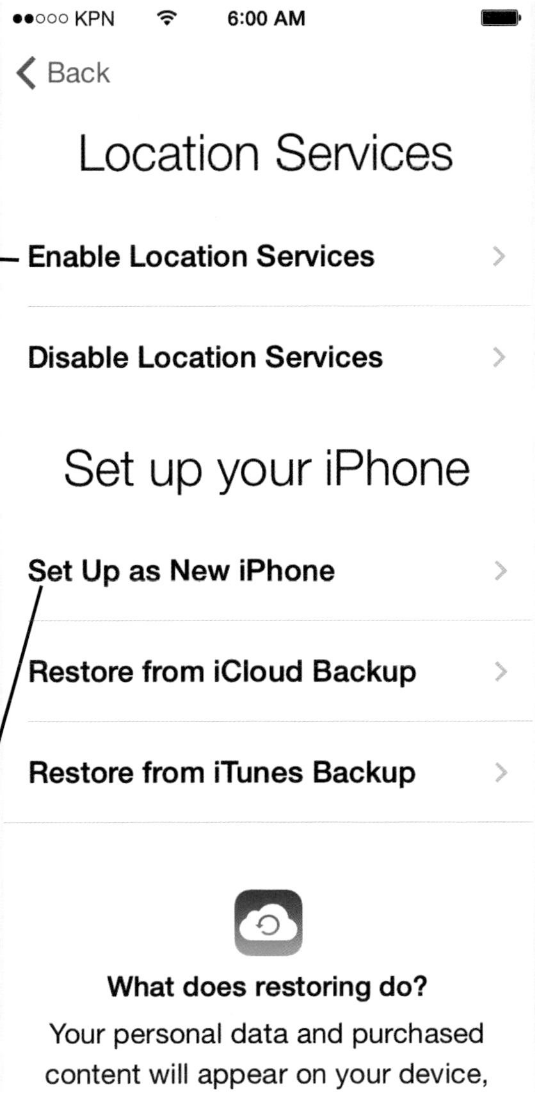

Set up your iPhone

Set Up as New iPhone

Restore from iCloud Backup

Restore from iTunes Backup

What does restoring do?

Your personal data and purchased content will appear on your device,

You will be asked whether you want to sign in with an existing *Apple ID* or if you want to create a new one. An *Apple ID* consists of a combination of an email address and a password. You need to have an *Apple ID* to be able to download apps from the *App Store* and when using certain applications. If you already have an *Apple ID*:

In this example we will assume you have not yet created an *Apple ID*:

Tap **Create a Free Apple ID**

If you already have an *Apple ID*, then tap **Sign In with Your Apple ID** and follow the instructions on the screen. Then continue reading at page 28.

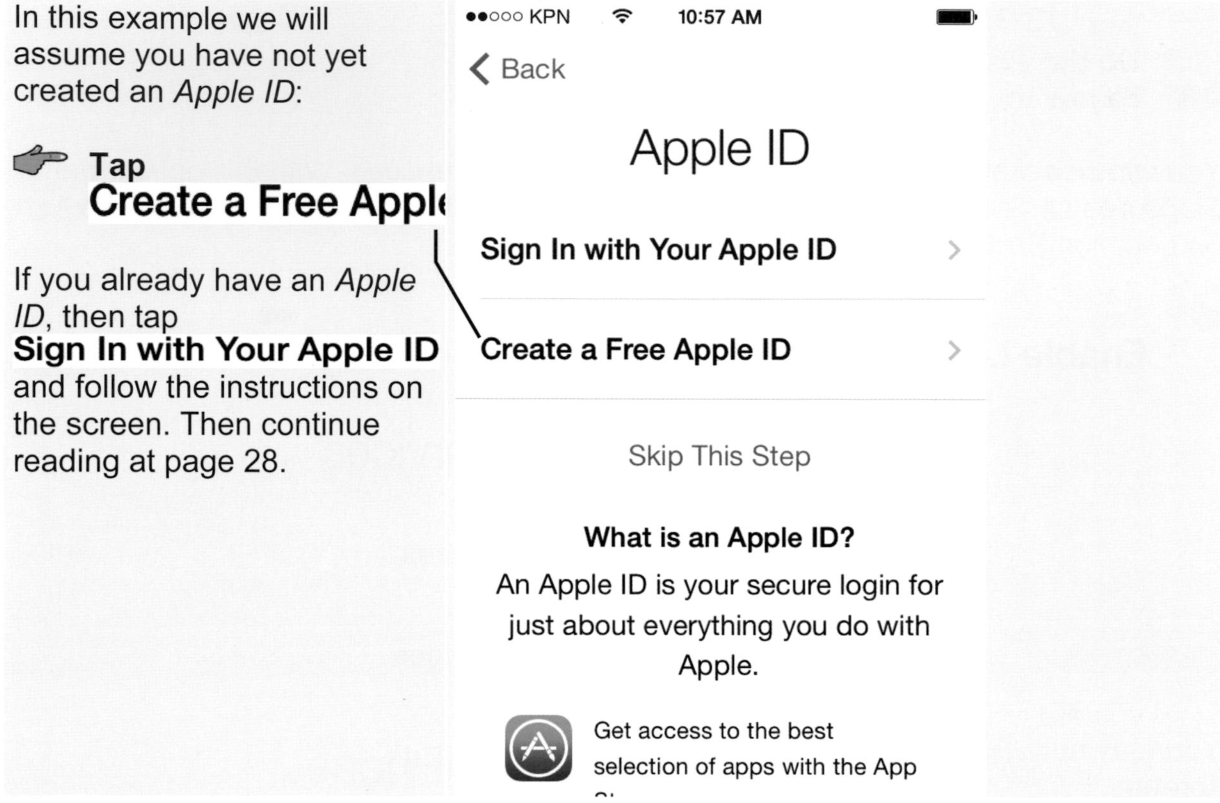

Tip

Skip

Although we recommend creating an *Apple ID* right away, so that you can understand all of the operations in this chapter, you can also decide not to create an *Apple ID*. In this case, you need to take into account that you may see some screens in this book that differ from the screens on your iPhone.

Tap Skip This Step

Tap Skip

Continue reading at page 28, with the Terms and Conditions

First, you need to enter your birth date:

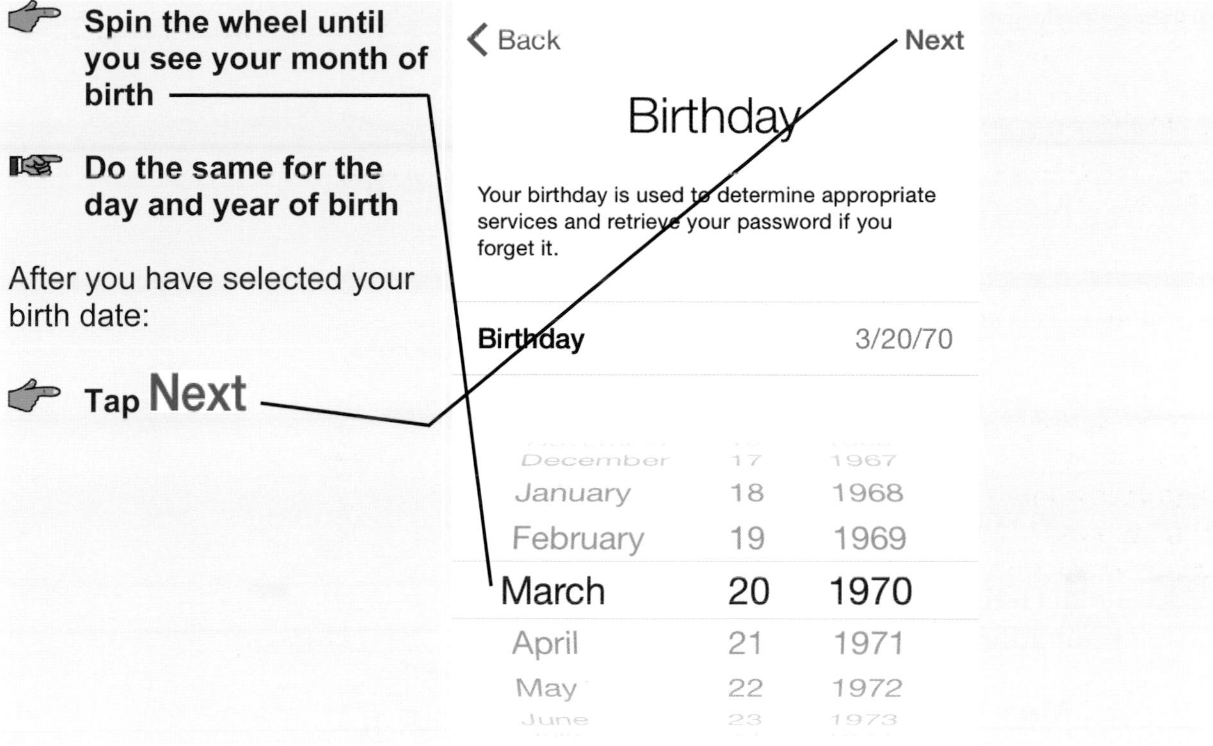

Spin the wheel until you see your month of birth

Do the same for the day and year of birth

After you have selected your birth date:

Tap Next

Now you are going to enter your name:

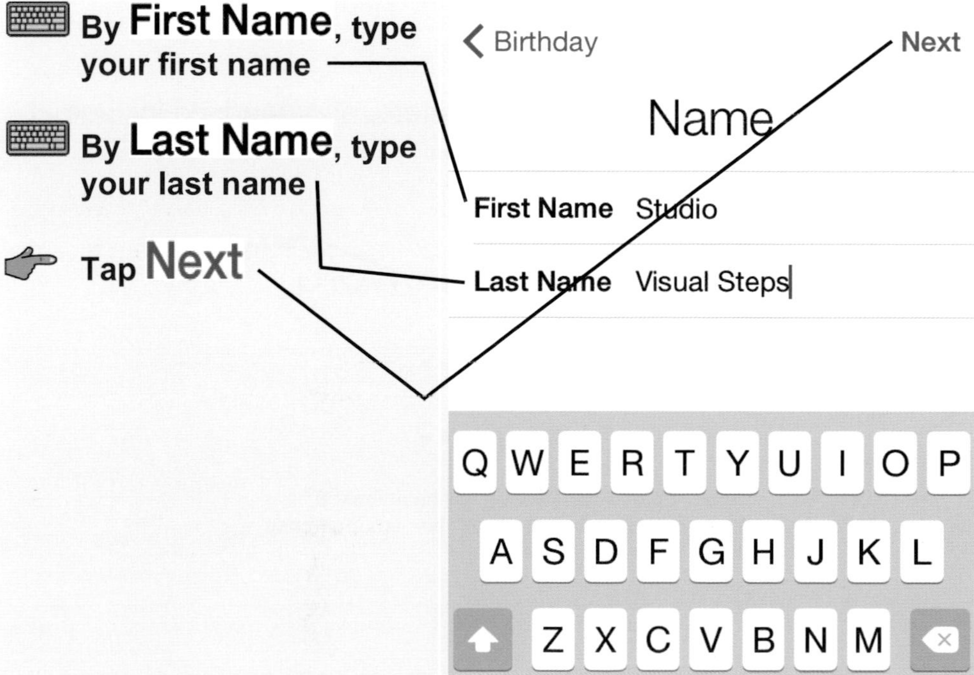

By First Name, type your first name

By Last Name, type your last name

Tap Next

In this book we assume you already have an email address and want to use this address for the options on the iPhone. It does not matter if you use this email address on your computer, or on another device:

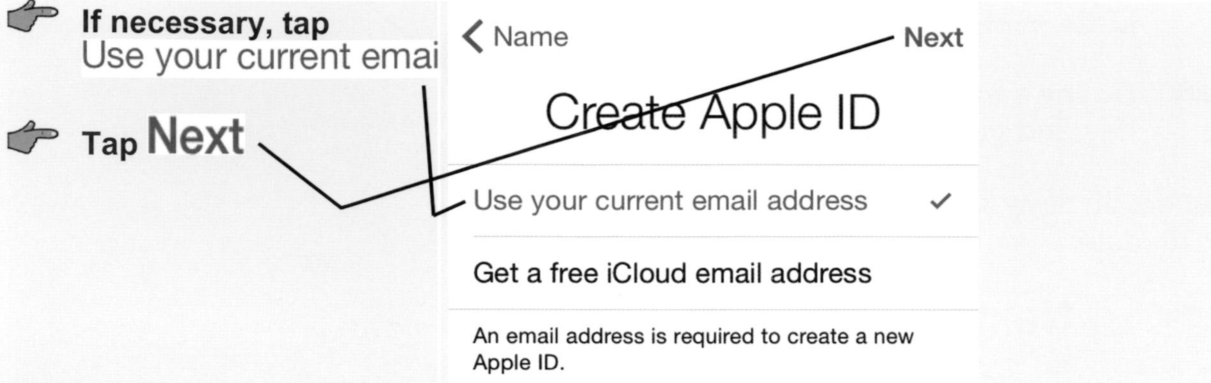

Now you can enter your email address:

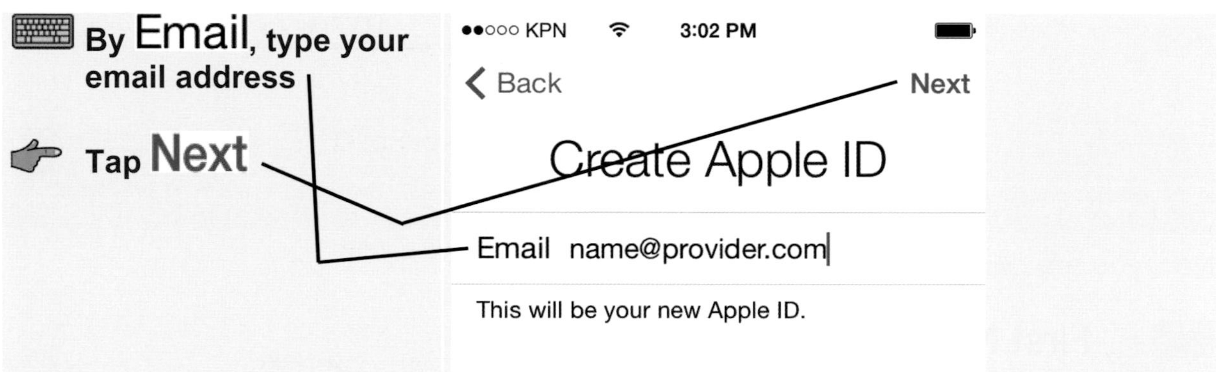

Your password needs to consist of at least eight characters, and needs to include at least one number, a capital letter and a lower case letter:

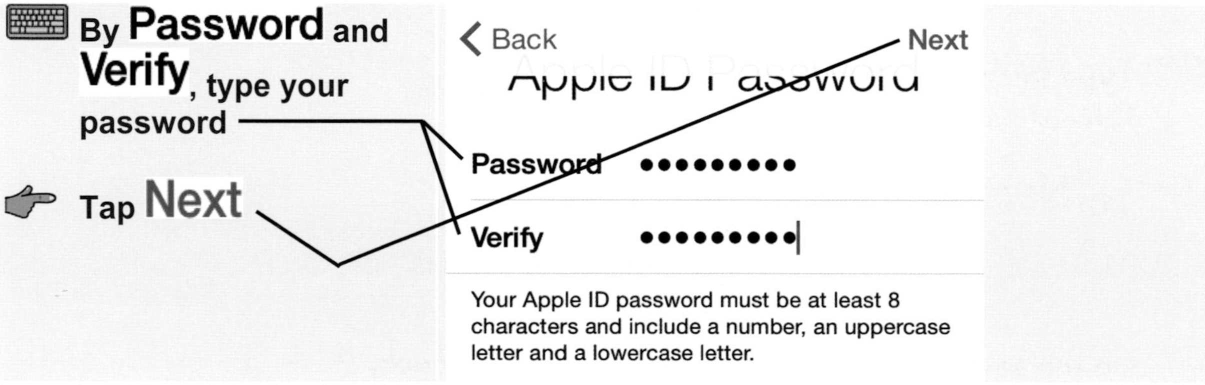

Next, select questions that will act as a hint to help you remember your password. You can use these security questions to retrieve your password, if you forget it:

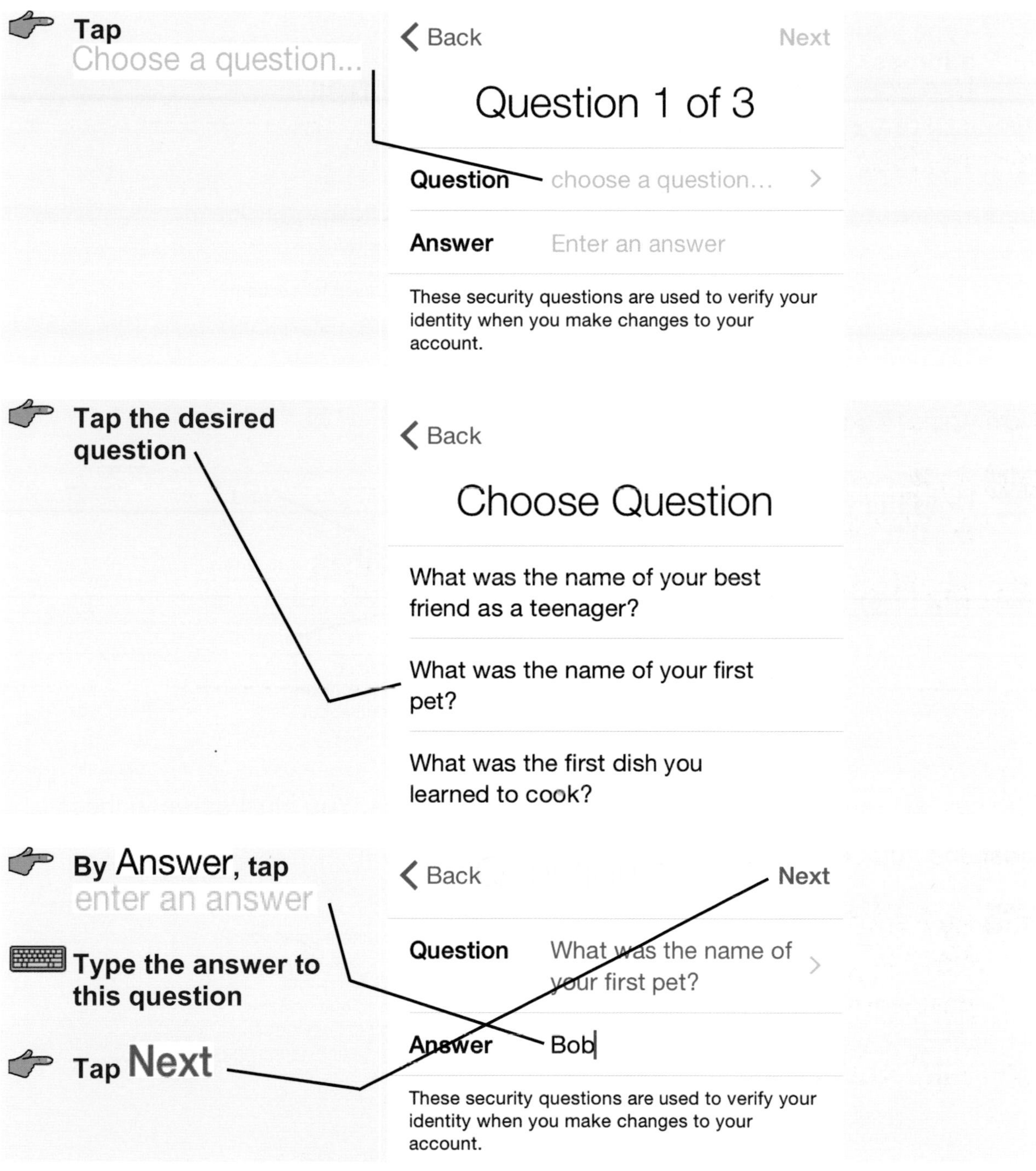
Tap
Choose a question...
Back
Next
Question 1 of 3
Question
choose a question...
Answer
Enter an answer
These security questions are used to verify your identity when you make changes to your account.
Tap the desired question
Back
Choose Question
What was the name of your best friend as a teenager?
What was the name of your first pet?
What was the first dish you learned to cook?
By Answer, tap
enter an answer
Type the answer to this question
Tap Next
Back
Next
Question
What was the name of your first pet?
Answer
Bob
These security questions are used to verify your identity when you make changes to your account.

Do the same with the other questions and answers

You can enter an email address in case you have forgotten your password. This will also provide extra security:

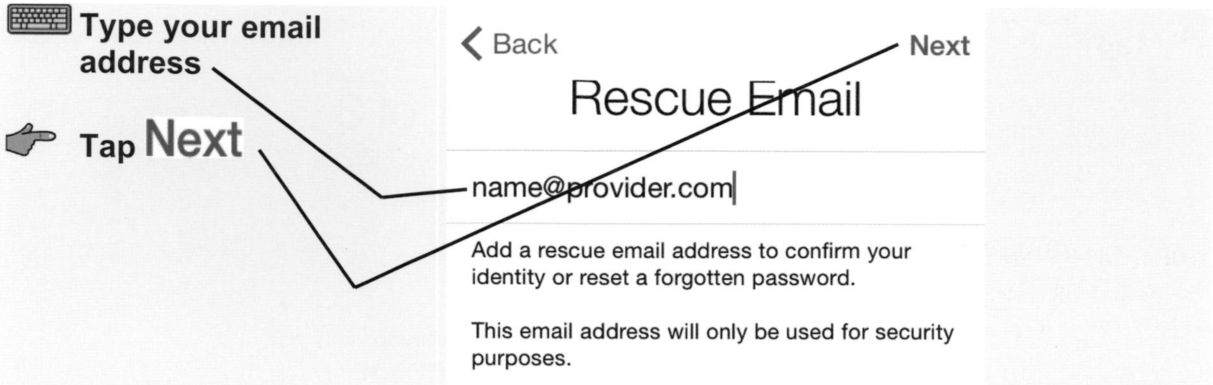

Type your email address
Tap Next
Back
Next
Rescue Email
name@provider.com
Add a rescue email address to confirm your identity or reset a forgotten password.
This email address will only be used for security purposes.

In the next screen you can choose whether you want to receive any email updates from Apple. If you do not want to do this:

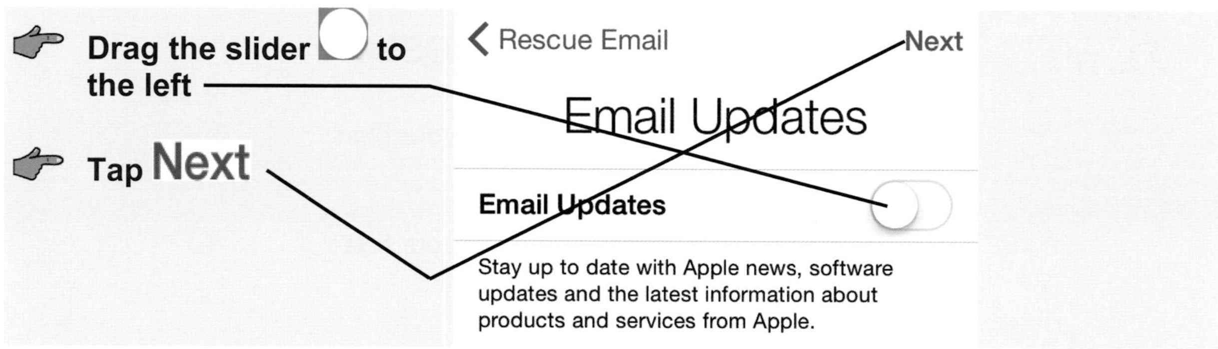

Drag the slider to the left
Tap Next
Rescue Email
Next
Email Updates
Email Updates
Stay up to date with Apple news, software updates and the latest information about products and services from Apple.

The next screen displays Apple's Terms and Conditions. You must agree to these terms in order to be able to work with your iPhone.

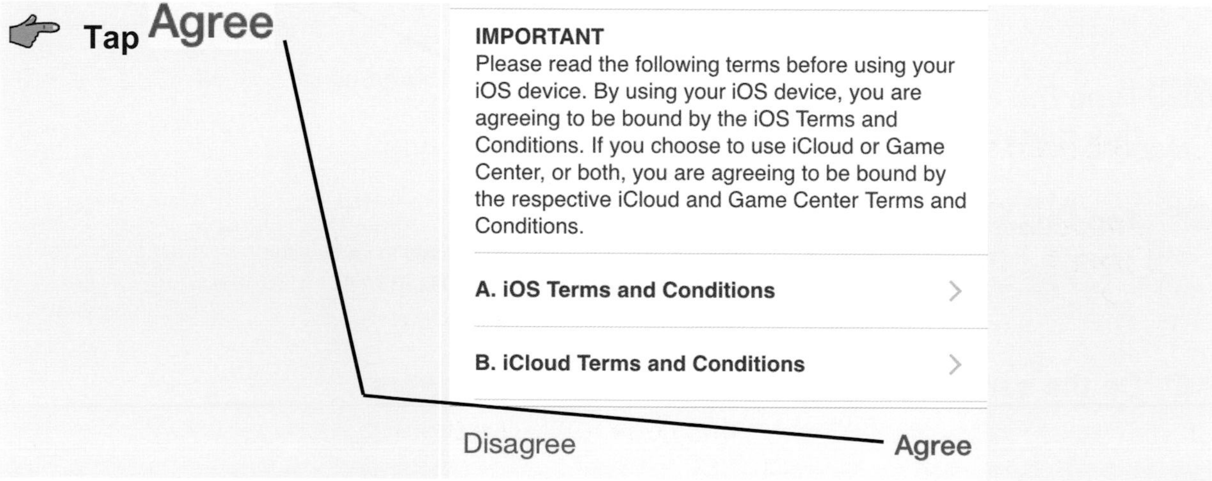

Tap Agree
IMPORTANT
Please read the following terms before using your iOS device. By using your iOS device, you are agreeing to be bound by the iOS Terms and Conditions. If you choose to use iCloud or Game Center, or both, you are agreeing to be bound by the respective iCloud and Game Center Terms and Conditions.
A. iOS Terms and Conditions
B. iCloud Terms and Conditions
Disagree
Agree

In this small window you are asked to confirm:

☛ **Tap** Agree

Terms and Conditions
I agree to the iOS, iCloud and Game Center Terms and Conditions, and the Apple Privacy Policy.
Cancel
Agree

Your new *Apple ID* will be created. This may take a little while:

It may take a few minutes to create your new Apple ID...

Apple will ask if you want to use *iCloud*. For now, this will not be necessary:

☛ **Tap**
Don't Use iCloud

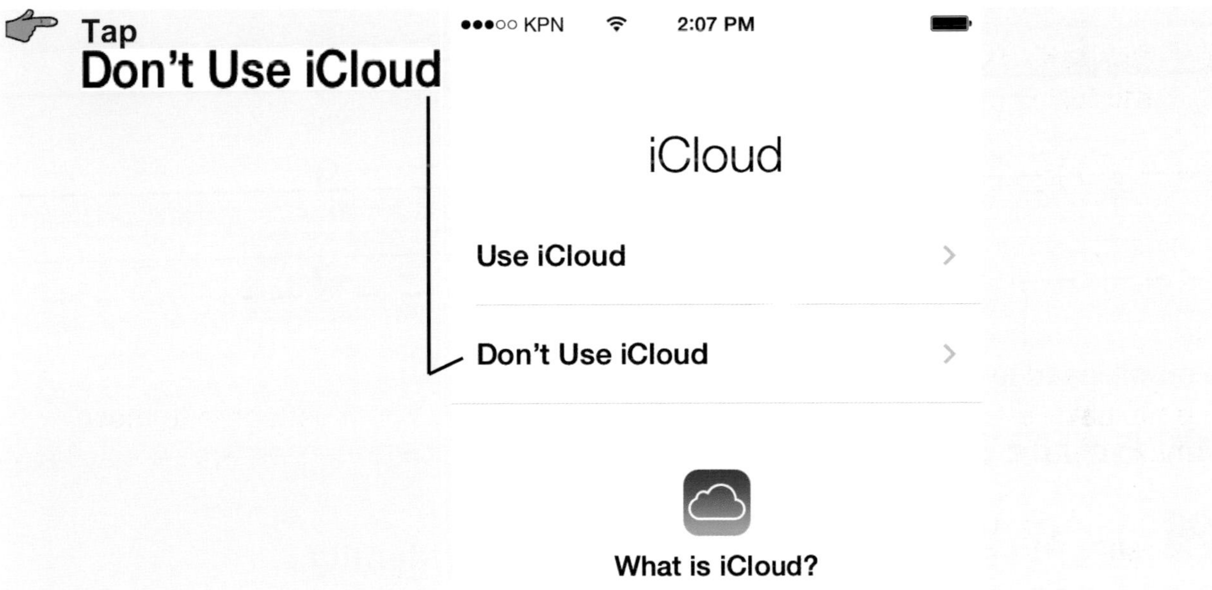

You might need to confirm that you don't want to use iCloud:

☛ **If necessary, tap**
Don't Use

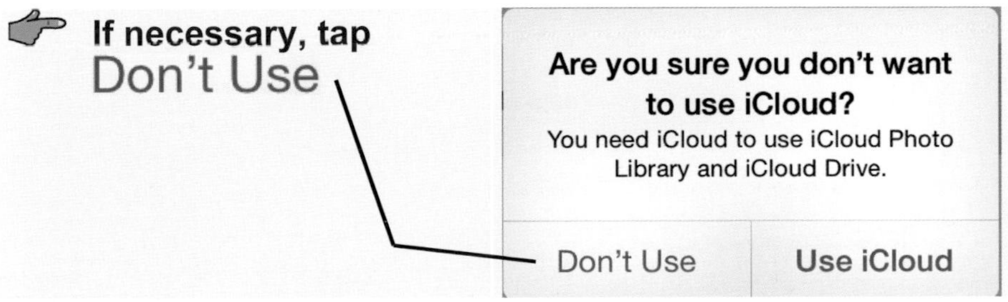

Are you sure you don't want to use iCloud?
You need iCloud to use iCloud Photo Library and iCloud Drive.
Don't Use
Use iCloud

You can enter a passcode with which you can unlock your iPhone. This is a security measure that prevents others from using your iPhone without your consent. In this example we will enter a passcode:

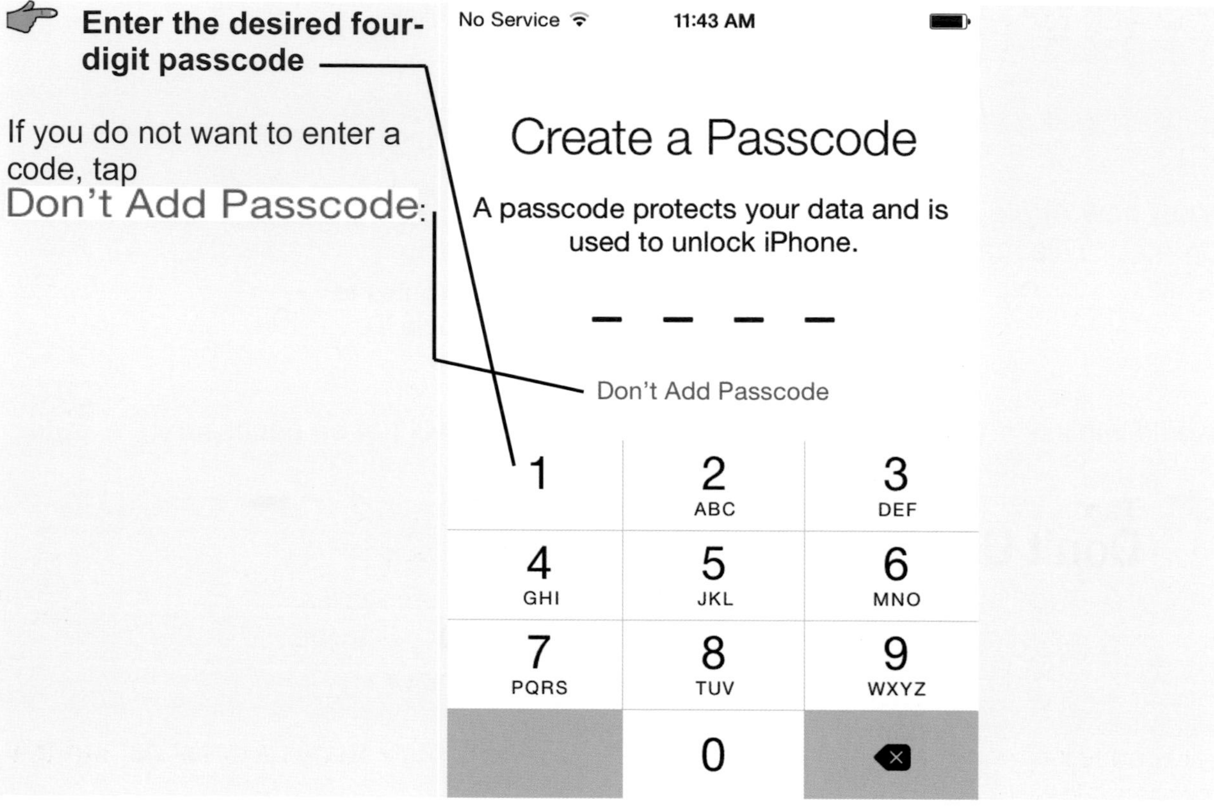

You will need to enter the code once more:

 **Enter the desired four-digit passcode again**

HELP! I see an option about fingerprint identity.

If you use the iPhone 5S, 6 or 6 Plus, you might see an option about using fingerprint identity instead of a passcode. In that case, follow the instructions onscreen if you wish to use the option.

In the next window you are asked if you want to assist Apple with the improvement of their products by sending them diagnostic and usage data. You do not want to send this:

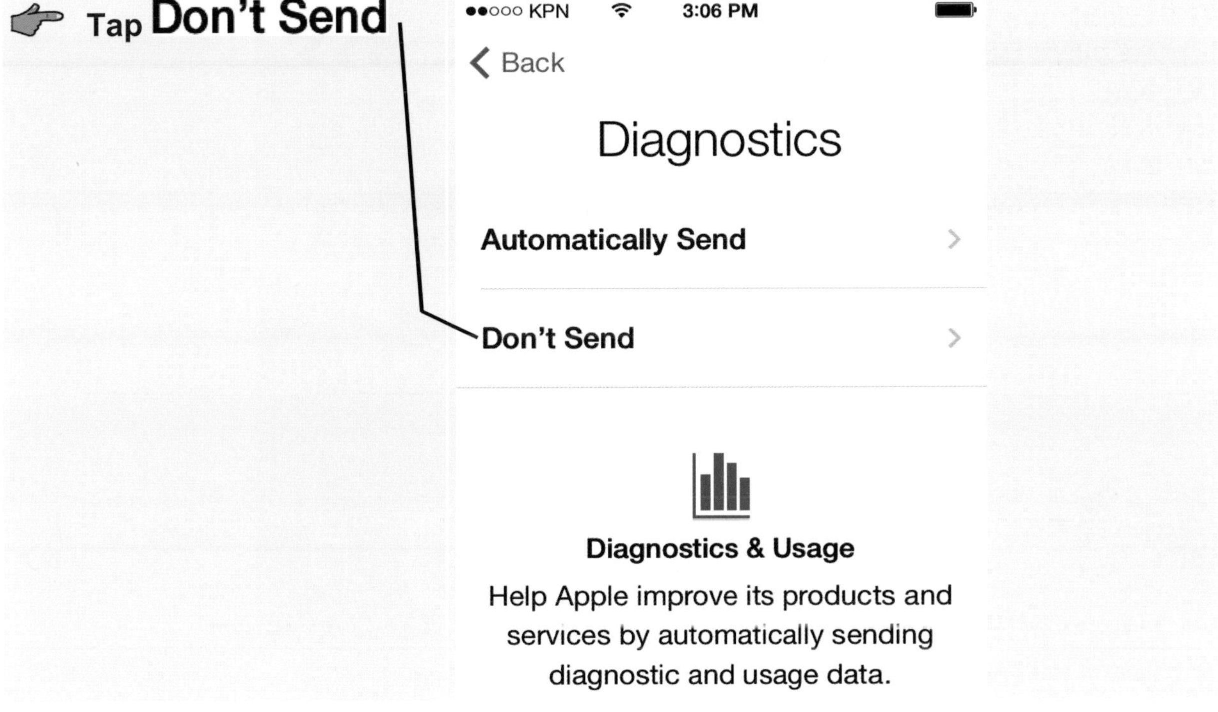

You have now completed the initial set up. There still is a little more to set up, but that comes later.

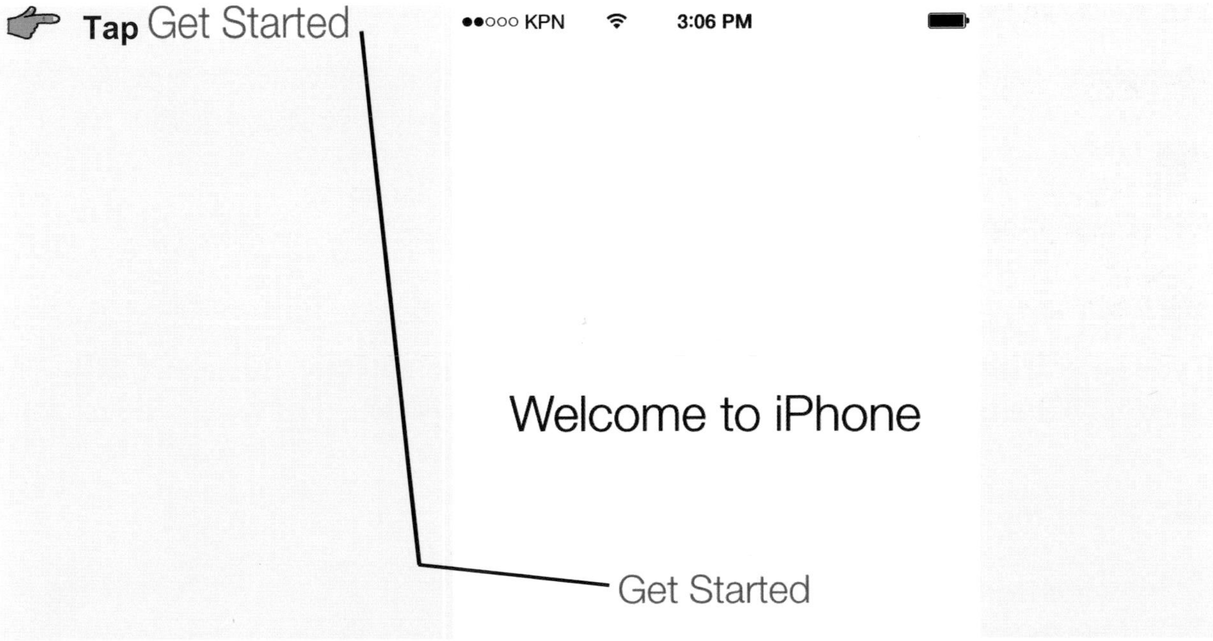

Now you will see the home screen with all the colored app icons:

The background of your iPhone might be slightly different.

HELP! Updates from my provider.

It is possible that you will see a message concerning an update for the settings of your provider. These provider settings updates are small files (approximately 10 Kb) that are installed on your iPhone.

The update has to do with the way in which your iPhone connects to the provider's cellular network. You need to install the most recent provider settings updates for your device, as soon as they are available:

Follow the onscreen instructions

HELP! My iPhone is locked.

If you do not use the iPhone for a while, it may lock automatically. By default, this will happen after one minute. This is how you unlock the iPhone:

 **Press the Home button** 

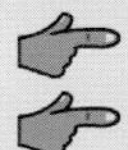 **Swipe from left to right over the screen**

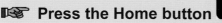

If necessary, enter the passcode

1.5 The Main Components of Your iPhone

In the diagrams below you will see the main components of the iPhone 4S, 5, 5S, 5C, 6 and 6 Plus. When instructions are given for a specific component, you can refer back to these diagrams to find the location of the component on your phone.

The iPhone 4S:

Source: User Guide iPhone

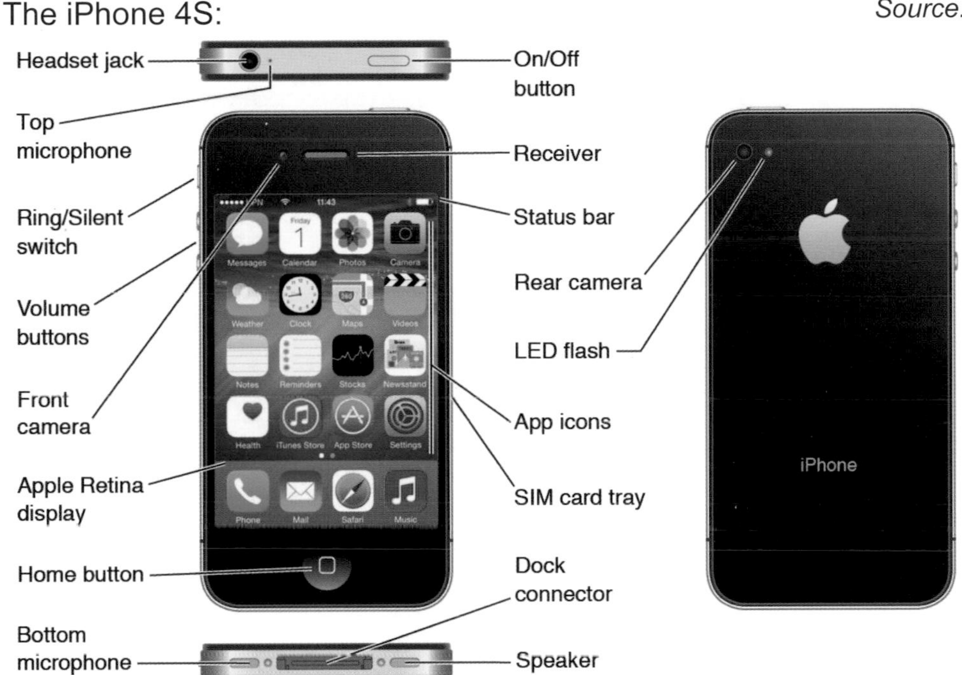

The iPhone 5, 5S and 5C are mostly similar:

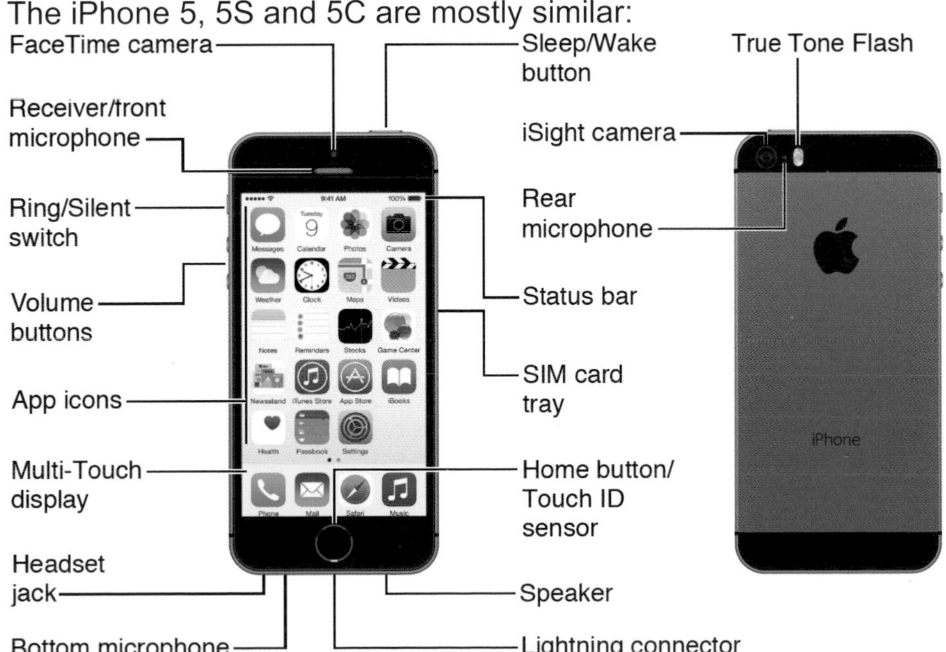

Source: User Guide iPhone

The iPhone 6 and 6 Plus are a little bit different.

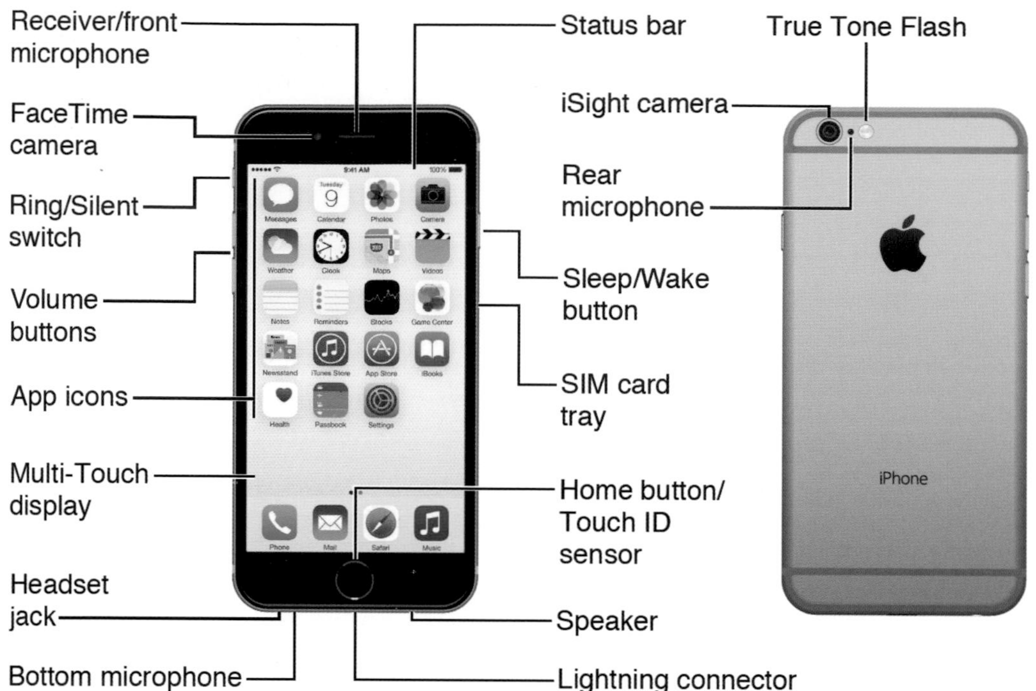

Source: User Guide iPhone

The status bar shows various symbols that give you information about the status of the iPhone and its connections. Below you will find a summary of the symbols used and what they indicate:

vodafone	Strength of the cell signal and the name of the cellular provider currently used.
3G / 4G	Shows that your carrier's 3G or 4G network is available and that you can connect to the Internet with this network.
	The iPhone is locked. This symbol is displayed when the lock screen appears.
	Shows that the iPhone is locked in portrait orientation.
	Battery is charging.
	Shows battery level.

- Continue on the next page -

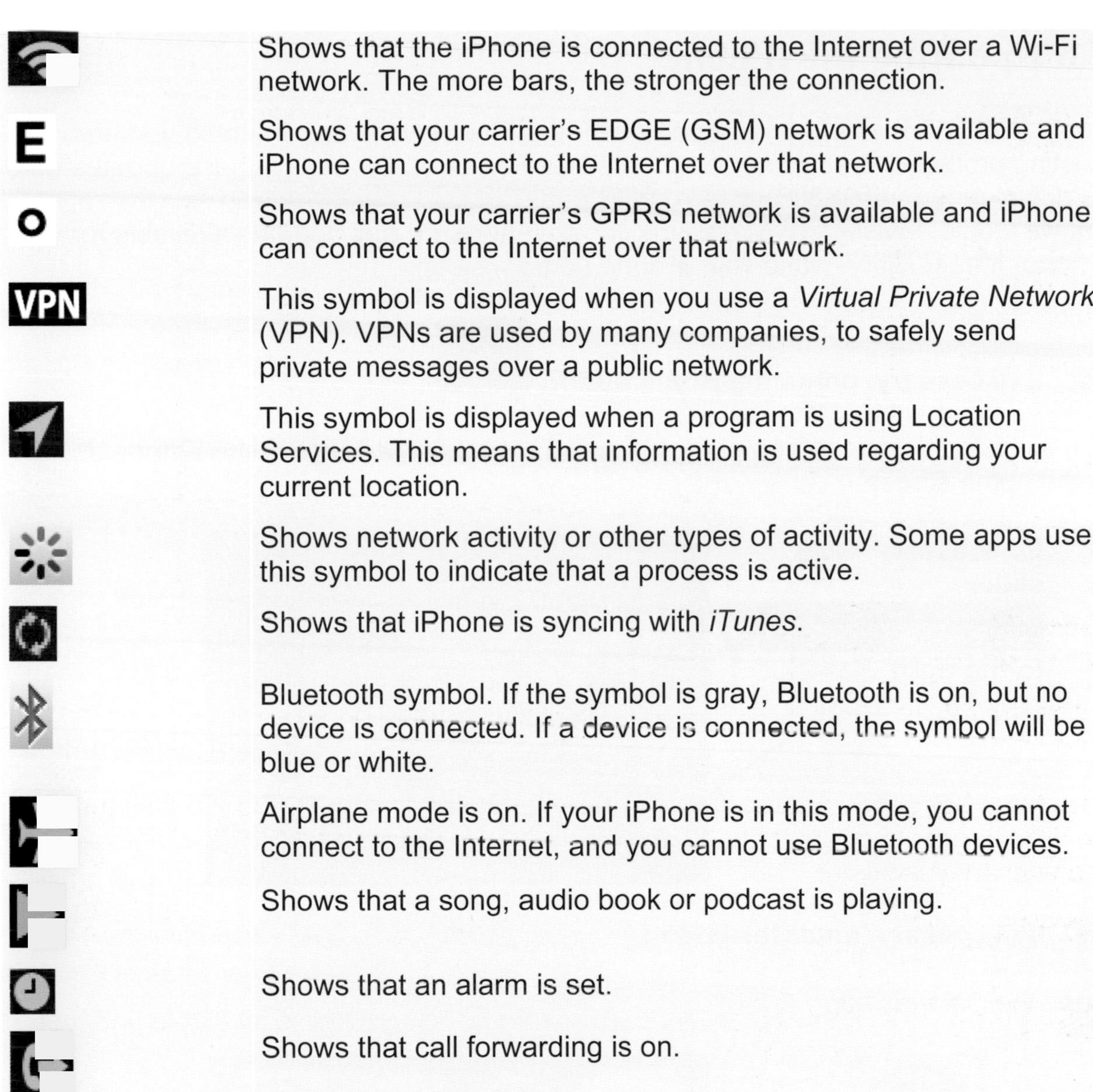

Shows that the iPhone is connected to the Internet over a Wi-Fi network. The more bars, the stronger the connection.

Shows that your carrier's EDGE (GSM) network is available and iPhone can connect to the Internet over that network.

Shows that your carrier's GPRS network is available and iPhone can connect to the Internet over that network.

This symbol is displayed when you use a *Virtual Private Network* (VPN). VPNs are used by many companies, to safely send private messages over a public network.

This symbol is displayed when a program is using Location Services. This means that information is used regarding your current location.

Shows network activity or other types of activity. Some apps use this symbol to indicate that a process is active.

Shows that iPhone is syncing with *iTunes*.

Bluetooth symbol. If the symbol is gray, Bluetooth is on, but no device is connected. If a device is connected, the symbol will be blue or white.

Airplane mode is on. If your iPhone is in this mode, you cannot connect to the Internet, and you cannot use Bluetooth devices.

Shows that a song, audio book or podcast is playing.

Shows that an alarm is set.

Shows that call forwarding is on.

Shows that the iPhone is connected to another iPhone providing a Personal Hotspot for your phone.

1.6 Updating the iPhone

Apple is regularly issuing new updates for the iPhone software. In these updates, existing problems are fixed or new functions are added. Normally, these updates will be downloaded automatically to your iPhone.
But we would advise you to regularly check if there are any updates available for your iPhone. If necessary, wake your iPhone up from sleep:

If necessary, press the Home button

You will see the lock screen of the iPhone. This is how you unlock the iPhone and go to the home screen:

If necessary, drag the slider slide to unlo **to the right**

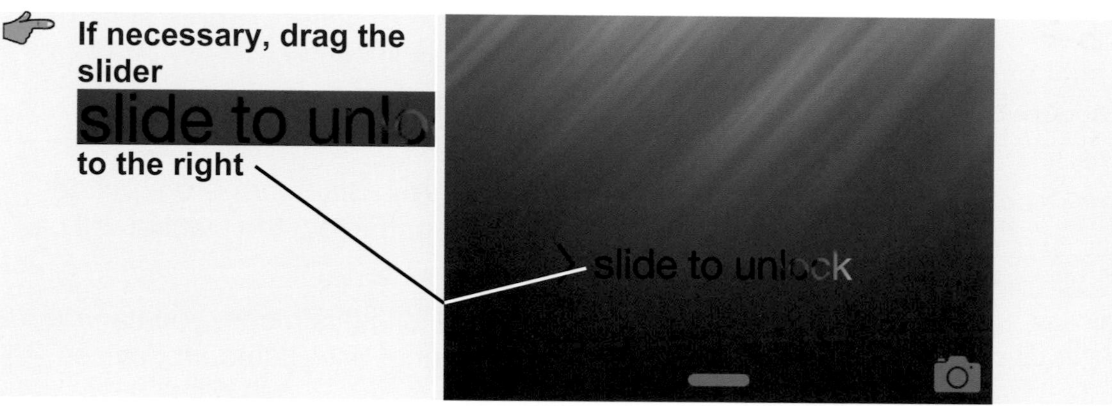

If necessary, enter the code

Open the *Settings* app:

Tap Settings

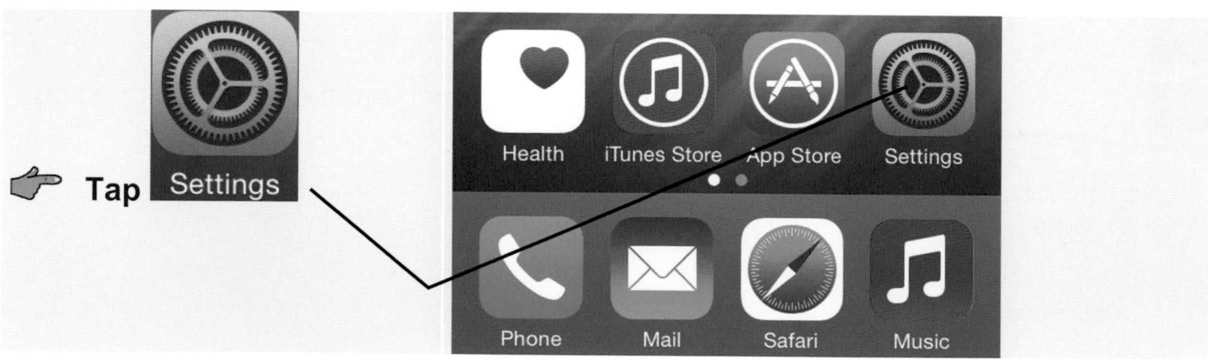

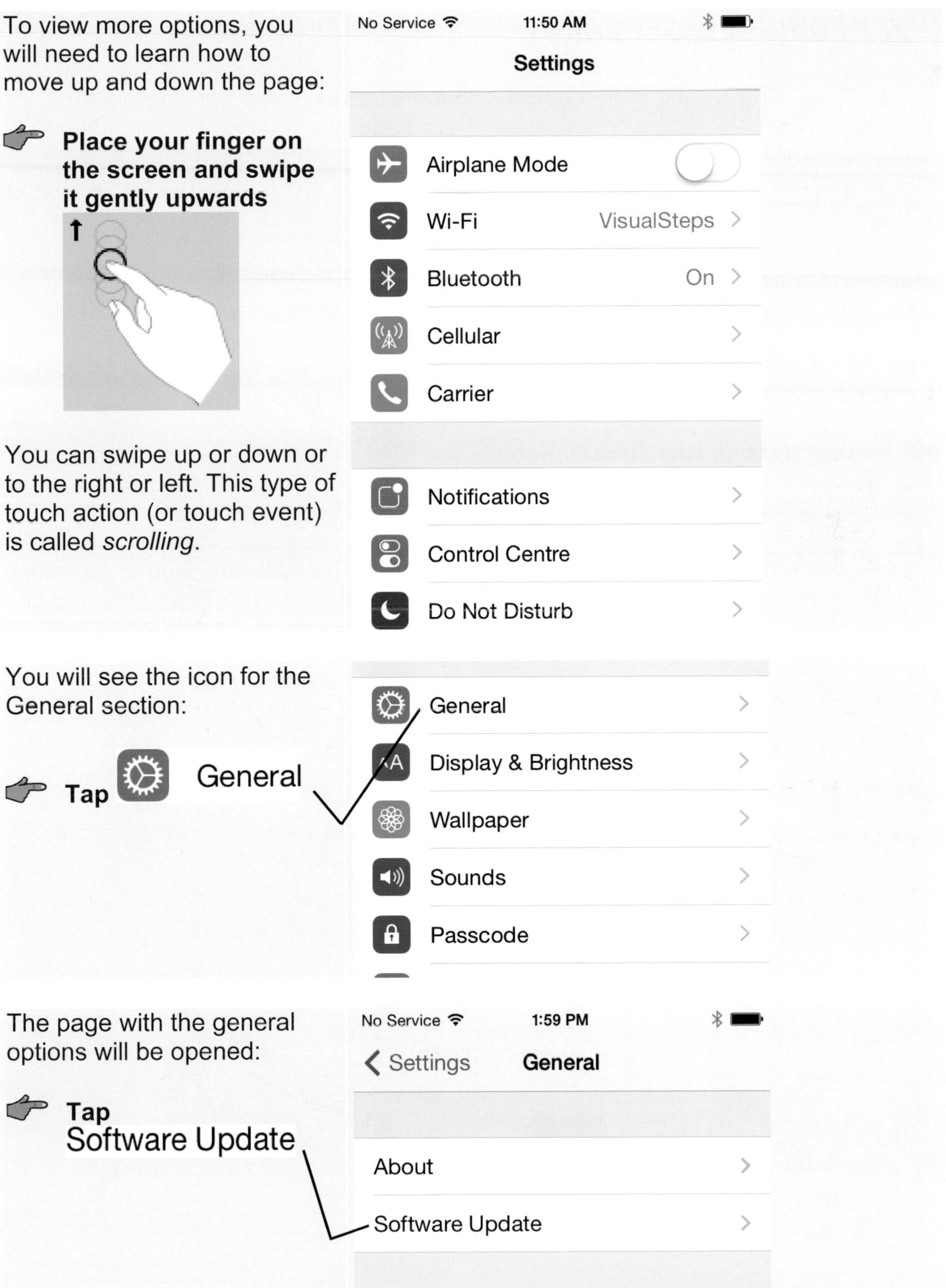

To view more options, you will need to learn how to move up and down the page:

Place your finger on the screen and swipe it gently upwards

You can swipe up or down or to the right or left. This type of touch action (or touch event) is called *scrolling*.

You will see the icon for the General section:

Tap General

The page with the general options will be opened:

Tap Software Update

Now the system will check if there is any new software for the iPhone:

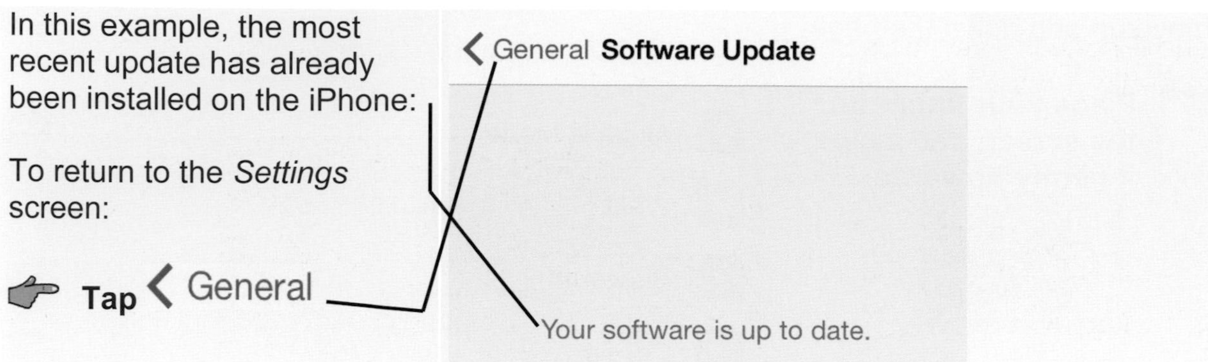

In this example, the most recent update has already been installed on the iPhone:
To return to the *Settings* screen:
Tap General
General Software Update
Your software is up to date.

If a newer version is found, you will see a message about the update.

Follow the onscreen instructions

When the update has been installed, you will return to the home screen.

It is also possible to install a new update with *iTunes*. Then you will need to connect the iPhone to your computer. You can read more about this in the *Tips* at the end of this chapter.

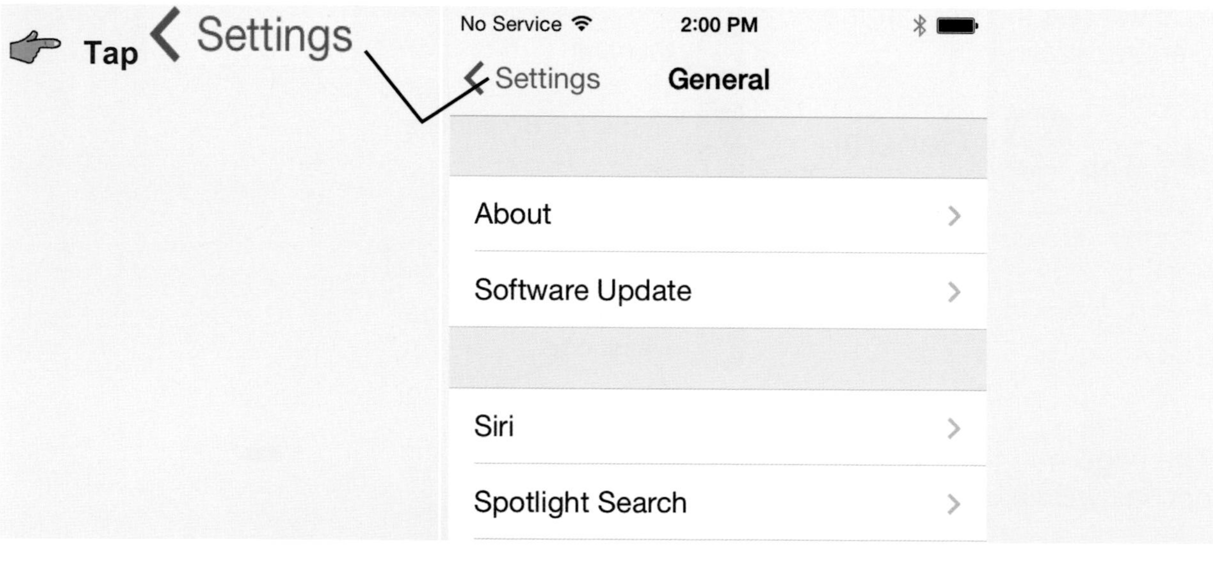

Press the Home button 

1.7 Basic Operations With the iPhone

The iPhone is easy to use. In this section you are going to practice some basic operations. Open the *Settings* app again:

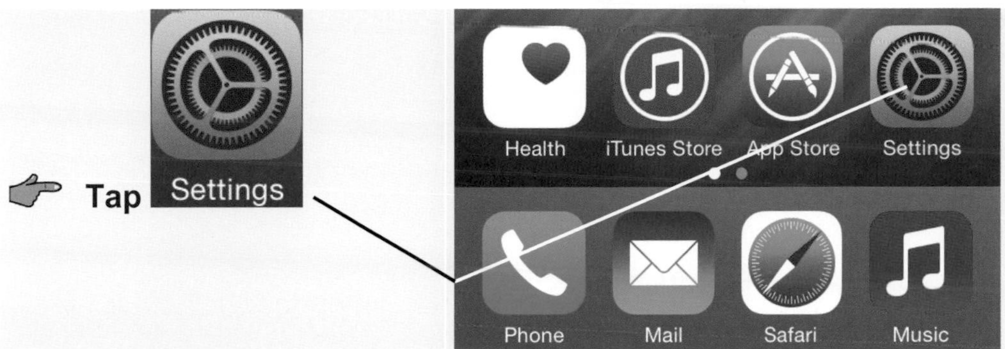

You can adapt the iPhone's lock screen and home screen according to your own taste by selecting a different wallpaper. Here is how you do that:

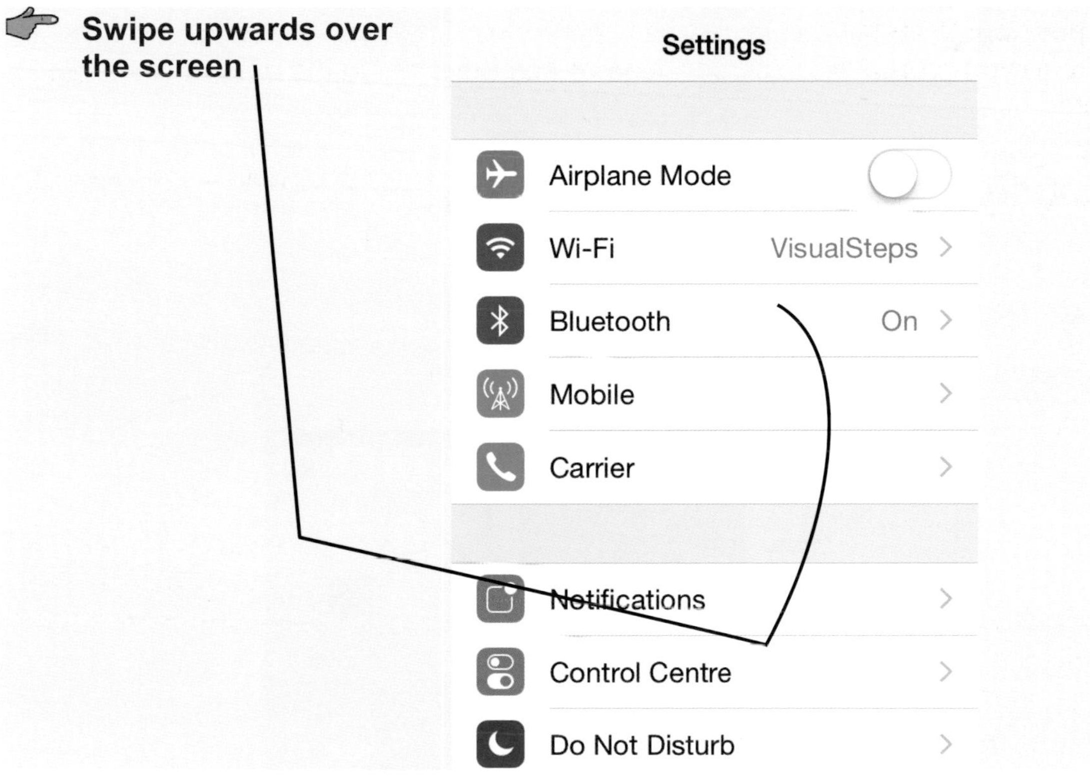

You can adapt the background (wallpaper) of the lock and home screens on your iPhone to your own taste, by selecting a different background. Here is how to do that:

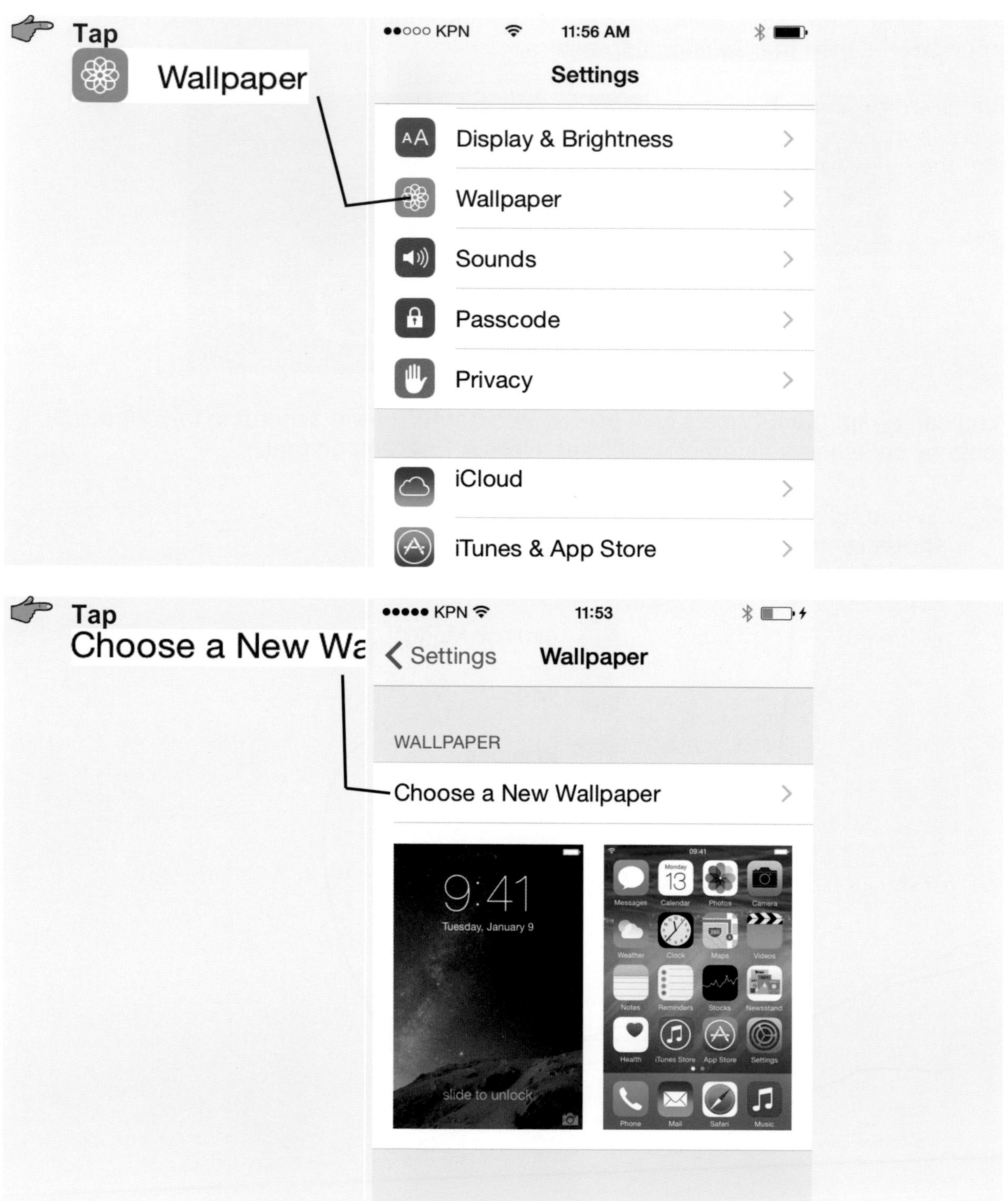

Select a wallpaper from one of the standard still wallpapers:

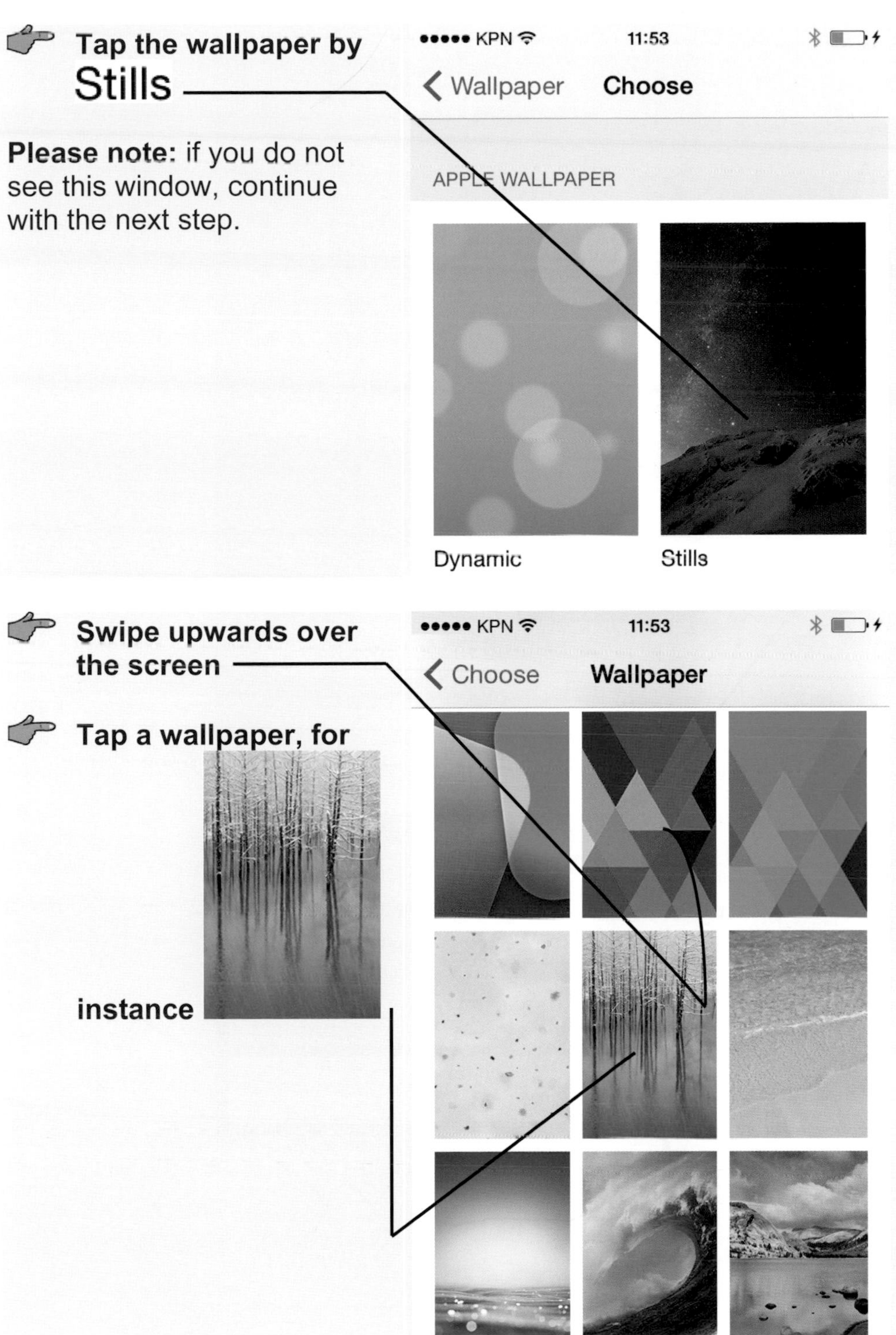

Tap the wallpaper by Stills

Please note: if you do not see this window, continue with the next step.

Swipe upwards over the screen

Tap a wallpaper, for instance

You will see a preview of the wallpaper. Now you can decide if you want to use this wallpaper for the lock screen, the home screen, or both:

- Tap Set

- Tap Set Lock Screen

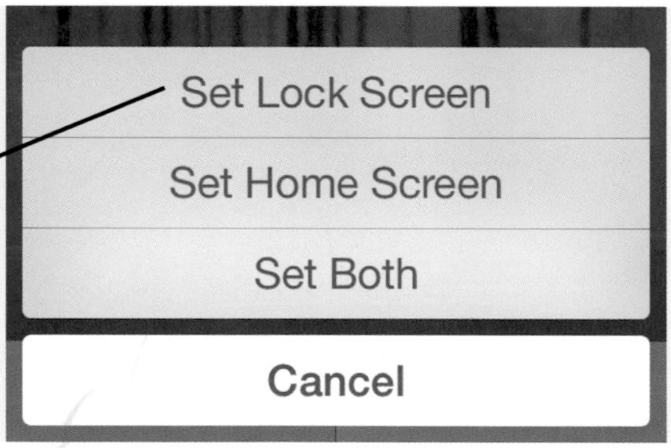

Now you will be back at the *Wallpaper* screen:

- Tap ‹ Choose

- Tap ‹ Wallpaper

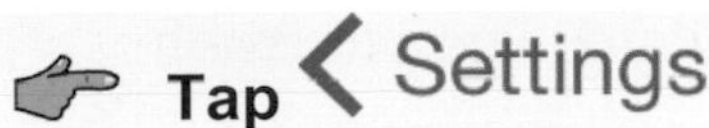

Tap < Settings

Check to see if the wallpaper of the lock screen has indeed been changed. Here is how to close the *Settings* app:

Press the Home button

Put the iPhone into sleep mode:

Press the On/Off button

Wake the iPhone up from sleep mode 1

1.8 Using the Keyboard

Your iPhone contains a useful onscreen keyboard, which will appear whenever you need to type something. For example, if you want to take notes in the *Notes* app. Here is how to open the *Notes* app:

Tap Notes

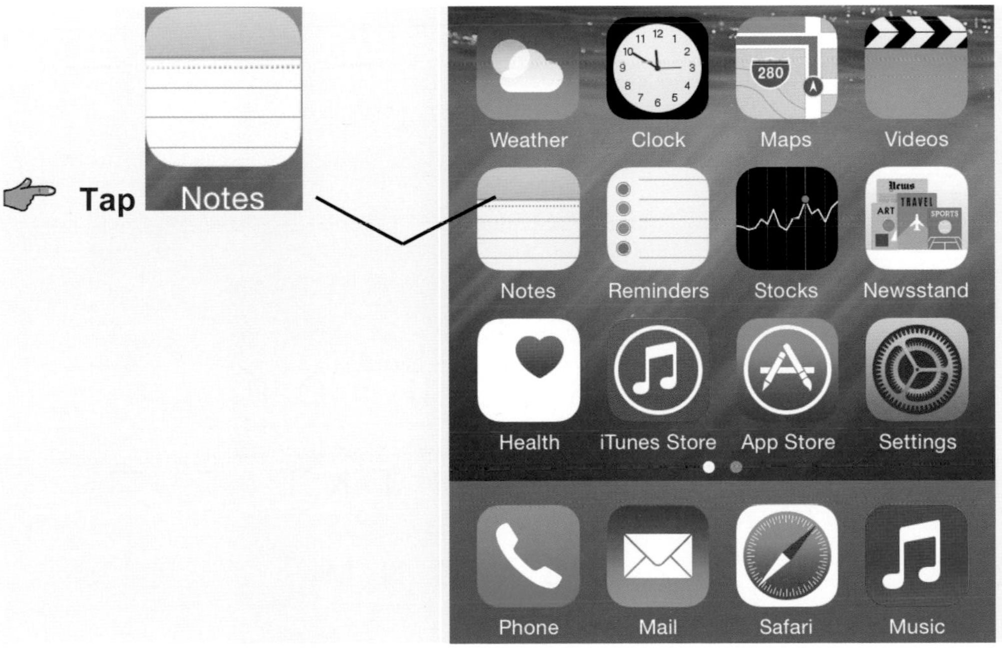

You will see a new, blank notes page with the onscreen keyboard. The onscreen keyboard works almost the same way as a regular keyboard. You simply tap the keys instead of pressing them. Just give it a try:

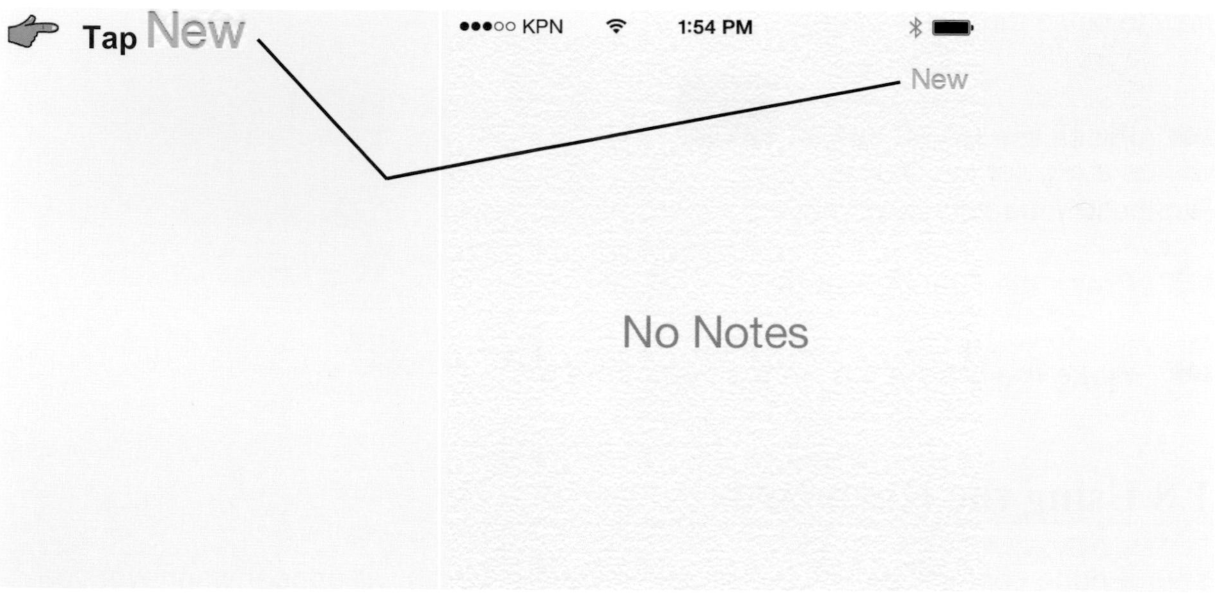

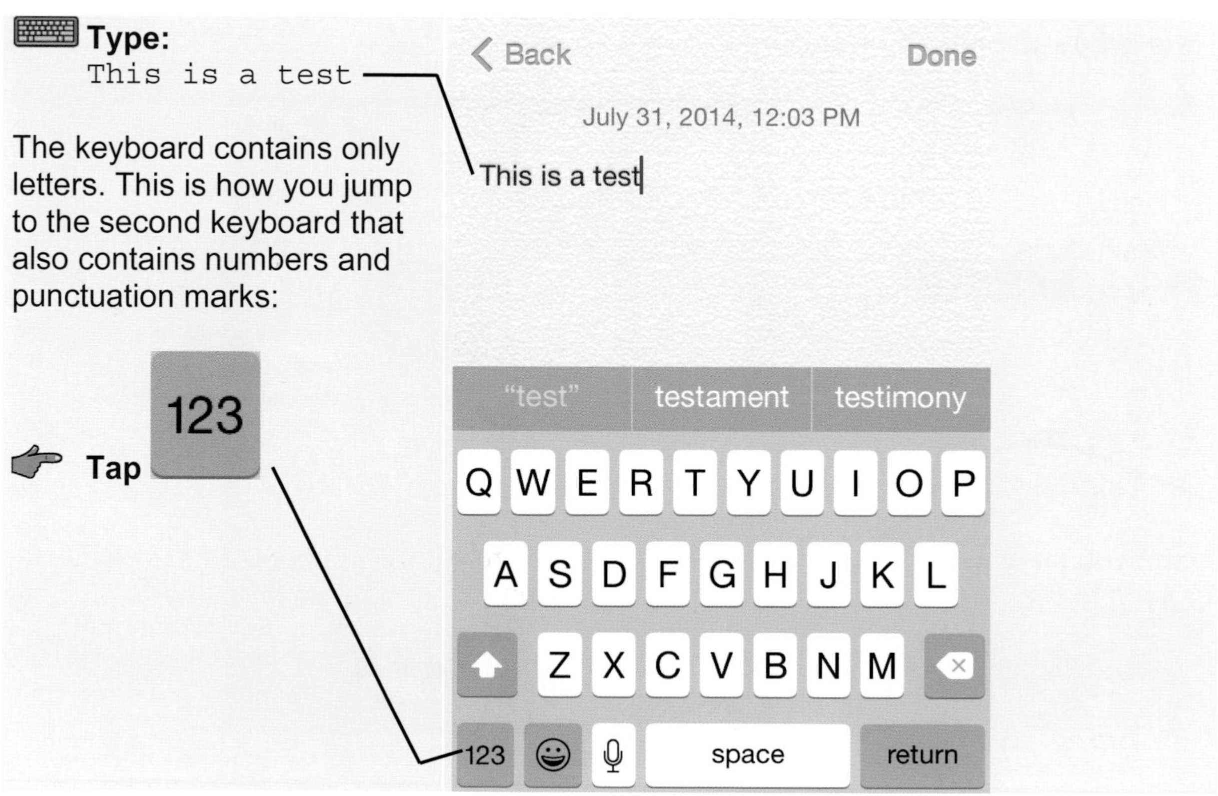

Type a period at the end of the sentence:

Type a period .

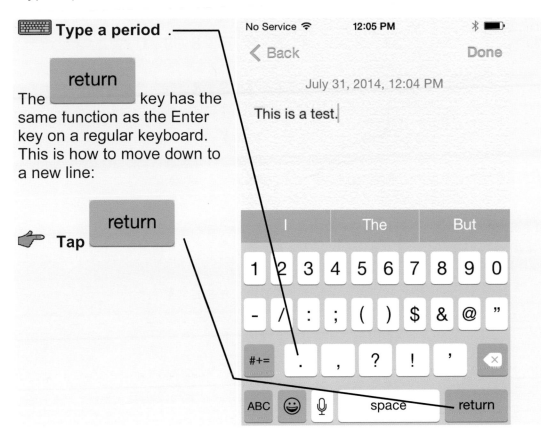

The return key has the same function as the Enter key on a regular keyboard. This is how to move down to a new line:

Tap return

Tip

Capital letters

New sentences will automatically start with a capital letter. This is how you type a capital letter in the middle of a sentence:

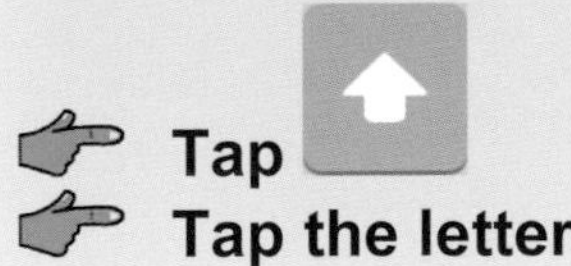

Tap the letter

When you start a new line, you will see the keyboard again with the letters. Now try jumping to the keyboard with the numbers and punctuation marks once more:

Type the first part of a simple sum:

Type: `12-10`

For the = symbol you need to use the third view of the onscreen keyboard:

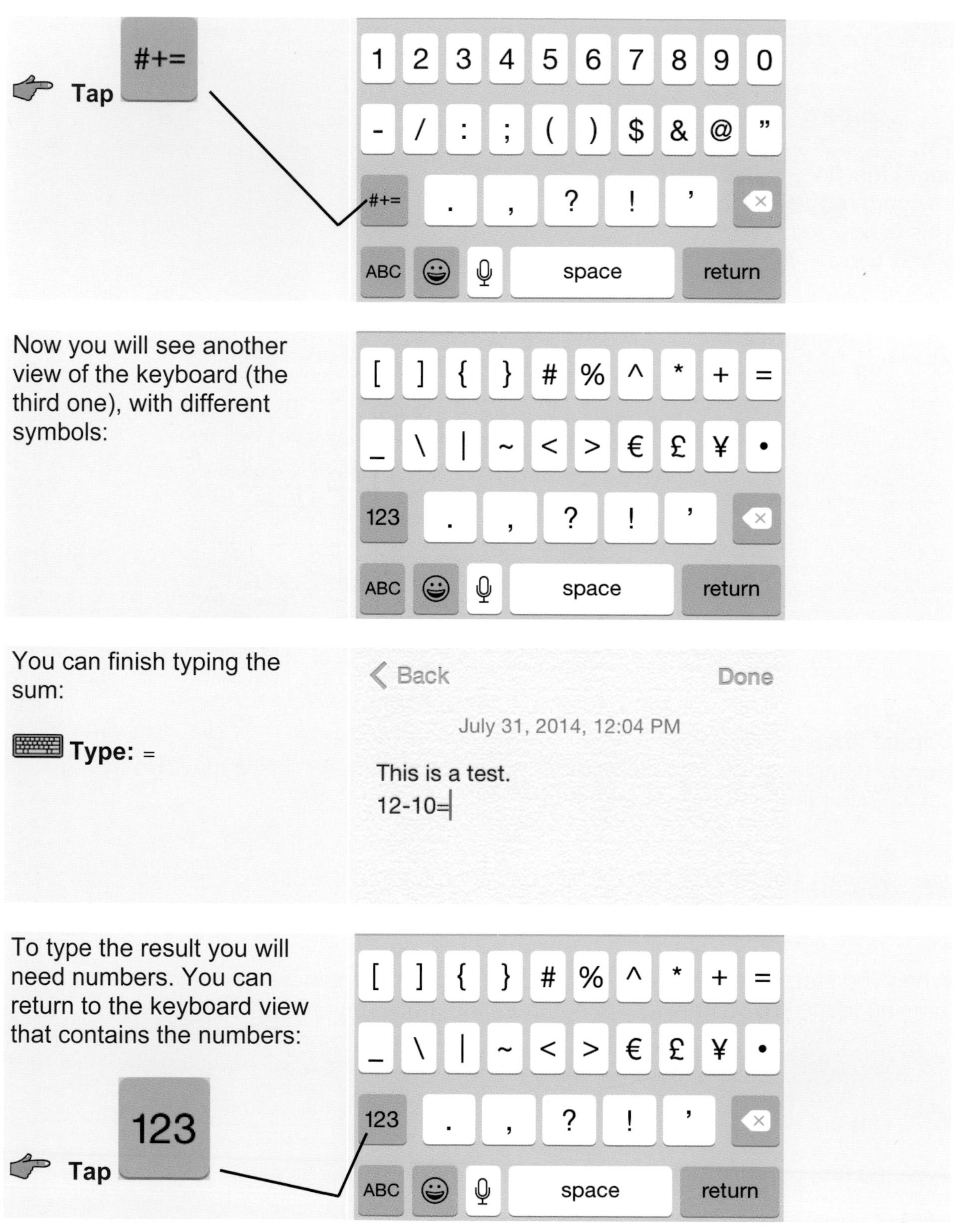

Tap **#+=**

Now you will see another view of the keyboard (the third one), with different symbols:

You can finish typing the sum:

Type: =

To type the result you will need numbers. You can return to the keyboard view that contains the numbers:

Tap **123**

Once again, you will see the onscreen keyboard with the numbers and punctuation marks:

Type: 3

This will make a typing error. You can correct that like this:

Tap

The wrong answer to the sum will be deleted.

Type: 2

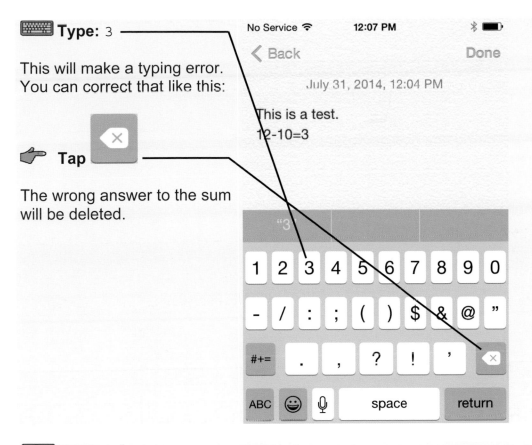

Now the answer is correct.

Tip

Back to the default view of the onscreen keyboard

This is how you go back to the default onscreen keyboard if you are viewing the keyboard with numbers and the special characters:

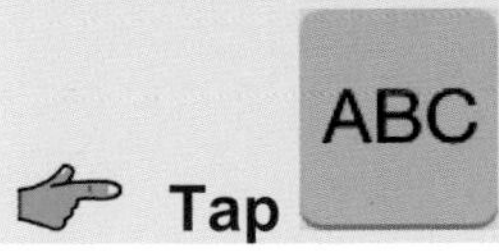

Now you can practice deleting the note. First, you need to stop editing the note:

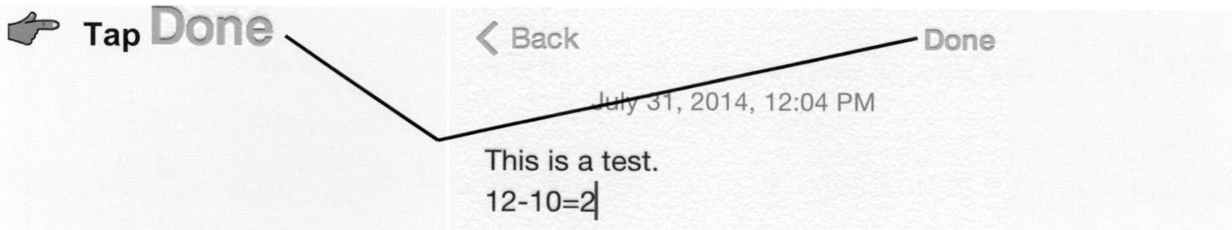

The onscreen keyboard has disappeared.

Tip

Display the onscreen keyboard again
This is how you display the onscreen keyboard again:

You can delete the note with a button at the bottom of the screen:

You need to confirm this operation:

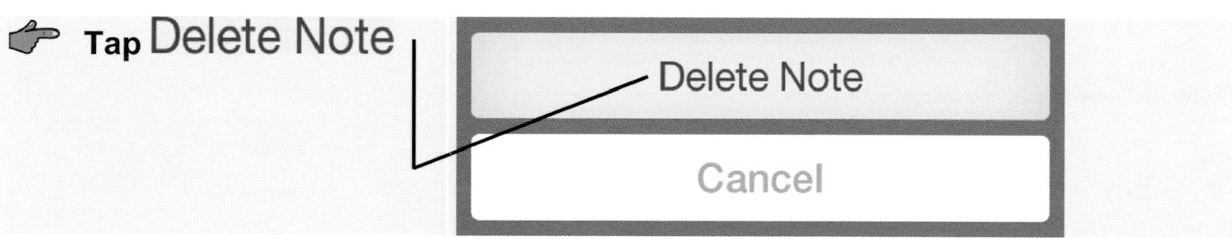

This is how you quit the *Notes* app:

Up to this point, you have performed some of the basic operations and have started to use some of the touch actions necessary to maneuver through the information on the iPhone screen. There are several other touch actions, such as scrolling sideways, zooming in and zooming out. We will discuss these at a later stage, as soon as you need to use them.

1.9 Connect to the Internet with Wi-Fi

You may have already connected to the Internet while you were setting up your iPhone. But it can happen that the default network is not available. Perhaps you are using the iPhone at a different location, for example a hotspot, or your own default network is temporarily down for some reason. If you have access to a wireless network, you can connect to the Internet with that.

Please note:

To follow the steps in this section, you will need to have access to a wireless network (Wi-Fi). If you do not (yet) have access, you can read through this section.

You will need to go to the *Settings* app:

Open the *Settings* app 3

To connect to a Wi-Fi-network:

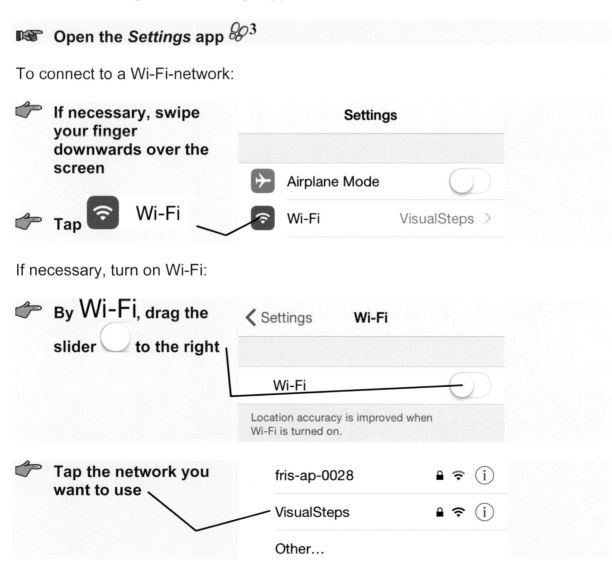

If necessary, swipe your finger downwards over the screen

Tap Wi-Fi

If necessary, turn on Wi-Fi:

By Wi-Fi**, drag the slider to the right**

Tap the network you want to use

If you see a padlock icon next to the network name, for instance VisualSteps, you will need a password to gain access to this network.

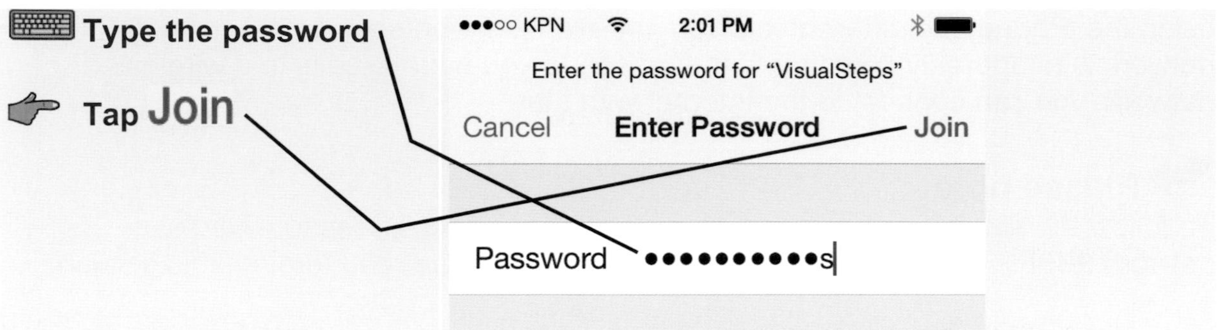

In future, the connection with known wireless networks will automatically be established as soon as you turn on Wi-Fi. You can check this, by turning off Wi-Fi first:

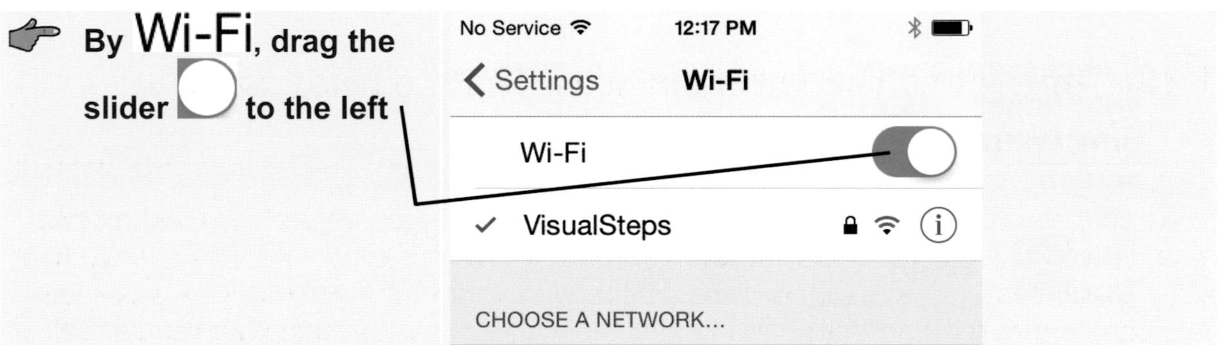

Now Wi-Fi has been turned off and you will see that the button looks like this. The icon has disappeared from the status bar.

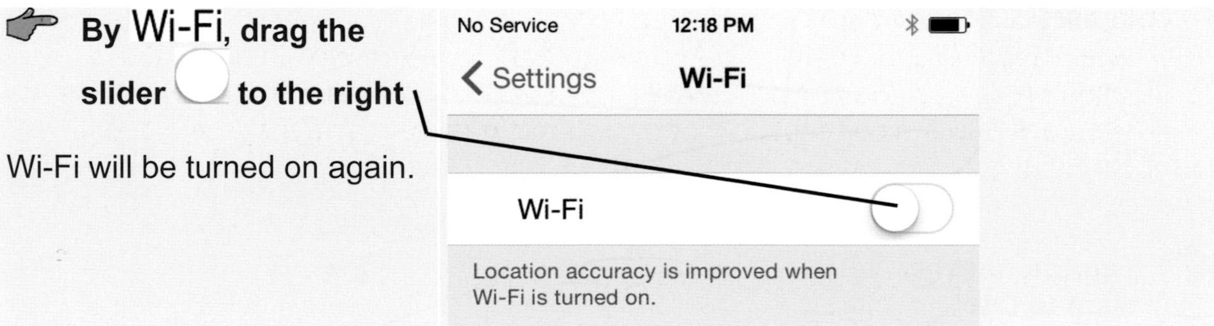

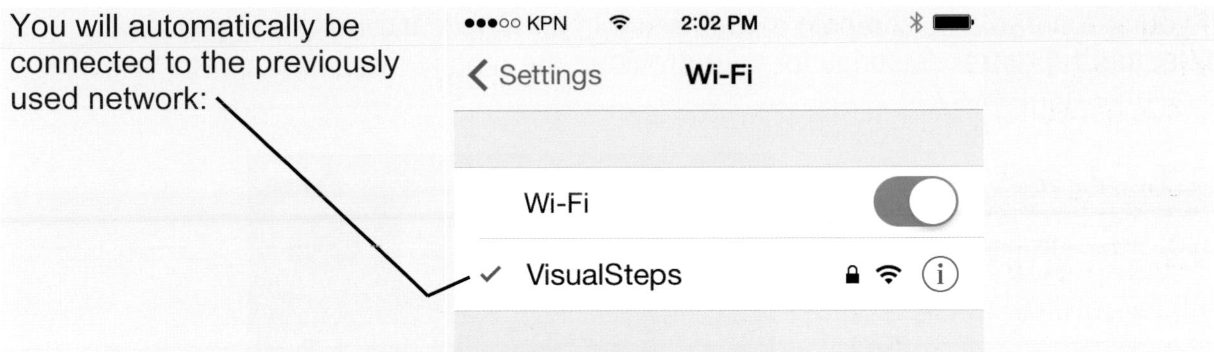

If you want, you can disable Wi-Fi again

1.10 Connect to the Internet with the Cellular Data Network

You can also connect to the Internet with a cellular data network (also called mobile data network). This is very useful when you do not have access to a Wi-Fi network. But you will need to have a data subscription with your mobile provider, or a prepaid SIM card where the Internet networking costs are handled through your regular cell phone account. If you do not (yet) have such a subscription, you can just read through this section.

 **Tip**

Enable mobile Internet

If you are using a prepaid card, you first need to activate the mobile Internet connection and select the correct settings for your iPhone. Some mobile providers will let you activate the connection by sending a text message to a specific phone number. Next, you will receive a text message in reply, containing the correct settings:

Follow the instructions in the next few screens

You can also go to your mobile phone provider's website, or phone the customer service for information about the settings for mobile Internet on your iPhone.

If your subscription or prepaid card is suitable for mobile Internet, and you have selected the correct settings for your provider, the mobile Internet connection will be available right away.

If the iPhone status bar displays the 3G (**3G**) or 4G (**4G**), EDGE (**E**), or GPRS (**O**) symbols, the device is connected to the Internet through the cellular data network.

 **Tip**

Check your subscription

Before you start using your iPhone for connecting to the Internet over the cellular data network, it is recommended that you check the fees for this type of connection. This will prevent you from getting unpleasant surprises.

Does your regular fee cover the expenses of connecting to the Internet? Or are you allowed unlimited use of the Internet at a fixed, monthly fee? Or do you pay for a fixed amount of data each month? What will it cost you if you exceed the limits?

If necessary, you can temporarily turn off the Internet connection over the cellular data network. In this way, you can prevent your children (or grandchildren) from using your prepaid account for playing games on your iPhone, for example, or you can block the use of the Internet while you are abroad.

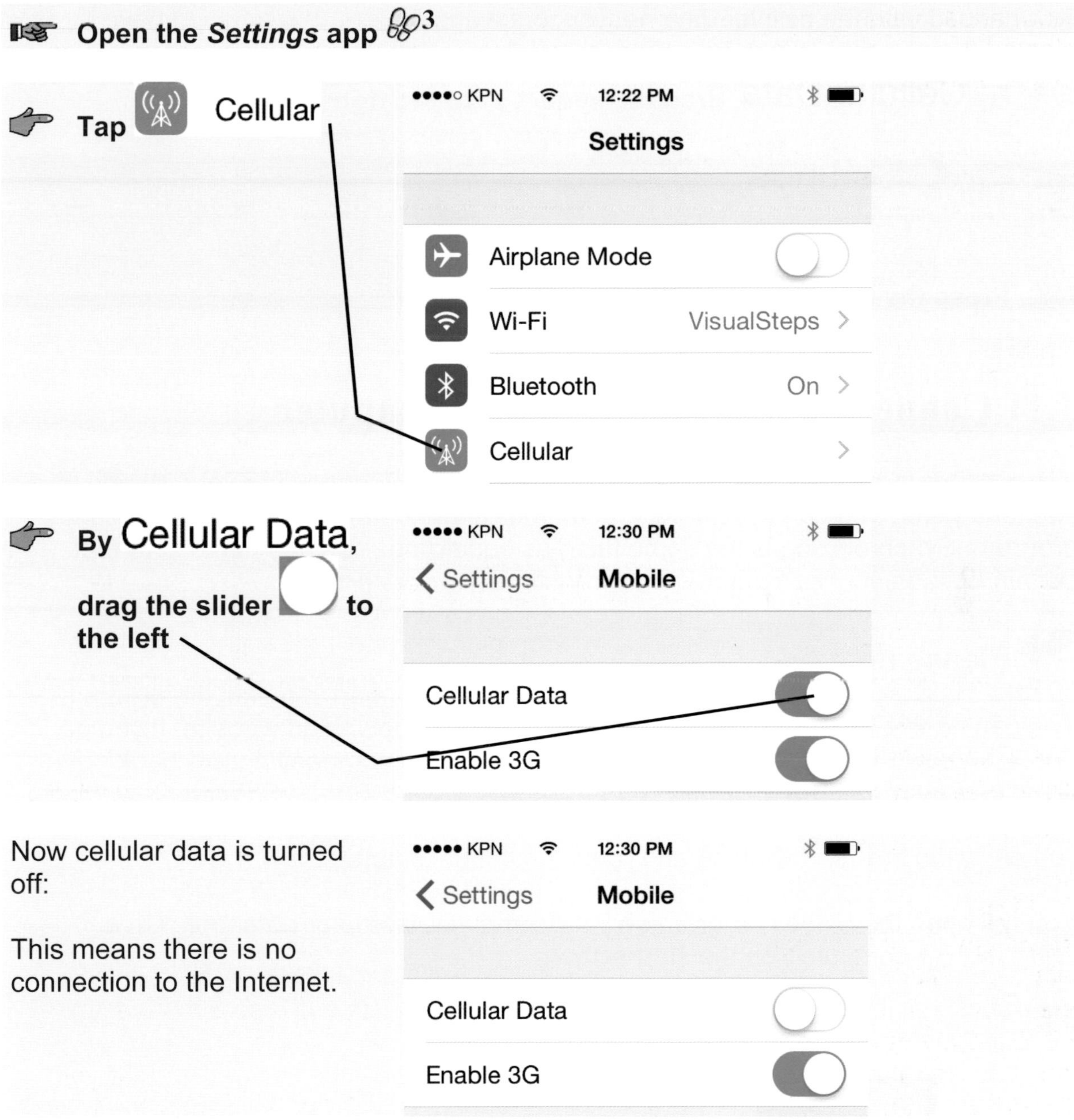

Please note:

If you use cellular data, by default, the Data Roaming function will be disabled. *Data roaming* means you can use the data network of a different provider, when your own provider's network is not available. Be careful: if you enable this function while abroad, the costs can be prohibitive.

You can activate the cellular data network once again:

1.11 Connecting the iPhone to the Computer

It is possible to connect the iPhone to the computer. By connecting your iPhone to your computer, you can synchronize data, music and other files through the *iTunes* program. Synchronizing is the same thing as equalizing. You can make sure that certain data on your computer is also transferred to your iPhone.

Please note:

If *iTunes* is not yet installed on your computer, you will need to install the program. You can do this by visiting the www.apple.com/itunes/download website. If you do not know how to install programs, check the website accompanying this book **www.visualsteps.com/iphone8**. There you will find the *Bonus Chapter Download and Install iTunes*. In *Appendix B Opening Bonus Chapters* at the end of this book, you can read how to download and open the bonus chapters.

You will open the *iTunes* program on your computer, laptop or notebook. On a *Windows 8.1* computer, on the start screen:

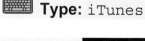

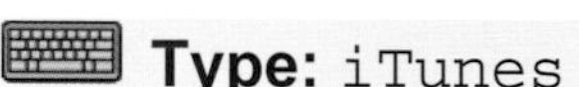

On a *Windows 7* or *Vista* computer:

You may see a window in which you are asked to accept the software license agreement:

If necessary, click **Agree**

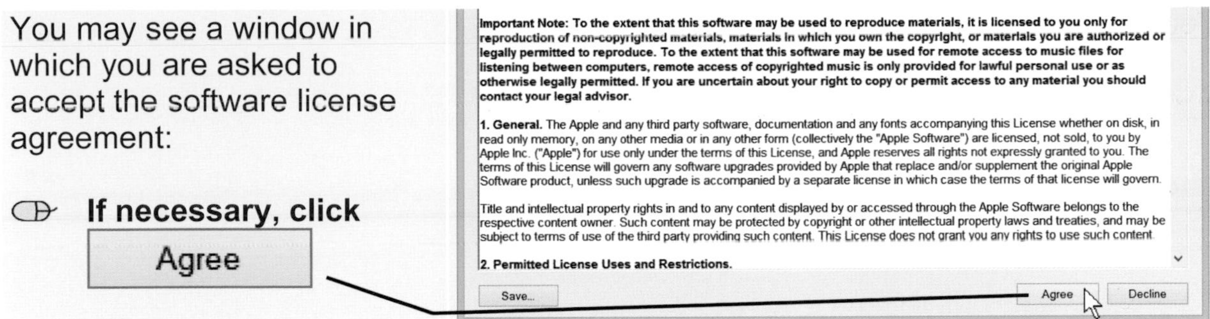

You may also see the window *iTunes Quick Tour*. You can close this window:

If necessary, close the window 5

You will see the opening window of *iTunes*:

Click **Agree**

Please note: you may see a different window on your own screen, but this will not affect the actions you need to perform in this section.

Now you can connect the iPhone. Here is how you do that:

Connect the broad end of the white Dock Connector-to-USB-cable to the iPhone

Connect the other end to one of your computer's USB ports

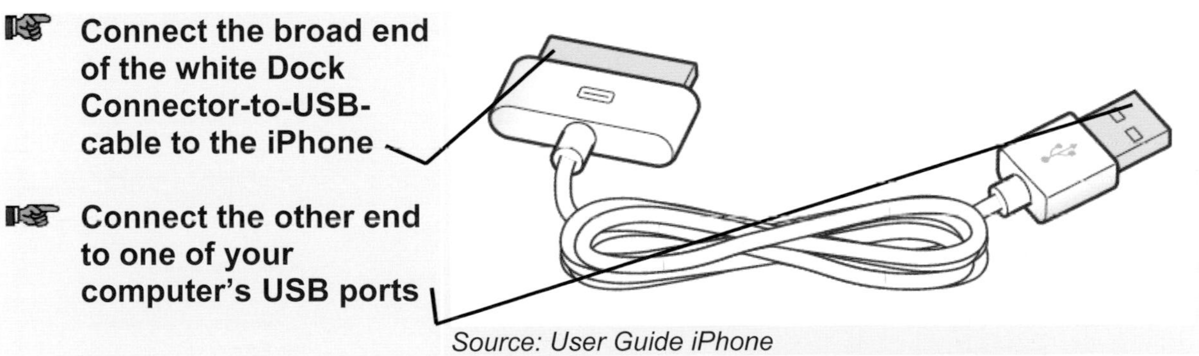

Source: User Guide iPhone

You may see a message like this at your computer screen:

Apple iPhone
Tap to choose what happens with this device.

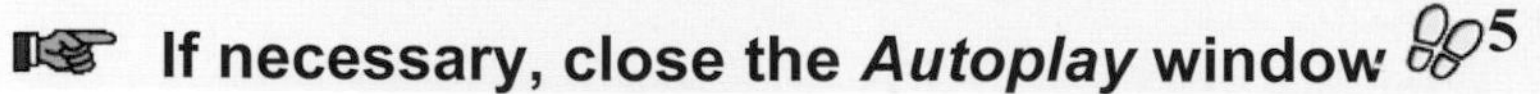

You may also see the *Autoplay* window.

If necessary, close the *Autoplay* window 5

After a while you will probably see this window:

Click Continue

If you see a different window, it will probably be the window on the bottom of this page, or the window in the Help frame on the next page. In that case, continue with the relevant window.

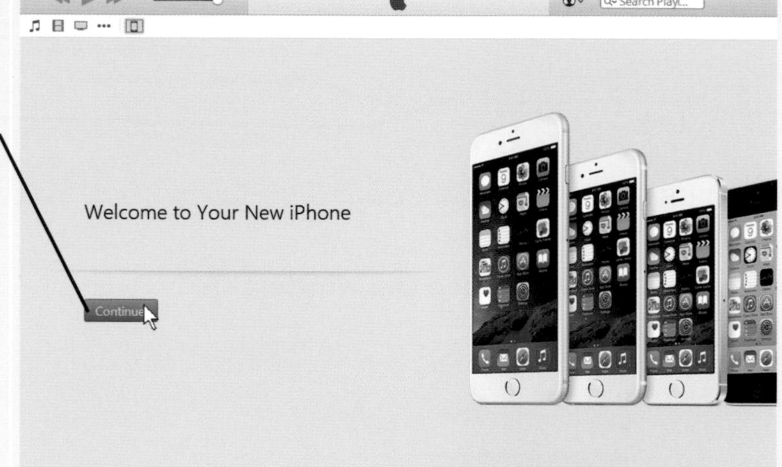

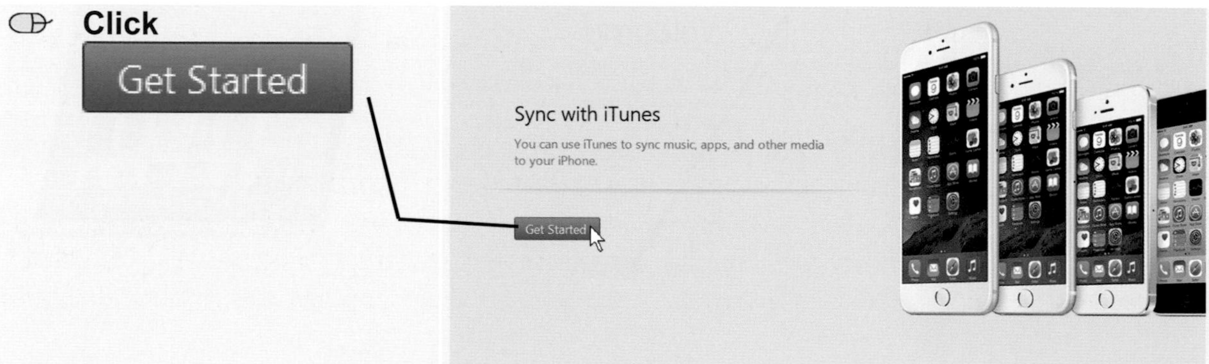

Now you will see this window:

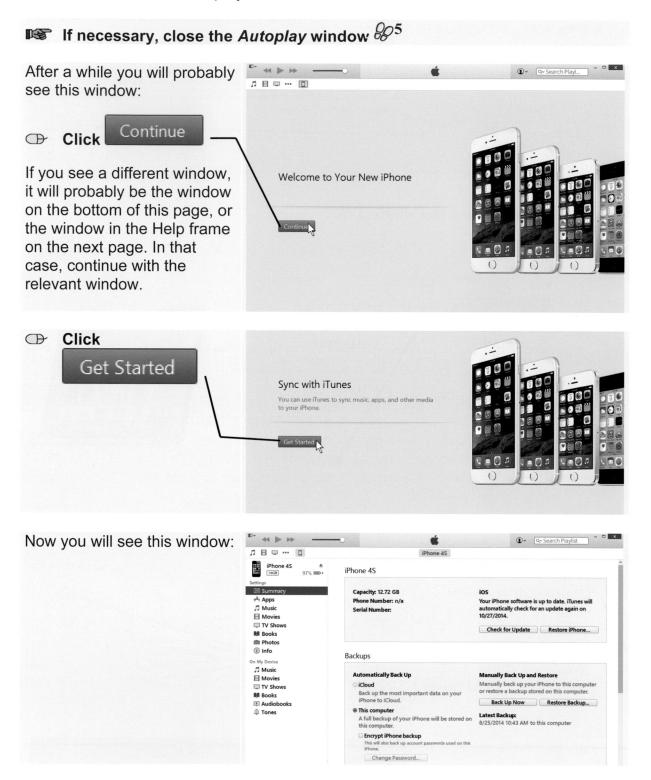

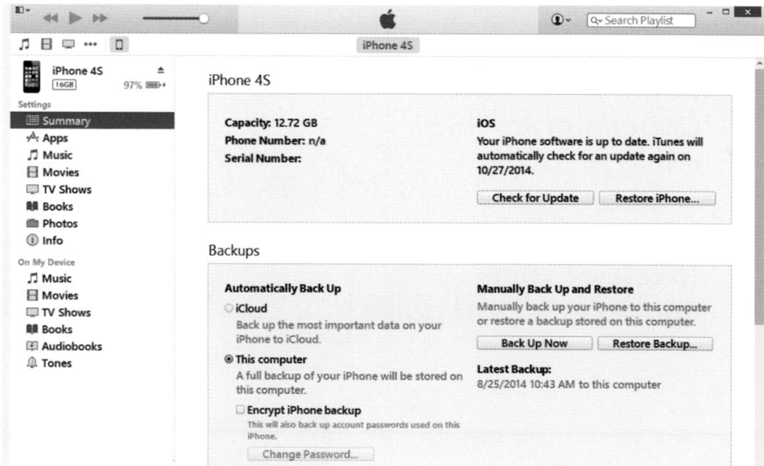

HELP! I see a different window.

If you have previously used your iPhone with *iTunes*, you will see a different window:

At the top left of the window:

Click

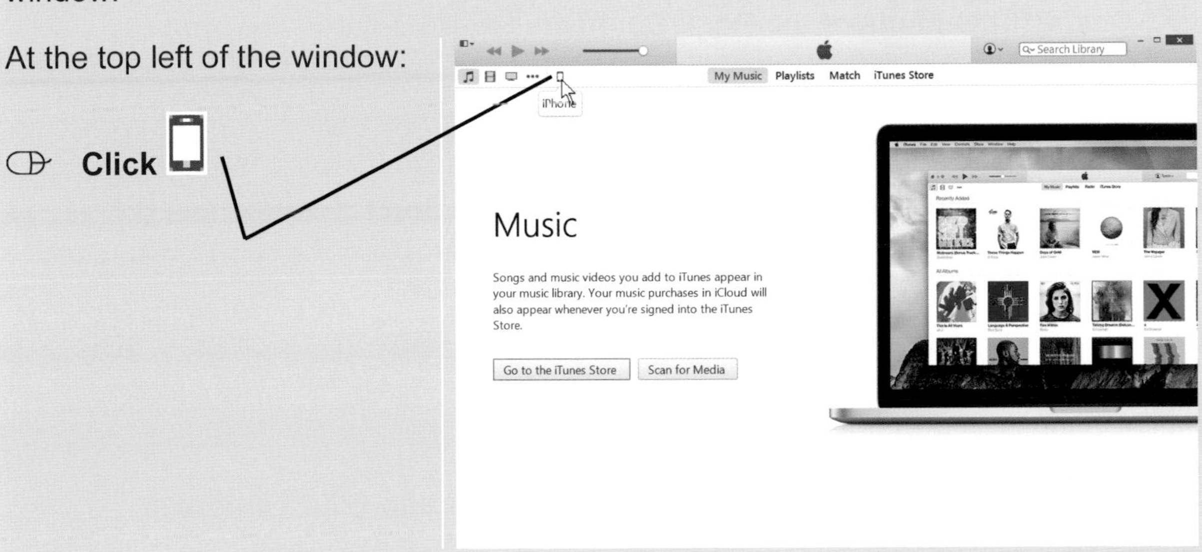

Now you will see the window described on the previous page and you can continue executing the operations on page 59.

HELP! I see a window with a registration message.

If you connect your iPhone for the first time, you may even see a different window altogether. You will be asked to register the iPhone. It is up to you whether you want to register. If you do, then just follow the operations in the various windows.

HELP! Update for provider settings.

You may see a message in *iTunes* regarding an update for the settings of your iPhone's provider. These types of updates are small files (approximately 10 kB) that should be installed on your iPhone.
The update has to do with the way in which your iPhone connects to the provider's cellular network. You should install the most recent provider settings updates for your device, as soon as they are available.

Follow the instructions in the next few windows

HELP! My iPhone does not appear in the window.

If your iPhone is not displayed in *iTunes*, you can try to do the following things:

- **Check if the plugs of the Dock Connector-to-USB-cable are properly connected**
- **Charge the iPhone's battery if it is nearly empty**
- **Disconnect other USB devices from your computer and connect the iPhone to a different USB port of the computer. Do not use the USB ports on the keyboard, in the monitor or in a USB hub**
- **Unlock the iPhone, if it is locked with an access code**

If the iPhone is still not recognized in *iTunes*:

- **Restart the computer and reconnect the iPhone to your computer**

If this does not work, then restart the iPhone. Here is how you do that:

- **Press and hold the on/off button pressed in until you see a slider appear on the screen (see *section 1.2 Turn On the iPhone or Wake It Up From Sleep Mode*)**
- **Drag this slider to the right**
- **Press and hold the on/off button pressed in for a second time, until you see the Apple logo**
- **Try to connect your iPhone once again**
- **If necessary, download and install the most recent version of the *iTunes* program from the www.apple.com/itunes/download website**
- **Try to connect your iPhone once again, preferably to a different USB port**

First, you need to enter an identifiable name for your iPhone:

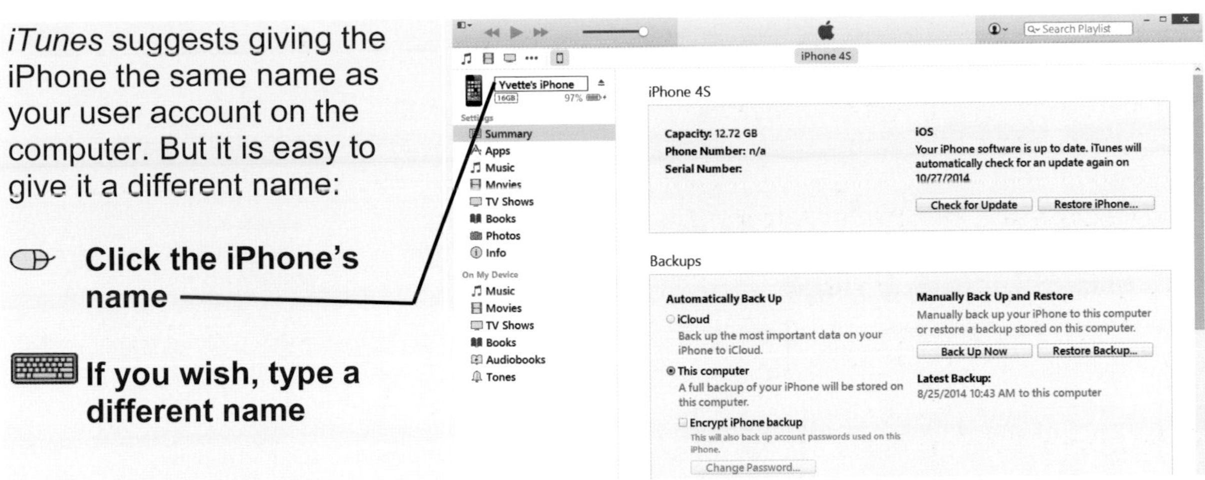

iTunes suggests giving the iPhone the same name as your user account on the computer. But it is easy to give it a different name:

- **Click the iPhone's name**
- **If you wish, type a different name**

Although *iTunes* does not automatically synchronize tracks, photos, or other items if you have not started such an operation yourself, *iTunes* started synchronizing by itself when you connected it to the computer. In this case, no data has been transferred to the iPhone, but a backup copy of the iPhone has been created:

When the synchronization is in progress, at the top of the screen you will see the progress of the synchronizing operation:

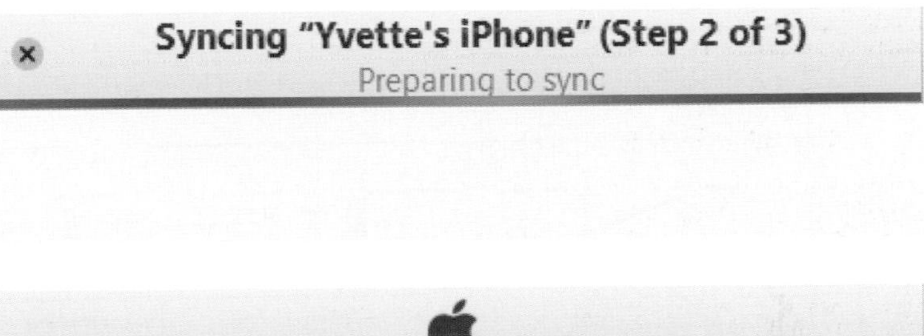

As soon as you see the Apple logo, you can continue:

Synchronizing means making sure the contents of your iPhone are identical to the contents of your *Library*. Songs, videos and apps that are no longer part of your library, will be removed from your iPhone during the synchronization process. You will be better able to control the contents of your iPhone if you disable the automatic synchronization and manually start the synchronization operation, whenever you feel like it. You are going to check the settings for automatic synchronization:

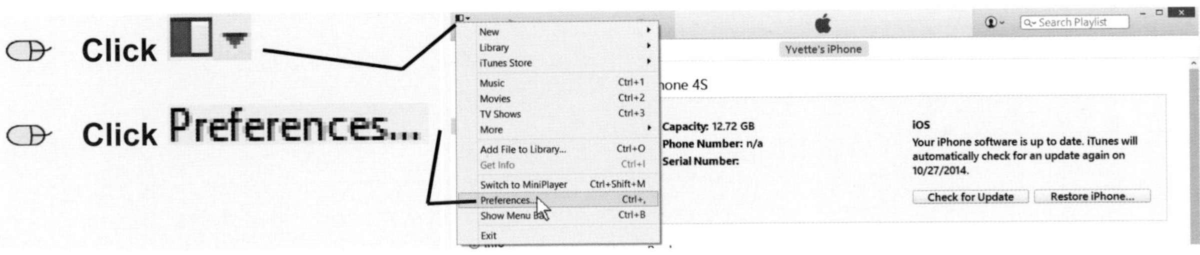

You will see a window with a set of buttons (icons) across the top:

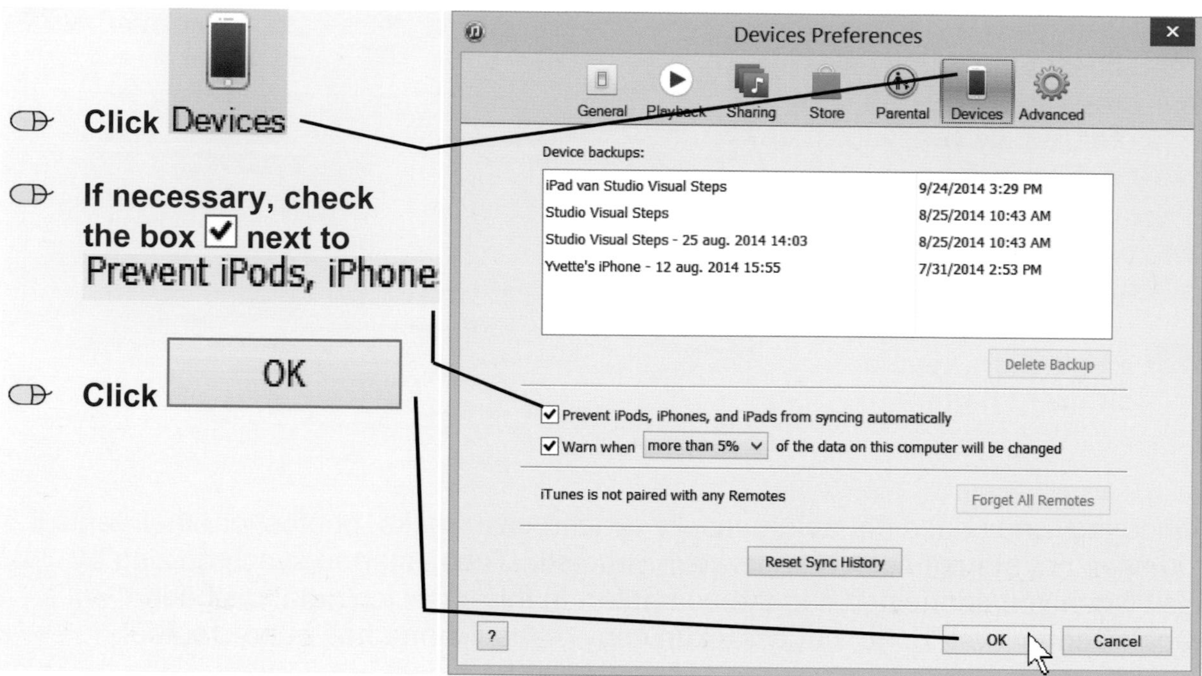

- Click Devices
- If necessary, check the box ☑ next to Prevent iPods, iPhone
- Click OK

You will see the *Summary* tab:

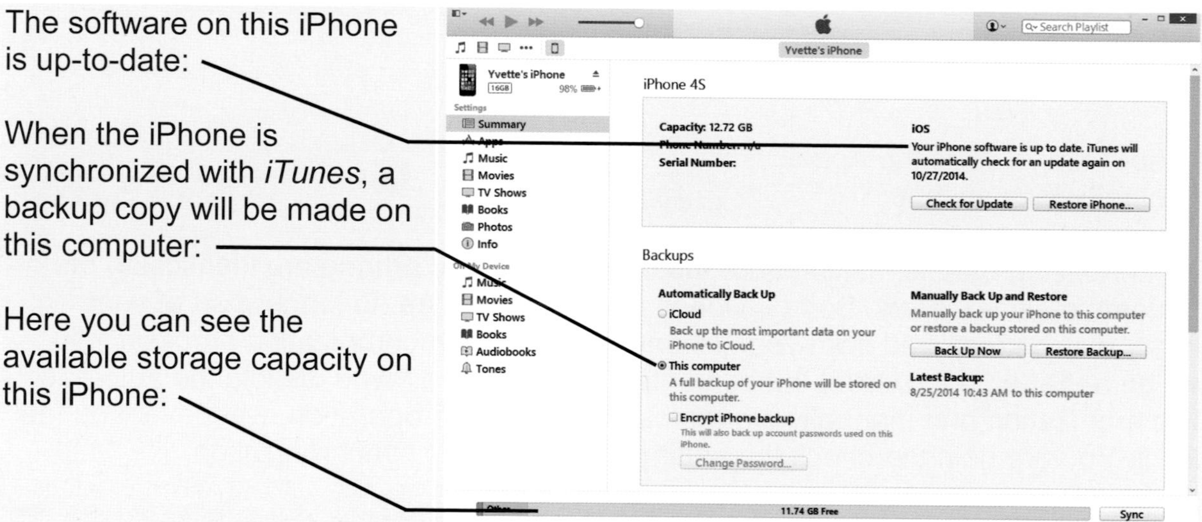

The software on this iPhone is up-to-date:

When the iPhone is synchronized with *iTunes*, a backup copy will be made on this computer:

Here you can see the available storage capacity on this iPhone:

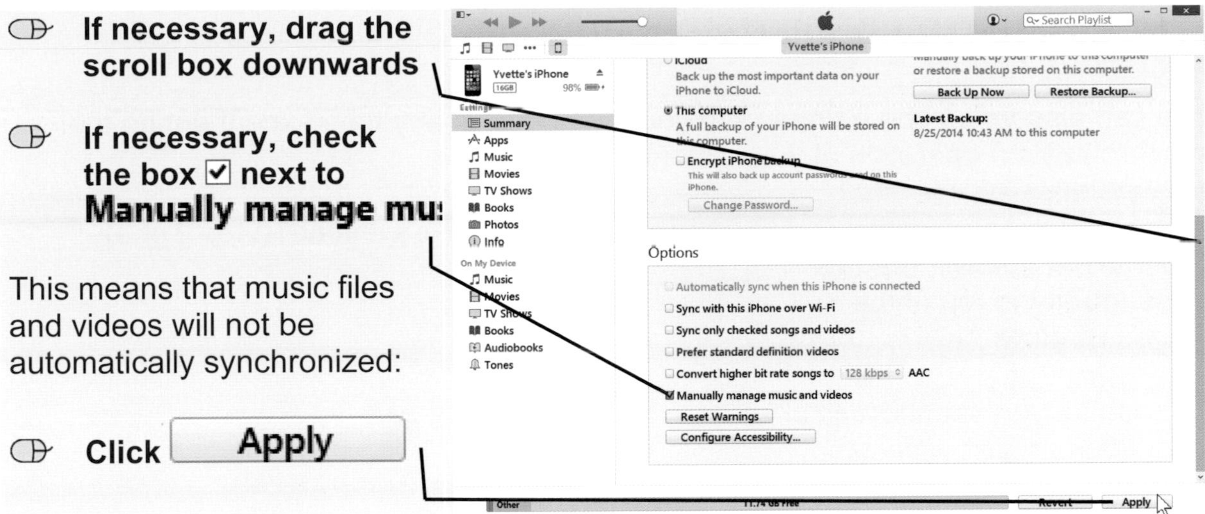

- **If necessary, drag the scroll box downwards**
- **If necessary, check the box ☑ next to Manually manage mu:**

This means that music files and videos will not be automatically synchronized:

- **Click Apply**

Tip

Wireless synchronization of the iPhone with iTunes

You have learned how to connect the iPhone to the computer with the so-called Dock Connector-to-USB-cable. But it is also possible to synchronize your iPhone with *iTunes* without using a cable.

On the *Summary* tab:

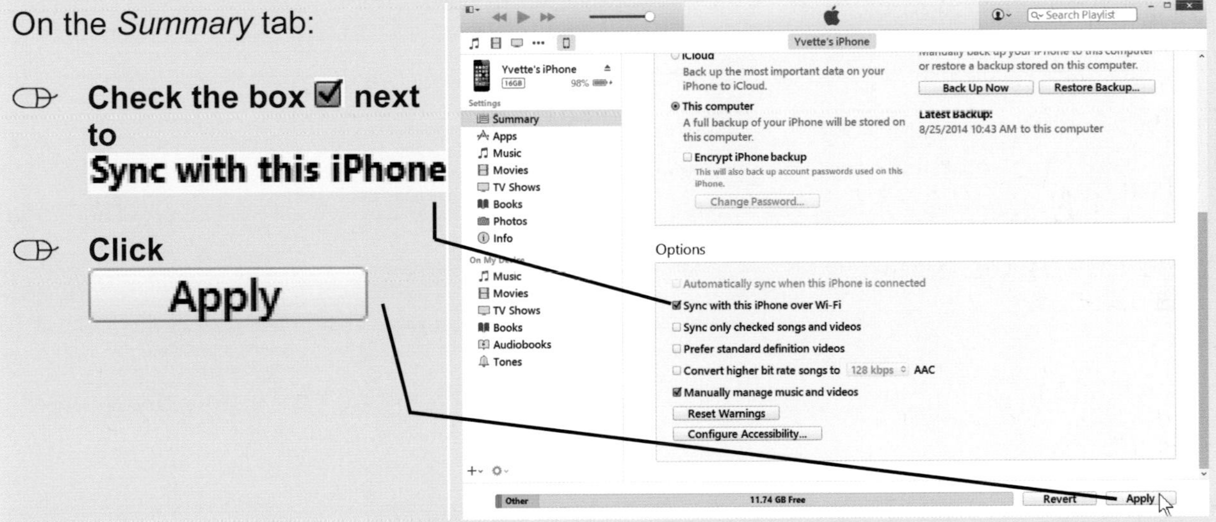

- **Check the box ☑ next to Sync with this iPhone**
- **Click Apply**

Each time the iPhone and the computer are connected to the same network, the iPhone will become visible in the *iTunes* program.

1.12 Safely Disconnecting the iPhone

You can disconnect the iPhone from your computer at any time except during the synchronization operation of your iPhone with *iTunes*.

When the synchronization is in progress, you will see this message at the top of the *iTunes* window:

As soon as you see the Apple logo, you can disconnect the iPhone:

This is how you disconnect your iPhone from *iTunes*:

By your iPhone's name:

Click ⏏

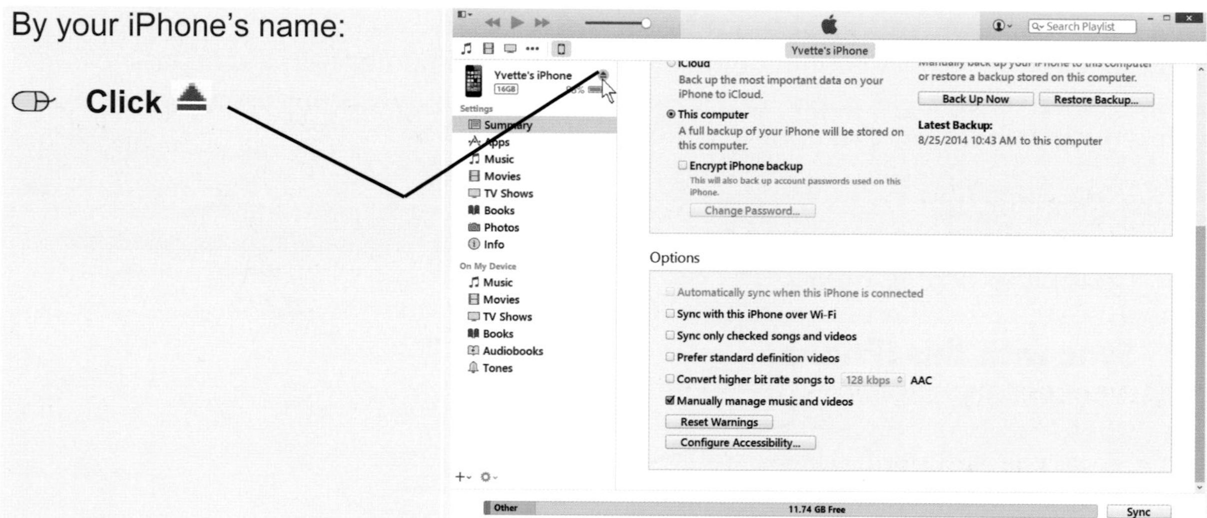

The iPhone is no longer visible in the *iTunes* window. Now you can safely disconnect the iPhone.

Disconnect the iPhone

You can close *iTunes*:

Close *iTunes* 5

1.13 Put the iPhone into Sleep Mode or Turn it Off

If you are not using the iPhone for a while, you still want to be able to receive incoming calls. If your iPhone is in sleep mode, you will always be within reach. This is how you put the iPhone into sleep mode:

Press the on/off button

The screen will be turned off.

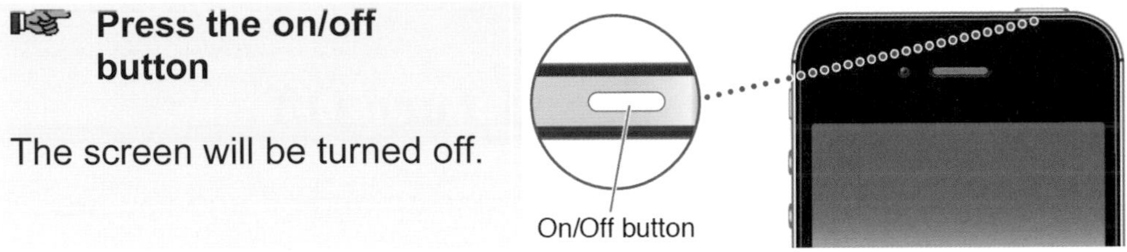

If you want to turn the iPhone off completely, you need to do this:

Press the on/off button until you see

Drag the slider to the right

If necessary, type your passcode

The screen will turn dark and the iPhone is turned off.

Please note:

If you turn off the iPhone completely, you will not be able to receive any calls!

If you want, turn your iPhone on again 1

In this chapter you have learned more about the main components of the iPhone, and have become acquainted with some of the basic operations for using this device. You have learned how to turn on the iPhone, how to connect it to the Internet, how to connect the iPhone to your computer and how to disconnect it again.

You can use the exercises on the following pages to practice and repeat these actions. In the *Background Information* and the *Tips* you will find additional information for this chapter.

1.14 Exercises

To be able to quickly apply the things you have learned, you can work through the following exercises. Have you forgotten how to do something? Use the numbers next to the footsteps 1 to look up the item in the appendix *How Do I Do That Again?* This appendix can be found at the end of the book.

Exercise 1: Turn On, Sleep Mode, and Turn Off

In this exercise you are going to practice turning the iPhone on and off and you are going to put it into sleep mode.

- If necessary, wake the iPhone up from sleep mode, or turn it on. 1
- Put the iPhone into sleep mode (lock the iPhone). 2
- Wake the iPhone up from sleep mode (unlock the iPhone). 1
- Turn off the iPhone. 2

Exercise 2: The Onscreen Keyboard

In this exercise you are going to type a short text with the onscreen keyboard.

- Turn on the iPhone. 1
- Open the *Notes* app 3 and open a new note. 7
- Type the following text:
  `The distance between Amsterdam and Paris is more than 310 miles. How many hours will it take to drive this by car?`
- Close the note. 8
- Delete the note. 9
- Go to the home screen. 10
- If you want, put the iPhone into sleep mode or turn it off. 2

1.15 Background Information

Dictionary

Airplane mode If your iPhone is in this mode, you will not have access to the Internet and you cannot use any Bluetooth devices.

App Short for *application*, a program for the iPhone.

App icons Colored icons which you can use to open various apps on the iPhone.

App Store Online store where you can download free and paid apps.

Auto-lock A function that makes sure that the iPhone is locked after a period of inactivity. The default period is one minute.

Bluetooth An open standard for wireless connections between devices which are in close proximity to each other. For example, with Bluetooth you can connect a wireless keyboard or a headset to the iPhone.

Data roaming Using the cellular data network of another provider when your own provider's network is not available. If you do this abroad this may result in extremely high costs.

EDGE Short for *Enhanced Data Rates for GSM Evolution*. It is an extension of GPRS, with which you can reach higher speeds in data traffic.

GPRS Short for *General Packet Radio Service*, a technique which is an extension of the existing GSM network. With this technology, cellular data can be sent and received more efficiently, quicker and cheaper.

Home button The button with which you return to the home screen. You can also use this button to unlock or wake up the iPhone.

- Continue on the next page -

Home screen	The screen with the app icons, which you see when you turn on and unlock the iPhone.
Hotspot	A place where wireless Internet access is offered.
iPhone	The iPhone is Apple's smartphone and has a touch screen.
iTunes	A program with which you can manage the contents of the iPhone. You can use *iTunes* to listen to audio files, view video files and import CDs. *iTunes* also has links to the *iTunes Store* and the *App Store*.
iTunes Store	Online store where you can download music, podcasts, movies, TV series, audio books and more (for a fee).
Library	The *iTunes* section where you store and manage your music, movies, books, podcasts and apps.
Location Services	With Location Services several apps, such as *Maps,* will be able to collect and use data regarding your location. The collection of location data will not be linked to your personal data. For instance, if you are connected to the Internet and have turned on Location Services, location information will be added to the photos and videos you make with your iPhone.
Lock screen	The screen you see when you turn on the iPhone. You need to unlock the iPhone on the lock screen, before you can use the phone.
Notes	An app with which you can write short notes.
Podcast	A kind of radio or TV program that can be downloaded for free from the *iTunes Store*.
SIM card	The small card that is used for cellular data traffic. The iPhone 4S uses a micro SIM card, this SIM card is also called a 3FF SIM card (Third Form Factor).The iPhone 6, 6 Plus, 5S, 5C and 5 use a nano SIM card (4FF).

- Continue on the next page -

Sim lock	A sim lock is a lock that is built-in in a cell phone or another mobile device; such a lock is meant to prevent the owner from inserting a SIM card issued by a different phone provider into the device. The reason for using a sim lock is the fact that the phone providers often offer the cell phones at a discount, along with a subscription. This is a way of holding on to their customers.
Sleep mode	You can lock the iPhone by putting it into sleep mode, if you do not use it for a while. If the iPhone is locked, nothing will happen when you touch the screen. You can still receive phone calls and you can also keep playing music. And you can also still use the volume control. You can lock your iPhone with the on/off button.
Smartphone	A cell phone that supports mobile Internet functions, along with the regular telephone functions. By using apps you can execute all sorts of tasks on a smartphone.
Synchronize	Literally: equalize. When you synchronize the iPhone with the *iTunes Library*, the contents of your iPhone will be made equal to the contents of your library. If you delete files or apps from your library, they will also be deleted from the iPhone, when you synchronize the device once again.
VPN	Short for *Virtual Private Network*. With VPN you can gain secure access to private networks, such as a company network.
Wi-Fi	Wireless network for the Internet.
3G	3G is the third generation of cell phone standards and technology. Because of higher speeds, 3G offers extensive options. For instance, you can use 3G to conduct phone conversations over the Internet.
4G	4G is the fourth generation of cell phone standards and technology. 4G is faster than 3G.

Source: User Guide iPhone, Wikipedia

1.16 Tips

Tip

Auto-lock

The default setting is for your iPhone to automatically lock and go into sleep mode after one minute of inactivity. This setting saves battery power, but you might like to keep your iPhone unlocked for a little while longer:

Open the *Settings* app 3

Tap

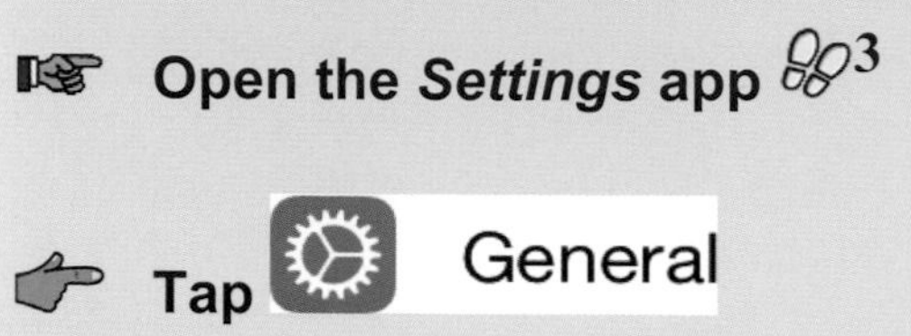

Swipe your finger upwards over the screen

Tap Auto-Lock

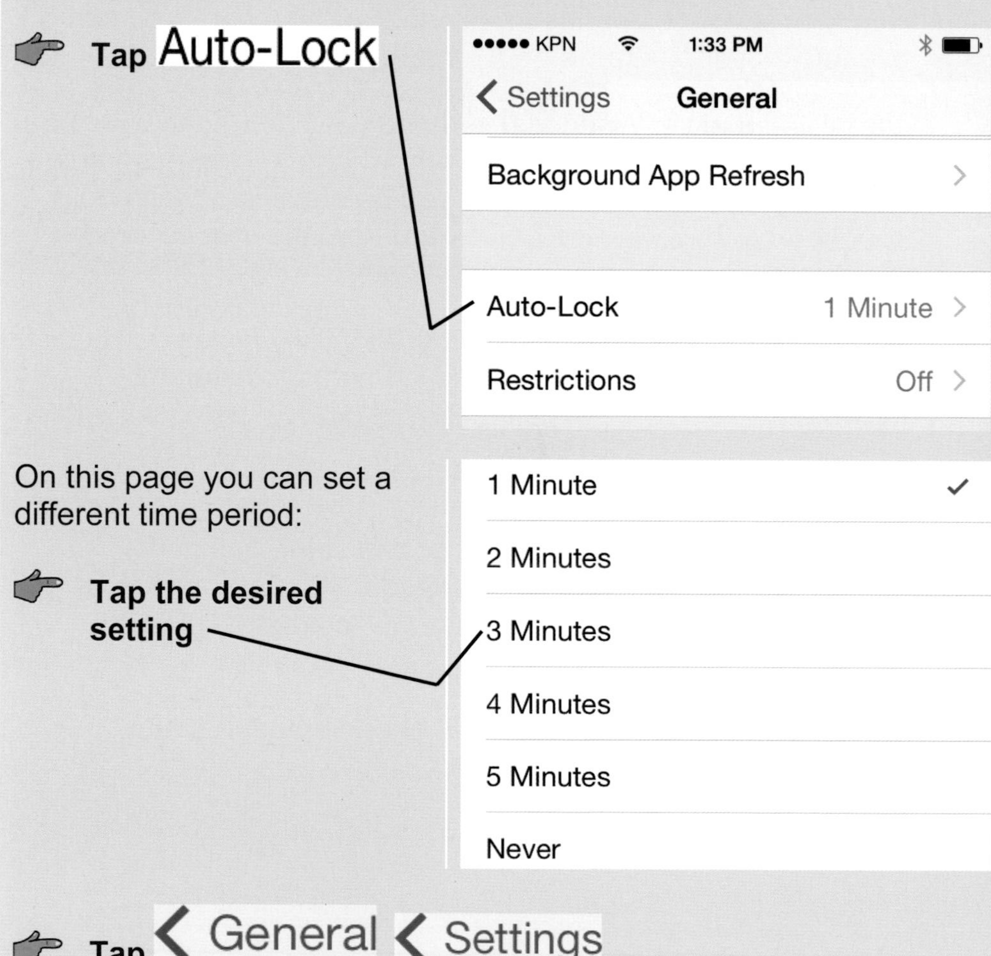

On this page you can set a different time period:

Tap the desired setting

Tap General, Settings

Go to the home screen 10

Tip

Turn off passcode protection for unlocking the iPhone
If you are annoyed by having to enter the passcode every time you unlock the iPhone, you can turn this option off, like this:

Open the *Settings* app 3

If, necessary, swipe your finger upwards over the screen

Tap Passcode

Type your passcode

On this screen you can set a different duration:

Tap Turn Passcode Off

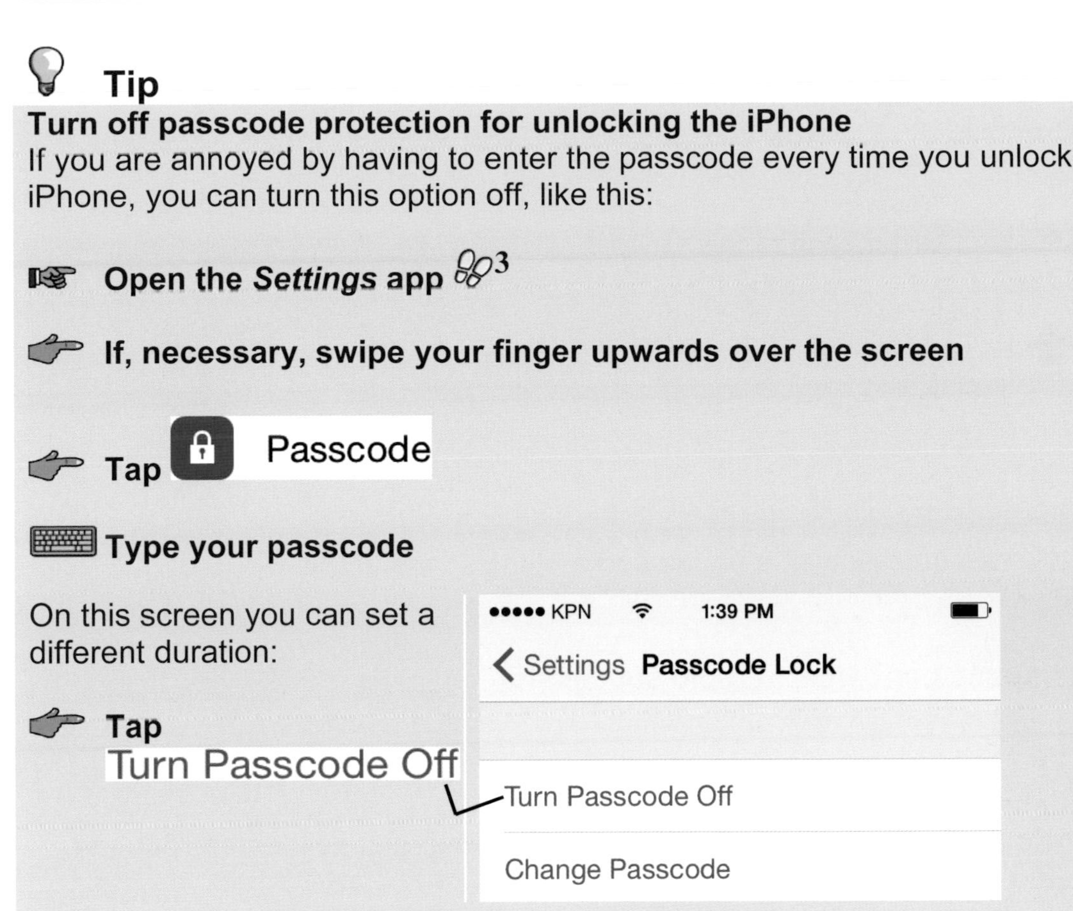

Type your passcode again

Tap 

Now you no longer need to enter a code if you want to unlock the device.

Tip

Activate Caps Lock
If you want to type only capital letters:

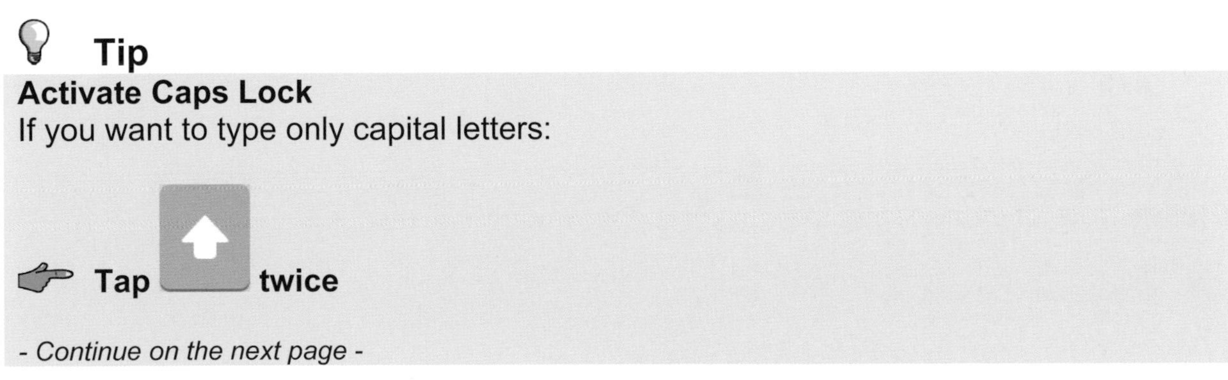

Tap **twice**

- Continue on the next page -

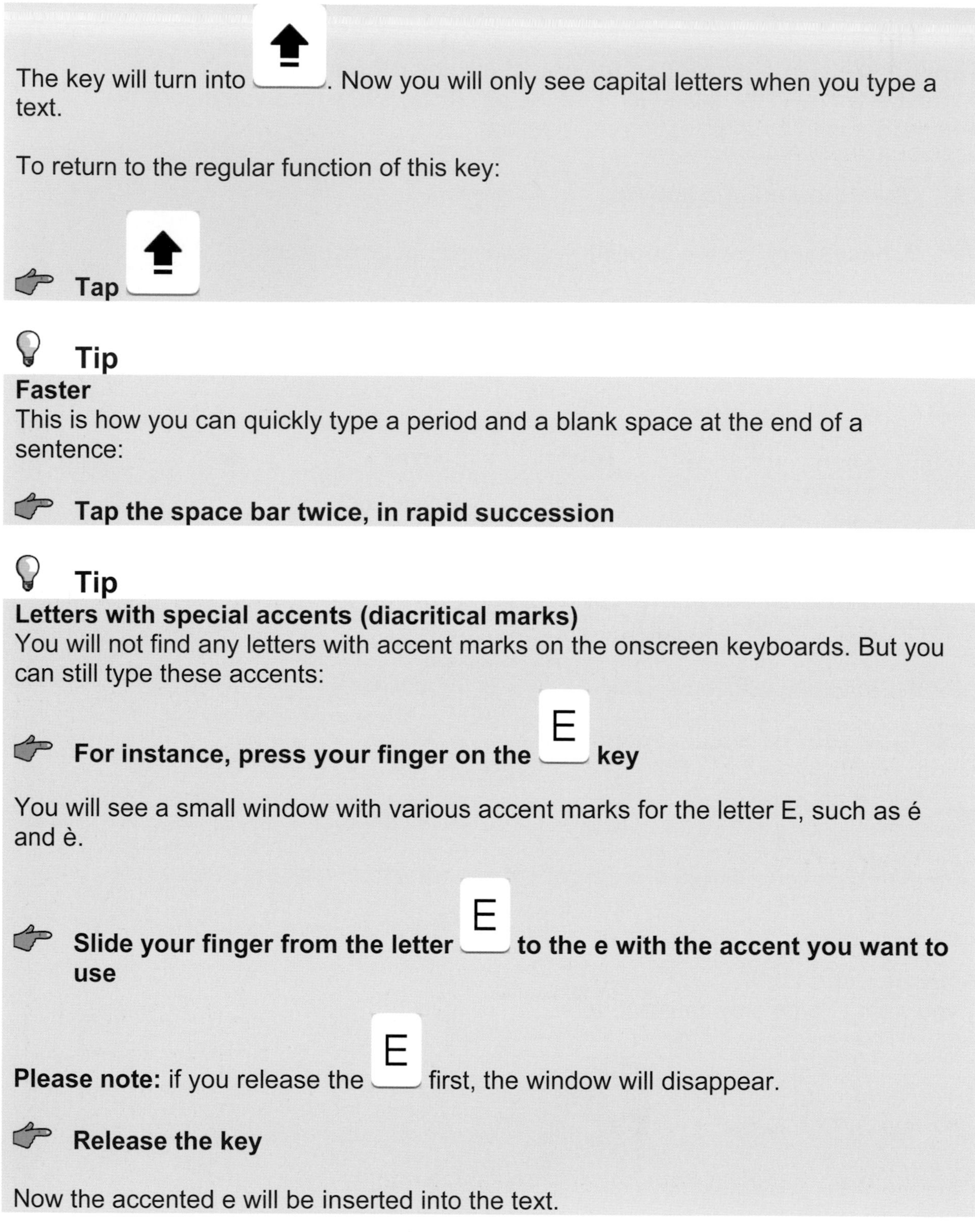

The key will turn into ⬆. Now you will only see capital letters when you type a text.

To return to the regular function of this key:

Tap ⬆

Tip

Faster

This is how you can quickly type a period and a blank space at the end of a sentence:

Tap the space bar twice, in rapid succession

Tip

Letters with special accents (diacritical marks)

You will not find any letters with accent marks on the onscreen keyboards. But you can still type these accents:

For instance, press your finger on the E **key**

You will see a small window with various accent marks for the letter E, such as é and è.

Slide your finger from the letter E **to the e with the accent you want to use**

Please note: if you release the E first, the window will disappear.

Release the key

Now the accented e will be inserted into the text.

Tip

Larger keys

If you hold the iPhone sideways, the keys on the onscreen keyboard will become larger:

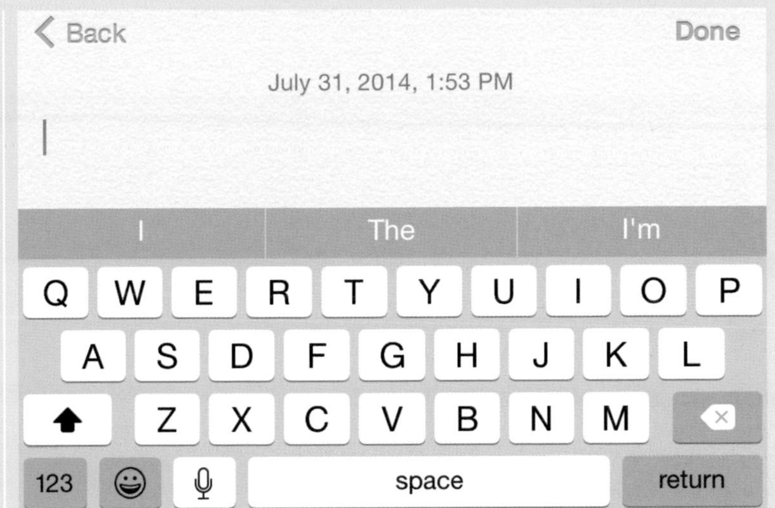

Tip

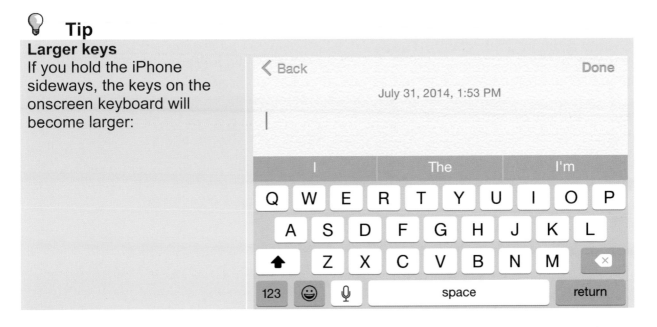

Update the iPhone through iTunes

If, at a certain point, there is no Wi-Fi connection available and you want to install a new software update, you can use *iTunes*:

- **Connect the iPhone to the computer**
- **If necessary, open *iTunes*** 11
- **If necessary, click**
- **Click**

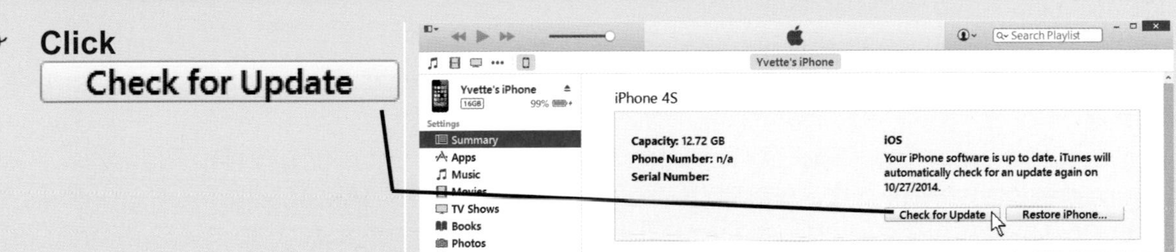

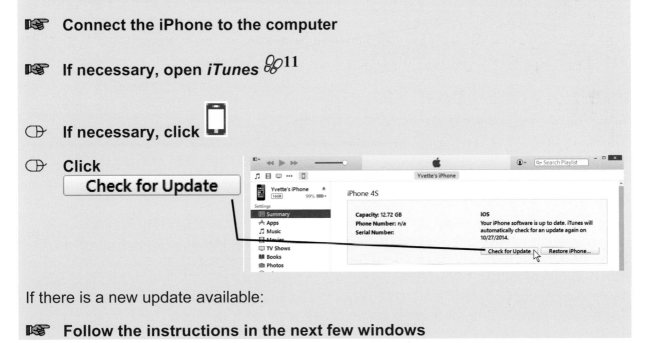

If there is a new update available:

- **Follow the instructions in the next few windows**

 **Tip**

Create a backup copy with iTunes

If you automatically or manually synchronize the iPhone with *iTunes*, a backup copy of your iPhone will be made. Among other things, *iTunes* will back up the photos, text messages, notes, the call history, the list with favorite contacts and the audio settings. Media files, such as songs and certain photos, will not be backed up. These files can be retrieved by synchronizing the iPhone with *iTunes* again.

If you do not synchronize your iPhone at all, you can also create a backup copy in this way:

- **Connect the iPhone to the computer**
- **If necessary, open *iTunes*** 11
- **If necessary, click**
- **Click** **Back Up Now**

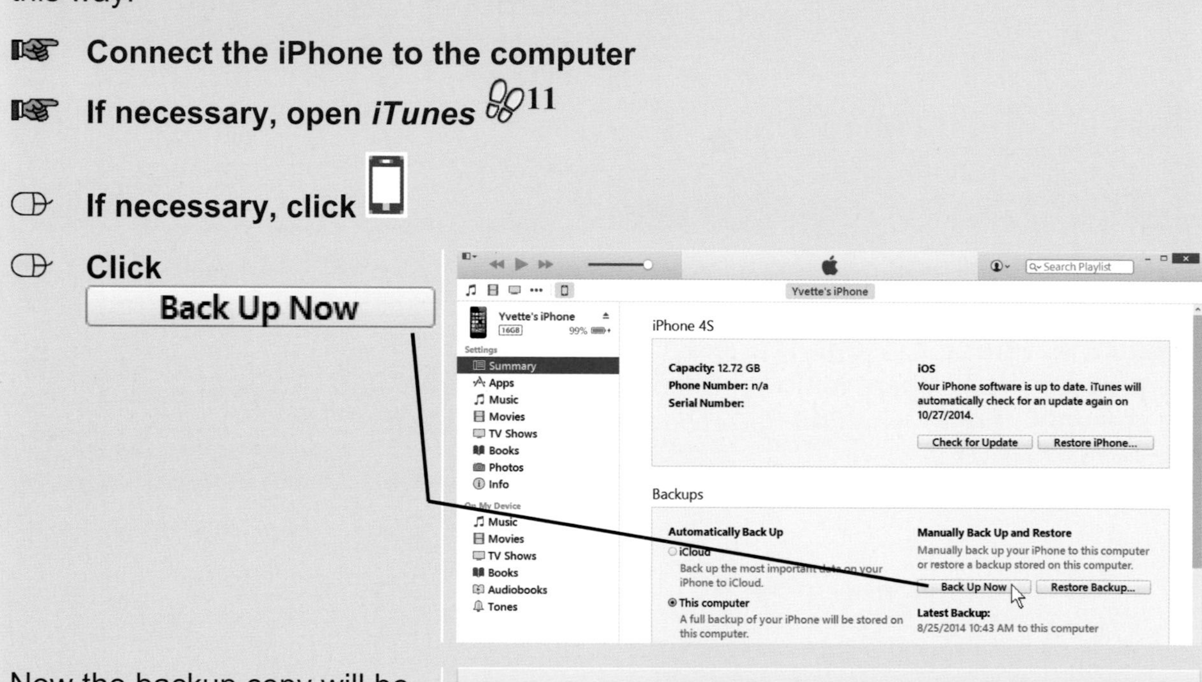

Now the backup copy will be made:

Backing up "Yvette's iPhone"...

 **Tip**

iCloud

iCloud is the online storage service provided by Apple. You could say that *iCloud* is a server somewhere in the world that offers you free storage space for your files. You can save a backup copy of your iPhone in *iCloud*, for example. But you can do much more with *iCloud*. You can also use it to save your photos, the music and apps you have purchased, your email messages, and your calendars and contact info. These files can be automatically synchronized with other devices, such as an iPhone and an iPod touch.
Do you want to know more about *iCloud*? Then download the free *Bonus Chapter iCloud* from the website accompanying this book. You can read how to do this in *Appendix B Opening Bonus Chapters.*

2. Making and Receiving Calls

Anytime you speak to enthusiastic iPhone users, you usually end up talking about the great apps that are available for the iPhone. You tend to almost forget that you can also use the iPhone for simply calling someone.

In this chapter you will learn how to use the *Phone* app to select a phone number, make a call and end the call. You will also learn how to add and edit contacts. By using the contacts list you can call someone quickly without having to enter the phone number manually each time.

The *FaceTime* app allows you to make free video conversations via Wi-Fi. During the conversation you will be able to see and hear the person on the other end of the line. You can start a *FaceTime* video conversation with other iPhone users or with people who use a *Mac* computer, an iPad or an iPod touch 4G.

Have you heard of something called *Skype?* This is a program that enables you to place free phone calls and chat with other *Skype* users. Once you have discovered how to use *FaceTime*, you will notice that *Skype* operates in a similar way. In the *Tips* at the end of this chapter you will find more information.

In this chapter you will learn how to:

- call someone;
- disconnect the call;
- answer a call;
- select a different ringtone;
- add a contact;
- edit a contact;
- call a contact;
- start a video conversation with *FaceTime*.

 **Please note:**

This book is intended to be used in a variety of English-speaking countries. Each country has its own phone number format as well as its own IDD (International Direct Dial) code. In this chapter, you may not see the particular number format that is used in the country where you live.

2.1 Making a Call

You open the *Phone* app from your iPhone's home screen.

Wake the iPhone up from sleep mode or turn it on [1]

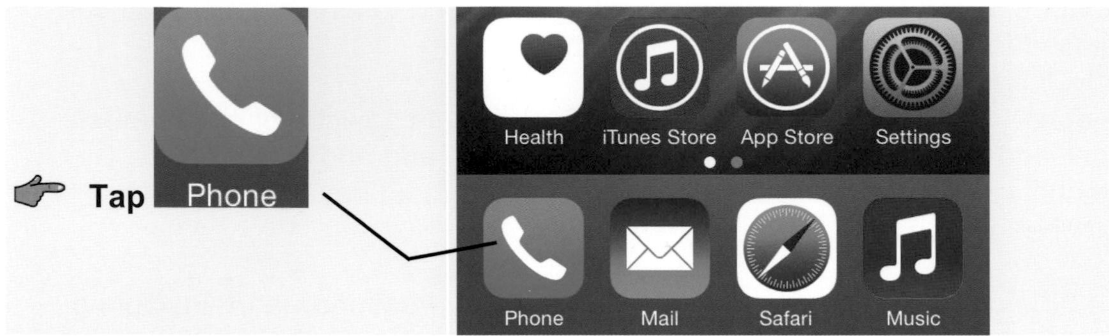

Enter the phone number of the person you want to call:

If necessary, tap
Keypad
Type the phone number
You will see the number you typed. The parentheses around the area code or cell phone prefix, hyphens and blank spaces will be inserted automatically according to the phone number format of your own country:
Tap
●●●●○ KPN NL
11:44
978123456
1
2 ABC
3 DEF
4 GHI
5 JKL
6 MNO
7 PQRS
8 TUV
9 WXYZ
*
0 +
#
Favourites
Recents
Contacts
Keypad
Voicemail

You will hear the phone ring.

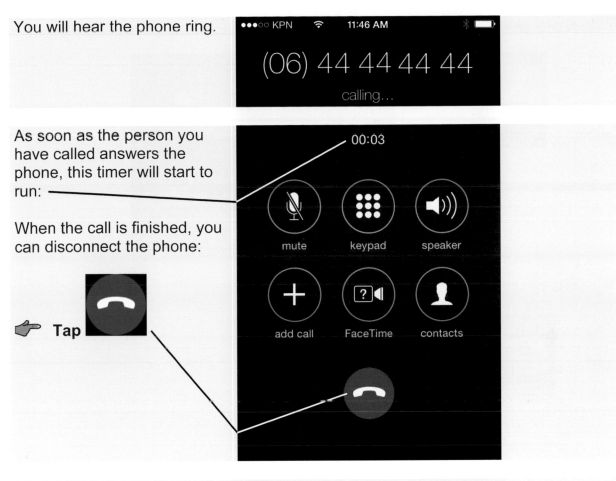

As soon as the person you have called answers the phone, this timer will start to run:

When the call is finished, you can disconnect the phone:

Tap

Go to the home screen 10

2.2 Answering a Call

If you receive a call yourself, you can answer the call in the following way. If the phone is locked:

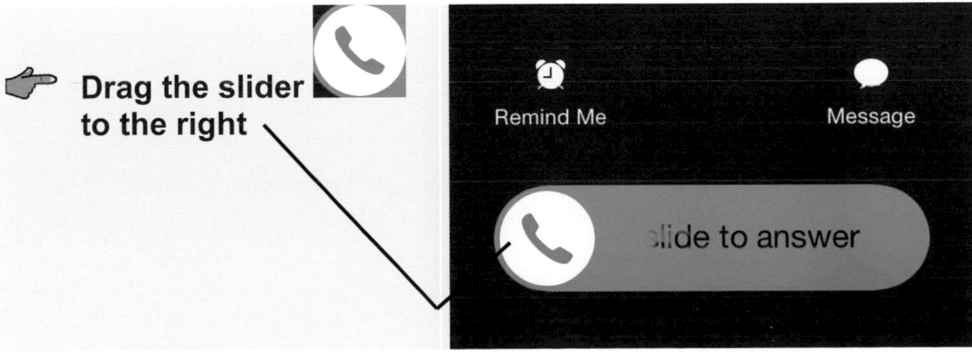

Drag the slider to the right

If the phone is unlocked:

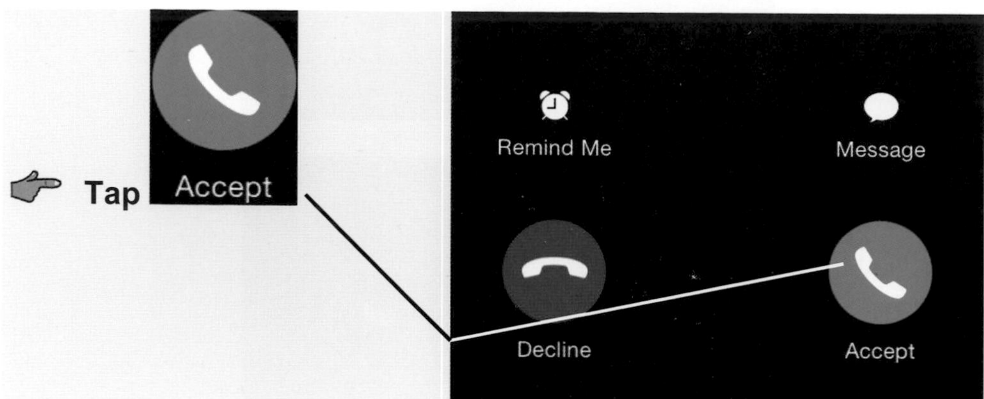

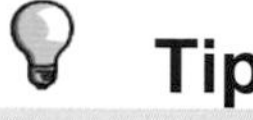

Tip

Ignore a call

With the Decline button you can directly send an incoming call to your voicemail service. This will only work if your phone is unlocked when the incoming call is received.

If your phone is locked, you can also ignore a call, like this:

Press the on/off button twice, in rapid succession

Tip

Mute the sound of incoming call

Is your phone ringing and do you want to silence the ringtone right away?

Press the on/off button

Or:

Press one of the volume control buttons

The caller will not notice this. The phone will keep ringing and you can answer the call before it is transferred to your voicemail.

2.3 Selecting a Different Ringtone

The iPhone is equipped with many different ringtones. You can easily select a different ringtone like this:

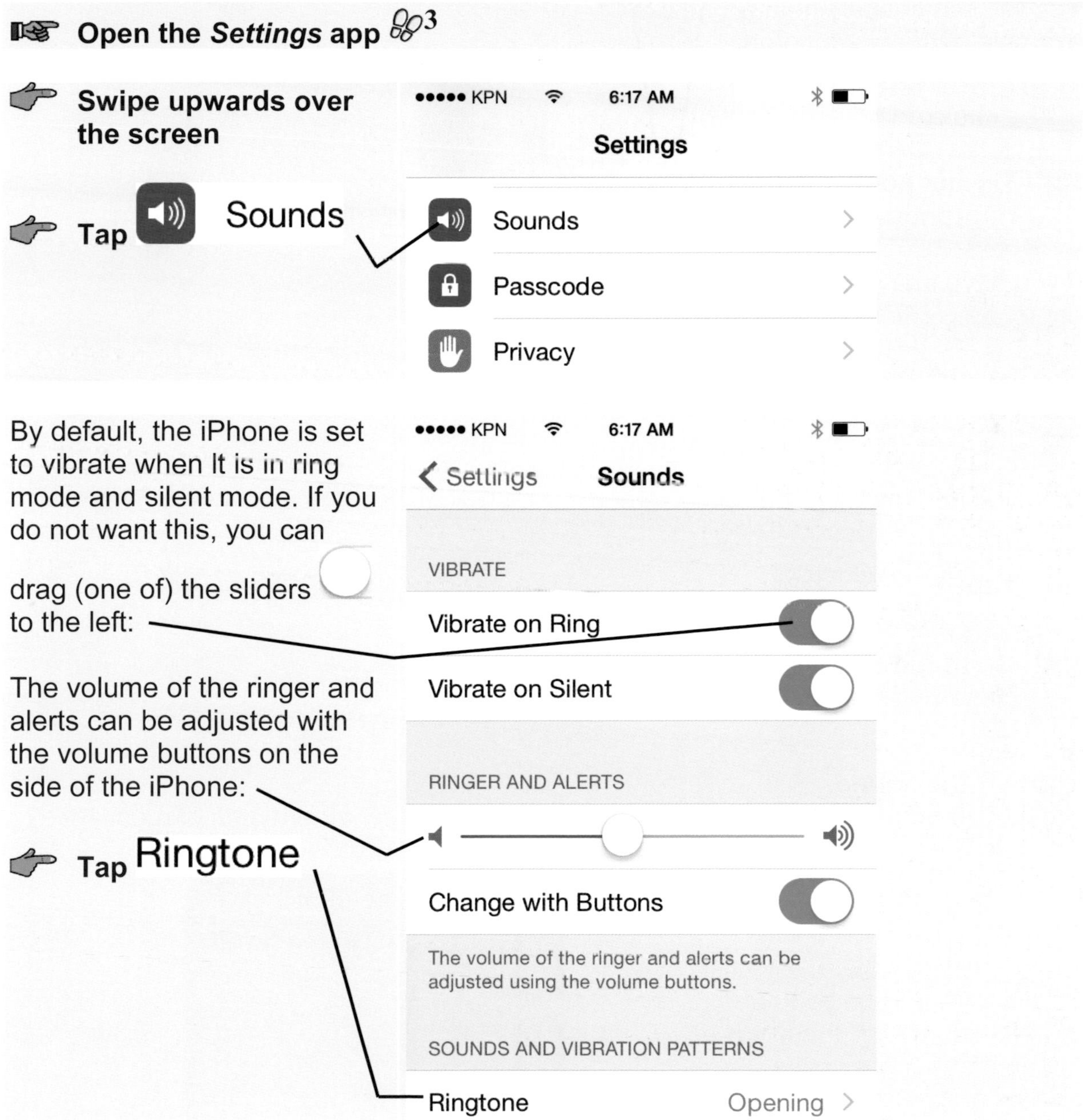

Open the *Settings* app 3

Swipe upwards over the screen

Tap Sounds

By default, the iPhone is set to vibrate when it is in ring mode and silent mode. If you do not want this, you can drag (one of) the sliders to the left:

The volume of the ringer and alerts can be adjusted with the volume buttons on the side of the iPhone:

Tap Ringtone

You will see a list of available ringtones:

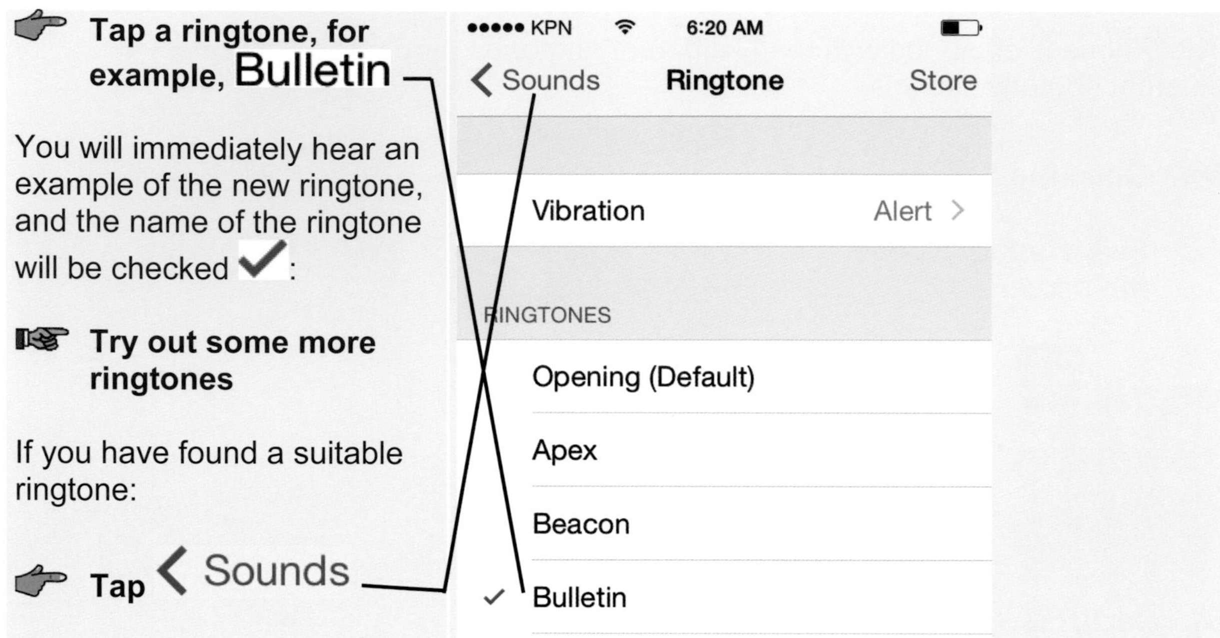

☛ **Tap a ringtone, for example,** Bulletin

You will immediately hear an example of the new ringtone, and the name of the ringtone will be checked ✔:

☞ **Try out some more ringtones**

If you have found a suitable ringtone:

☛ **Tap** < Sounds

Now you can return to the home screen:

☛ **Tap** < Settings

☞ **Go to the home screen** 10

Tip

Turn off the sound

Would you prefer not to be disturbed by the ringtone or by other types of messages?

Then you can use the switch on the side of the iPhone to mute the sound:

This is useful when you need to make sure your phone will not go off during a movie, performance or a meeting.

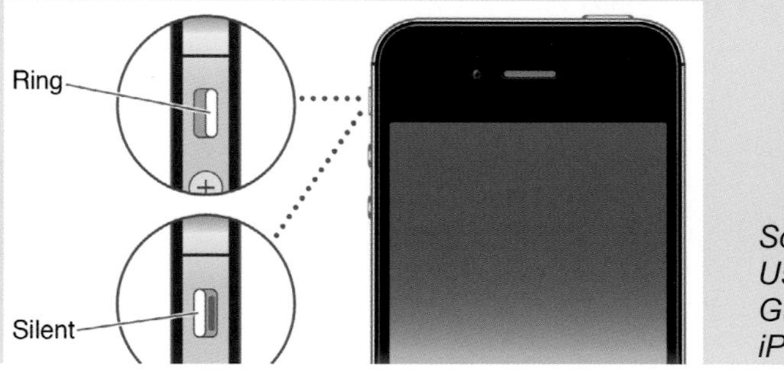

Source: User Guide iPhone

2.4 Adding a Contact

In the *Phone* app you can also add contacts. Here is how to do that:

Open the *Phone* app [3]

Tap Contacts

In this example we have not yet stored any contacts. You are going to add a new contact:

Tap +

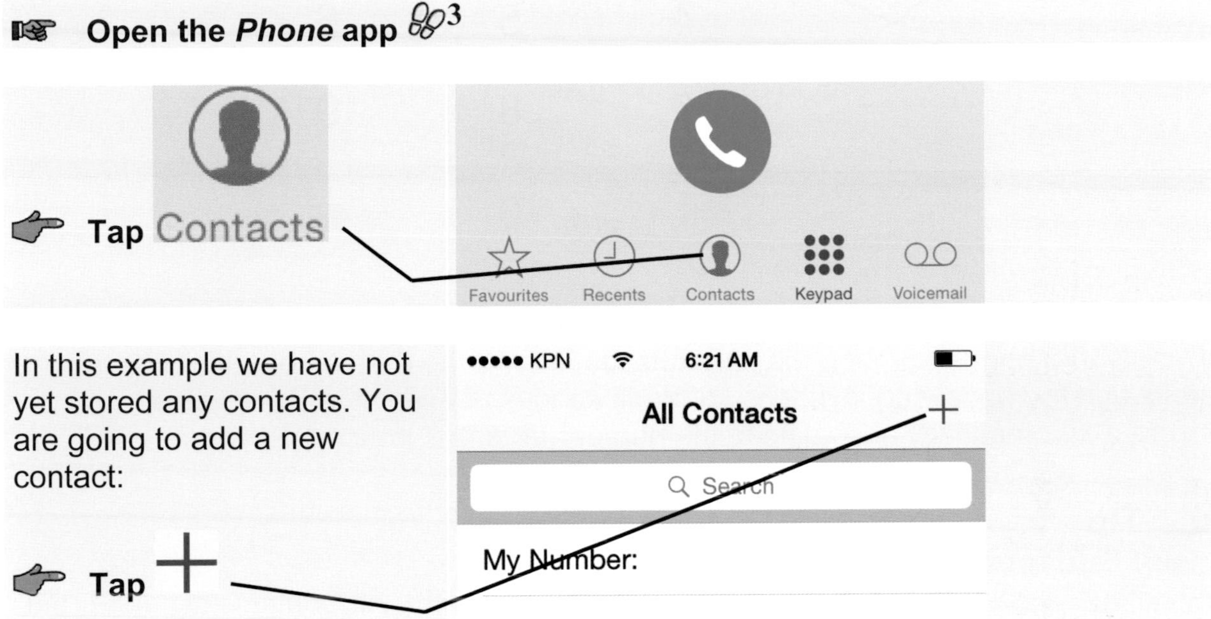

In this example we will add a fictitious contact. But if you prefer, you can enter the data from a real contact right away by using the onscreen keyboard:

Tap First

Type the first name of your contact

Tap Last

Type the last name of your contact

Tap add phone

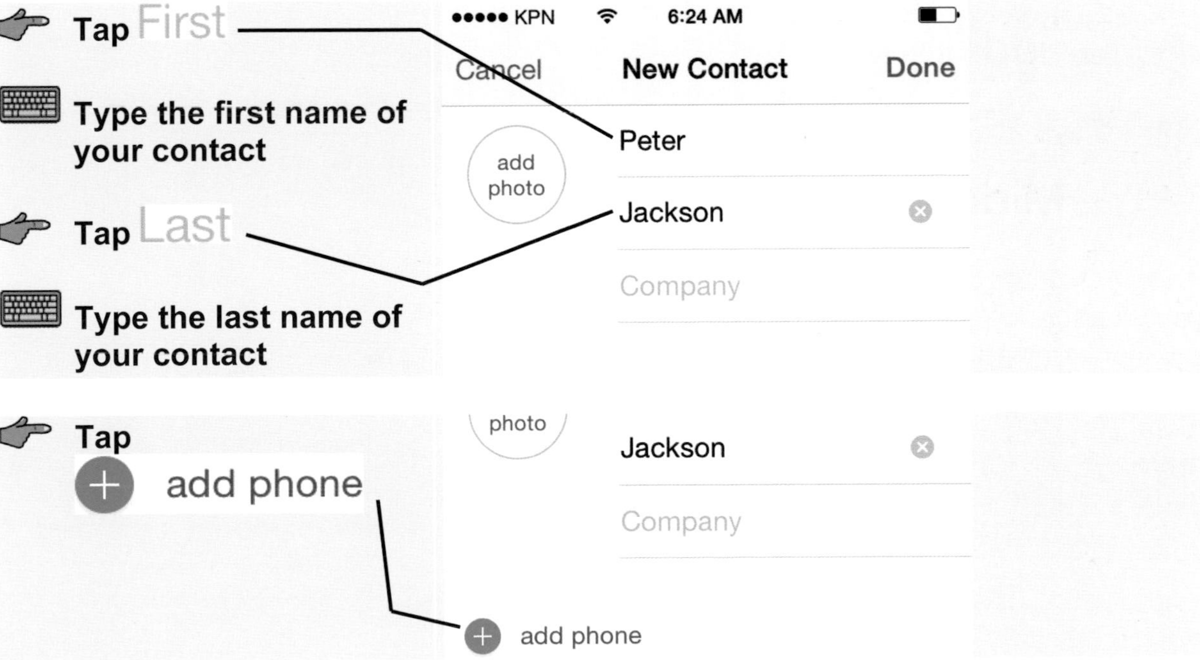

Type the cell phone number of your contact

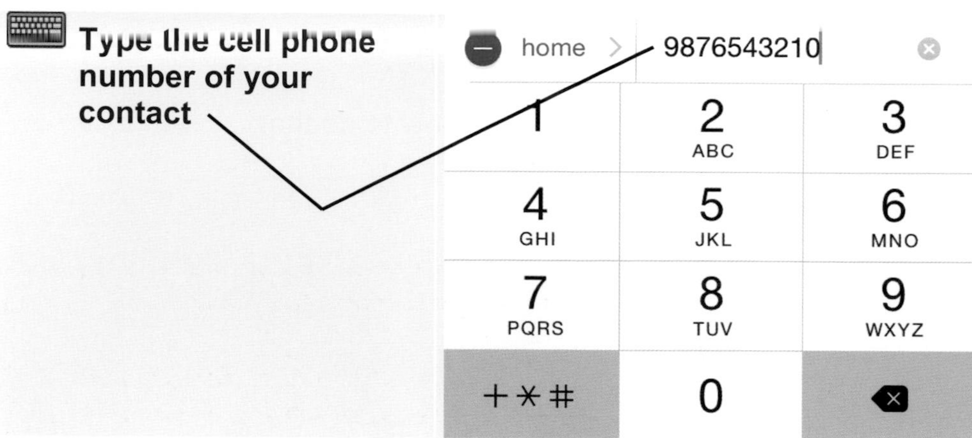

Please note:

If you type a phone number, the parentheses around the area code or cell phone prefix and the necessary hyphens, or blank spaces between the digits will be inserted automatically according to the number format of the country where you live.

Tip

Insert field for connecting name

By default, a contact called 'de Vere' will be inserted in the All Contacts list under the letter 'D'. If you prefer to find this contact under the letter 'V', you can add a field to the contact data and use this field for a connecting or middle name:

Drag the page all the way upwards

Tap add field

You will see a window listing the fields you can add:

Tap Middle

The field called *Middle name* will be added. You can use this field for additions to a last name, such as 'de', 'del', 'dela', 'le', 'la', 'van', 'el' and more.

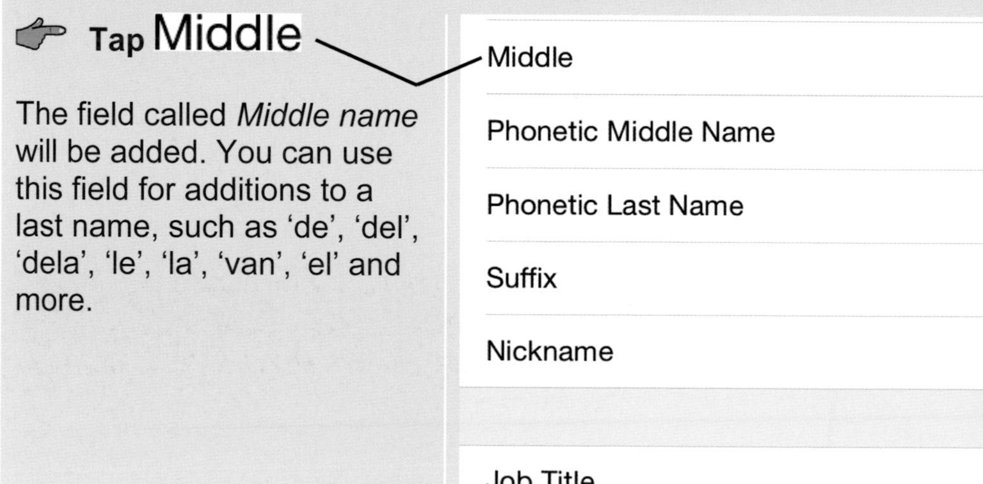

You can modify these labels yourself, and change them into a mobile number, or a work-related phone number, for example:

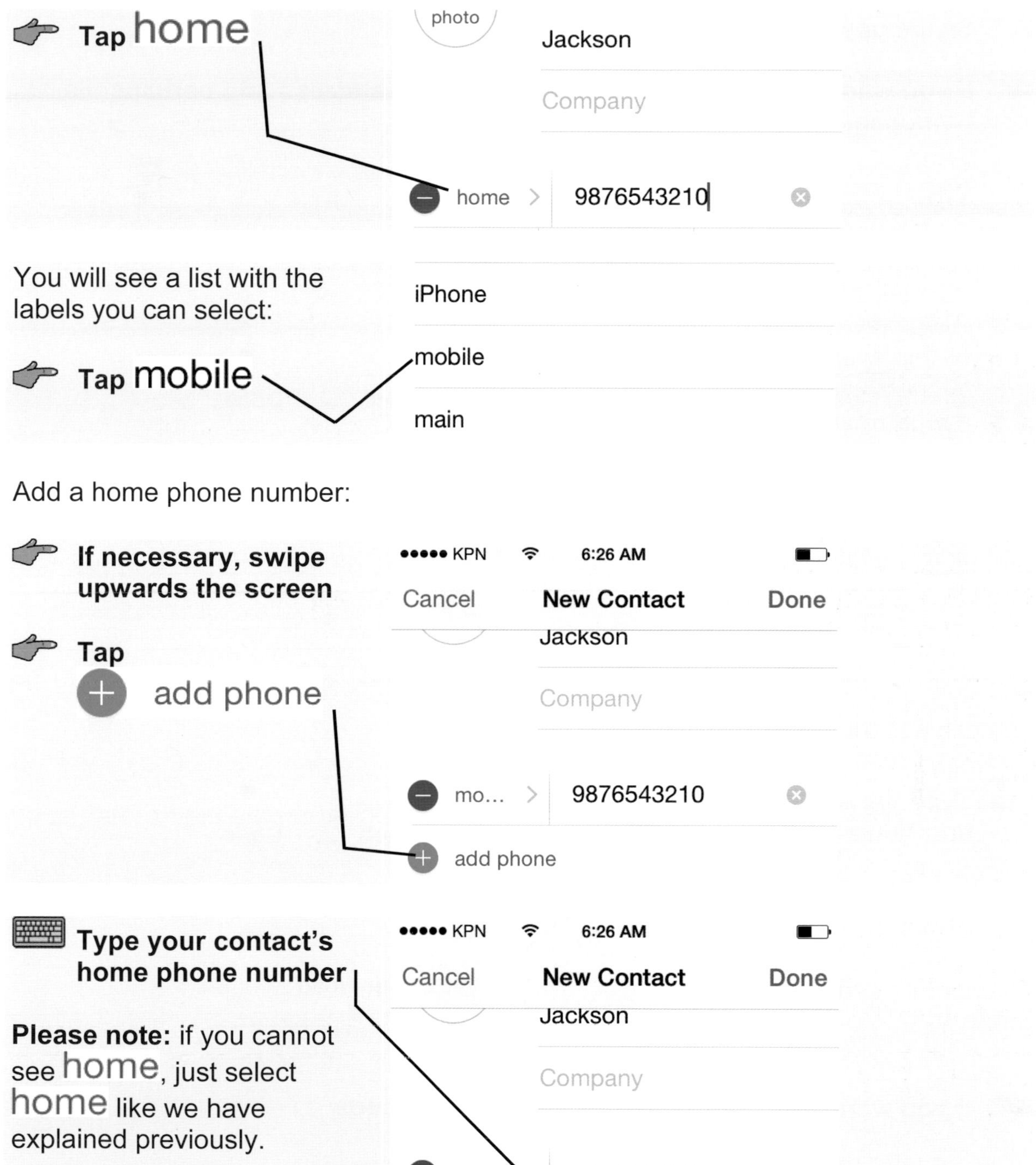

- **Tap** home

You will see a list with the labels you can select:

- **Tap** mobile

Add a home phone number:

- **If necessary, swipe upwards the screen**
- **Tap** add phone
- **Type your contact's home phone number**

Please note: if you cannot see home, just select home like we have explained previously.

You can add lots of other information concerning your contact. It is up to you to decide how much information to enter and whether any extra fields are needed.

Swipe upwards the screen

If you want, you can add your contact's email address and perhaps his homepage (website address)

Tip

Change labels
You can also change the label for the email address just as easily, for instance from home to work.

You will find even more fields:

Swipe upwards over the screen

Tap add address

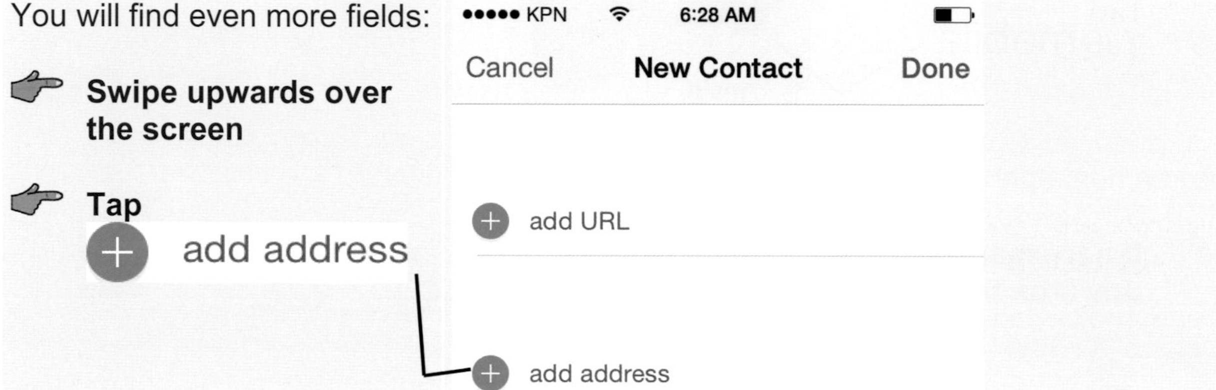

You can add the home address:

Type the street name and home address

You will immediately see a new line for the street name:

You do not need to use this line.

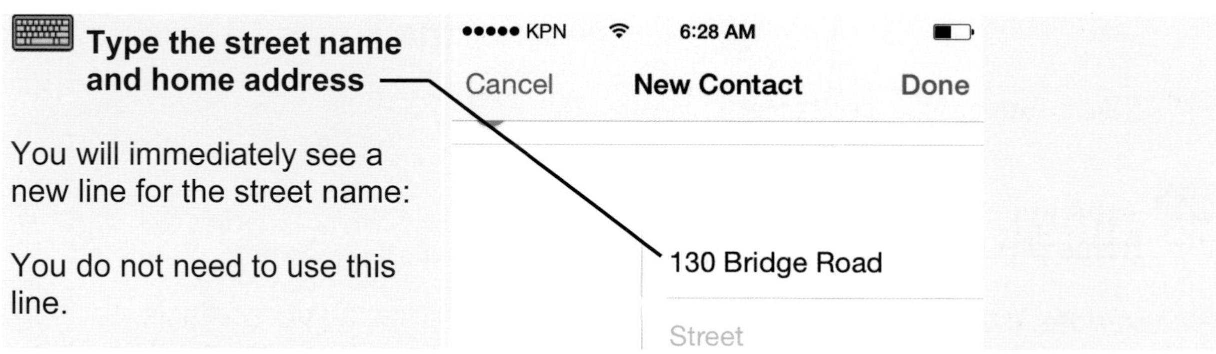

If you want, add your contact's city and area code

You can save the data:

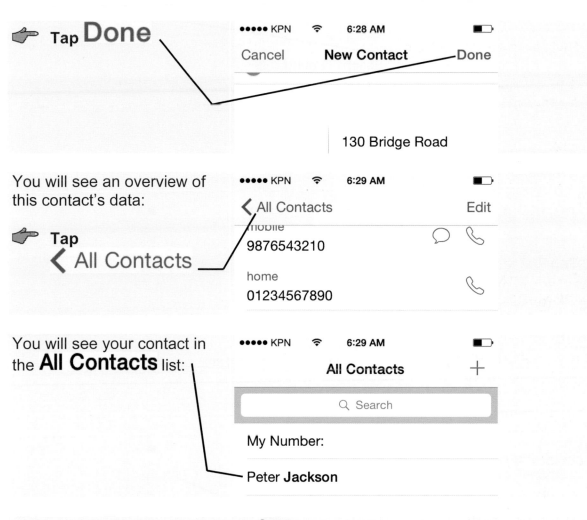

☞ **Tap** Done

You will see an overview of this contact's data:

☞ **Tap** ‹ All Contacts

You will see your contact in the **All Contacts** list:

☞ **Add another four contacts** 14

2.5 Editing a Contact

After a while, you may need to edit the information from one of your contacts. Perhaps someone has moved and has a new address or a new phone number. This is how you open the contact's data for editing:

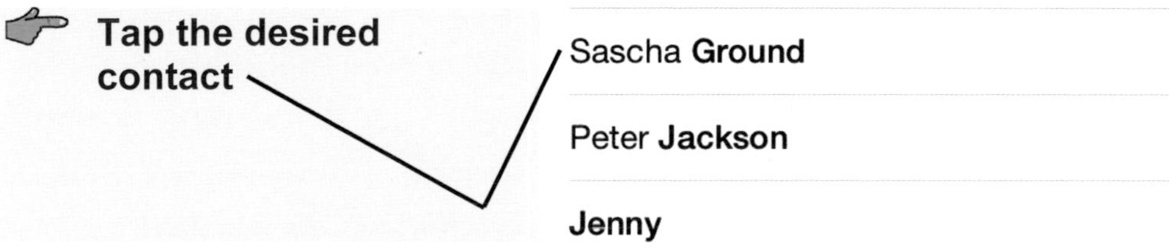

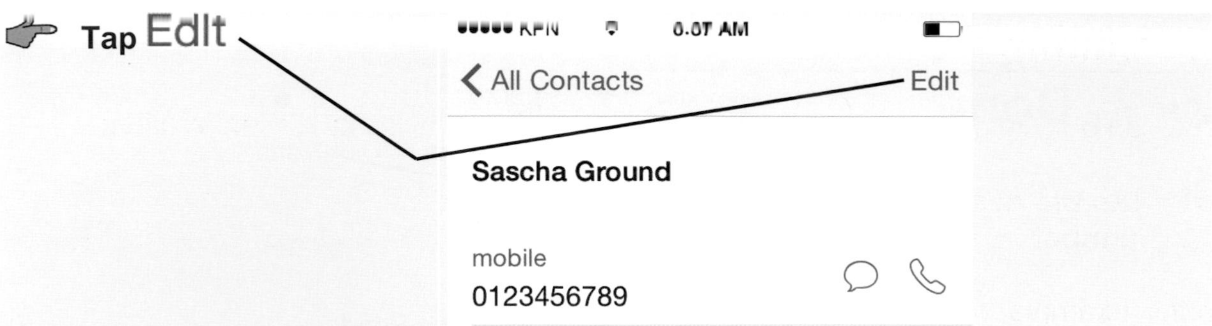

This is how you change the phone number:

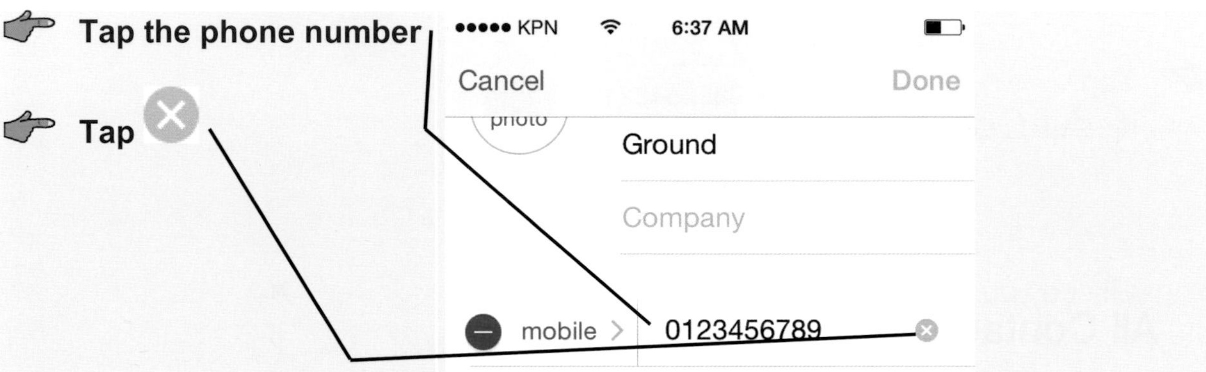

The phone number will be deleted:

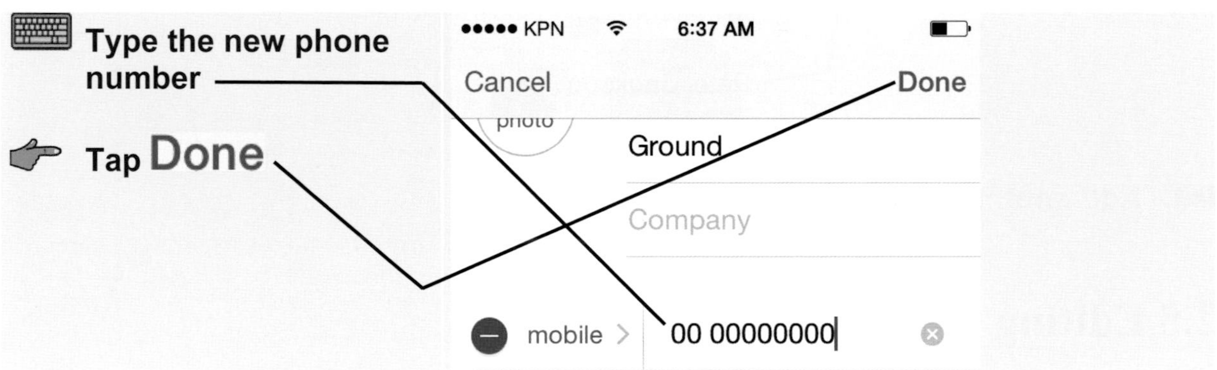

Now you will again see a summary of all the data for this particular contact.

2.6 Calling a Contact

You can quickly call one of your contacts directly from the contact's information:

Tap the desired phone number

In this example, only one phone number is entered for this contact:

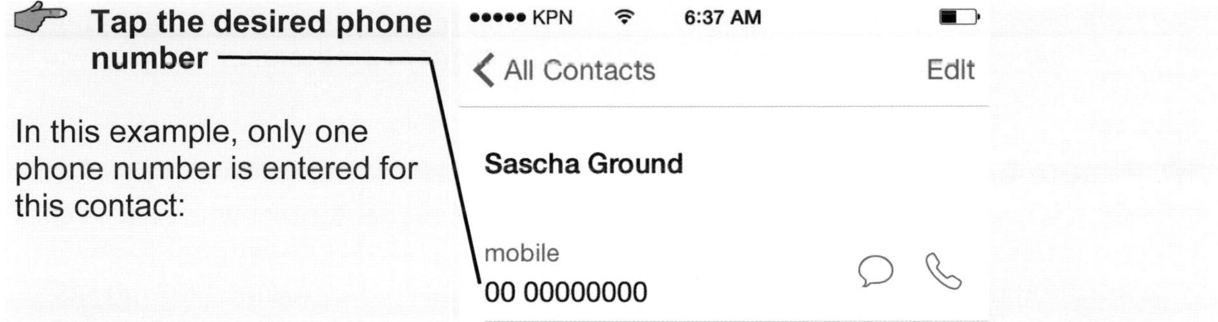

The number is called:

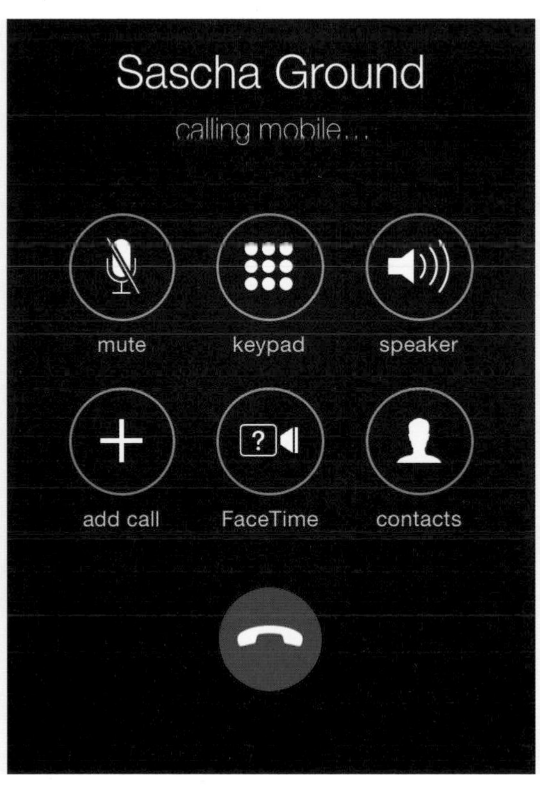

2.7 FaceTime

With the *FaceTime* app you can use your iPhone to start a video conversation for free through Wi-Fi. You will be able to see and hear your companion. By default, *FaceTime* uses the front-facing camera, so your companion will be able to see your face. During the conversation you can switch to the camera on the back and show your friend your surroundings.

Please note:

To follow the examples in this section you will need to have a contact who is able to use *FaceTime* and who is within reach. You will also need to know whether this contact can be reached by *FaceTime* through his cell phone number or through his email address. If you do not have a contact that uses *FaceTime*, you can just read through this section.

First, you are going to take a look at the *FaceTime* settings:

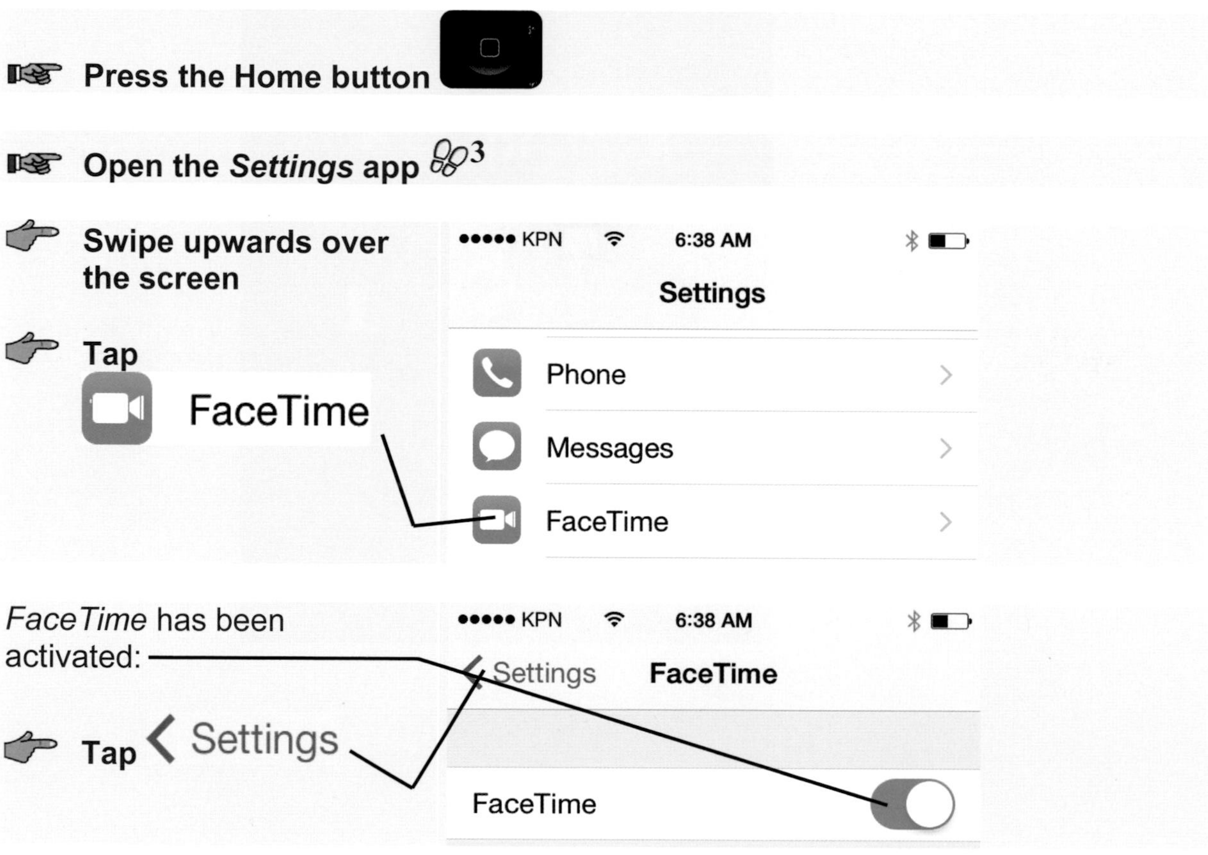

Go to the home screen 10

You can hold a video conversation with anyone who owns an iPhone, an iPad, an iPod touch or a *Mac* computer. You can start a *FaceTime* video call from the contacts list:

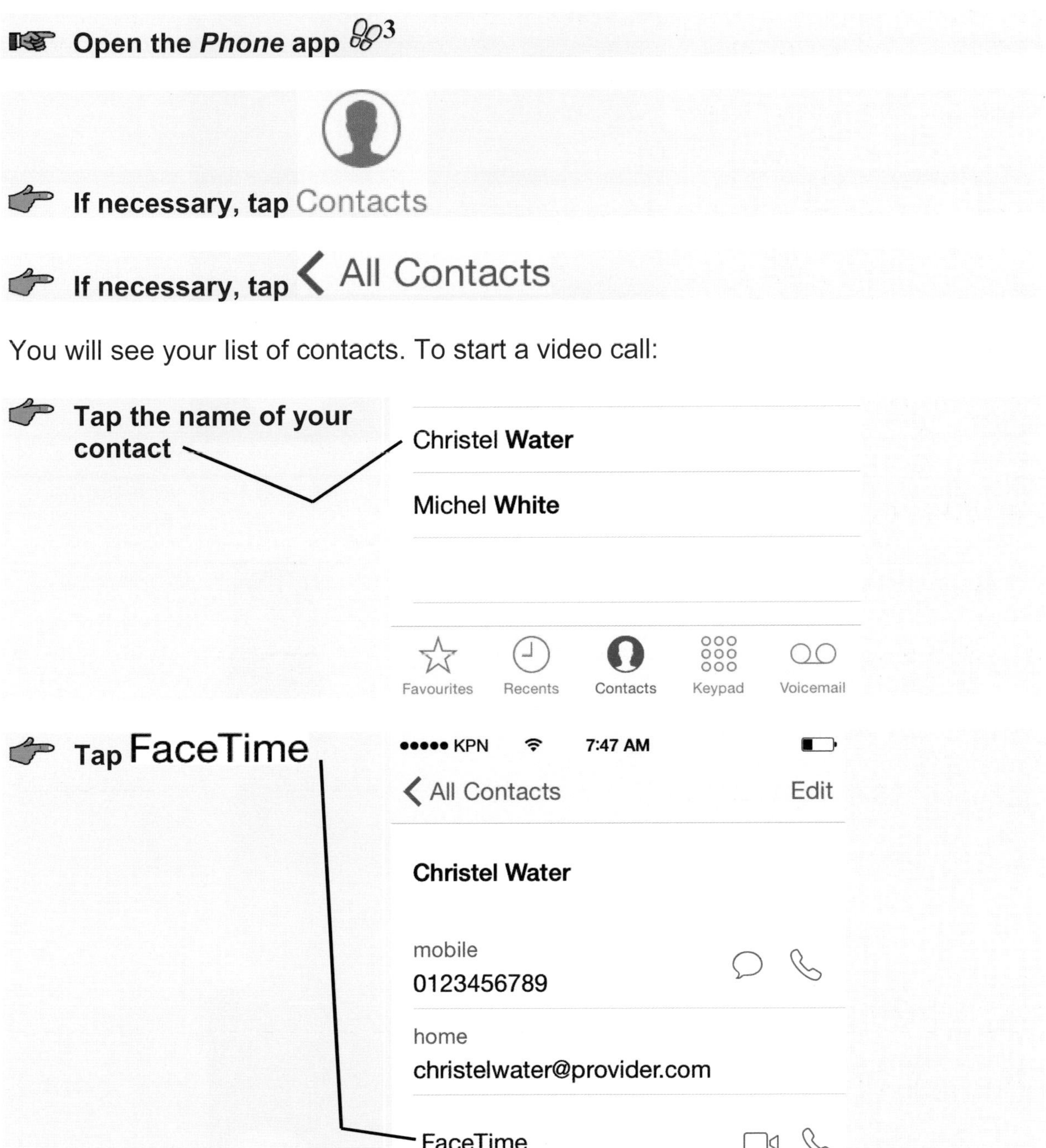

Open the *Phone* app [3]

If necessary, tap Contacts

If necessary, tap < All Contacts

You will see your list of contacts. To start a video call:

Tap the name of your contact

Tap FaceTime

The phone tries to establish a connection. You will hear the phone ring and see yourself on the screen:

When the connection has been made, you will be able to see and hear your contact:

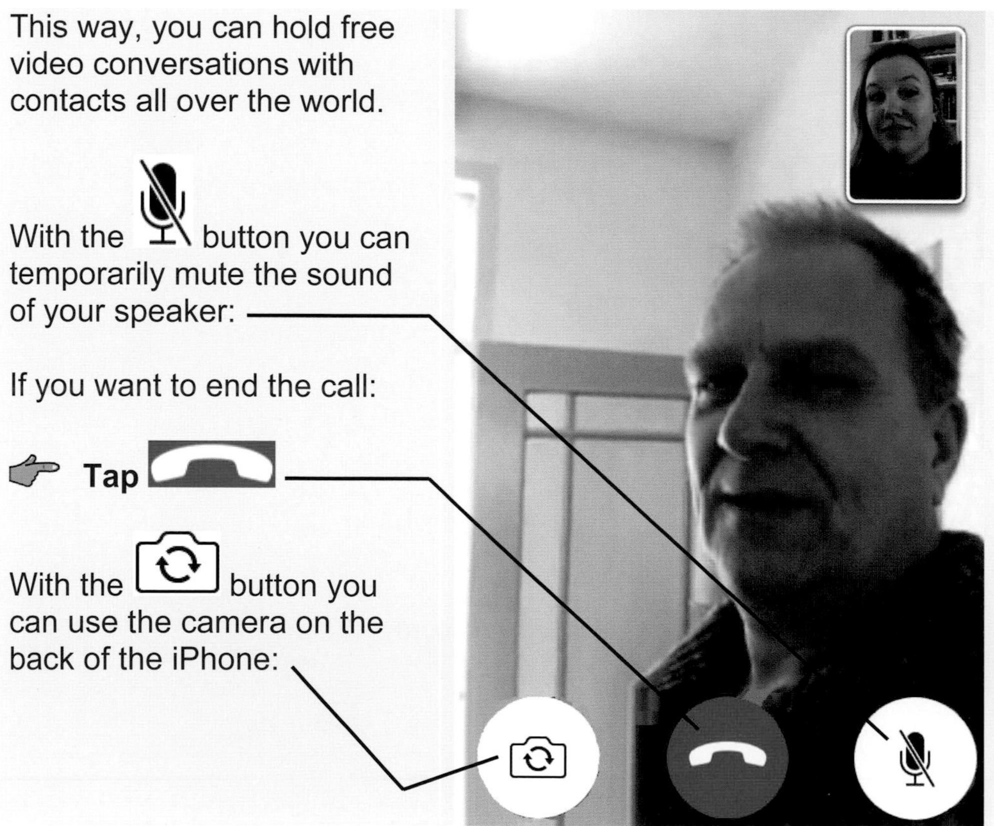

This way, you can hold free video conversations with contacts all over the world.

With the button you can temporarily mute the sound of your speaker:

If you want to end the call:

Tap

With the button you can use the camera on the back of the iPhone:

☞ **Go to the home screen** 10

In the previous chapter you have practiced turning off the iPhone. From now on we will always lock the iPhone (this means putting it into sleep mode), so that you will be able to accept calls.

☞ **If you want, put the iPhone into sleep mode** 2

In this chapter you have learned how to call someone with your iPhone and how to use the *Phone* and *FaceTime* apps. You have also seen how to store and edit contacts. In the following exercises you can practice these actions once more.

2.8 Exercises

To be able to quickly apply the things you have learned, you can work through the following exercises. Have you forgotten how to do something? Use the numbers next to the footsteps 1 to look up the item in the appendix *How Do I Do That Again?* This appendix can be found at the end of the book.

Exercise 1: Calling

In this exercise you are going to practice calling with the iPhone.

- If necessary, wake the iPhone up from sleep mode. 1
- Open the *Phone* app. 3
- Call a friend, acquaintance or family member. 16
- Disconnect the call. 17
- Go to the home screen. 10

Exercise 2: Contacts

In this exercise you are going to practice storing and editing contacts.

- If necessary, wake the iPhone up from sleep mode or turn it on. 2
- Open the *Phone* app. 3
- Add a new contact. 14
- Open the contact's data. 18
- Change the *mobile* label to *home*. 19
- Save the changes. 20
- Go to the home screen. 10
- If you want, lock the iPhone (sleep mode). 2

2.9 Background Information

Dictionary

Caller ID	A function that displays your phone number to the person who is calling you. If you have activated caller ID, you will be able to see the number of the person who is calling you, provided this person has not disabled the caller ID function.
Car kit	A Bluetooth device which allows you to use your cell phone in hands free mode, in your car. You will hear the conversation over the car's audio speakers or over a separate speaker in the device. You can speak into a microphone which is suspended somewhere near your head.
Contacts	A section of the *Phone* app in which you can add and manage contacts.
FaceTime	An app that lets you hold free video conversations over the Internet with contacts all over the world.
Field	You can use a field to add data for your contacts. For example, *First name* and *Zip code* are fields.
Forward	Reroute incoming calls to another cell phone or a land line.
Headset	A Bluetooth headset is a device to be worn on your head or in your ear that enables hands free phone conversations. The headset includes a microphone and speaker.
iPad	A tablet computer manufactured by Apple.
iPod touch	A portable media player with a touch screen, made by Apple.
Label	A field name.
Phone	An app with which you can call and start a *FaceTime* conversation.
Ringtone	A melody or sound you hear whenever somebody calls you.
Skype	A program you can use to make free phone calls over the Internet.
Swap calls	With this function you can answer an incoming call while having another conversation.
Video call	A conversation with a contact, using a video and an audio connection.

Source: User Guide iPhone, Wikipedia

2.10 Tips

Tip

Call options

While you are talking, the screen of the iPhone will turn off when you press the phone to your ear. As soon as you take the iPhone away from your ear, you will see a number of call buttons on your screen:

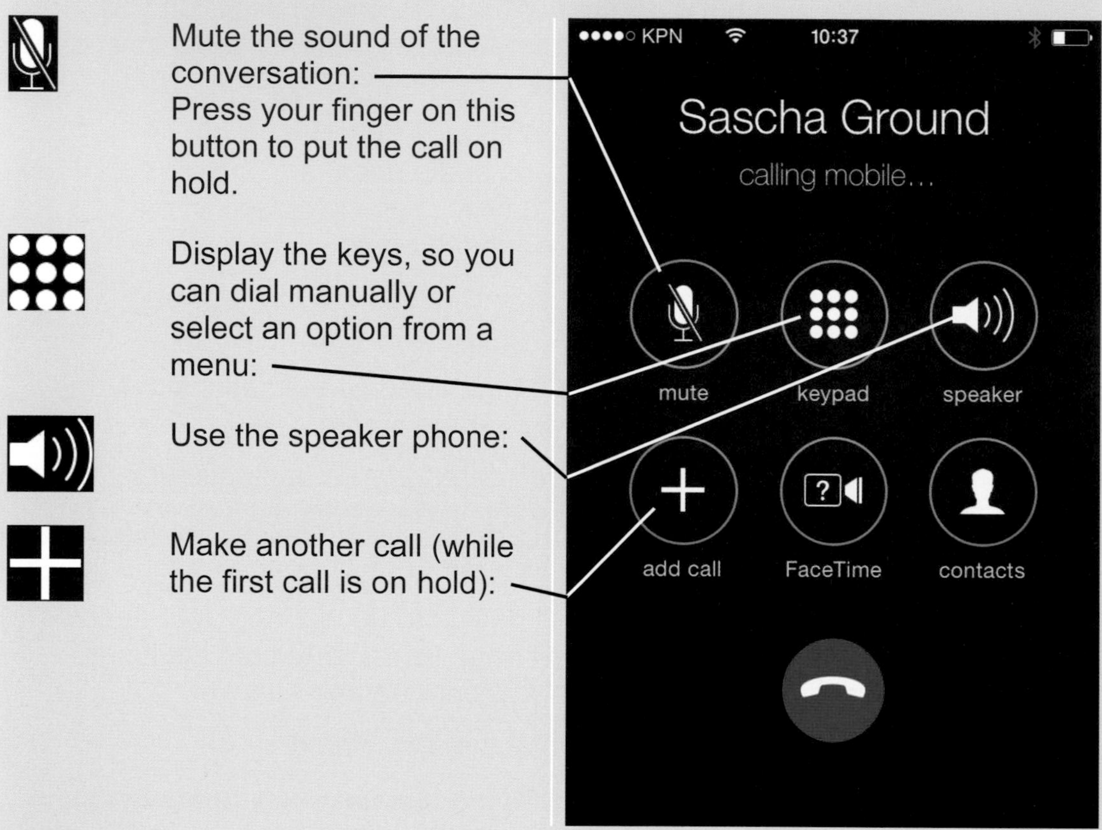
Mute the sound of the conversation:
Press your finger on this button to put the call on hold.
Display the keys, so you can dial manually or select an option from a menu:
Use the speaker phone:
Make another call (while the first call is on hold):
●●●●○ KPN
10:37
Sascha Ground
calling mobile...
mute
keypad
speaker
add call
FaceTime
contacts

Start a video call with *FaceTime* with the current caller. If the button displays a question mark, you will not be able to use *FaceTime* with this contact.

With this button you can view your contact info during a call. For example, if you want to look up a phone number while calling somebody.

Tip

Add a contact from the list of recent calls

If you have been called by someone who is not included in your contacts list, you can quickly add this person to your contacts:

☞ **Open the *Phone* app** 3

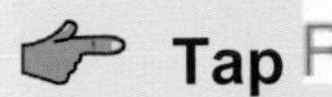

Tap Recents

You will see the list with recent calls:

By the desired number, tap ⓘ

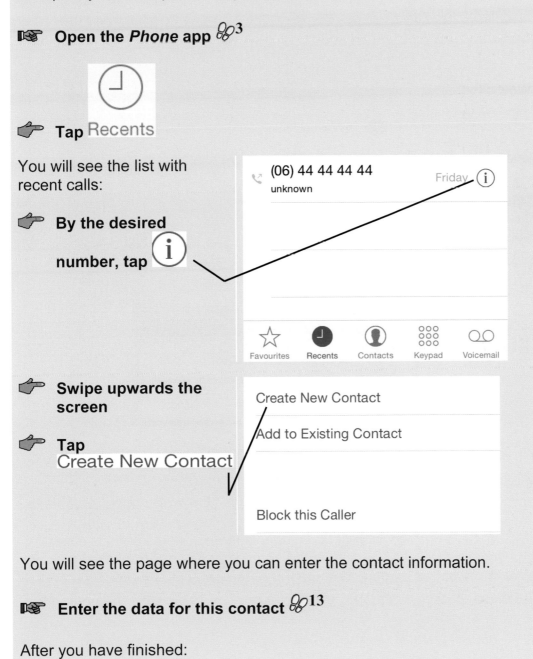

Swipe upwards the screen

Tap Create New Contact

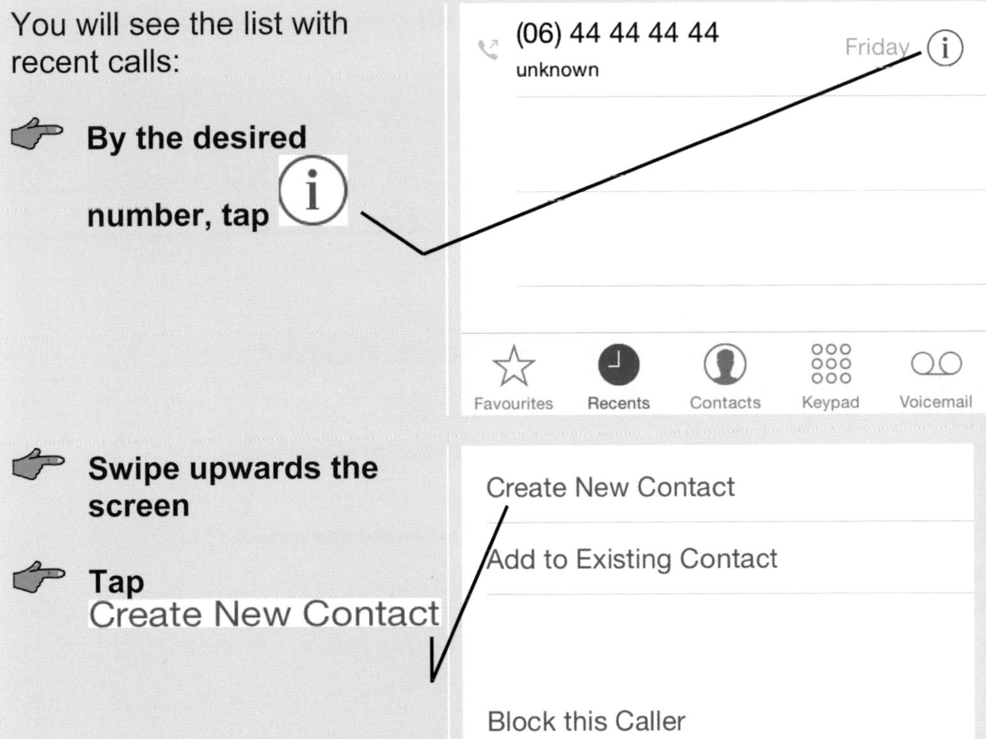

You will see the page where you can enter the contact information.

☞ **Enter the data for this contact** 13

After you have finished:

Tap Done

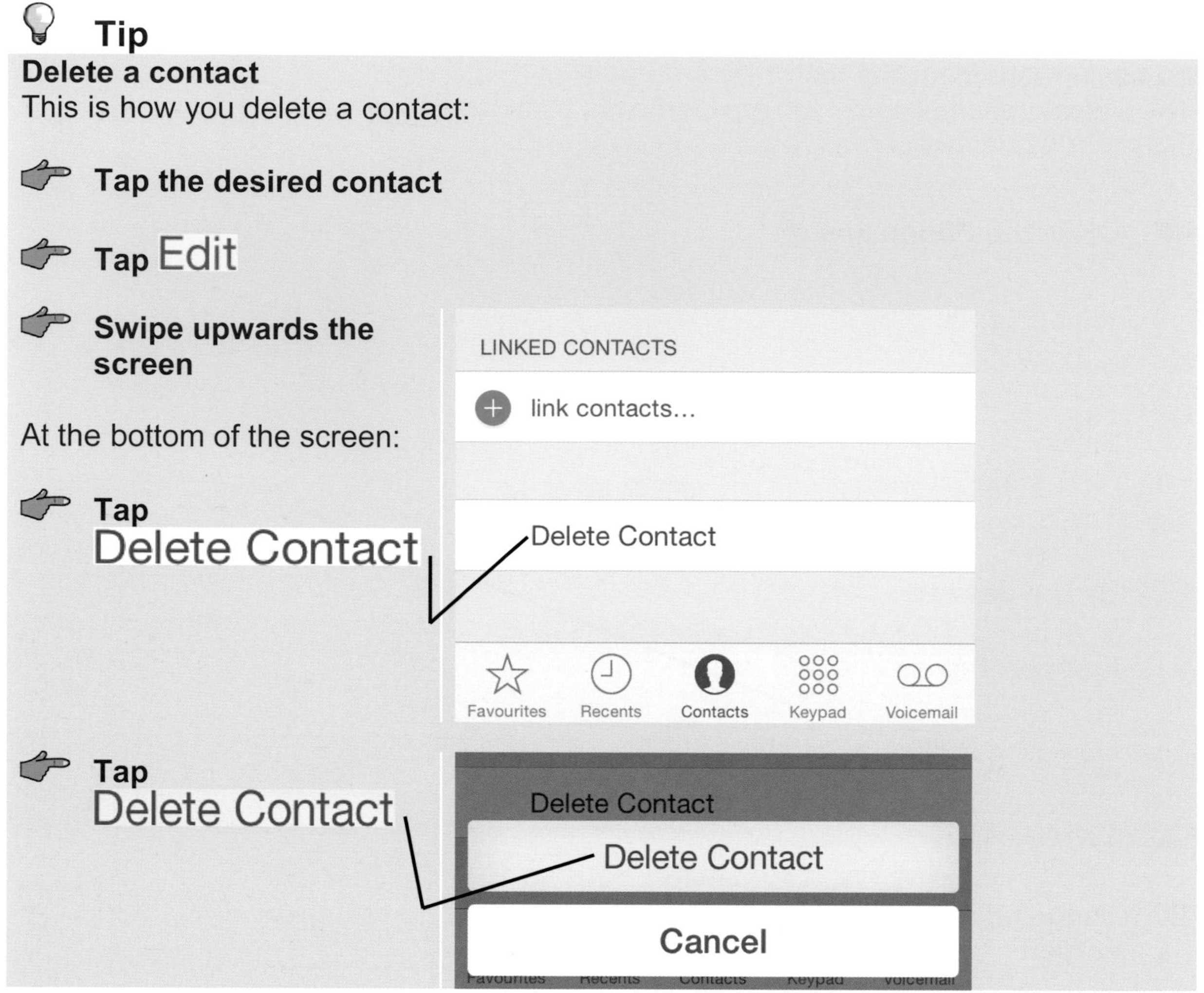

Tip

Delete a contact
This is how you delete a contact:

- **Tap the desired contact**
- **Tap** Edit
- **Swipe upwards the screen**

At the bottom of the screen:

- **Tap** Delete Contact
- **Tap** Delete Contact

Tip

Synchronize contacts
Do you manage your contacts already on your computer? Then you might be able to synchronize these contacts with your iPhone. You can synchronize with contacts from *Microsoft Outlook*, *Windows Contacts*, *Google Contacts*, and *Yahoo! Address Book*. You can synchronize your contacts in the same way as your bookmarks in *Internet Explorer* or *Safari*, as explained in the *Tip* at the back of *Chapter 5 Surfing with Your iPhone*.

Tip

Delete recent calls

The iPhone maintains a list of all recent calls. This is how you can delete a call from the list of recent calls:

☞ **Open the *Phone* app** ⁸⁸3

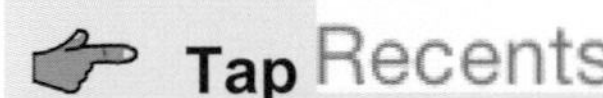

👉 **Tap** Recents

👉 **Tap** Edit

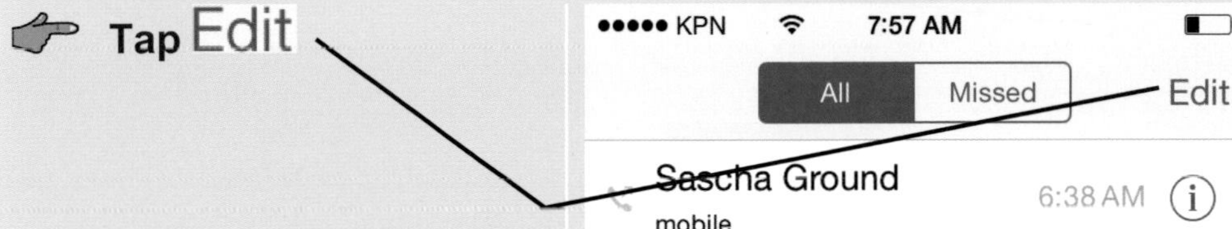

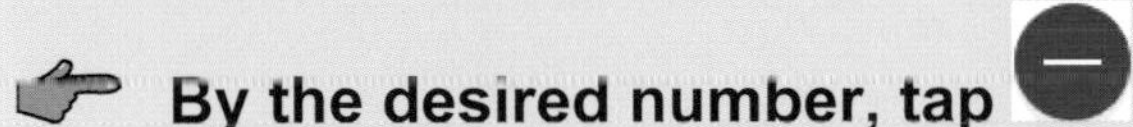

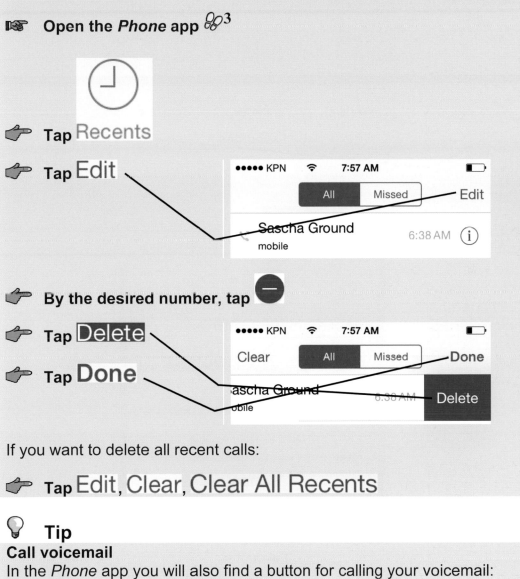

👉 **By the desired number, tap**

👉 **Tap** Delete

👉 **Tap** Done

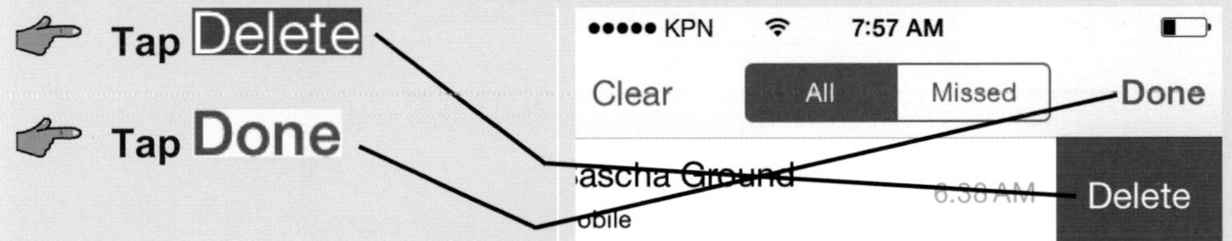

If you want to delete all recent calls:

👉 **Tap** Edit, Clear, Clear All Recents

Tip

Call voicemail

In the *Phone* app you will also find a button for calling your voicemail:

👉 **Tap** Voicemail

The correct number for your provider's voicemail will be dialed automatically.

Tip

Add favorites

If you have a few contacts that you call often, you can add them to the list of favorites. Then you will not need to scroll endlessly through the entire contacts list to find their phone number. This is how you add a contact to the favorites:

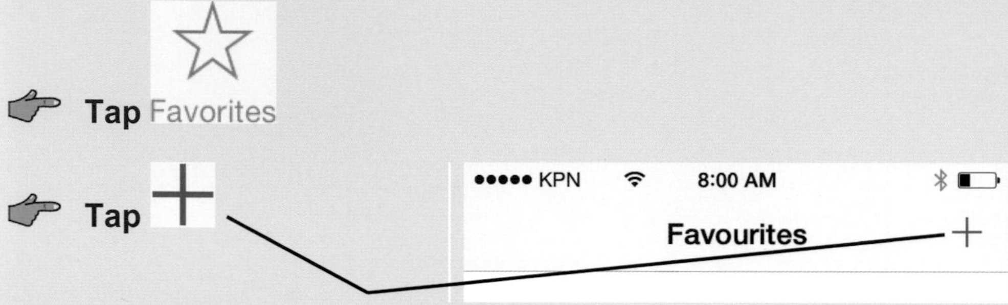

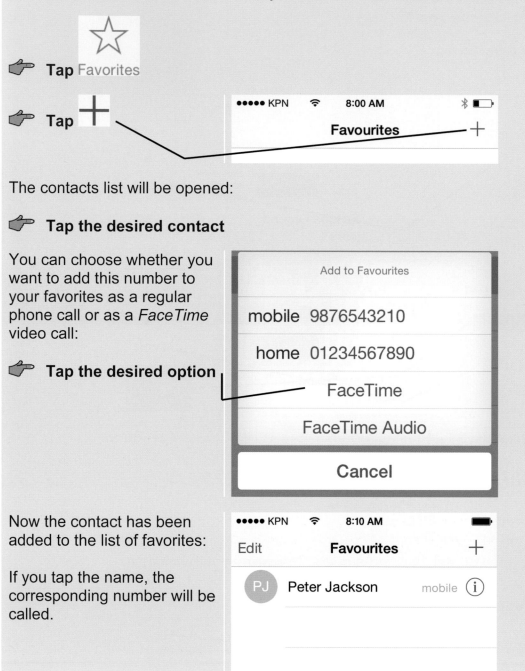

The contacts list will be opened:

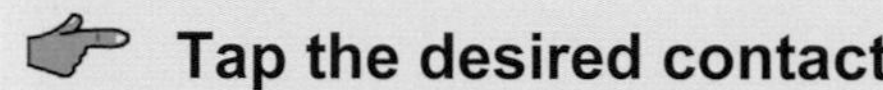

Tap the desired contact

You can choose whether you want to add this number to your favorites as a regular phone call or as a *FaceTime* video call:

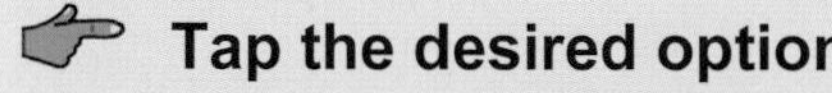

Tap the desired option

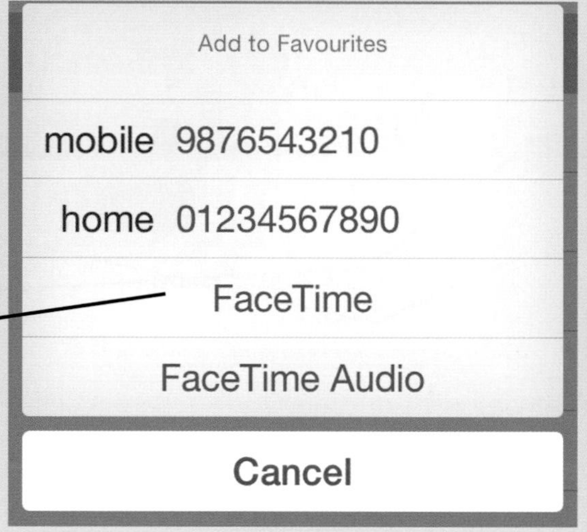

Now the contact has been added to the list of favorites:

If you tap the name, the corresponding number will be called.

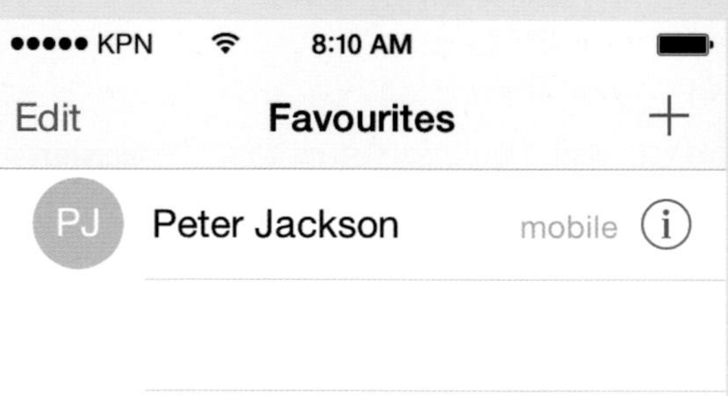

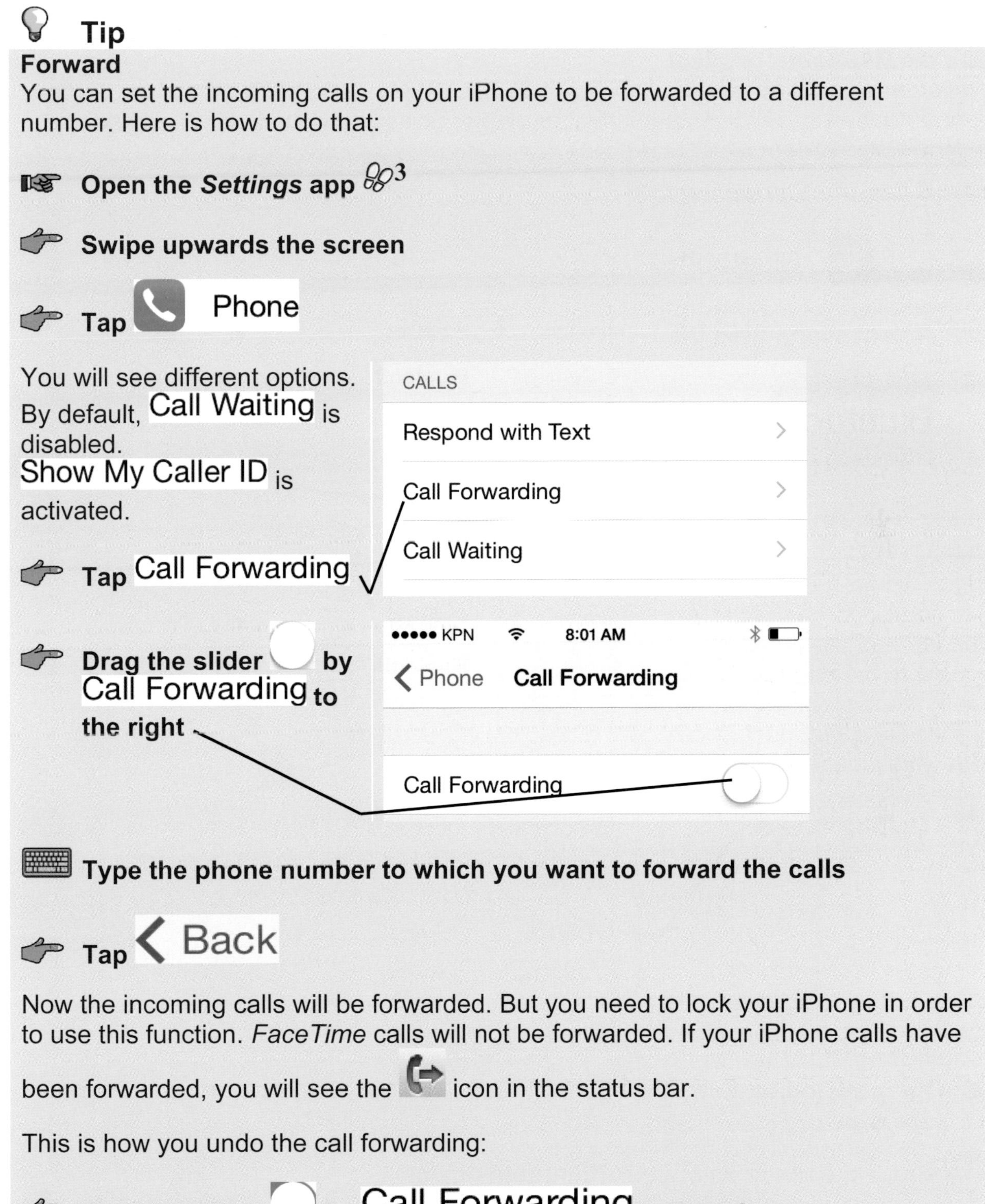

Tip

Forward

You can set the incoming calls on your iPhone to be forwarded to a different number. Here is how to do that:

- **Open the *Settings* app** 3
- **Swipe upwards the screen**
- **Tap** Phone

You will see different options. By default, Call Waiting is disabled. Show My Caller ID is activated.

- **Tap** Call Forwarding

- **Drag the slider by** Call Forwarding **to the right**

- **Type the phone number to which you want to forward the calls**
- **Tap** Back

Now the incoming calls will be forwarded. But you need to lock your iPhone in order to use this function. *FaceTime* calls will not be forwarded. If your iPhone calls have been forwarded, you will see the icon in the status bar.

This is how you undo the call forwarding:

- **Drag the slider by** Call Forwarding **to the left**
- **Tap** Phone, Call Forwarding

Tip

Use the Bluetooth headset

While driving a car it is mandatory that you use the hands free function. You can use your iPhone with a Bluetooth headset or car kit. This is how you activate Bluetooth:

Open the *Settings* app 3

Tap Bluetooth

If necessary, drag the slider by Bluetooth **to the right**

You will see the icon appear in the status bar. At once, the system will start looking for Bluetooth devices with which it can connect.

Tap the device

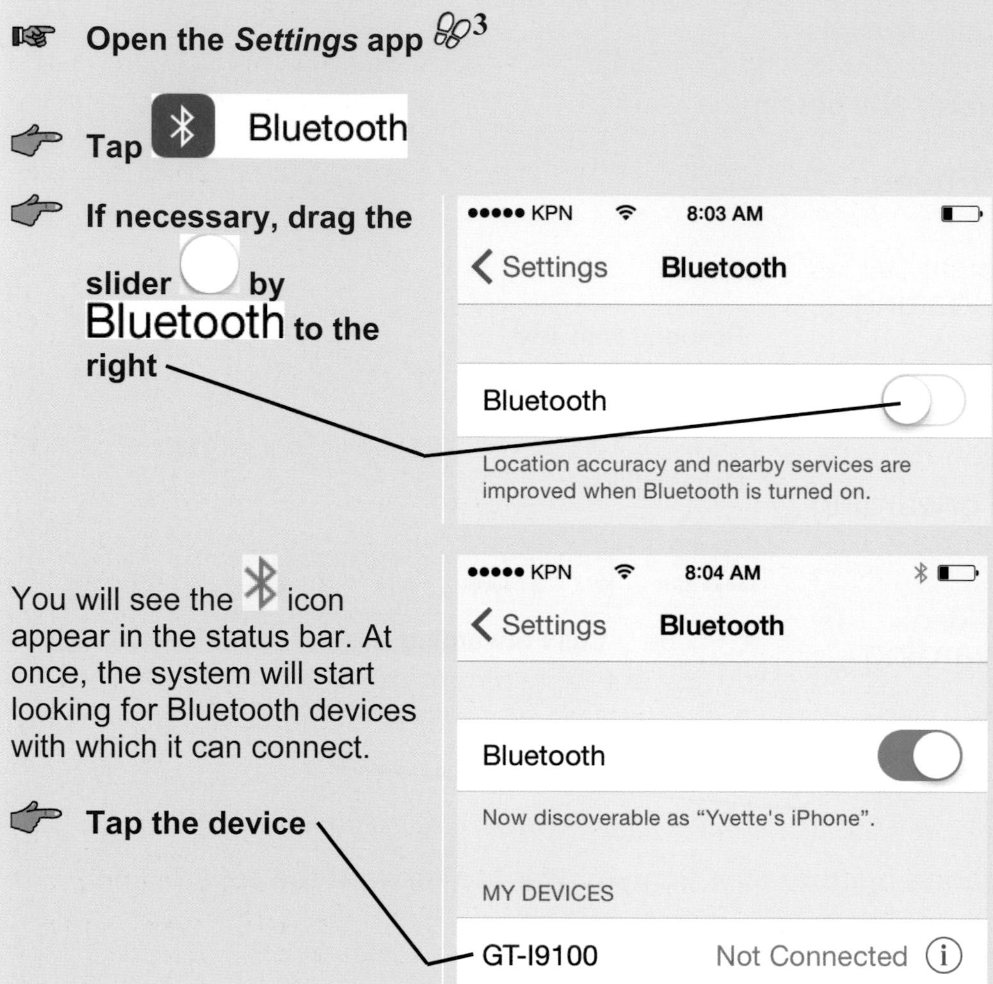

If you are using your headset or car kit for the first time or if it is set with a password, you will need to connect the device to the iPhone. Here is how to do that:

Keep the on/off button of the Bluetooth device pressed in, until the light stays on

Enter the pin code of your Bluetooth device

Usually, the default pin code is 0000. If this does not work, read the manual.

- Continue on the next page -

A connection has been made with the Bluetooth headset. The icon in the status bar on top of the screen has turned blue.

Now you can start calling with the headset. Read the manual of the headset or car kit to find out how you should accept and end calls.

Once you have linked the Bluetooth device to the iPhone with the pin code, you can use the connection much quicker. After you have activated Bluetooth on the iPhone:

Keep the on/off button of the Bluetooth device pressed in for a moment, until the lamp starts to blink

The iPhone will connect to the device right away. If you no longer need to use the Bluetooth device:

Keep the on/off button of the Bluetooth device pressed in until the lamp turns dark

Drag the slider by Bluetooth **to the left**

Tap < Settings

Please note: keep in mind that your iPhone's battery life will be much shorter if you keep the Bluetooth connection activated.

Tip

Add a photo

If you have a picture of your contact stored on your iPhone, you can add this photo to the contact information. In *Chapter 8 Photos and Video* you will learn how to take pictures with your iPhone and how to transfer pictures to your iPhone. This is how you add an existing photo to one of your contacts:

Tap the desired contact

Tap Edit, add photo

- Continue on the next page -

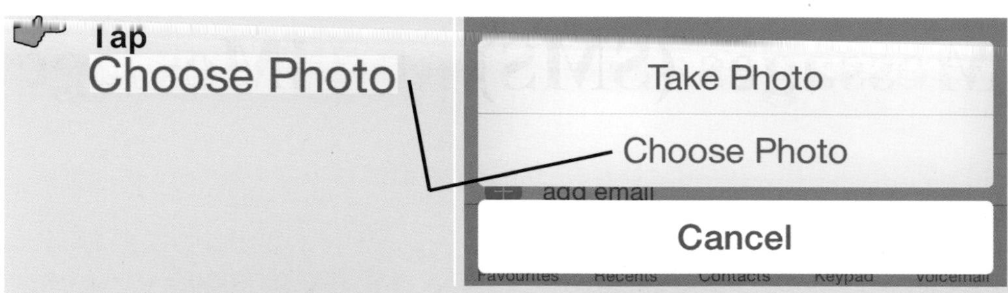

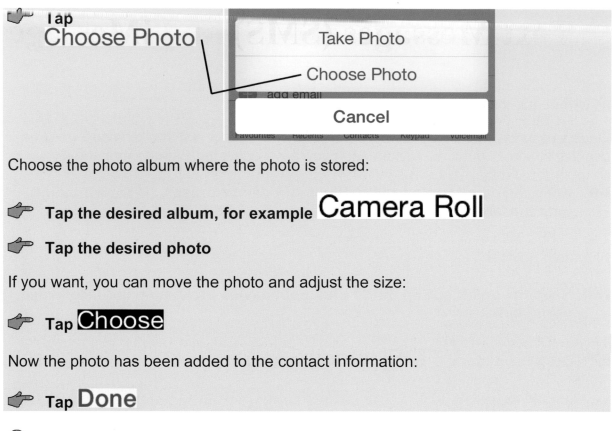

Tap Choose Photo

Choose the photo album where the photo is stored:

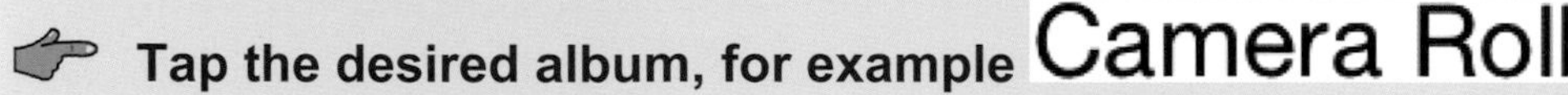

Tap the desired album, for example Camera Roll

Tap the desired photo

If you want, you can move the photo and adjust the size:

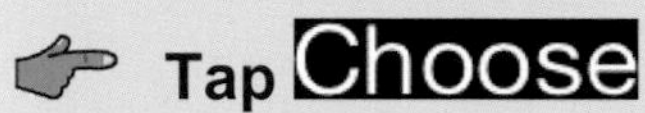

Tap Choose

Now the photo has been added to the contact information:

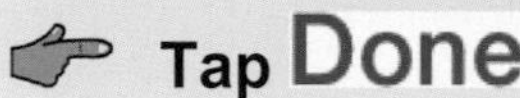

Tap Done

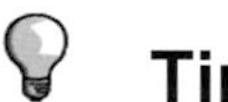

Tip

Skype

You can also conduct video conversations with the free app from the well-known *Skype* program. With this app you can phone other *Skype* users. You can download this app from the *App Store*. In *Chapter 7 Downloading and Managing Apps* you can read how to download apps.

The *Skype* app works simular to the *FaceTime* app.

At the bottom of the *Skype* screen you will see some buttons that are similar to the buttons in *FaceTime*:

3. Text Messages (SMS) and iMessage

Just like other types of cell phones, the iPhone can also send text messages (SMS). You can use the *Messages* app to send messages. SMS is short for *short message service*, in other words, a service that lets you send short text messages. In this chapter you will learn how to send and receive a text message.

For sending an SMS text message you normally pay a fixed fee to your mobile service provider, or a fixed amount will be deducted from your account. Usually, you do not need to pay when you receive a text message, except for receiving messages from paid service providers. Be sure to check the information from your mobile provider about your own pricing plan.

When you send a text message to another iPhone, iPad or iPod Touch user, the system will automatically try to send your message as an *iMessage*. Such a message is sent over the cellular data network or Wi-Fi, which means you will not be charged for the costs of the text message.

You can also send a photo or video along with your SMS or *iMessage* text messages. In the *Tips* at the end of this chapter you can read how to do this.

In this chapter you will learn how to:

- send an SMS or *iMessage* text message;
- receive an SMS or *iMessage* text message;
- view the settings for *iMessage*;
- delete a single message or a conversation;
- add a photo to the text message.

3.1 Sending a Message

You can open the *Messages* app from your iPhone's home screen.

Wake the iPhone up from sleep mode or turn it on 1

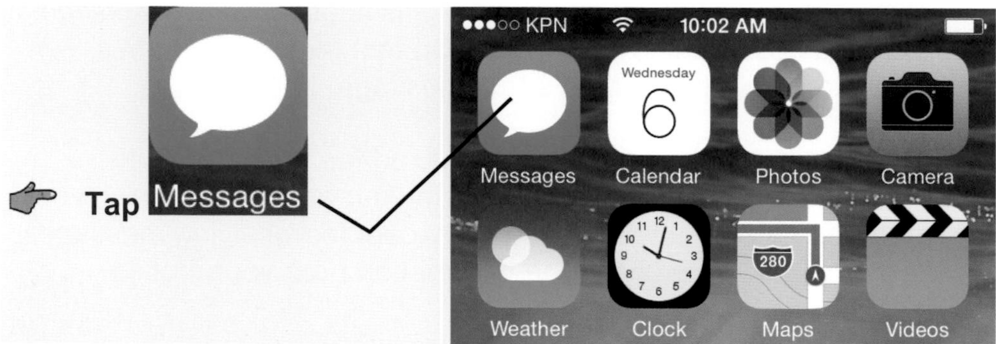

You will see the *New Message* page:

Type the first letter of a contact's name
Right away, you will see a list with all the contacts whose first name starts with this letter:
Tap the desired contact
KPN 10:02 AM
New Message
Cancel
To: l
Lisa Band

Tip

Type a phone number
Instead of selecting a contact, you can also enter a phone number by To:. If necessary, the parentheses around the area code or mobile prefix (7) will automatically be added.

HELP! I see a different page.

If you have already sent or received any text messages with your iPhone, you will see an overview of these messages. Here is how to open a new message:

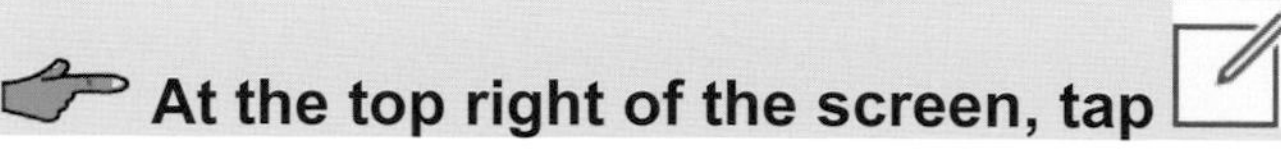

At the top right of the screen, tap

If you want, you can add other recipients. For now, this will not be necessary.

👉 **Tap** Text Message

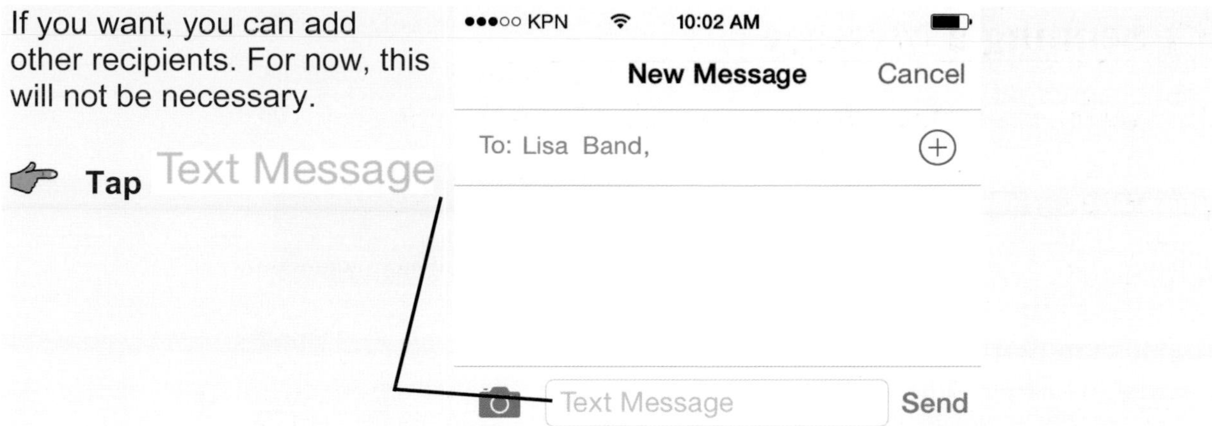

Tip

SMS or iMessage

If you see Text Message, your message will be sent as a regular SMS text message, and you will usually pay a fee for such a message.

If you see iMessage, it means the recipient uses an iPhone, iPad or iPod Touch and *iMessage* has been activated both on your phone and on the recipient's phone. You message will be sent for free over the cellular data network (3G or 4G) or Wi-Fi network. With 3G/4G you will pay a fee for the data traffic, but a text message only uses about 140 bytes, which is very little.

Creating a text message for an SMS or for *iMessage* is done in exactly the same way. In *section 3.4 iMessage* you can read more about the *iMessage* feature.

Type your message, for instance:
`This is my first SMS sent with my iPhone! Greetings from Yvette`

Replace the name 'Yvette' with your own name to finish the message.

👉 **Tap** Send

As soon as the message has been sent, you will hear a sound signal, at least, if the sound on your iPhone is turned on.

A sent SMS text message is displayed in green.

A message that is sent as an *iMessage* will be blue:

This is my first iMessage sent with my iPhone!

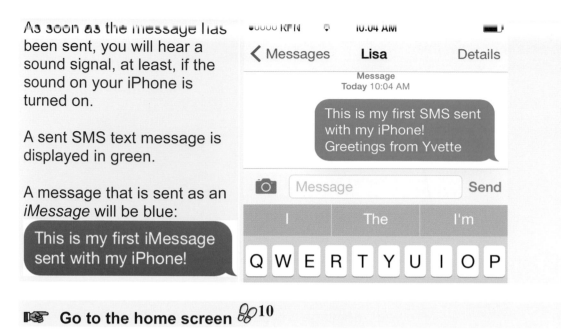

☞ **Go to the home screen** 10

3.2 Receiving a Message

You will hear a sound signal whenever you receive a text message, at least, if the sound on your iPhone is turned on.

If your phone is locked, the screen of your iPhone will light up and you will see the message right away:

If you do not wake your iPhone up at once (unlock), the same thing will happen again after two minutes.

You can go straight to the received messages and reply:

Swipe from left to right over the message

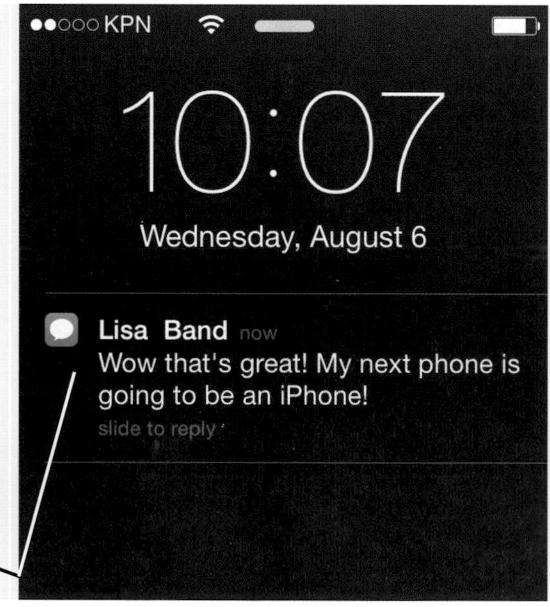

You will see that the answer is displayed below your message:

KPN
10:07 AM
Messages
Lisa
Details
Greetings from Yvette
Wow that's great! My next phone is going to be an iPhone!

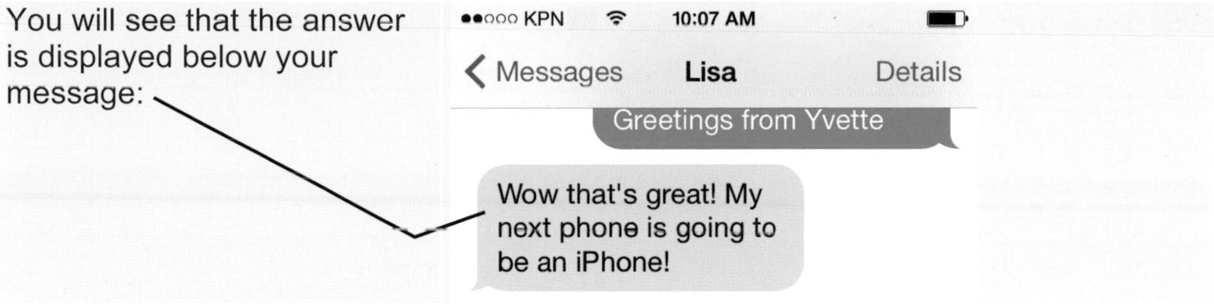

If you have waited a while longer before unlocking your iPhone, you will not see the message immediately:

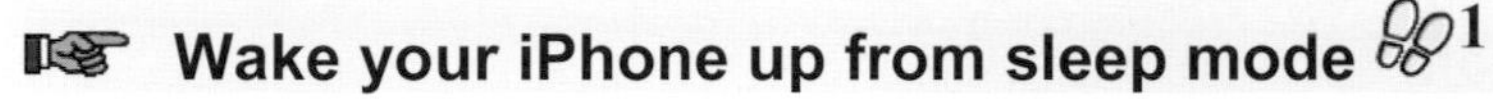

Wake your iPhone up from sleep mode 1

The symbol (called a *badge*) indicates that you have received one new message:

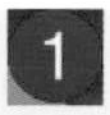

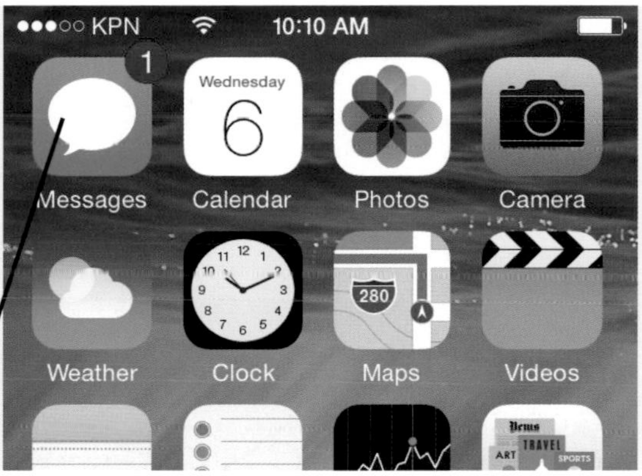

KPN
10:10 AM
1
Messages
Wednesday
6
Calendar
Photos
Camera
Weather
Clock
280
Maps
Videos

Tap
1
Messages

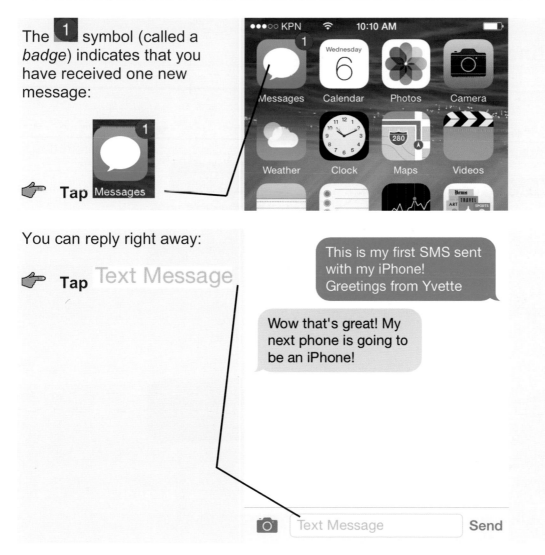

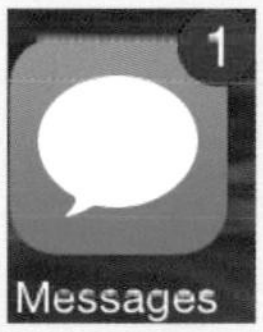

You can reply right away:

Tap Text Message

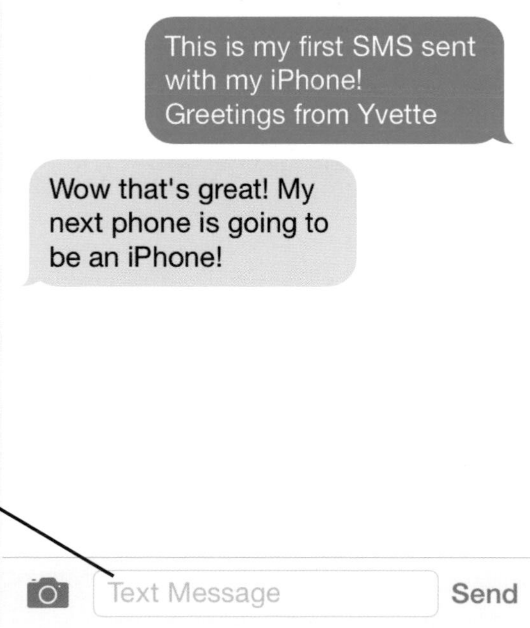

This is my first SMS sent with my iPhone! Greetings from Yvette
Wow that's great! My next phone is going to be an iPhone!
Text Message
Send

Type your message

Tap Send

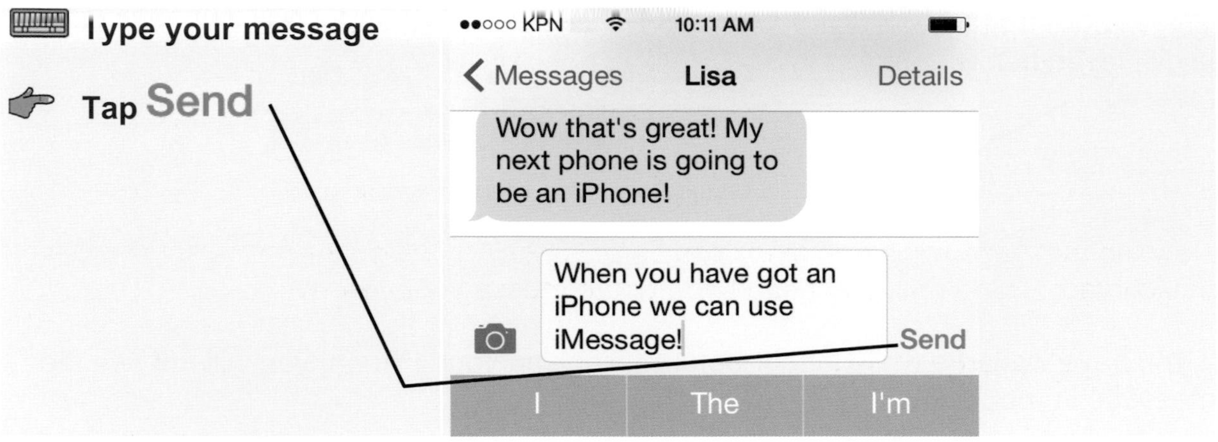

In this way you can create and entire conversation.

3.3 Deleting a Message

You can also delete a message. This is how you do that:

Put your finger on the message

Tap More...

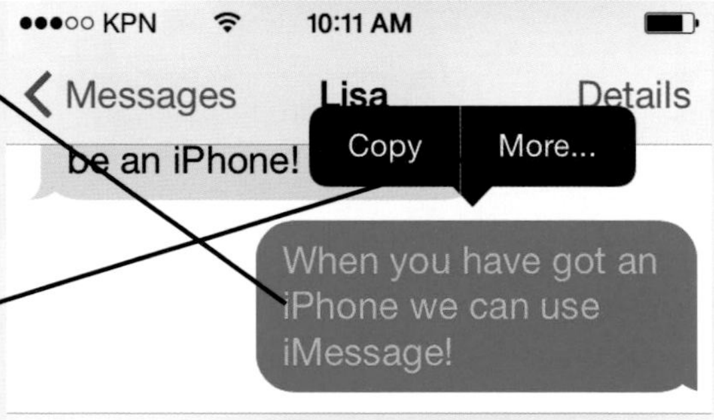

Tap

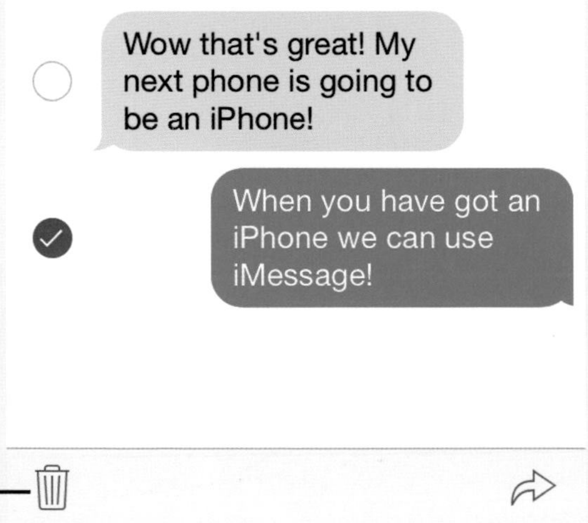

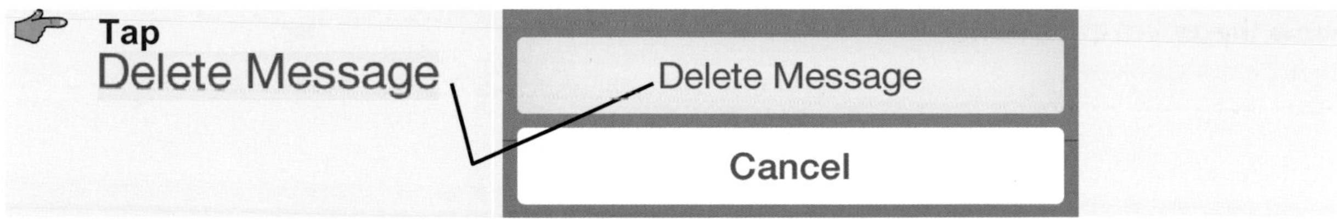

Now the message will be deleted. You can also delete the entire conversation with this contact. To do this, you need to go to the messages overview:

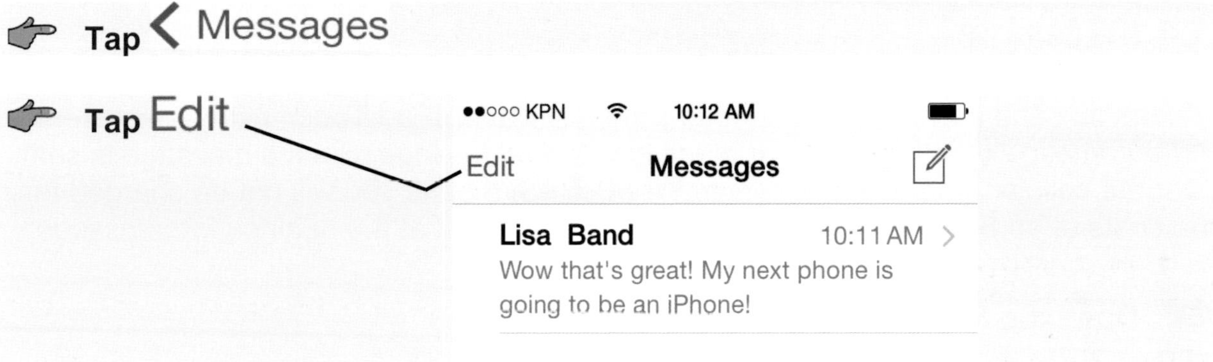

Select the conversation you want to delete:

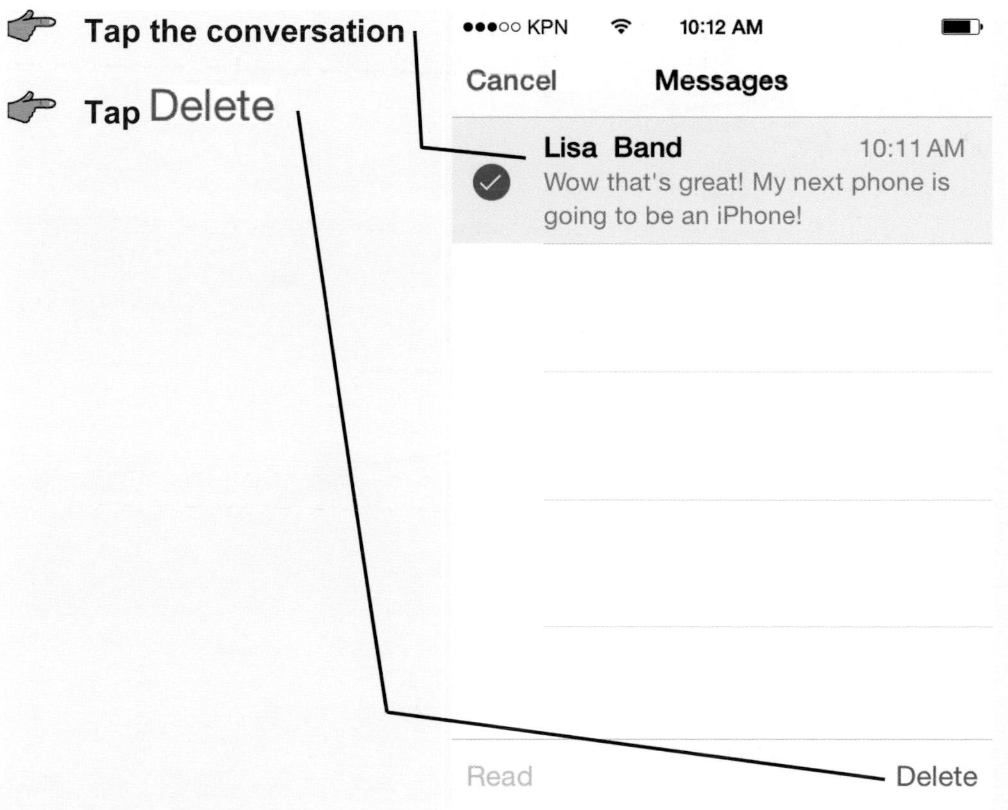

Now the entire conversation has been deleted:

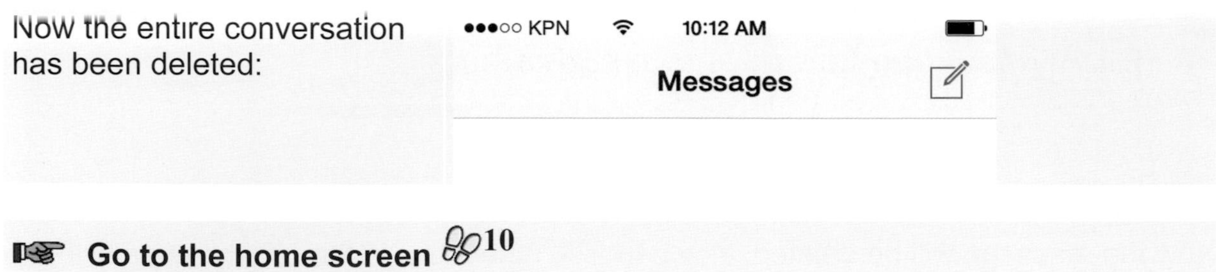

Go to the home screen [10]

3.4 iMessage

When you send a message to another iPhone, iPad or iPod Touch user, the system will automatically try to send your message as an *iMessage*. Such a message is sent over the cellular data network or over Wi-Fi, which means you will not be charged for the costs of an SMS text message. You can take a look at the settings for *iMessage*:

Open the *Settings* app [3]

Swipe upwards over the screen

Tap Messages

iMessage has been activated:

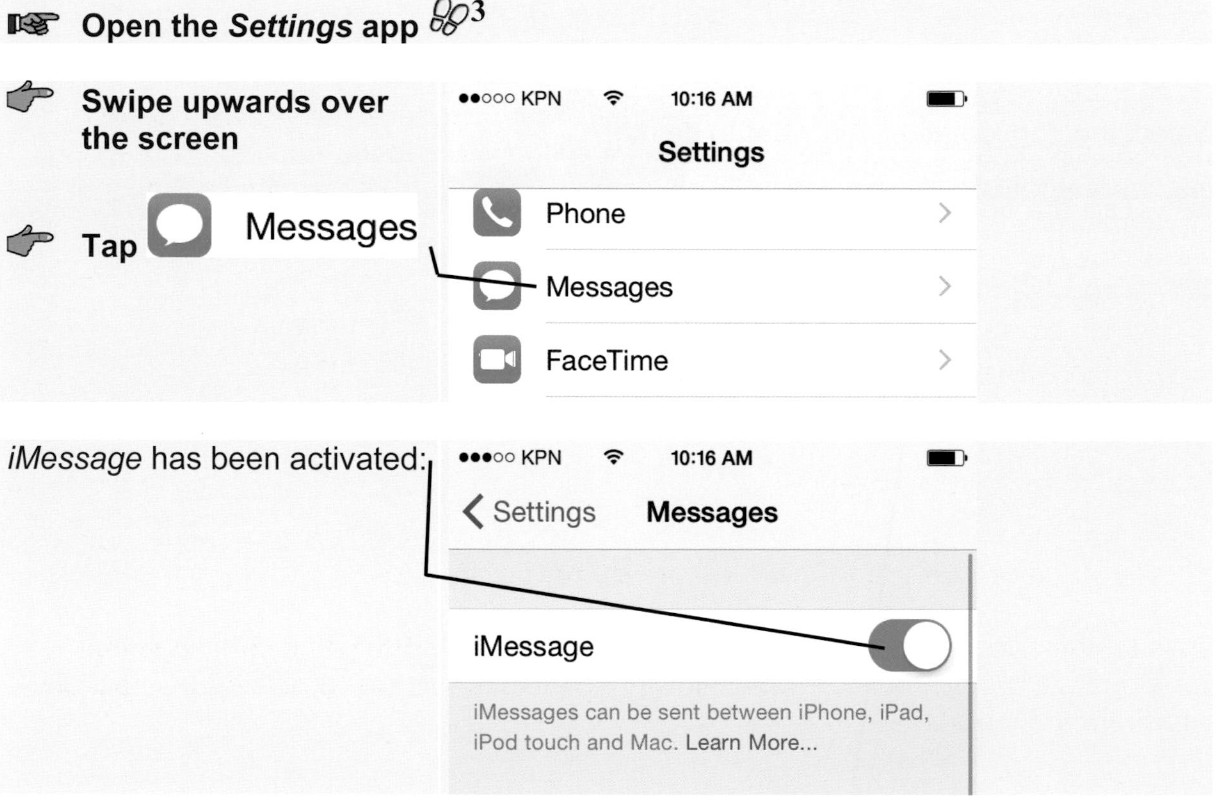

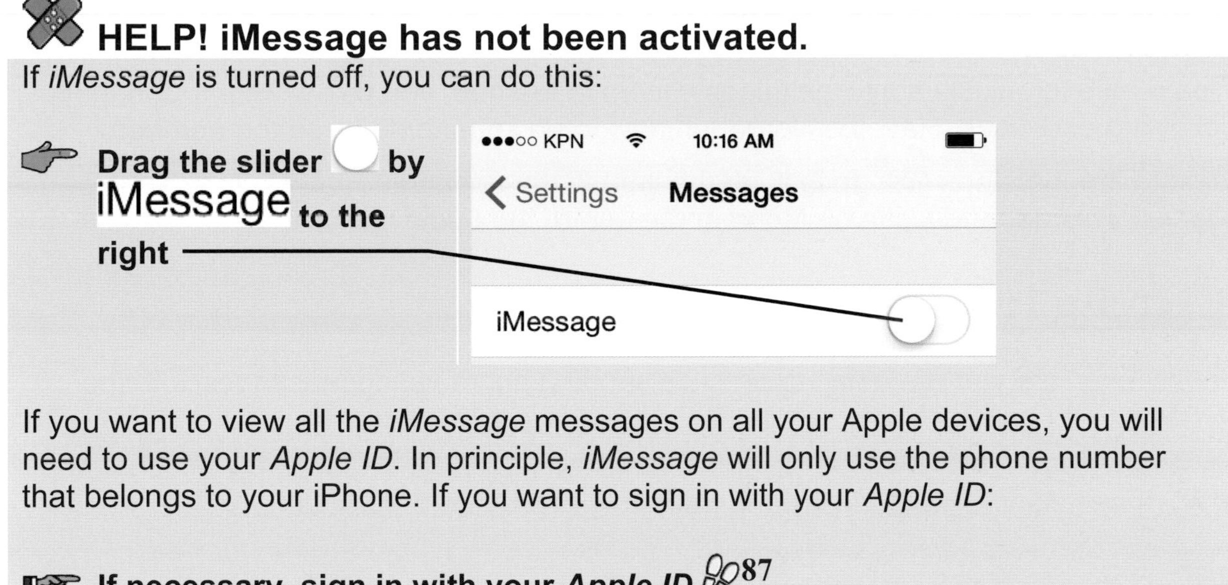

HELP! iMessage has not been activated.

If *iMessage* is turned off, you can do this:

Drag the slider by iMessage to the right

If you want to view all the *iMessage* messages on all your Apple devices, you will need to use your *Apple ID*. In principle, *iMessage* will only use the phone number that belongs to your iPhone. If you want to sign in with your *Apple ID*:

If necessary, sign in with your *Apple ID* 87

If you send a message and you see iMessage appear in the text box, instead of Text Message, your contact will also be using *iMessage*. Your message will automatically be sent as a free-of-charge *iMessage*. You do not need to do anything else, the operations for sending SMS text messages and *iMessage* messages are identical.

You can now return to the home screen:

Tap Settings

Go to the home screen 10

If you want, put the iPhone into sleep mode 2

In this chapter you have learned how to send and receive SMS and *iMessage* text messages with your iPhone. In the following exercises you can practice these actions by repeating them again.

3.5 Exercises

To be able to quickly apply the things you have learned, you can work through the following exercises. Have you forgotten how to do something? Use the numbers next to the footsteps 1 to look up the item in the appendix *How Do I Do That Again?* This appendix can be found at the end of the book.

Exercise 1: Send and Delete a Message

In this exercise you are going to practice sending and deleting messages with the iPhone.

- If necessary, wake the iPhone up from sleep mode or turn it on. 1
- Open the *Messages* app. 3
- Open a new text message. 22
- Select a contact. 23
- Type the message. 24
- Send the message. 25
- Delete the text message you just sent. 26
- Go back to the messages overview screen. 27
- Delete a conversation with a contact. 28
- Go to the home screen. 10
- If you want, put the iPhone into sleep mode. 2

3.6 Background Information

Dictionary

Android	Operating system for mobile phones manufactured by *Google*, the counterpart of the *iOS* system manufactured by Apple.
Conversation	A view in which all the messages you have sent to and received from the same contact are listed one below the other.
Emoji	A Japanese term for emoticon. Literally, *e* means 'image' and *moji* means 'letter'. The special *Emoji* keyboard contains all sorts of symbols you can use in your messages.
Emoticon	An image with which you can express an emotion.
iMessage	A function that allows you to send free text messages over 3G, 4G or Wi-Fi to other iPhone, iPad and iPod touch users. If you send the message over 3G or 4G you will only be charged for the costs of the data traffic, but usually a text message does not cost very much as its data size is only about 140 bytes.
Messages	An app that can be used to send text messages, through SMS or (if possible) *iMessage*.
MMS	Short for *multi media messaging*. A service that allows you to send and receive text messages with attachments. An attachment can consist of a photo or an audio clip. For each MMS message you send, you pay a fixed fee to your cellular service provider.
SMS	Short for *short message service*, a service used to send and receive short text messages (up to a maximum of 160 characters) over the cellular phone network. Your cellular service provider will charge you a fixed fee for each SMS text message sent. A text message that is longer than 160 characters will be divided into two SMS messages. This means you will pay for two text messages. Receiving an SMS message is free of charge.
WhatsApp Messenger	A message service for *Android* cell phones, comparable to *iMessage*. With the *WhatsApp* app you can also use *WhatsApp Messenger* on your iPhone. You can download this app from the *App Store*.

Source: User Guide iPhone, Wikipedia

3.7 Tips

Tip

Add a photo to a message

This is how to attach a photo to an SMS or *iMessage* text message. In *Chapter 8 Photos and Video* you will learn more about making photos.

- **Tap**

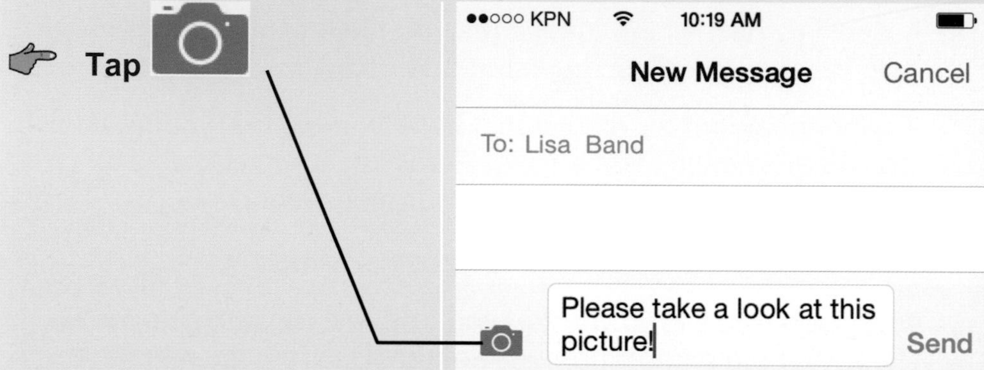

You can take a new picture, or use an existing photo:

- **Tap the desired option, for example** Photo Library
- **Tap the desired album**
- **Tap the desired photo**
- **Tap** Choose

The photo has been added to the message. You can send the message now:

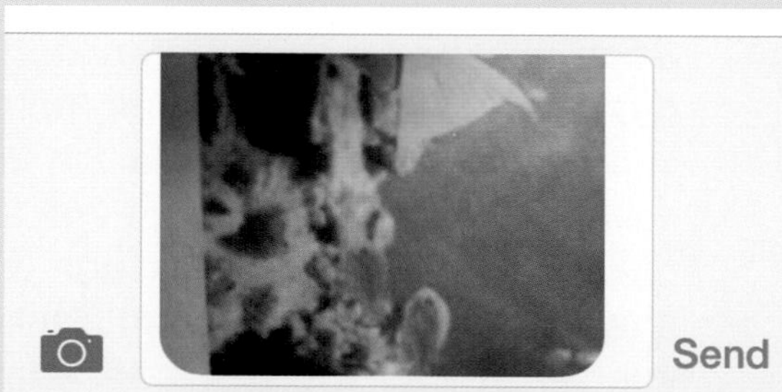

If you add a photo to an SMS text message, the message will be sent as an MMS message. Your cellular service provider will charge a higher fee for such a message. With *iMessage* the photo will be sent over the Wi-Fi or 3G/4G data network. If the message is sent over 3G or 4G you will pay the costs for the data traffic.

Tip

Use emoticons

Have you ever received a message with a small image in the text, such as 😃 or 😳? You can also use these symbols (emoticons):

Open a new message 22

Type your message

Using emoticons in your text messages is very easy:

Tap 😀

You will see the *Emoji* keyboard. This is how you add a symbol:

Tap the desired symbol

You will see that the symbol is immediately inserted into your message:

Here are some other categories of *Emoji* keyboards:

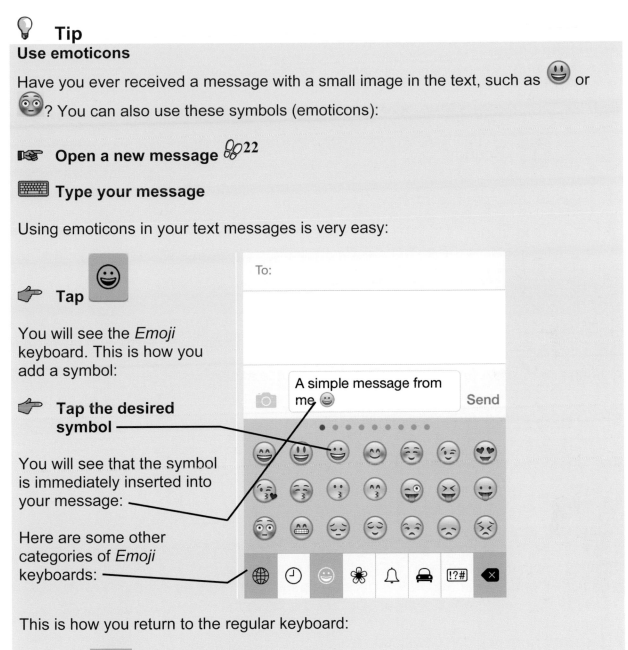

This is how you return to the regular keyboard:

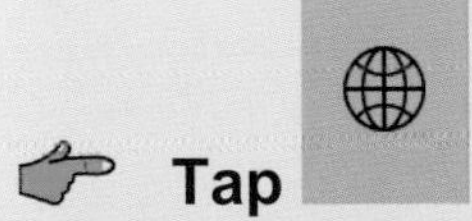

Please note: If you send an SMS text message that contains *Emoji* symbols, the message will be encoded in a different way. Instead of 160 characters you will only still have 70 characters available for typing your text message. This means that if your message is longer than 70 characters, you will be charged for two separate SMS messages.

 **Tip**

Adjust the sound
You can change the sound signal you hear when you receive a new message:

- **Open the *Settings* app** 3
- **Tap** Sounds
- **Swipe upwards the screen**
- **Tap** Text Tone

You will see a long list of available sounds:

- **Tap the desired sound, for example** Aurora

Right away, you will hear a sound sample of the sound and you will see a checkmark ✓ next to the name. If you want to use this sound:

- **Tap** < Sounds, < Settings
- **Go to the home screen** 10

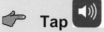

 **Tip**

WhatsApp Messenger
You can also use the popular message service *WhatsApp Messenger* on your iPhone. This service has been developed for *Android* devices, but you can also use it on the iPhone. *WhatsApp Messenger* works the same way as *iMessage*. The messages are sent free of charge, over the cellular data network 3G/4G or over Wi-Fi.
In the *App Store* you can download *WhatsApp Messenger*. In *Chapter 7 Downloading and Managing Apps* you can read how to do this.

 **Tip**

Message not delivered
Due to technical problems, or if the cellular network is extremely busy, it may happen that an SMS message cannot be delivered.

You will see an exclamation mark (!) next to the message. You can try sending the message again by tapping (!) and Try Again.

4. Sending Emails with Your iPhone

The *Mail* app is one of the standard apps installed on your iPhone. With *Mail* you can compose, send and receive email messages, just like you do on a regular computer. In this chapter you will learn how to set up your email account. We will explain how to do this for popular Internet Service Providers, such as AT&T and Verizon and for web-based accounts such as *Hotmail*. If you are using multiple email accounts, you can set all of them up to use on your iPhone.

Writing an email with your iPhone is very easy. In this chapter you will practice writing an email and learn how to select, copy, cut and paste text using the iPhone's onscreen keyboard. You will also get acquainted with the autocorrect function.

Furthermore, we will explain how to send, receive and delete email messages.

In this chapter you will learn how to:

- set up an email account;
- set up an *Outlook.com*, *Hotmail* or *Gmail* account;
- send an email message;
- receive an email message;
- reply to an email;
- move an email message to the *Trash* folder;
- permanently delete an email message.

4.1 Setting Up an Email Account

In order to use email on your iPhone, you need to set up at least one email account. In this section you will learn how to do this for an account with an Internet Service Provider (ISP) such as AT&T and Verizon. To set up your account, make sure you have the necessary account information from your ISP provider handy. This includes the server information, user name and password.

Wake the iPhone up from sleep mode [1]

Open the *Settings* app [3]

Swipe upwards over the page

Tap Mail, Contacts, C

Tap Add Account

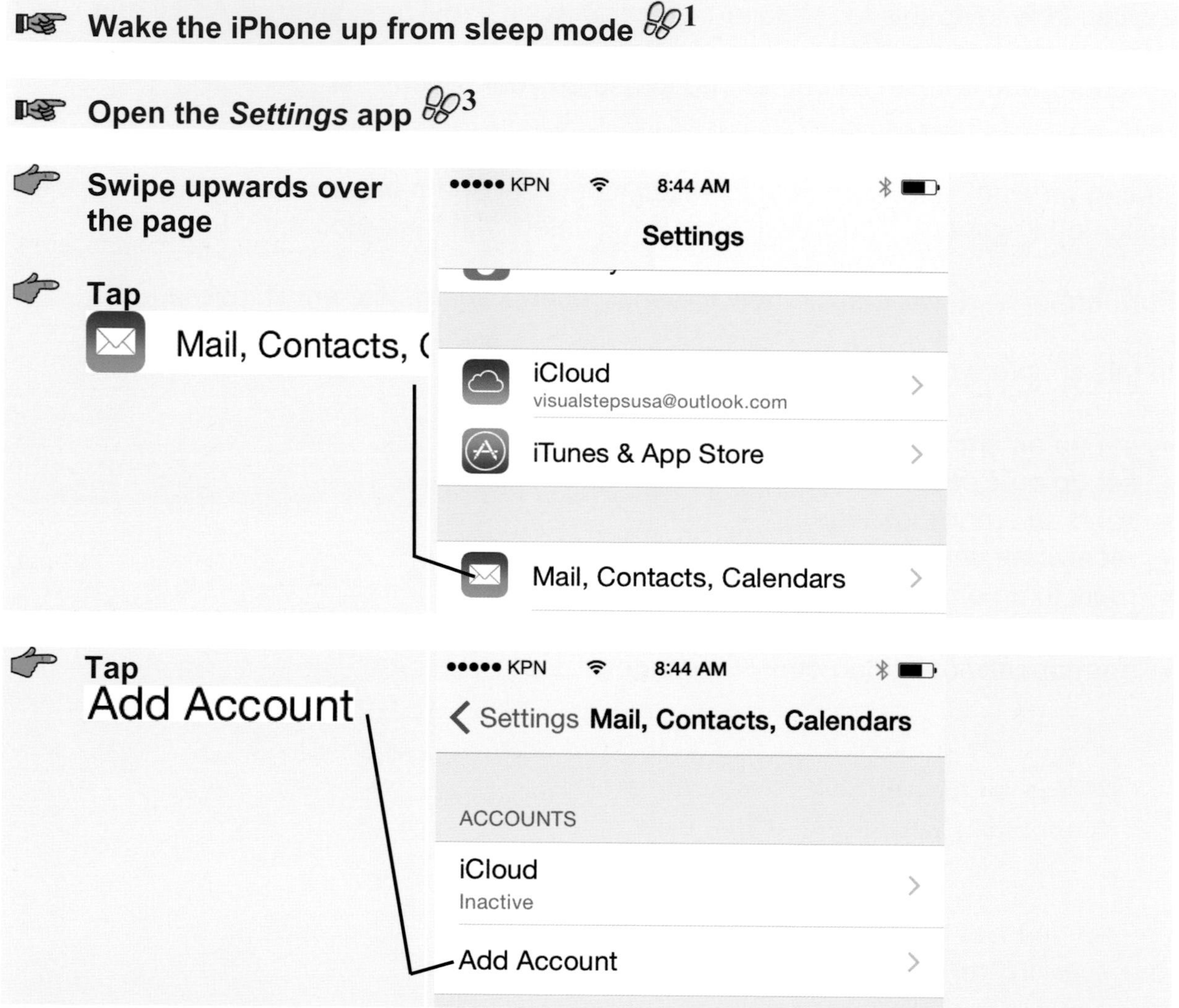

Please note:

Do you have an *Outlook.com, Hotmail* or *Gmail* account, you can skip this section and continue further in *section 4.2 Setting Up an Outlook.com, Hotmail or Gmail Account.*

You can choose from various well-known web-based providers. If you have an account with one of these popular providers, you only need your user name and password. If your provider is not included in this list:

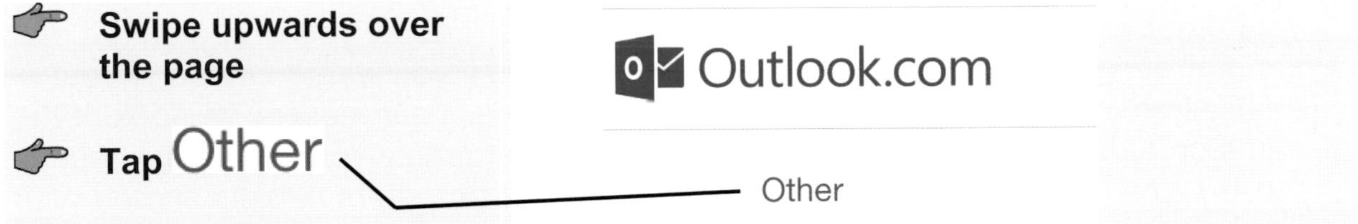
Swipe upwards over the page
Tap Other
Outlook.com
Other

You can now add your email account:

Tap Add Mail Account

Now you will see a screen where you need to enter some basic information concerning your email account. To do this, you can use the onscreen keyboard from the iPhone:

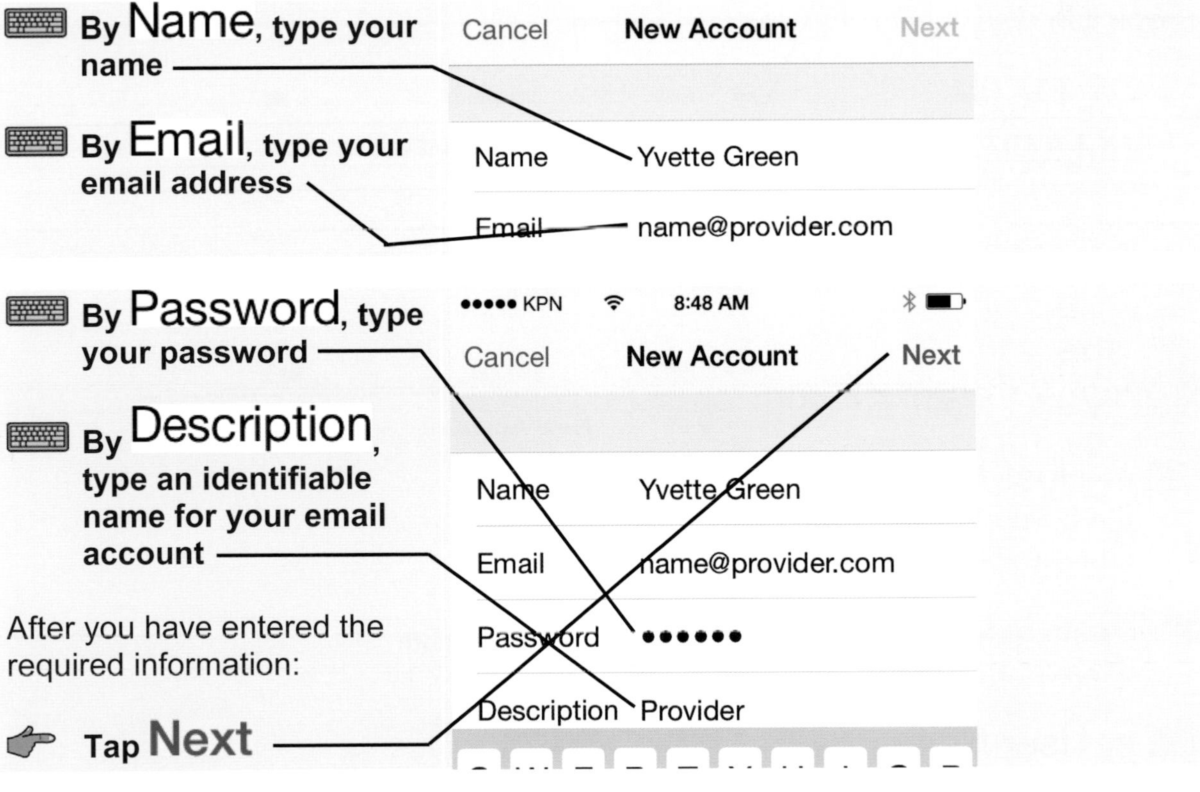
By Name, type your name
By Email, type your email address
Cancel
New Account
Next
Name
Yvette Green
Email
name@provider.com
By Password, type your password
By Description, type an identifiable name for your email account
After you have entered the required information:
Tap Next
••••• KPN
8:48 AM
Password
••••••
Description
Provider

Tip

Onscreen keyboard
Have you forgotten how to operate the onscreen keyboard on the iPhone? Then read how to do that by going back to *section 1.8 Using the Keyboard*.

Now you can select whether you want to set your email account as an *IMAP* or *POP* account:

- IMAP stands for *Internet Message Access Protocol*. This means you can manage your email messages on the mail server. Messages read by you will be stored on the mail server until you delete them. IMAP is useful if you want to manage your emails from different computers, tablets and a phone. Your mailbox will look the same on each device. When you create folders to organize your email messages, these same folders will also be visible on the other computers, tablets and on your iPhone. If you want to use IMAP, you will need to set up your email account as an IMAP account on each computer, tablet or phone you use.

- POP stand for *Post Office Protocol*. This is the traditional way of managing email messages. After you have received your messages, they will immediately be deleted from the mail server. But on your iPhone, the default setting for POP accounts is for leaving a copy of your message stored on the server, even after you have received your email messages. This means you will also be able to receive these messages on your computer. In the *Tips* at the end of this chapter you can read how to change these settings.

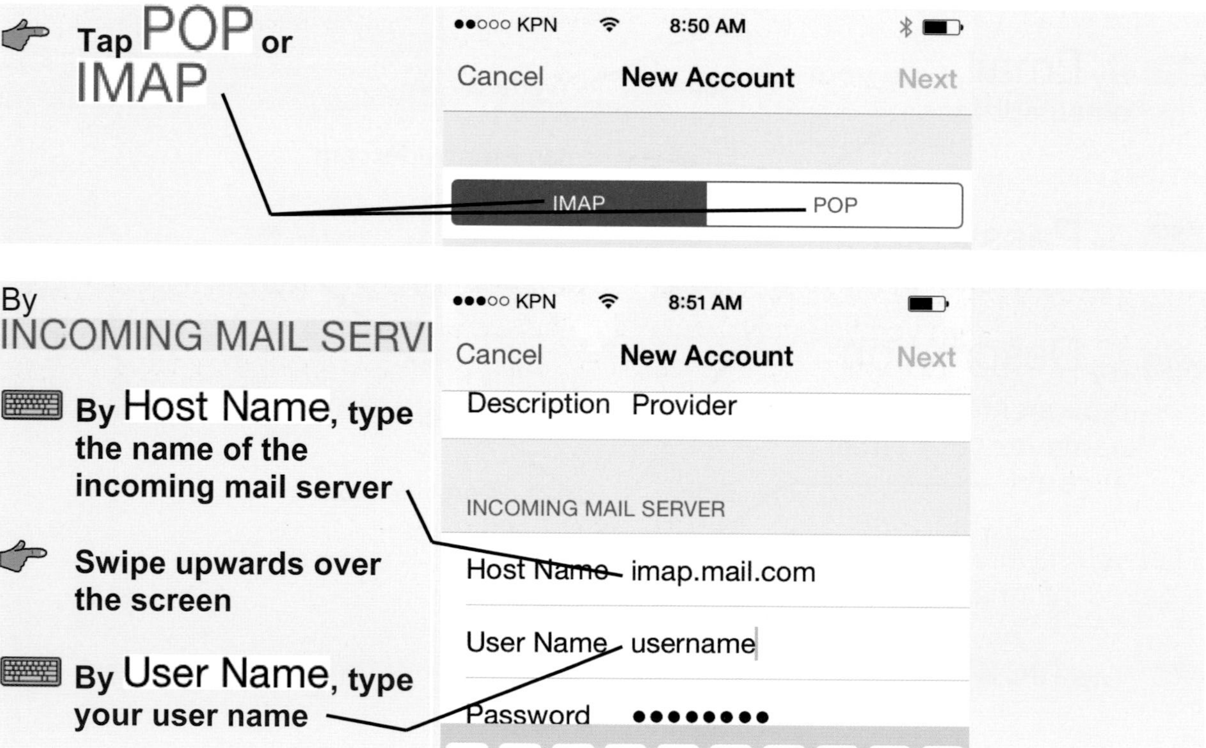

Swipe upwards over the screen

By OUTGOING MAIL SERVE

By Host Name, type the name of the outgoing mail server

If by OUTGOING MAIL SERVE you see the text Optional in the fields for the user name and password, you do not need to enter this information.

Tap Next

Tap Save

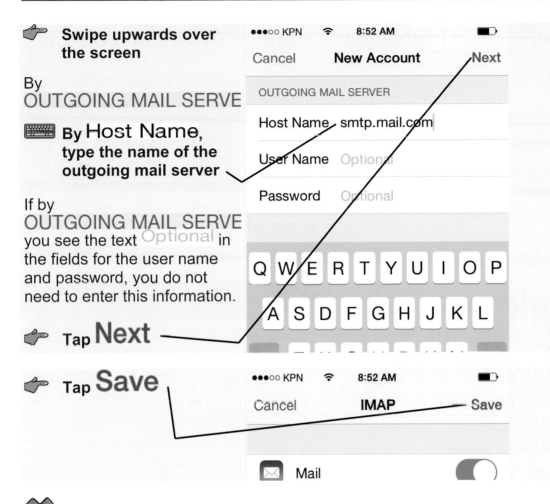

HELP! It does not work.

Because of the popularity of the iPhone, many providers such as AT&T and Verizon have put instructions on their websites about setting up an email account for the iPhone. Just look for something like 'email settings iPhone' on your provider's website and follow the instructions listed.

Your email account has been added:

Tap < Settings

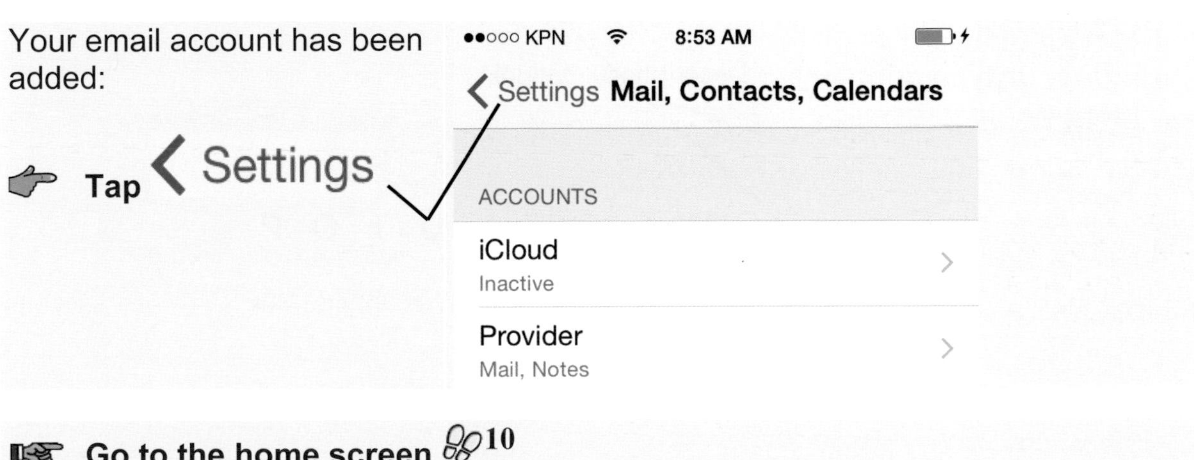

Go to the home screen 10

4.2 Setting Up a Outlook.com, Hotmail or Gmail Account

If you have a *Outlook.com* or *Hotmail* account, you can set this up on your iPhone too. You can set up a *Gmail* account on a similar way.

If necessary, open the *Settings* app 3

Tap Add Account

Tap Outlook.com

If you use *Gmail*, tap Google Mail.

In this example we have used an email address that ends with hotmail.com.

By Email**, type your email address**

By Password**, type your password**

By Description **you can just leave the name, or type another identifiable name**

Tap Next

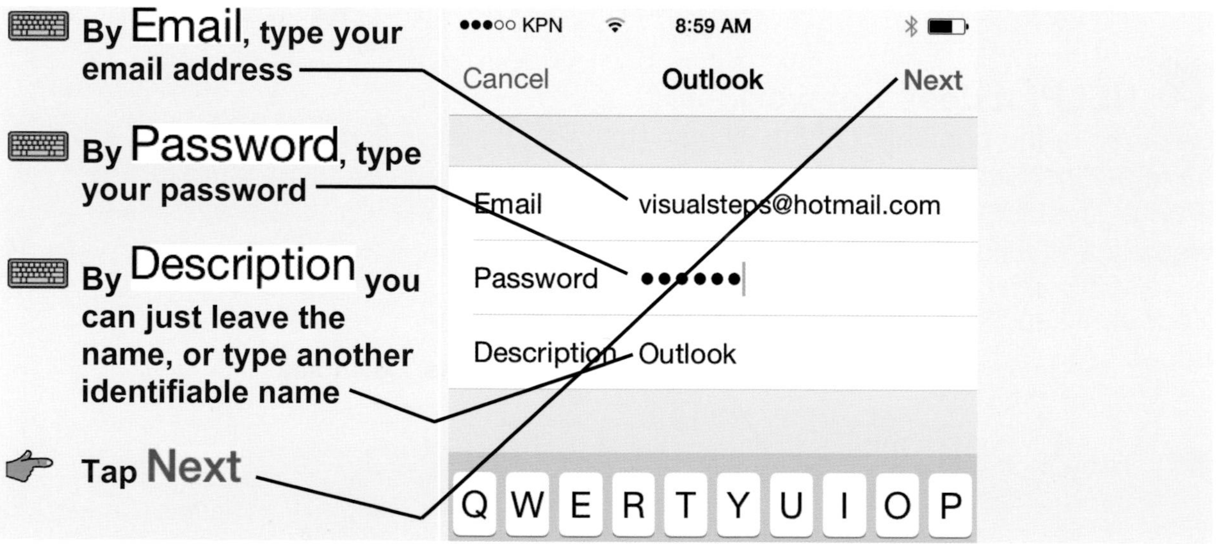

The iPhone will automatically recognize the server.

On this page you can select an option to synchronize your contacts and calendars too, besides your email. You do not need to change these settings:

Tap Save

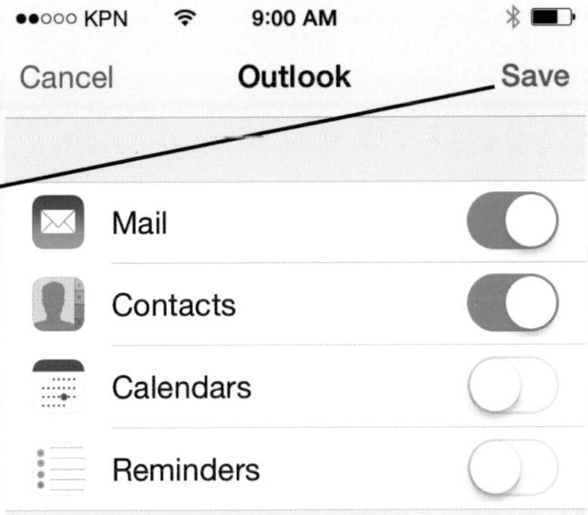

You will see that the account has been added:

Tap < Settings

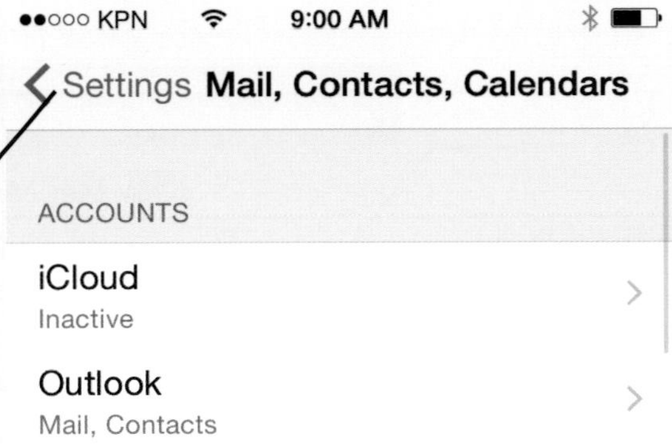

Go to the home screen 10

4.3 Sending an Email

Just to practice, you can now write an email and send it to yourself. First, you need to open the *Mail* app:

Tap

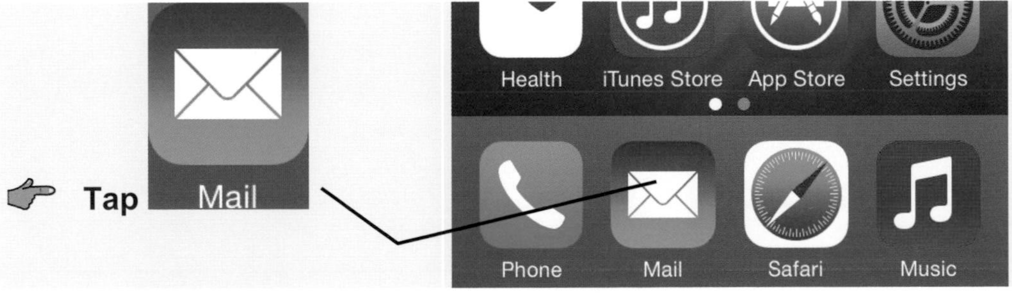

The app will first check for new messages. In this example there are no new messages, but you may find some new ones in your own *Mail* app. Go ahead and open a new, blank email:

At the bottom of the screen:

Tap

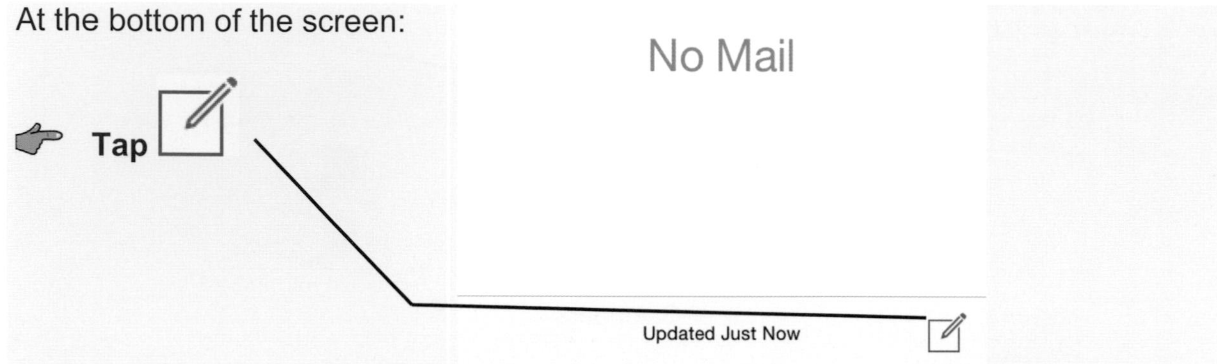

A new message will be opened. Now you are going to send yourself a sample message:

By To:, type your email address

A soon as you start typing in the To: field, the @ sign will appear on the onscreen keyboard:

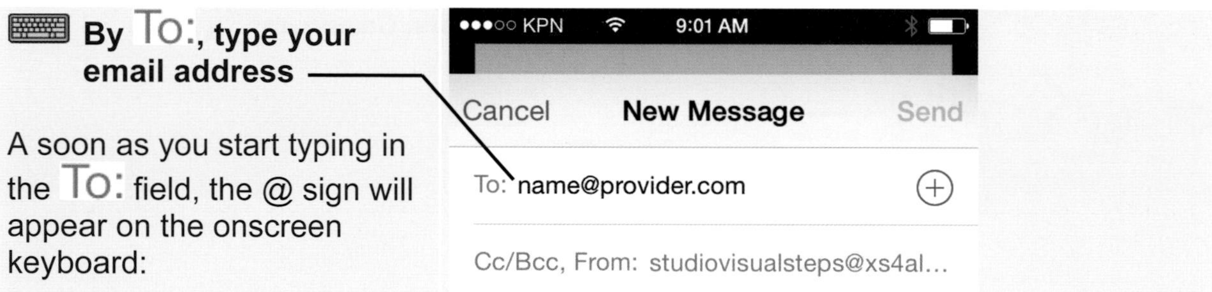

Tip

Contacts

With the button you can open the list of contacts. You can select the recipient from this list by tapping his or her name.
When you type the first letter of a stored contact's first name, you will see a relevant selection from the list. The same thing will happen when you type the first letter of an email address you have stored.
If you need to review, see *Chapter 2 Making and Receiving Calls* to learn how to add new contacts to this list.

By Subject: **type:** `Test`

Tap the white area to enter your message

Type: `This is a test.`

Continue typing on a new line:

Tap return

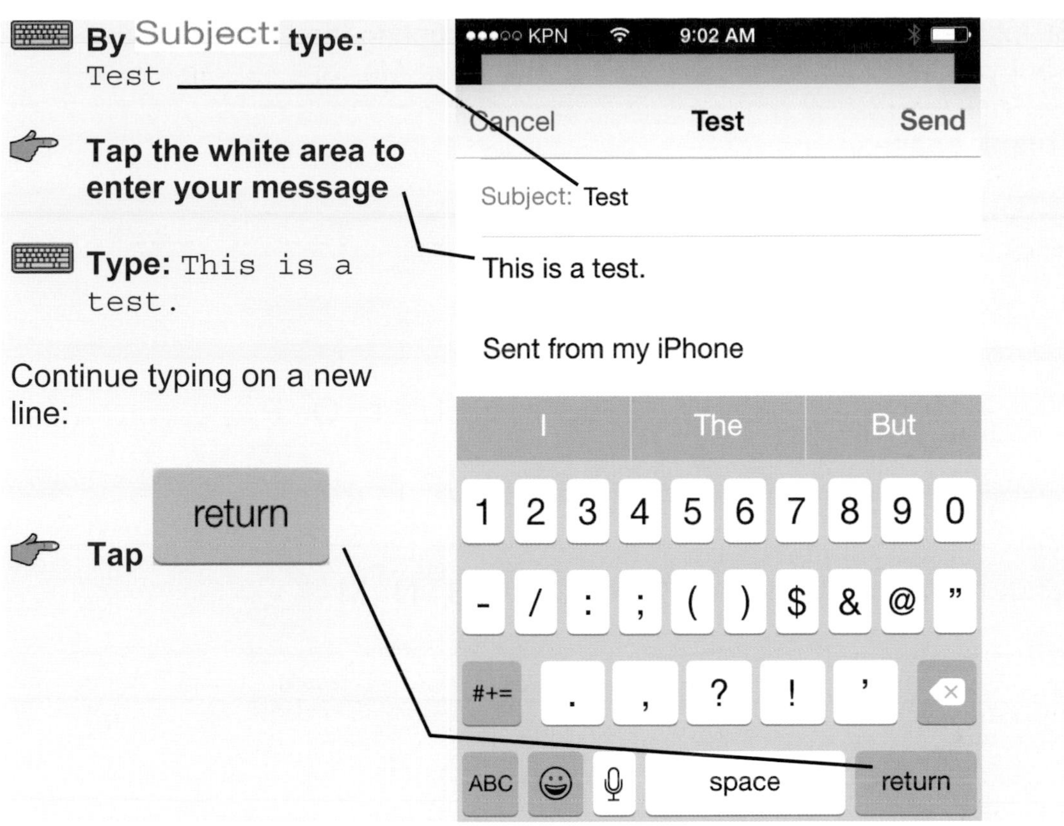

The iPhone contains a dictionary that will help you while you are typing. Just see what happens when you make a spelling mistake intentionally:

Type: `Type a speling`

You will see that while you are typing, the app suggests this correction spelling:

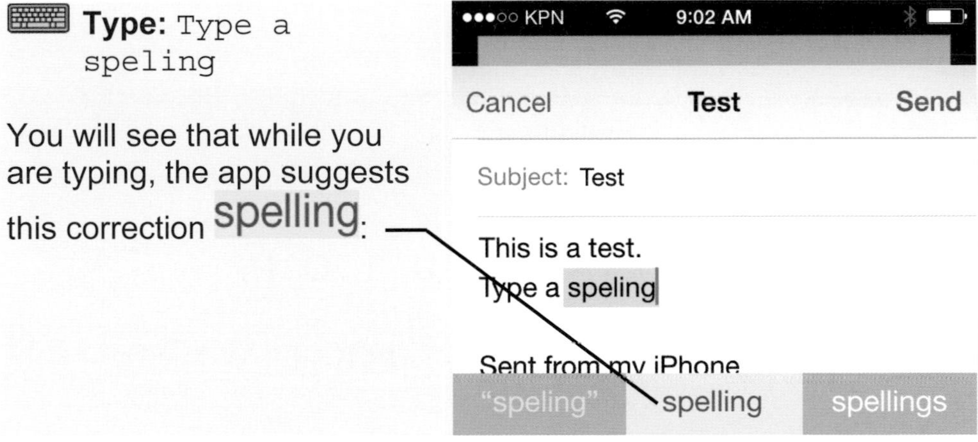

You can accept the suggested correction without interrupting the typing of your message:

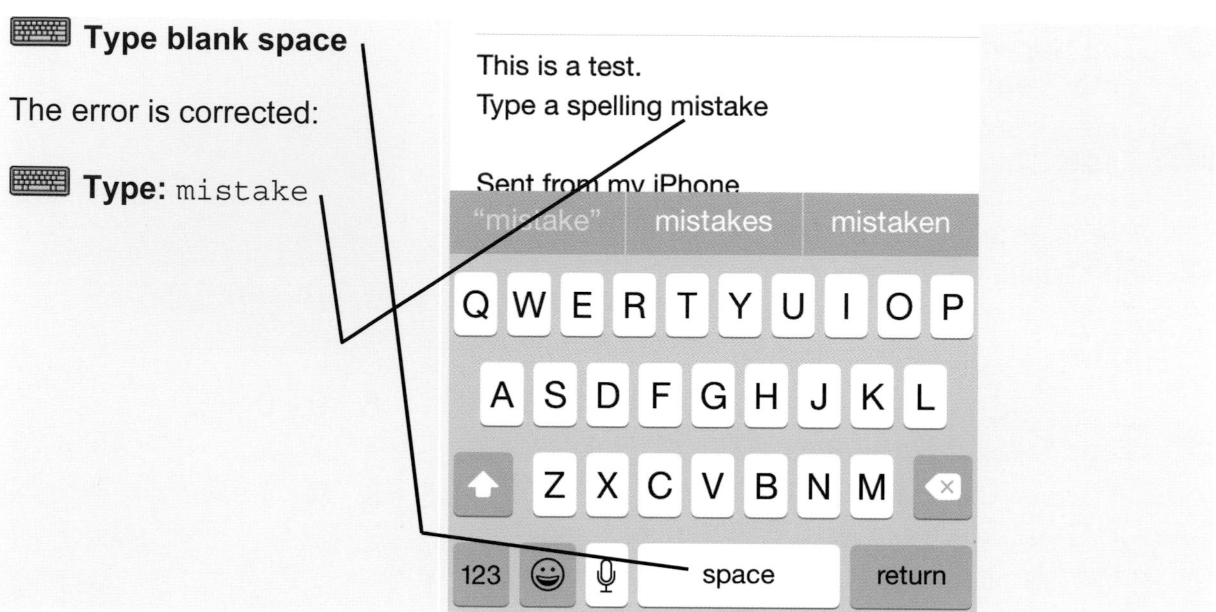

Tip

Accept correction
A suggested correction will also be accepted if you type a period, comma or another punctuation symbol.

Tip

Refuse correction
You can also refuse to accept a suggested correction. This is how you do it:

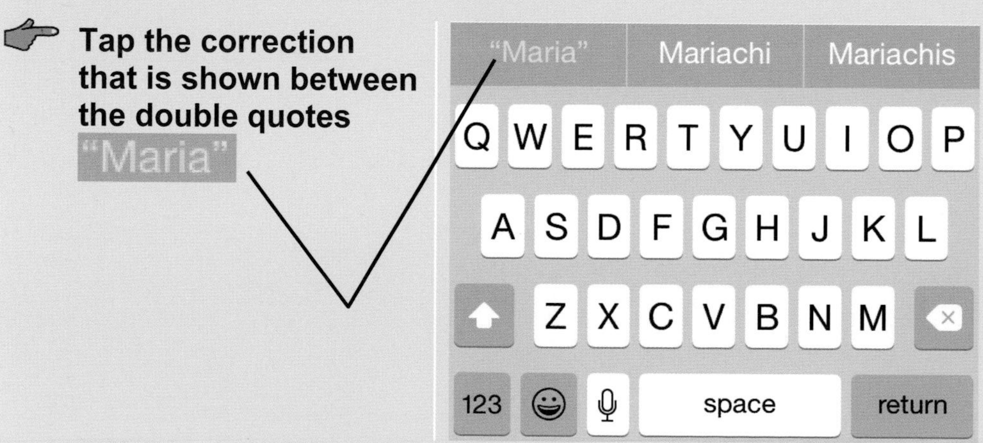

You need to do this before you type a blank space, period, comma or other punctuation symbol, otherwise the correction will be accepted.

Tip

Turn off Auto-Correction function

In the *Tips* at the back of this chapter you can read how to disable the Auto-Correction function while typing.

If you are not satisfied with your message, you can quickly delete the text by using the backspace key:

- **Press your finger on** ⌫ **until both lines have been deleted**

You will see that at first, the deletion will take place one letter at a time. When you reach the next line, the words will be deleted one by one.

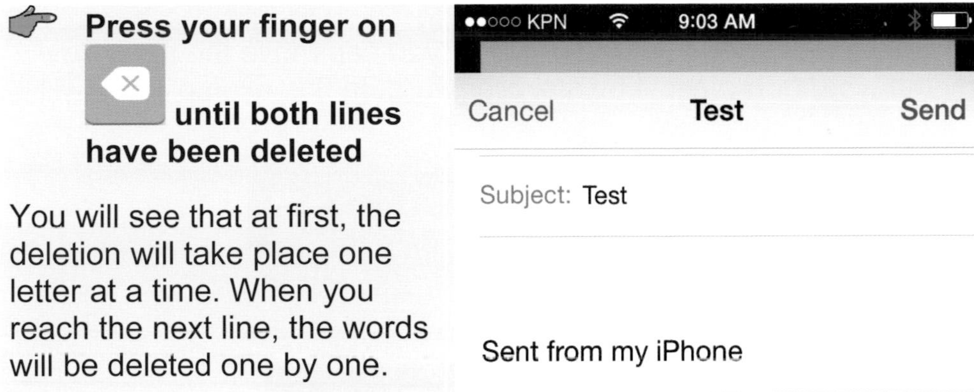

In *Mail* you can also copy, cut and paste. You can do this for a single word or with an entire text. Here is how to select a word:

- **Put your finger on the word** iPhone

You will see a magnifying glass which contains the selected word:

- **Release your finger from the screen**

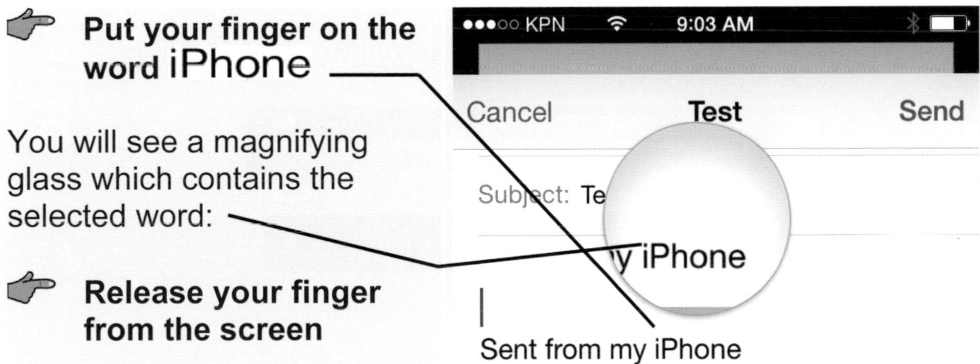

A pop-up menu appears. You can select the one word, multiple words or the entire text. Try selecting just one word:

- **Tap** Select

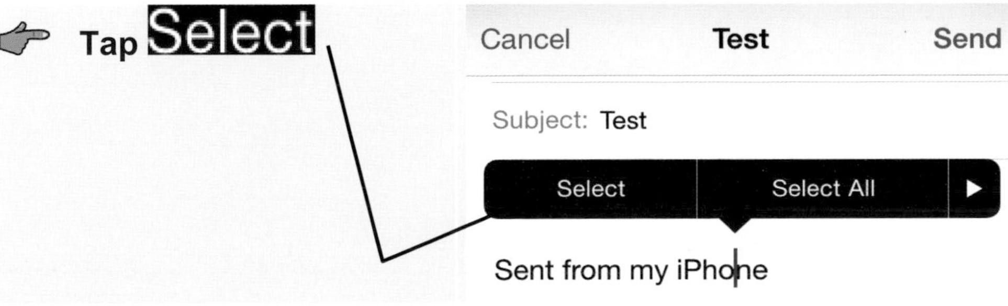

Tip

Magnifying glass
With the magnifying glass, you can easily position the cursor on the exact spot inside a word, or between two words. This is helpful when you want to edit or correct text. Move your finger along, until you can see the correct position of the cursor in the magnifying glass, then release your finger. You will not need to use the Select or Select All buttons. You can just go on typing.

The word has been selected. To select multiple words, you can move the pins. Now you can cut or copy the word or replace it by a similar word. In this example you will copy the word:

- Tap **Copy**

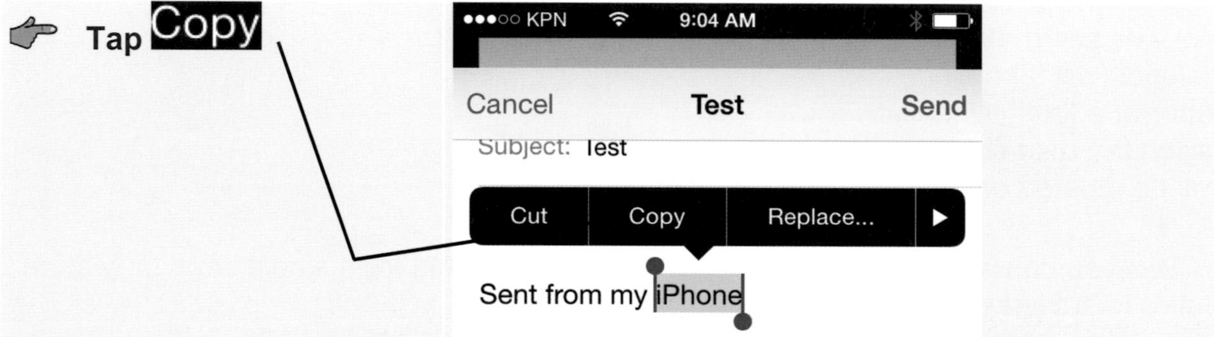

The word has been copied to the clipboard. Now you can paste it into the text:

- **Put your finger on the first line**

You may need to keep your finger there for a moment.

Again, you will see the magnifying glass.

- **Release your finger**
- Tap **Paste**

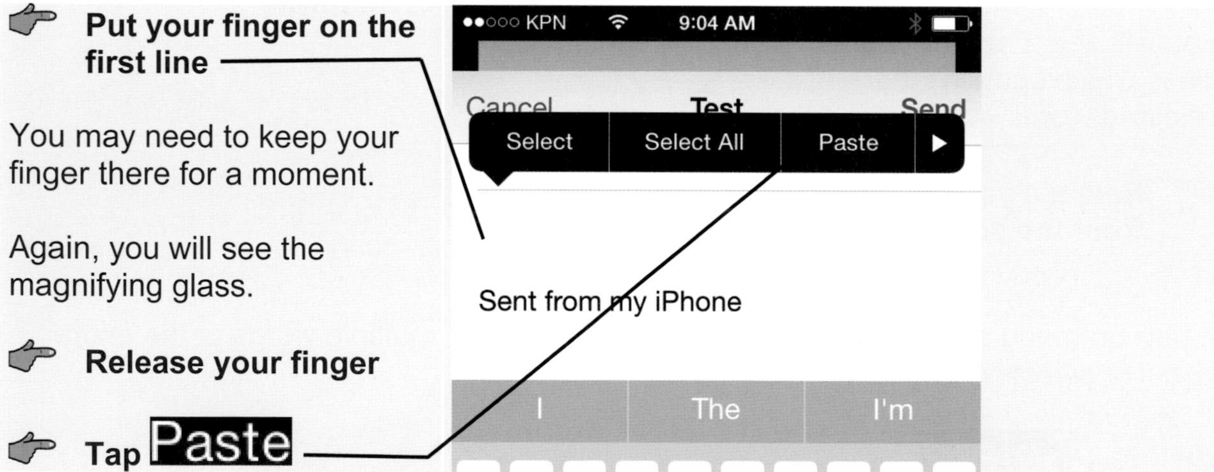

Now the copied word has been pasted to the first line:

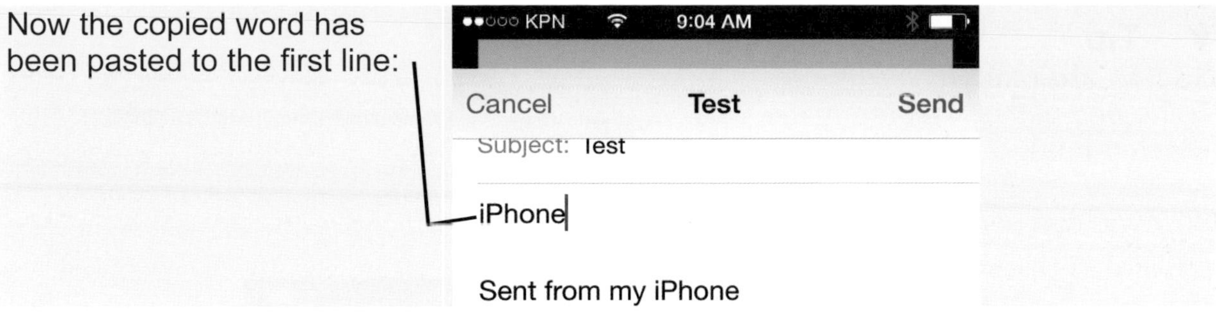

You can also format the text in an email message. Here is how to do that:

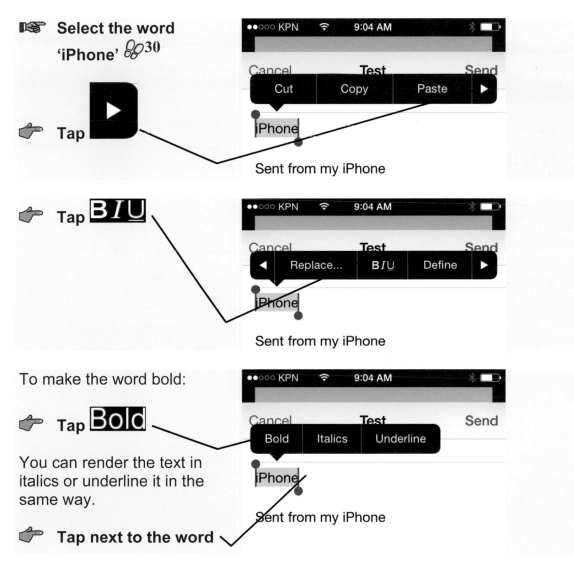

Select the word 'iPhone' 30

Tap ▶

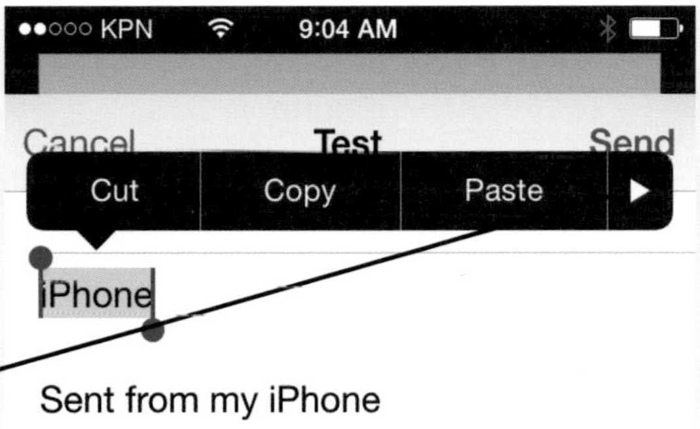

Tap B *I* U

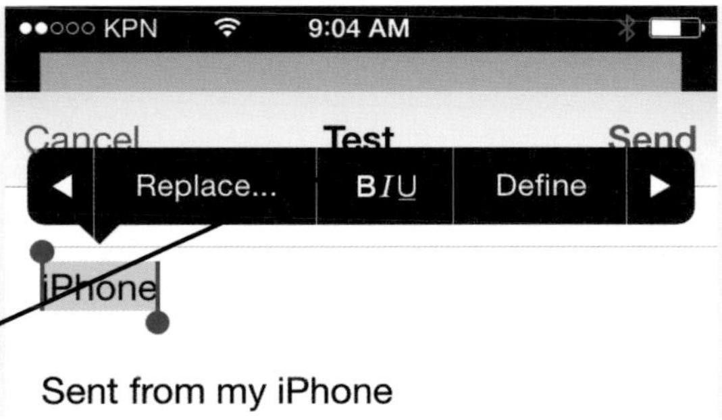

To make the word bold:

Tap Bold

You can render the text in italics or underline it in the same way.

Tap next to the word

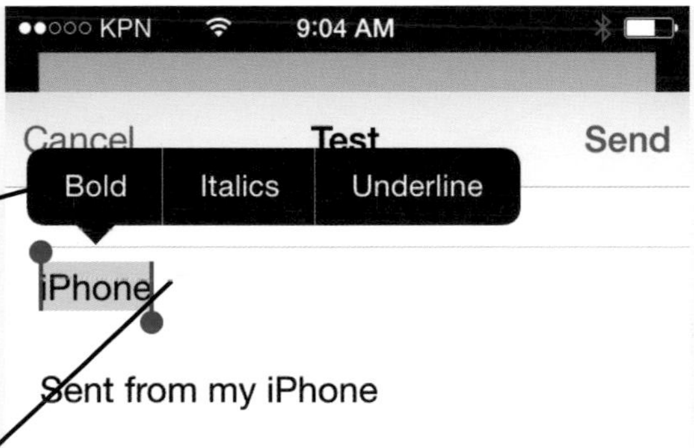

Tip

Add an attachment

At the end of this chapter, in the *Tips*, you can find more information about email attachments.

Now you can send your test email message:

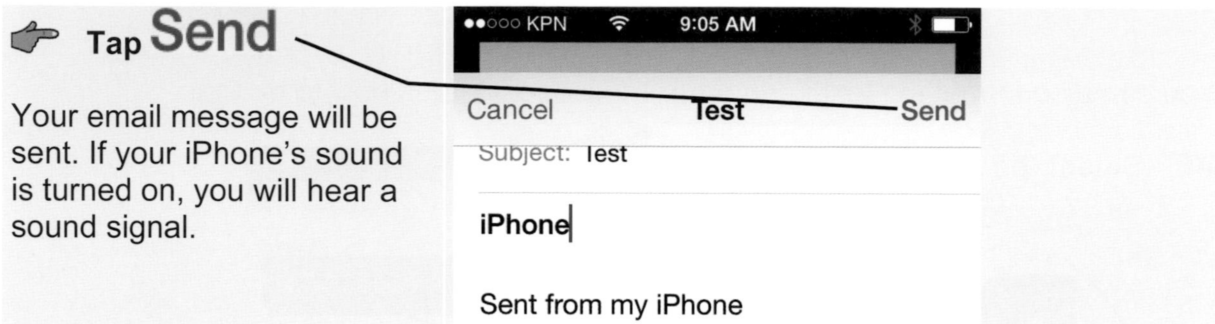

Tap Send

Your email message will be sent. If your iPhone's sound is turned on, you will hear a sound signal.

4.4 Receiving an Email

Shortly afterwards, your email message will be received. You may hear another sound signal. This is how you open the *Inbox* folder, where your incoming messages are stored:

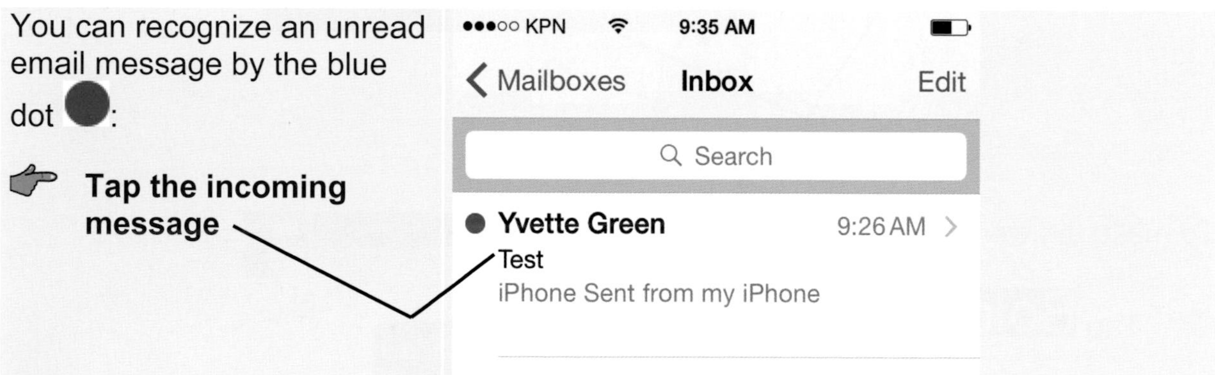

You can recognize an unread email message by the blue dot:

Tap the incoming message

HELP! I do not see a new message.

When you do not see a new email message:

 **Swipe downwards the screen**

You will see the contents of the message:

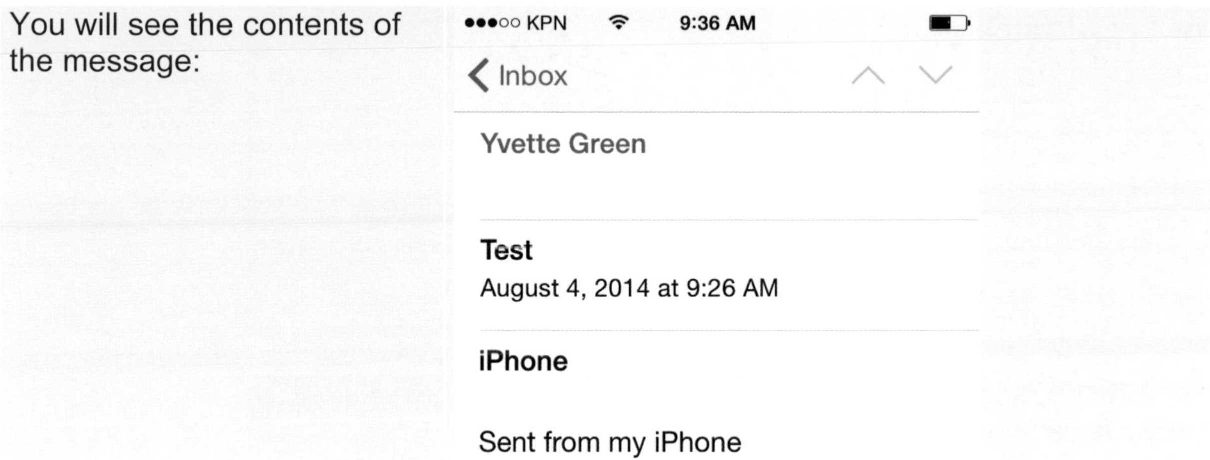

In the toolbars above and below a message you will see a number of buttons. These are the functions of the various buttons:

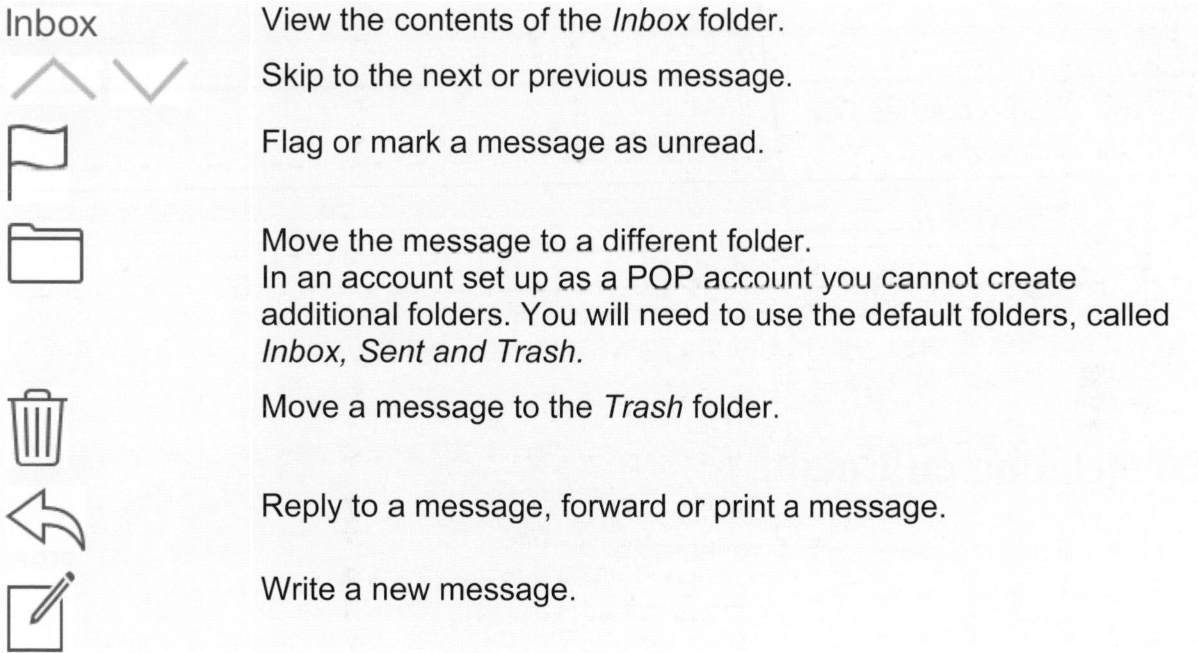

Inbox — View the contents of the *Inbox* folder.

Skip to the next or previous message.

Flag or mark a message as unread.

Move the message to a different folder.
In an account set up as a POP account you cannot create additional folders. You will need to use the default folders, called *Inbox, Sent and Trash.*

Move a message to the *Trash* folder.

Reply to a message, forward or print a message.

Write a new message.

4.5 Replying To an Email

This is how you reply to an email. At the bottom of the screen:

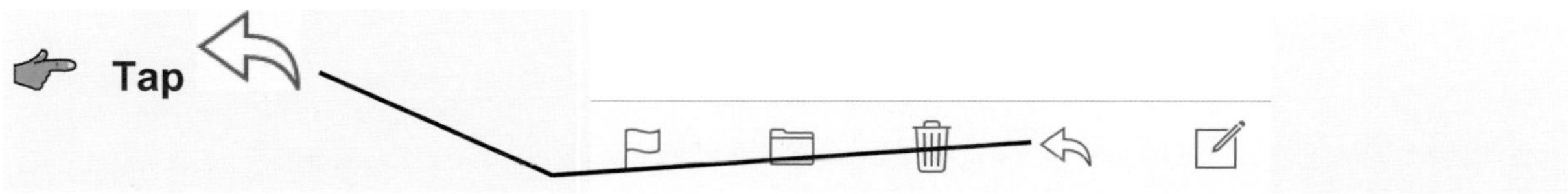

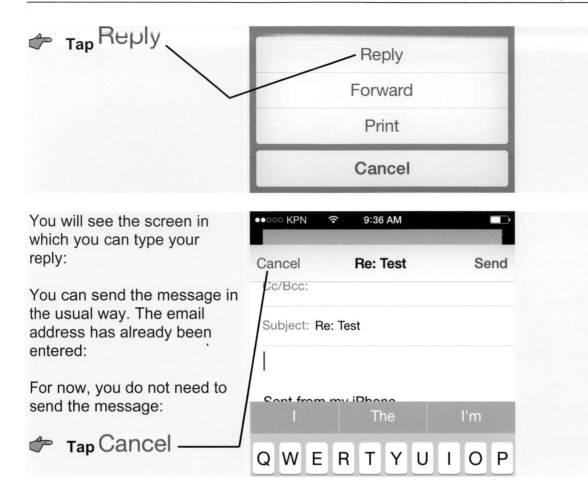

Tap Reply

You will see the screen in which you can type your reply:

You can send the message in the usual way. The email address has already been entered:

For now, you do not need to send the message:

Tap Cancel

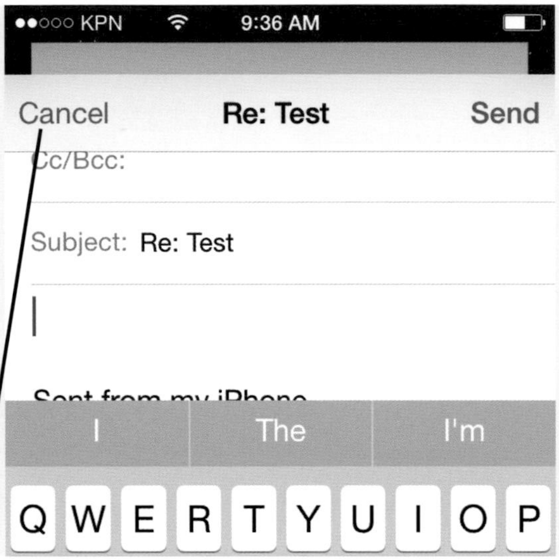

You will see the screen again with the message you have previously sent to yourself.

4.6 Deleting an Email

You are going to delete your test message:

At the bottom of the screen:

Tap

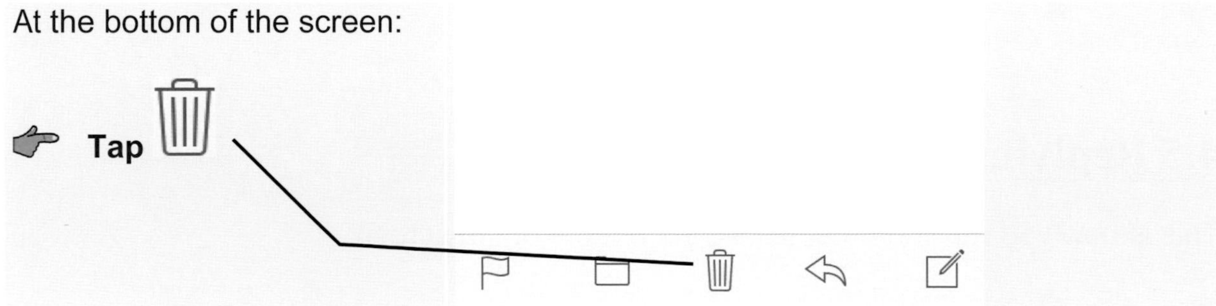

Now the email has been moved to the *Trash* folder. You can check to make sure:

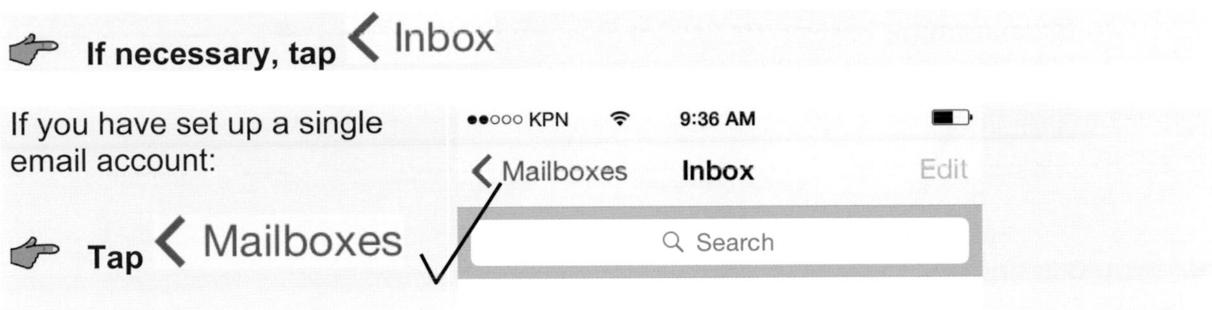

If necessary, tap Inbox

If you have set up a single email account:

Tap Mailboxes

If necessary, tap the description of your account once more

You will some folders:

If necessary, swipe upwards the screen

Tap Trash

Please note:

If you have set up multiple email accounts, you need to tap the name of your account first before you see the *Trash* folder.

The deleted message has been moved to the *Trash* folder:

Tap Edit

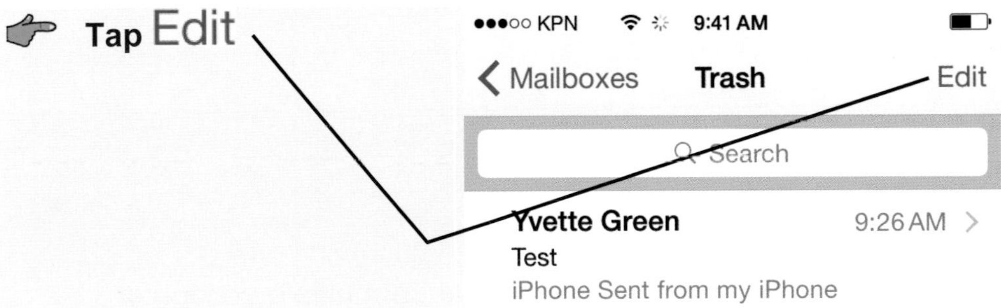

Here is how to permanently delete the message:

Tap the message

You will see a checkmark on the left side of this message.

Now you can decide whether to delete the message, move it to a different folder or mark it as read.

You are going to delete the message.

At the bottom of the screen:

Tap Delete

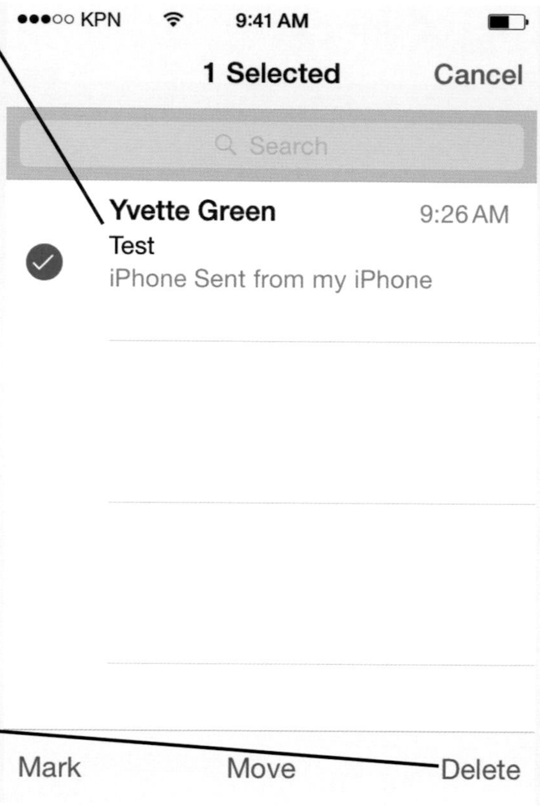

Tip

Delete all messages

If you want to delete all the messages, you do not need to tap the message. This is what you do instead:

Tap Edit

Tap Delete All

If you are sure:

Tap Delete All

This is how you return to the *Inbox* folder if you have set up multiple accounts:

If necessary, tap the description of your account

If you have set up a single account:

Tap ‹ Mailboxes

If necessary, swipe downwards the screen

Tap Inbox

As soon as you open the *Inbox*, the app will automatically check for new messages. At the bottom of the screen you will see the message Checking for Mail....

You can also manually check for new messages by swiping downwards over the screen.

Go to the home screen [10]

If you want, put your iPhone into sleep mode [2]

In this chapter you have learned how to set up your email account on your iPhone. You have practiced sending, receiving and deleting email messages. On the next page you will find some additional exercises.

4.7 Exercises

To be able to quickly apply the things you have learned, you can work through these exercises. Have you forgotten how to do something? Use the numbers next to the footsteps 1 to look up the item in the appendix *How Do I Do That Again?* This appendix can be found at the end of the book.

Exercise 1: Writing and Correcting an Email Message

In this exercise you are going to write a new email and then practice correcting, copying and pasting.

- If necessary, wake the iPhone up from sleep mode or turn it on. 1
- Open the *Mail* app. 3
- Open a new message. 32
- By To:, type your own email address. 33
- By Subject:, type this text: `Practice` 34
- Type this text in the message, including the typing mistake: 35
  `By practicing a lot I become very skillled`
- Do not accept the suggested correction for skilled. 36
- Delete the words `very skilled` with the backspace key. 29
- Type this text: 35
  `more skilful using the keyboard.`
- Go to a new line. 37
- Select the word ‘practicing’. 30
- Copy the word ‘practicing’. 38
- Paste the word ‘practicing’ on the second line. 39

Exercise 2: Sending and Receiving an Email Message

In this exercise you will practice sending and receiving the email message that was written in the previous exercise.

- Send the email. [40]
- View the incoming message. [41]

Exercise 3: Permanently Deleting an Email Message

You do not need to save the practice message. In this exercise you will delete the message completely.

- Delete the message. [42]
- View the contents of the *Trash* folder. [43]
- Permanently delete the message. [44]

Exercise 4: Checking for New Messages

In this exercise you will check to see if you have received any new email messages.

- Go back to the *Inbox*. [45]
- Manually check for new mail. [46]
- Go to the home screen. [10]
- If you want, put the iPhone into sleep mode. [2]

4.8 Background Information

Dictionary

Account A combination of a user name, a password and possibly other information that allows you access to closed or protected online computing services. A subscription with an Internet Service Provider (ISP) is also called an account.

Contacts A standard app on the iPhone that allows you to manage, view and edit your contacts.

Fetch The traditional way of receiving new email messages. First, you open your mail program and connect to the mail server. Then you can set up the mail program to automatically check for new messages with fixed intervals, once the mail program is opened.

Gmail A free email service provided by *Google*, the manufacturers of the well-known search engine.

Hotmail A free email service of *Microsoft*.

IMAP IMAP stands for *Internet Message Access Protocol*. This means you can manage your email messages on the mail server. Messages read by you will be stored on the mail server until you delete them. IMAP is useful if you want to manage your emails from different devices. Your mailbox will look the same on each computer, tablet or phone. When you create folders to organize your email messages, these same folders will also be visible on the other computers, tablets and on your iPhone. If you want to use IMAP, you will need to set up your email account as an IMAP account on each device you use.

Inbox A folder in *Mail* where you can view all the email messages you have received.

Mail A standard app on the iPhone with which you can send and receive email messages.

- Continue on the next page -

Outlook.com	A free email service of *Microsoft*.
POP	POP stand for *Post Office Protocol*. This is the traditional way of managing email messages. After you have received your messages, they will immediately be deleted from the mail server. But on your iPhone, the default setting for POP accounts is for leaving a copy of your messages stored on the server even after you have received them.
Push	When push is on, data is automatically sent (pushed) to your iPhone from the application server even when the specific app is not open.
Signature	A standard closing signature that is automatically appended to all your outgoing email messages.
Synchronize	Literally this means: make even. You can synchronize your iPhone with the contents of your *iTunes Library* and also the data from your email accounts.
Trash	A folder in *Mail* in which the deleted messages are stored. A message is permanently deleted when you delete it from the *Trash* mailbox.
VIP	With this feature you can automatically route mail from people you designate as 'VIPs' into the special folder *VIP* in the *Mail* app.

Source: User Guide iPhone, Wikipedia.

4.9 Tips

Tip

Email from Apple

While creating your *Apple ID*, you have received one or more email messages from Apple. In these messages you are asked to verify the email address. Here is how you do that:

Open the *Mail* app 3

Open the most recent message from Apple 41

Tap the verify link

A web page will be opened. You will need to sign in with your *Apple ID* and password in order to verify your email address:

Sign in with your *Apple ID* and password and verify the address

You will see a confirmation message:

Go to the home screen 10

Tip

Signature

By default, each email you send will end with the text *Sent from my iPhone*. This text is called your *signature*. You can replace this text by a standard ending for your messages or by your name and address. This is how to change your email signature:

Open the *Settings* app 3

Tap 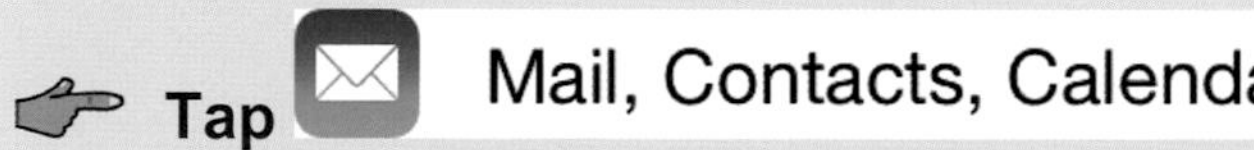

Swipe upwards over the screen

Tap Signature

- Continue on the next page -

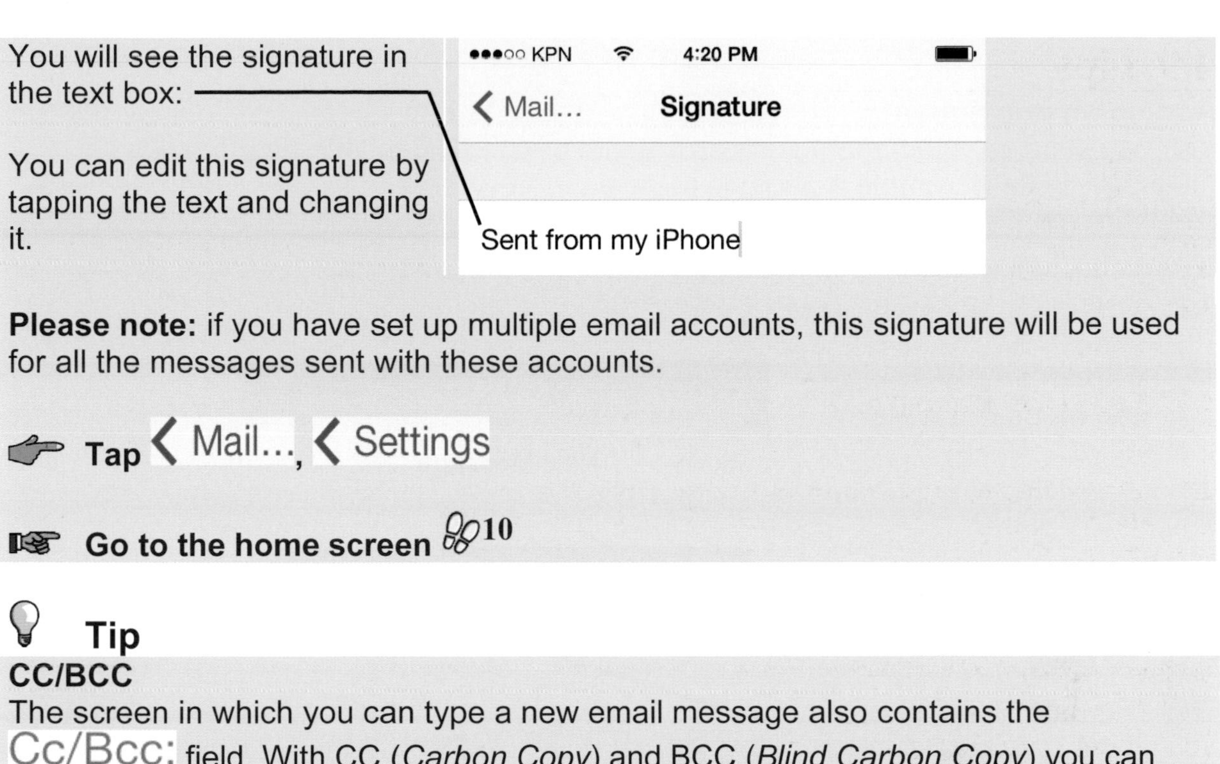

You will see the signature in the text box:

You can edit this signature by tapping the text and changing it.

Please note: if you have set up multiple email accounts, this signature will be used for all the messages sent with these accounts.

Tap Mail..., Settings

Go to the home screen 10

Tip

CC/BCC

The screen in which you can type a new email message also contains the Cc/Bcc: field. With CC (*Carbon Copy*) and BCC (*Blind Carbon Copy*) you can send others a copy of your message. The recipients in the BCC field will not be visible to the other recipients of this message. But if you use the CC field, every recipient can view the other recipients.

Tap Cc/Bcc:

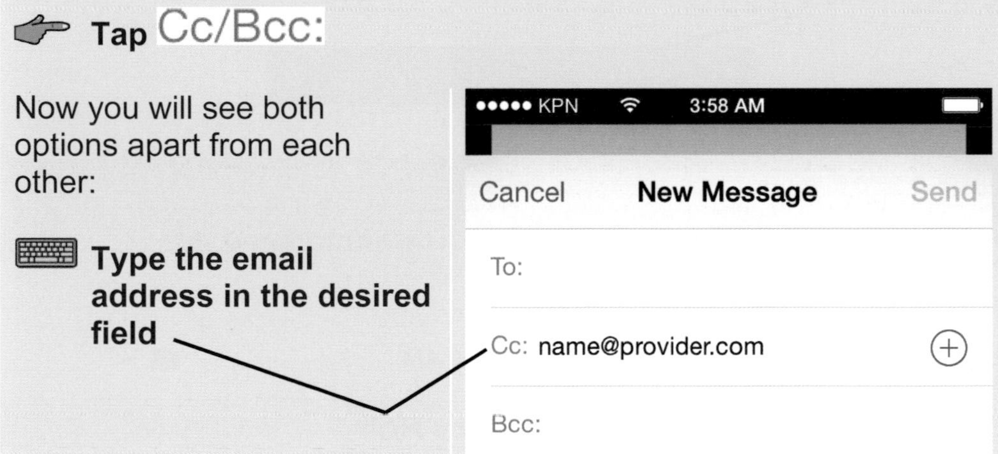

Now you will see both options apart from each other:

Type the email address in the desired field

Tip

Adding an attachment

You can send an attachment such as a photo or short video with your email message. In this example a photo is being sent. In *Chapter 6 Photos and Video* you can learn more about working with photos and video.

Open a new email message 32

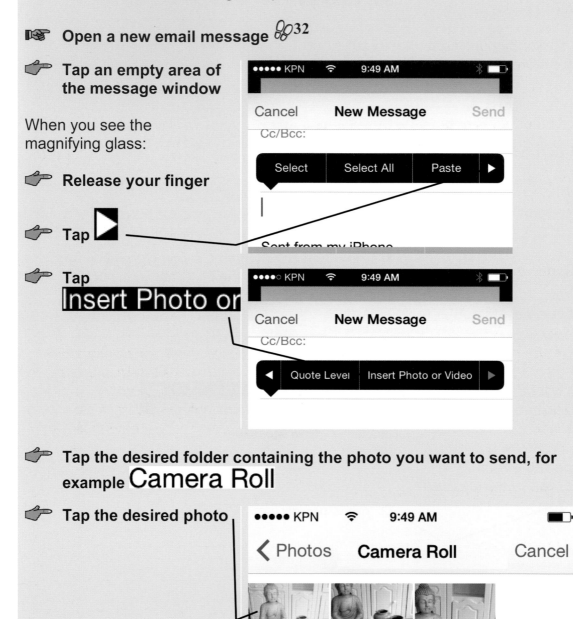

Tap an empty area of the message window

When you see the magnifying glass:

Release your finger

Tap ▶

Tap Insert Photo or

Tap the desired folder containing the photo you want to send, for example Camera Roll

Tap the desired photo

- Continue on the next page -

 **Tap** Choose

The photo will be added to the email message.

You can also send a photo using the *Photos* app. See *section 8.10 Sending a Photo by Email* for more information.

If you have other types of documents such as a text file or a PDF file stored on your iPhone, you can send these as attachments as well. You do this using a slightly different method. Instead of using the Mail app, you open the document with the app you normally use to view or edit the document. For PDFs this can be iBooks for example. Once the document is opened, tap and Mail.

 **Tip**

Opening attachment

Once you have used email on your iPhone for a little while, you will eventually receive a message with an attachment. This can be in the form of a photo, video or other type of document such as a text file. Most of these types of files can be opened directly on your iPhone. In this tip we will show you how to open a *Word* document that has been received as an attachment to an email. For other types of files, the procedure is pretty much the same.

Open the email with the attachment 41

The attachment icon is shown underneath the message.

 **Tap the icon**

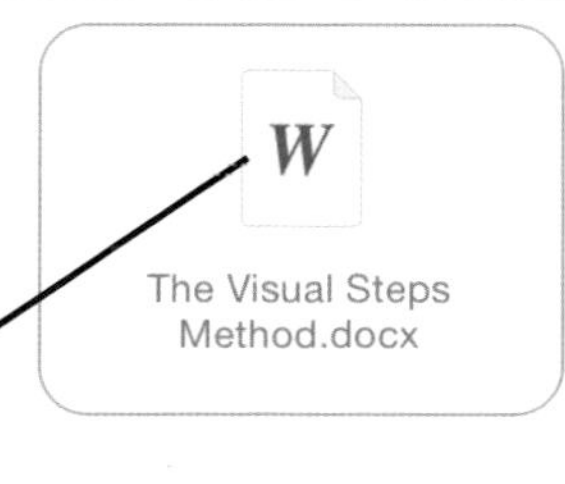

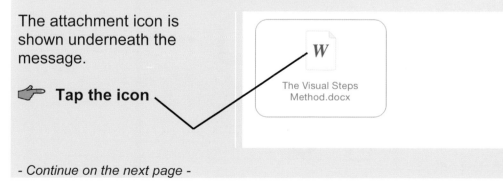

- Continue on the next page -

The *Word* document opens and you can start to read it.

When you have finished, you can close the document. You will return to the *Mail* app once more:

Tap the screen

Tap <

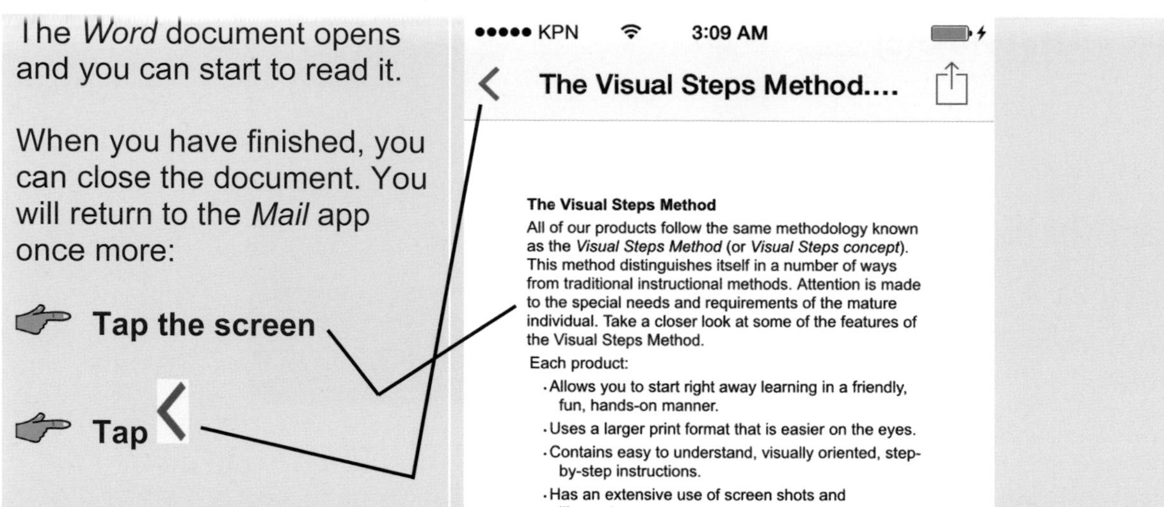

If desired, you can use this document with other apps or even print it. To do this, you tap [share icon] and select one of the options shown.

If you have received a document that you want to open in a specific app, such as *iBooks* for a PDF file, then you need to select the app from the list of available options shown.

Hold your finger on the icon for a moment until a small window appears

Tap the desired app, Open in iBooks **for example**

The document will be opened in the selected app.

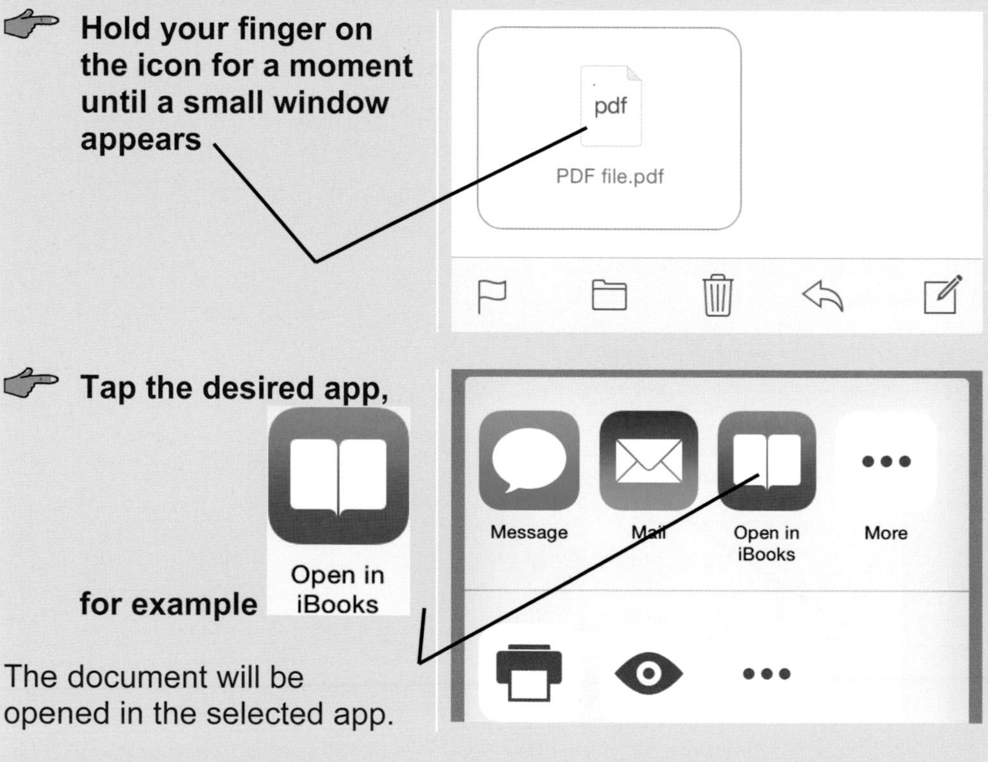

- *Continue on the next page* -

In the case of a photo, you also have the option of saving it to your iPhone:

- **Tap the photo and hold your finger on it until a small window appears**

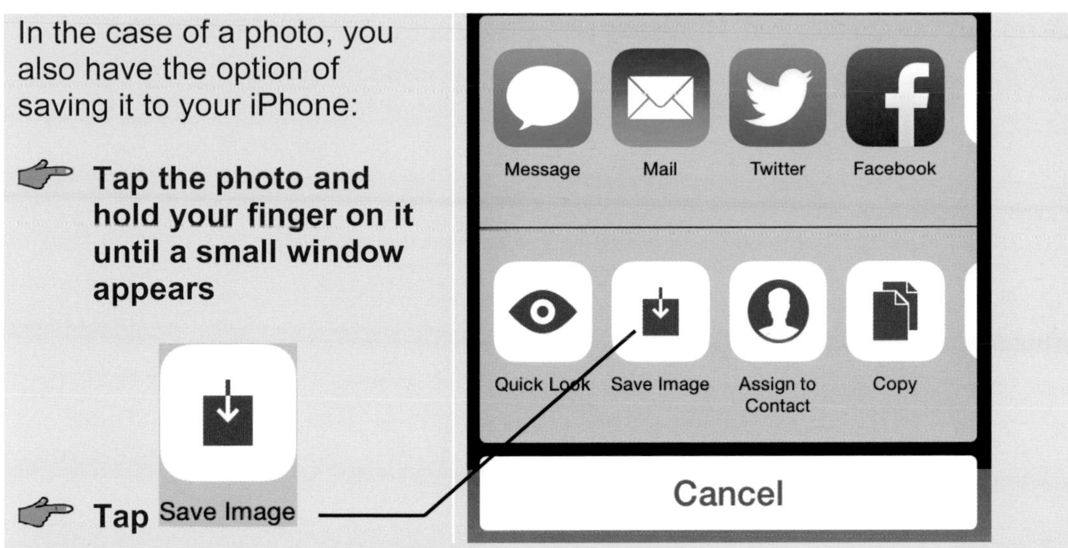

- **Tap** Save Image

The photo is saved on your iPhone. You can find the photo in the app *Photos* in the album *Camera Roll*.

Tip

Disable Auto-Correction function

The Auto-Correcting function on the iPhone may sometimes lead to unwanted corrections. The dictionary will not recognize all the words you type, but will suggest a correction nevertheless. This may lead to some strange corrections, which you might accept without knowing it, every time you type a period, a comma or a blank space. This is how you disable the Auto-Correction function:

- **Open the *Settings* app** 3

- **Tap** General

- **Swipe upwards the screen**

- **Tap** Keyboard

- **By** Auto-Correction, **drag the slider to the left**

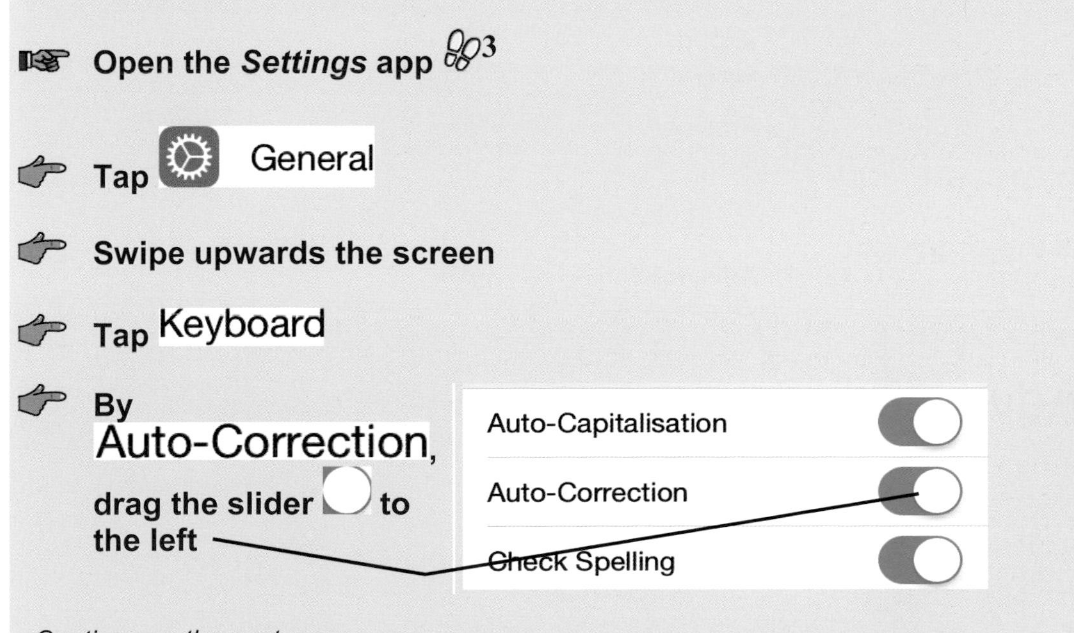

- Continue on the next page -

Now you will no longer see any suggestions for corrections. To save the changes:

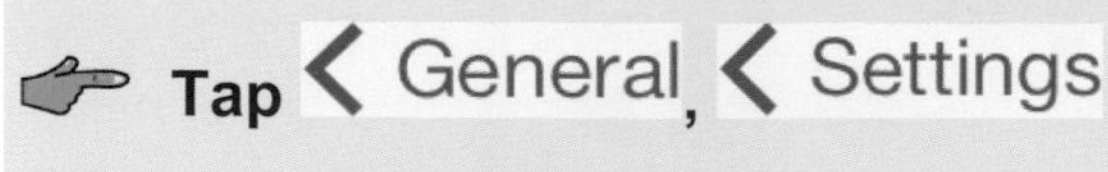

Tap < General, < Settings

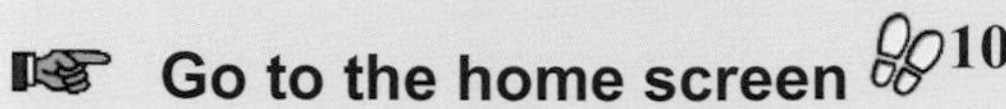

Go to the home screen 10

Tip

Should I save my emails on the server or not?
For POP email accounts you can modify the settings yourself and choose to save a copy of the received emails on the mail server. If a copy is stored, you will also be able to retrieve the email messages on your computer, even after you have retrieved them on your iPhone. Here is how to modify the settings to suit your own preferences:

Open the *Settings* app 3

Tap Mail, Contacts, Calendars

Tap your POP email account

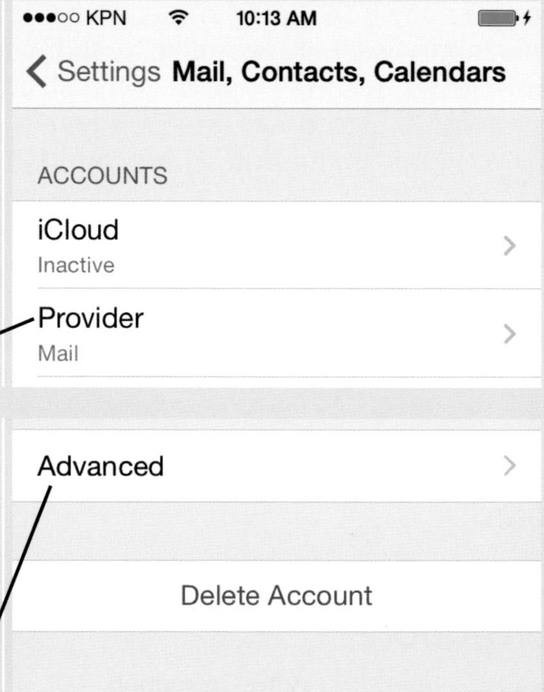

You will see the page with your account information. At the bottom of the screen:

Tap Advanced

- Continue on the next page -

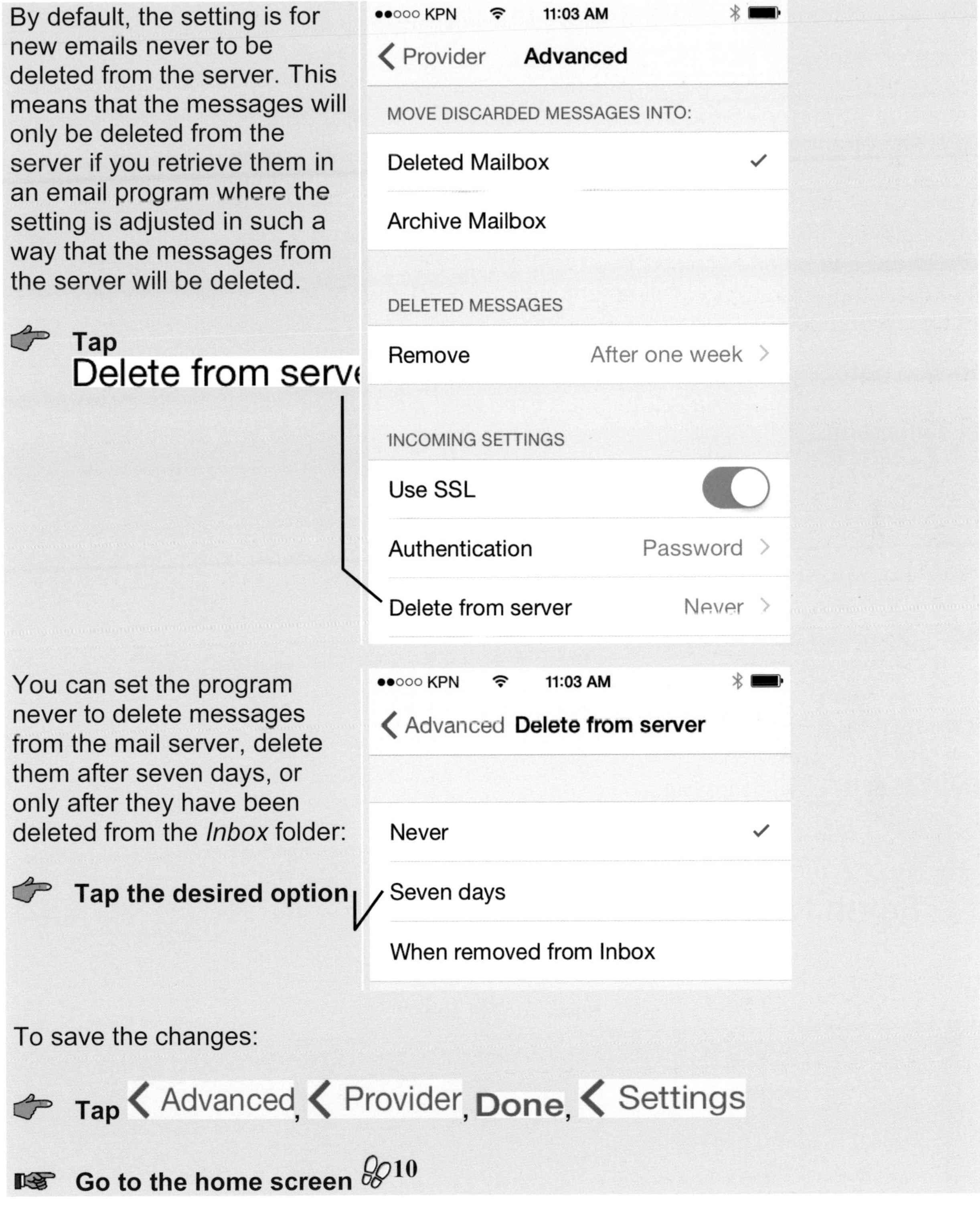

By default, the setting is for new emails never to be deleted from the server. This means that the messages will only be deleted from the server if you retrieve them in an email program where the setting is adjusted in such a way that the messages from the server will be deleted.

- **Tap** Delete from server

You can set the program never to delete messages from the mail server, delete them after seven days, or only after they have been deleted from the *Inbox* folder:

- **Tap the desired option**

To save the changes:

- **Tap** Advanced, Provider, **Done**, Settings

- **Go to the home screen** 10

 **Tip**

Push or fetch

If you always manage your emails on your computer, you will be accustomed to receiving your email through *fetch*. You open your email program, connect to the mail server and the new messages arrive very quickly. You can set the program to check for new messages at regular intervals, at least when the program is opened. With *push*, new messages will be sent to your email program by the mail server, immediately after their arrival, even if your email program is closed or if your iPhone is locked. The email accounts you have set up with the *Microsoft Exchange* and *Yahoo!* templates support the push functions. For other types of email accounts, fetch will be used.

Please note: if you connect to the Internet over 3G or 4G and you do not have an account with unlimited data traffic at a fixed rate, it is recommended to disable the push functions. This is because you pay for the amount of data you download. If long emails with large attachments are pushed to your iPhone, the costs can be quite high. In this case, it is better to manually receive your messages after you have made a connection using Wi-Fi.

This is how to view the settings for push or fetch:

Open the *Settings* app 3

Tap Mail, Contacts, Calendars

By default, Push is set up for all email accounts:

Tap Fetch New Data

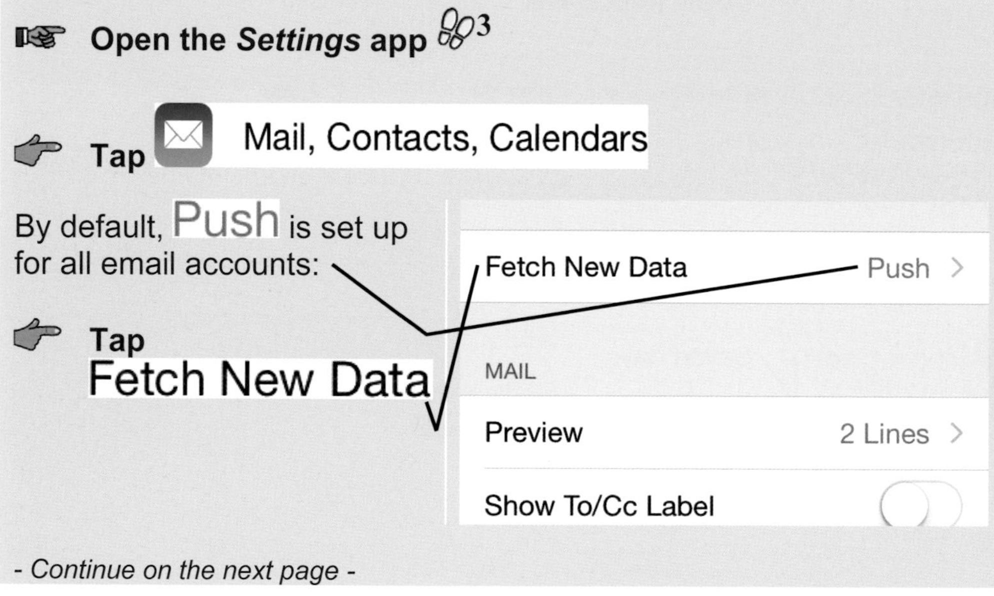

- Continue on the next page -

If you want to disable push:

Drag the slider to the left

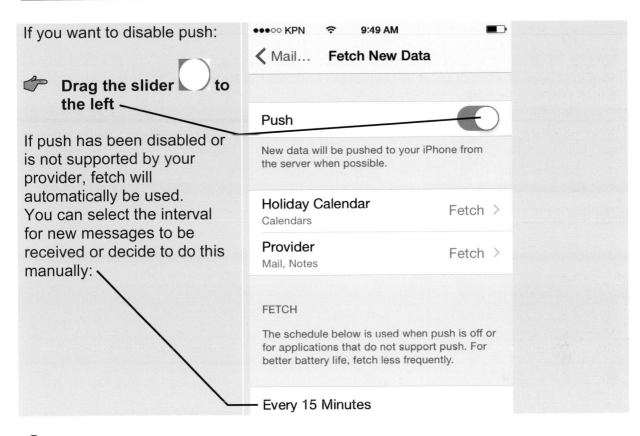

If push has been disabled or is not supported by your provider, fetch will automatically be used. You can select the interval for new messages to be received or decide to do this manually:

●●●○○ KPN 9:49 AM

Mail... **Fetch New Data**

Push

New data will be pushed to your iPhone from the server when possible.

Holiday Calendar
Calendars
Fetch

Provider
Mail, Notes
Fetch

FETCH

The schedule below is used when push is off or for applications that do not support push. For better battery life, fetch less frequently.

Every 15 Minutes

Tip

Multiple email accounts

If you have set up multiple email accounts on your iPhone, your *Inbox* will look different.

If you tap All Inboxes, you will see all the incoming messages of the accounts:

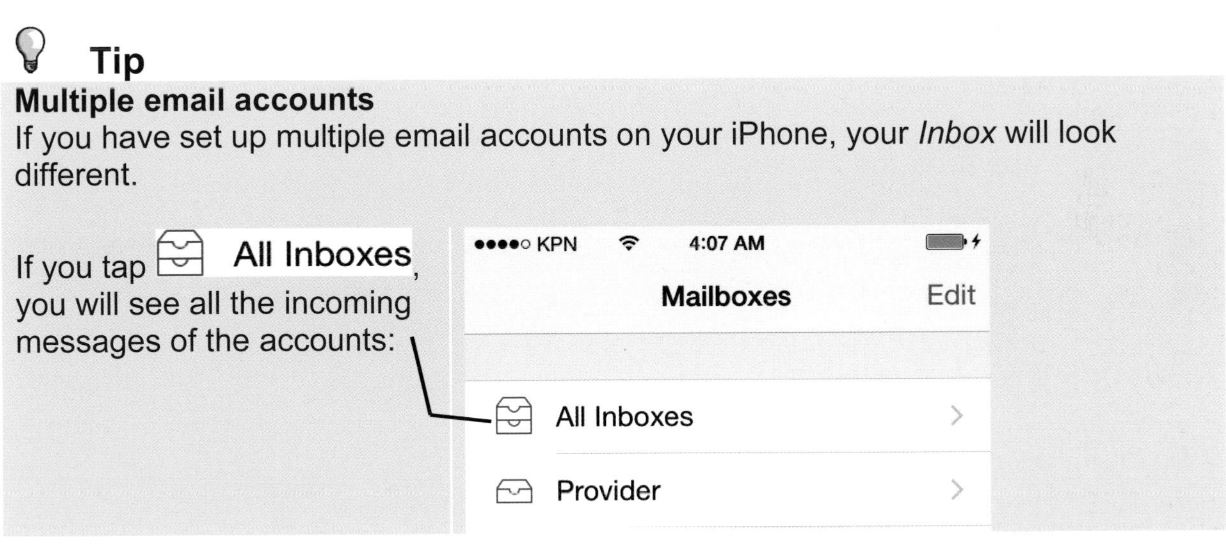

Tip

Moving email messages to folders

You can also move your emails to different folders. If you have not yet created any folders you can do this in the *Mailboxes* window:

Please note: creating new folders is only possible in an *IMAP* account. In an *POP* account this is not possible.

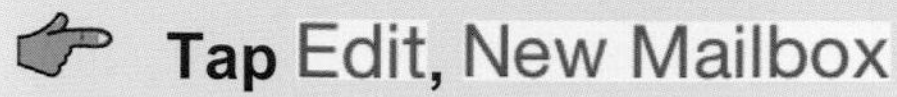

Tap Edit, New Mailbox

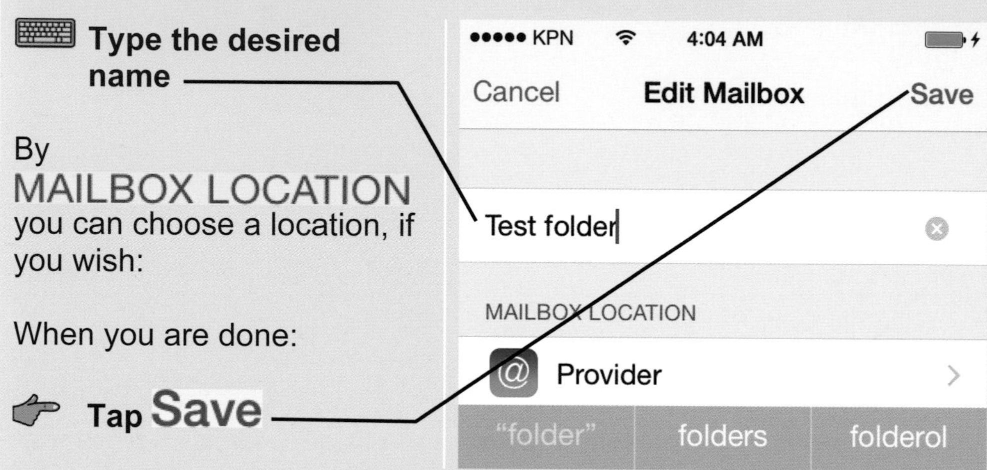

Type the desired name

By MAILBOX LOCATION you can choose a location, if you wish:

When you are done:

Tap Save

In the next screen:

Swipe upwards the screen

You will see the new folder:

Tap Done

This is how you move an email:

Open an email message 41

At the bottom of the screen:

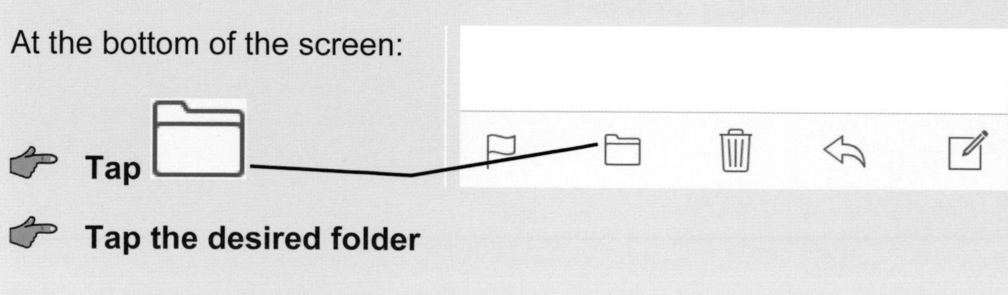

Tap

Tap the desired folder

The email will be moved.

 **Tip**

VIP

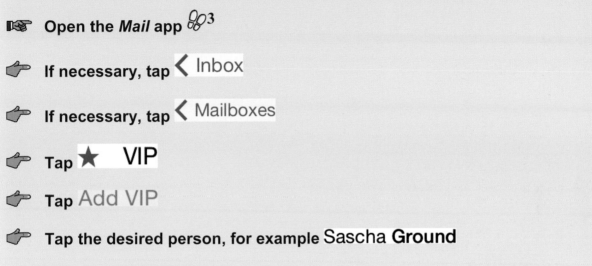

With the new feature VIP you can automatically route mail from people you designate as 'VIPs' into the special folder *VIP* in the *Mail* app. Even if you have more than one email account set up for your iPhone, all mail from your VIPs will automatically appear in the *VIP* folder. Here is how you add someone to the VIP list:

Open the *Mail* app 3

If necessary, tap < Inbox

If necessary, tap < Mailboxes

Tap ★ VIP

Tap Add VIP

Tap the desired person, for example Sascha **Ground**

In *Chapter 2 Making and Receiving Calls* you learned how to add new people to the list in the *Contacts* app.

Notes

Write your notes down here.

5. Surfing with Your iPhone

In this chapter you will get to know *Safari*, the web browser made by Apple. You can surf the Internet on your iPhone using *Safari*. If you also use the Internet on your computer, you will see that you can just as easily surf on your iPhone. The big difference is that you do not use a mouse on the iPhone. You surf by touching your iPhone's screen.

You will learn how to open a web page and get acquainted with a couple of new touch operations to zoom in, zoom out and scroll. We will also discuss how to open a link (also called a hyperlink) and how to use stored web pages, called bookmarks.

In *Safari* you can open multiple pages at once. In this chapter you will learn how to quickly switch between these open pages.

While you are surfing you may also want to modify a certain setting or do something else entirely. This does not pose any problems because your iPhone can perform multiple tasks simultaneously. You can easily switch from one app to another.

In this chapter you will learn how to:

- open a web page;
- zoom in and zoom out;
- scroll;
- open a link on a web page;
- open a link in a new tab;
- switch between opened web pages;
- add bookmarks;
- search;
- switch between recently used apps;
- change the search engine.

5.1 Opening a Web Page

This is how you open *Safari*, the app that is used to surf the Internet:

If necessary, wake the iPhone up from sleep mode [1]

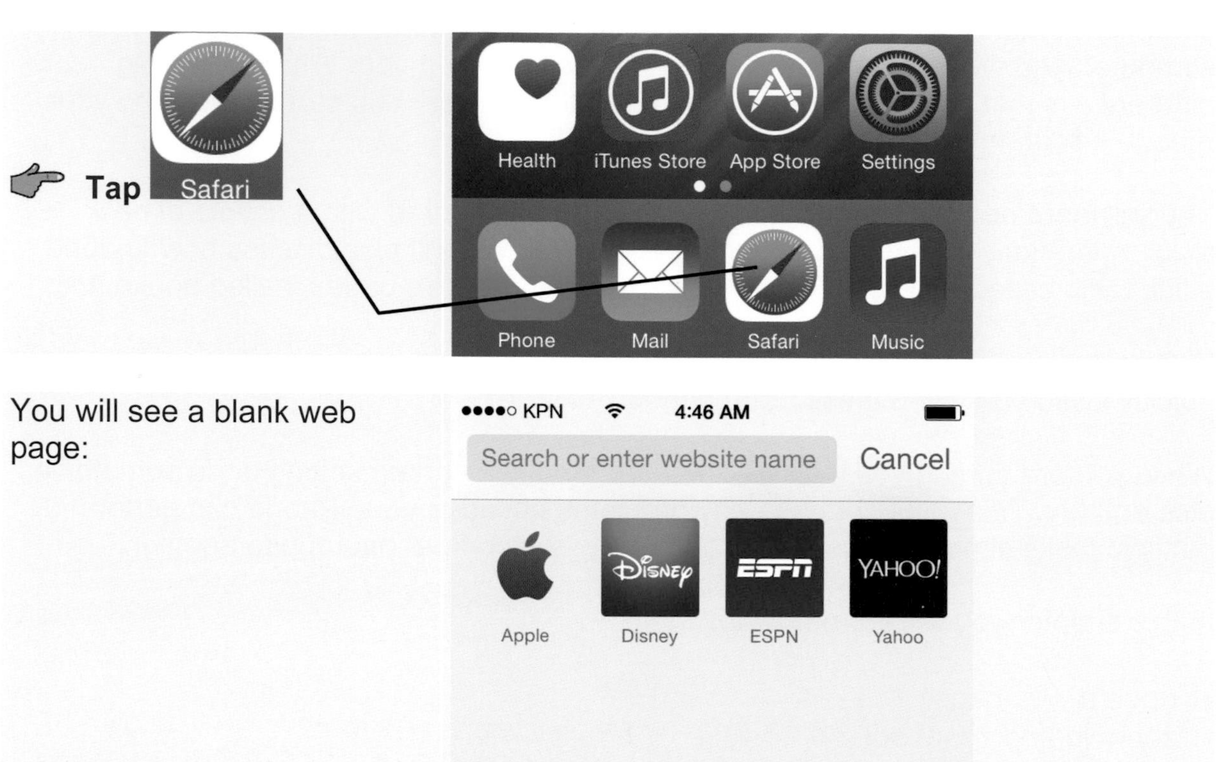

Tap Safari

You will see a blank web page:

This is how to display the onscreen keyboard so that you can type the web address:

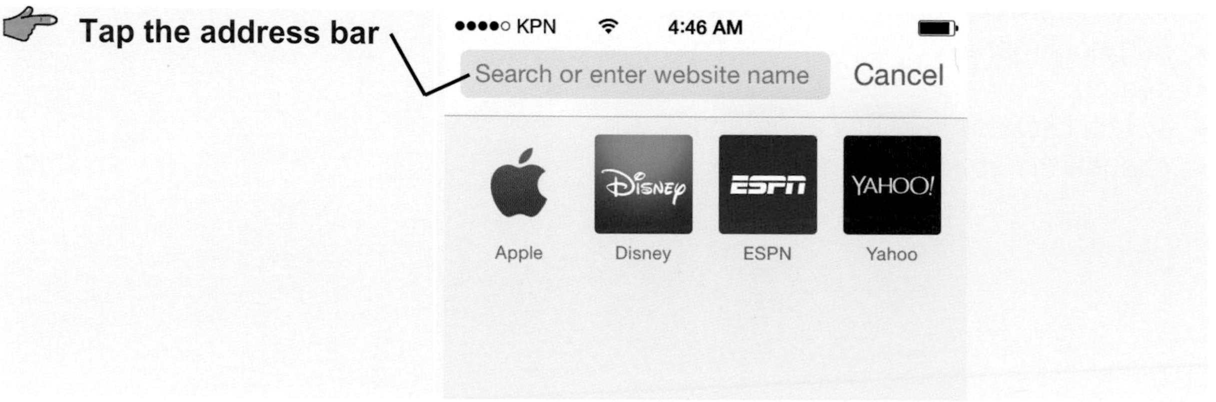

Tap the address bar

To practice, you can take a look at the Visual Steps website:

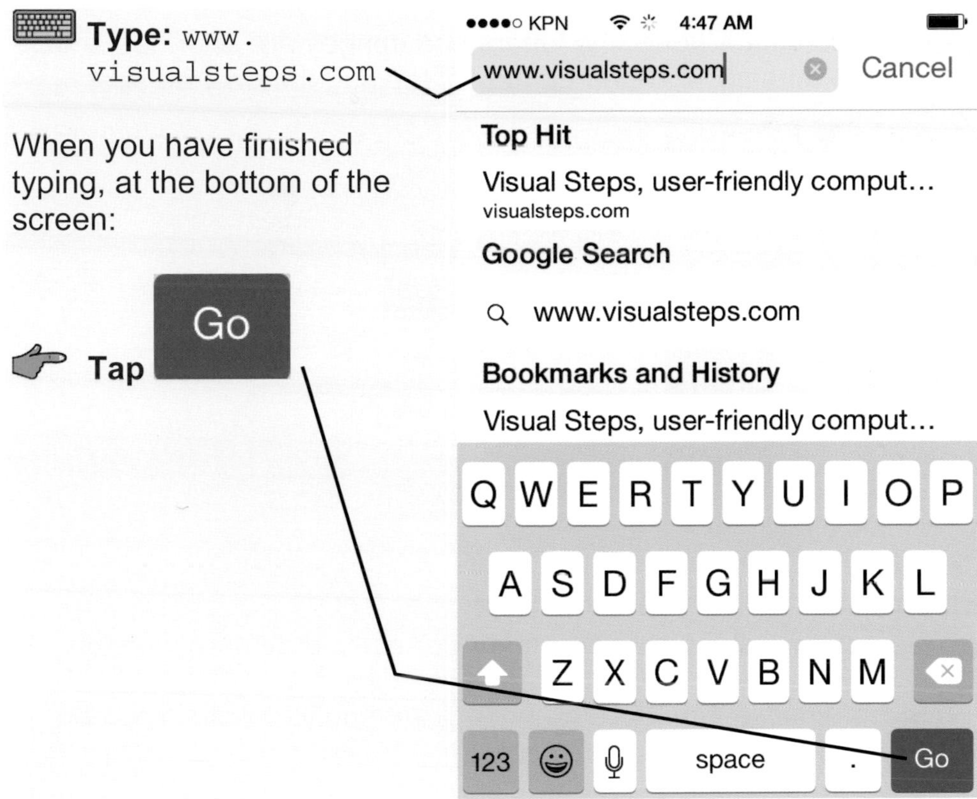

Type: www.visualsteps.com

When you have finished typing, at the bottom of the screen:

Tap Go

HELP! A web address has already been entered.

If you see a web address in the address bar, you can delete it like this:

Tap

You will see the Visual Steps website:

5.2 Zooming In and Zooming Out

When you view a website on your iPhone, the letters and images are often too small. You can zoom in by double-tapping. You can do this by tapping the desired spot twice, in rapid succession:

Double-tap on the menu on the left side of the page

HELP! A different web page is opened.

If the action of double-tapping has not been executed correctly, a different window may be opened. If that is the case, tap < at the bottom left and try again. You can also practice double-tapping a blank area of the screen.

Now you will see that the web page has been enlarged:

Double-tap the menu once more

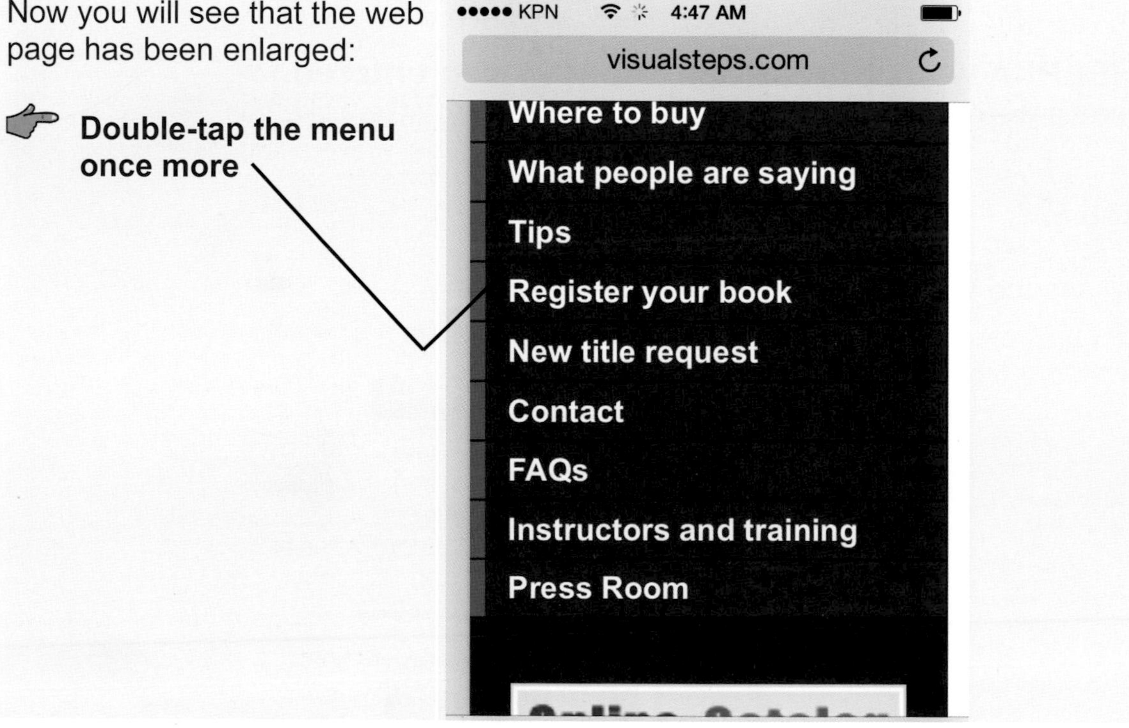

Now you can zoom out again to the regular view. But there is another method for zooming in and out. With this method, you need to use two fingers:

Move your thumb and index finger away from each other on the screen

This is called the pinch movement.

You will see that the web page becomes larger again. You can zoom out by reversing the pinch movement:

Move your thumb and index finger towards each other on the screen

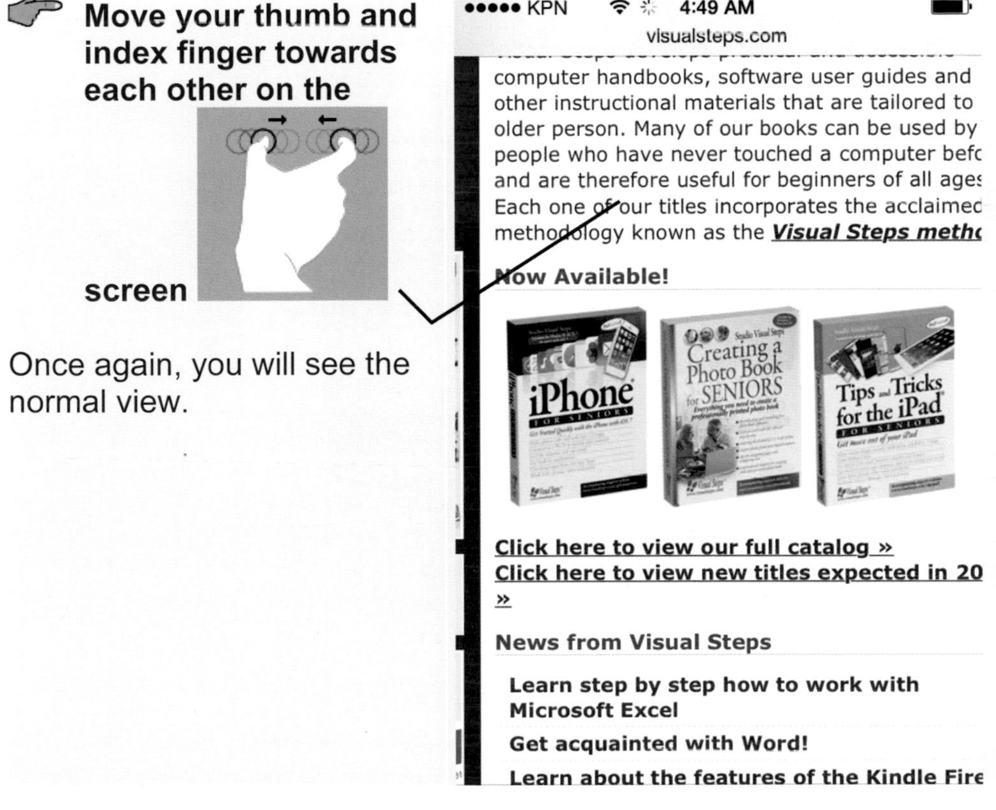

Once again, you will see the normal view.

You can return to the view you had after zooming in for the first time:

Double-tap the text in the upper part of the web page

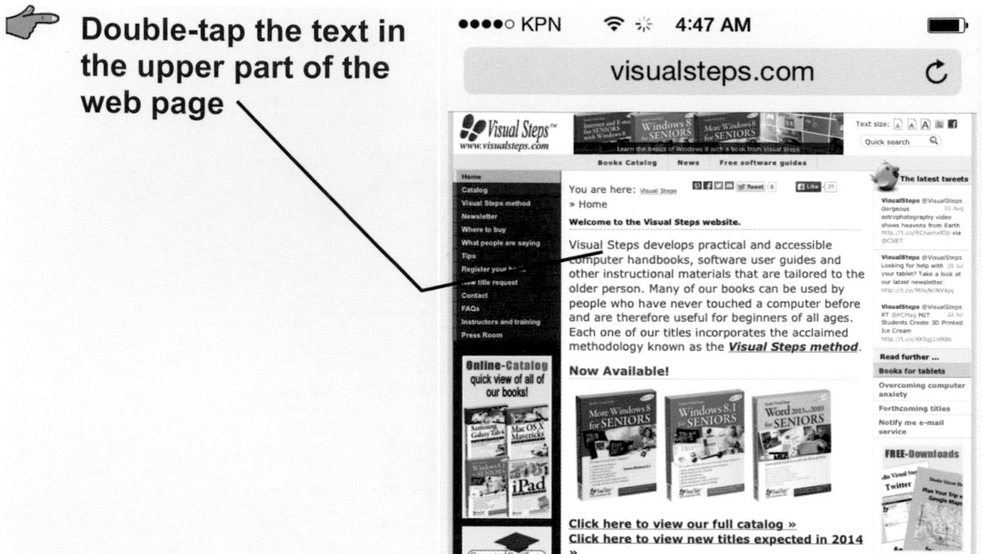

Now you will see the view after zooming in once:

5.3 Scrolling

Scrolling enables you to view different parts of the web page. On your iPhone you use your fingers to scroll:

Drag your finger upwards a bit over the screen

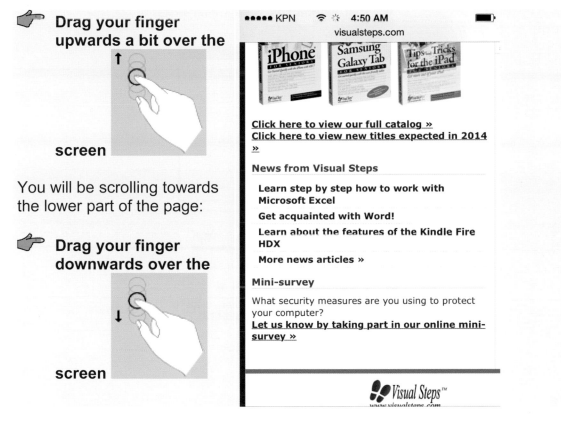

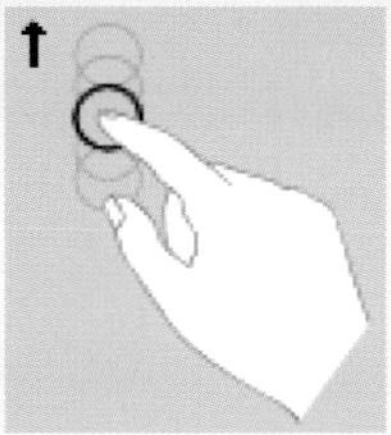

You will be scrolling towards the lower part of the page:

Drag your finger downwards over the screen

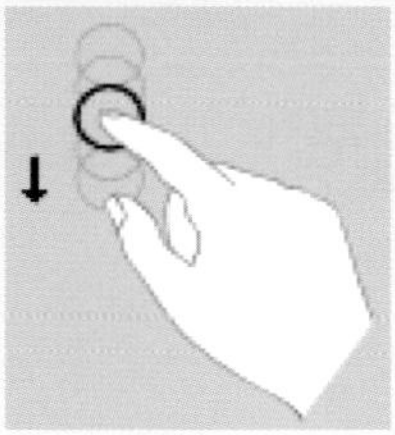

Now you will be scrolling towards the upper part of the page.

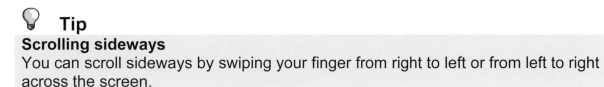

Tip

Scrolling sideways

You can scroll sideways by swiping your finger from right to left or from left to right across the screen.

If you want to scroll quickly through a lengthy page, you can make a swiping movement:

Move your finger upwards in a swiping gesture, over the screen

You will be quickly scrolling towards the bottom of the page:

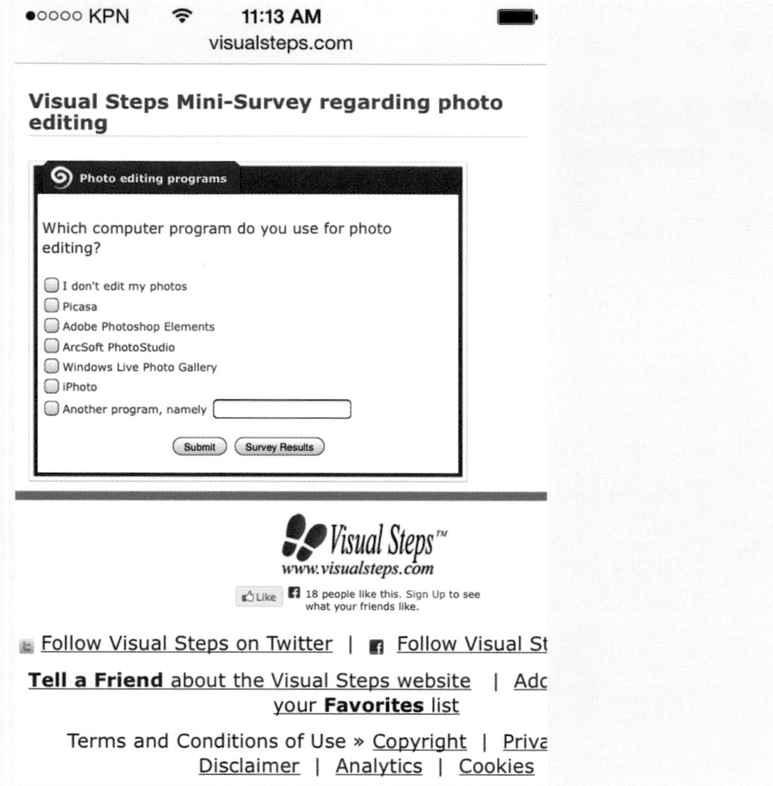

Tip

Moving in other directions
You can also scroll quickly in other directions by swiping upwards, to the left or to the right.

This is how you go to the top of the page at once:

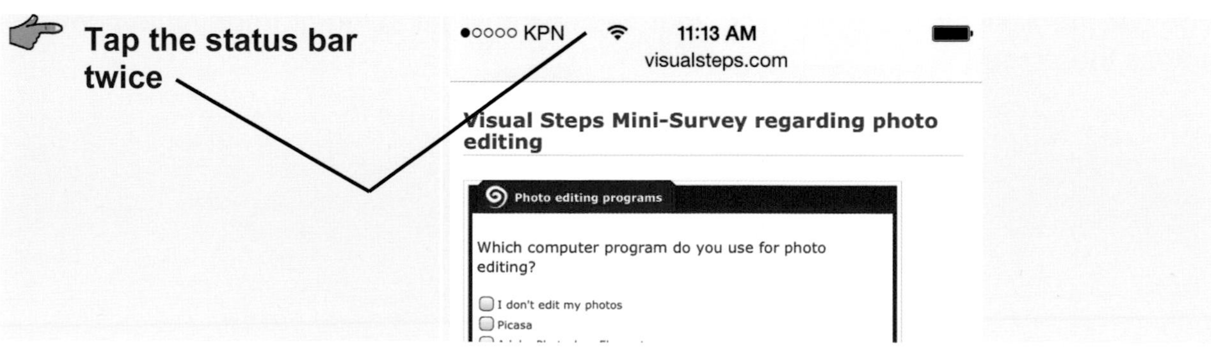

5.4 Opening a Link on a Web Page

If a page contains a link, you can open it by tapping the link. Just try this with the menu:

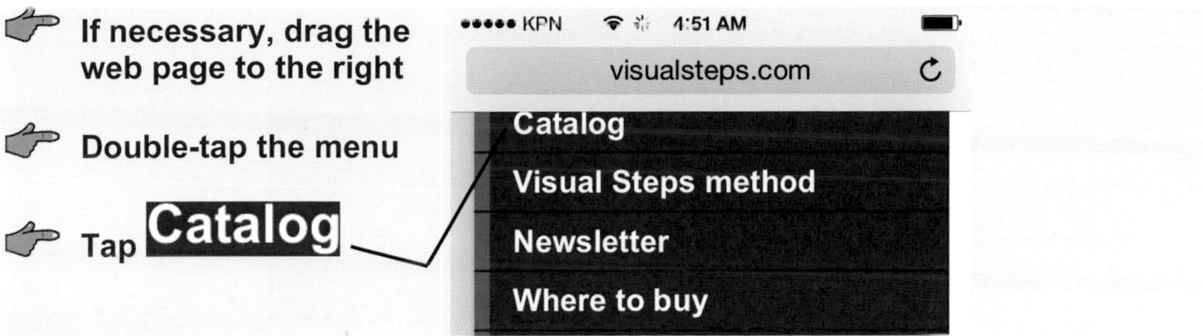

If necessary, drag the web page to the right

Double-tap the menu

Tap Catalog

 **HELP! I have not succeeded in tapping the link.**

If you find it hard to tap the right link, you can zoom in a bit further or turn the iPhone to the horizontal view. The links become larger and tapping them becomes easier.

Now the catalog page will be opened. You can view the current list of the Visual Steps books:

You will see that the new page is displayed in the normal size (zoomed out):

5.5 Opening a Link in a New Tab

You can also open a link in a new tab:

Double-tap the menu

You will zoom in on the menu:

Put your finger on **Where to buy**

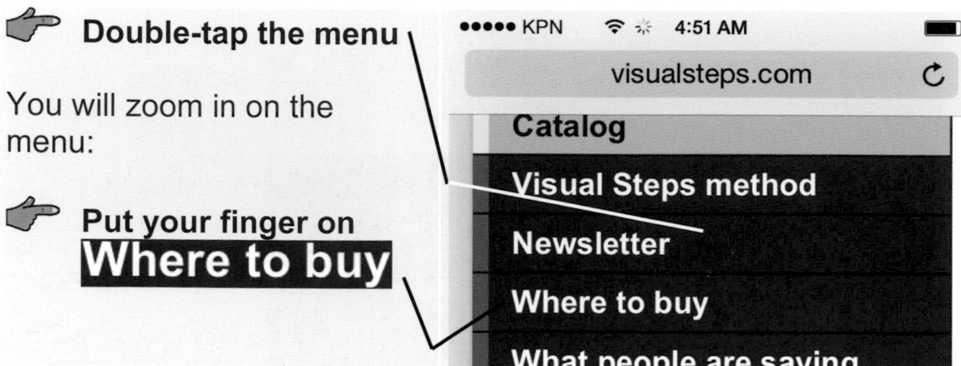

After a while a pop-up menu will appear:

Tap Open in New Tab

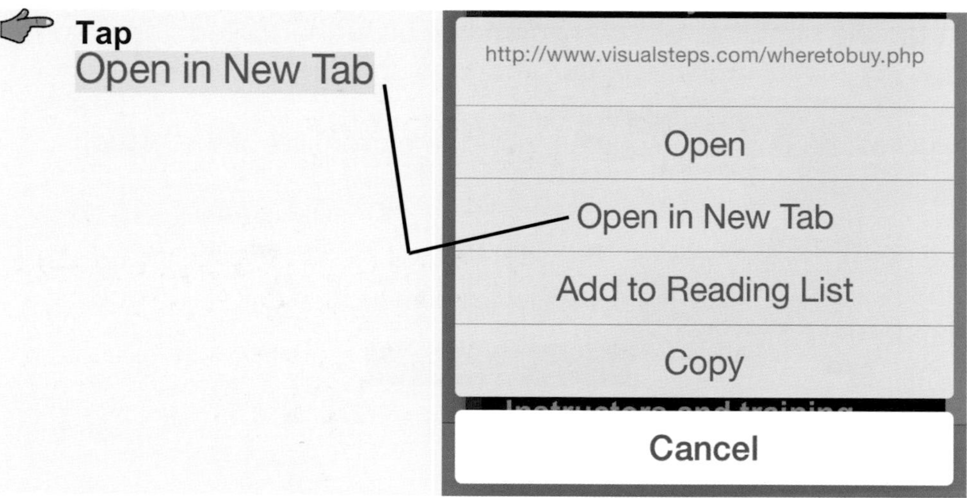

A second tab is opened:

Now you will see the page with information on where to buy the Visual Steps books:

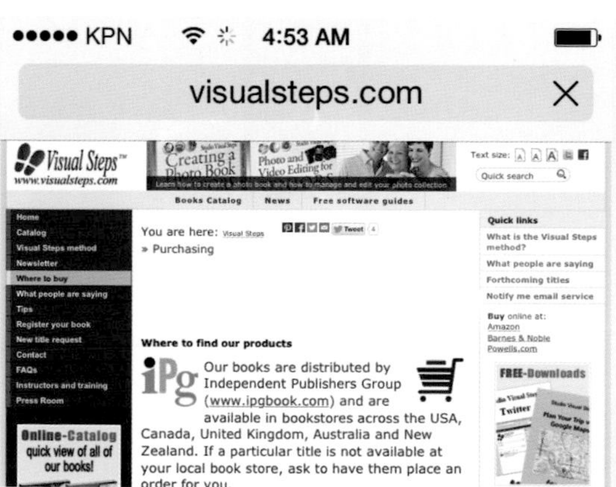

This is how you close an open tab:

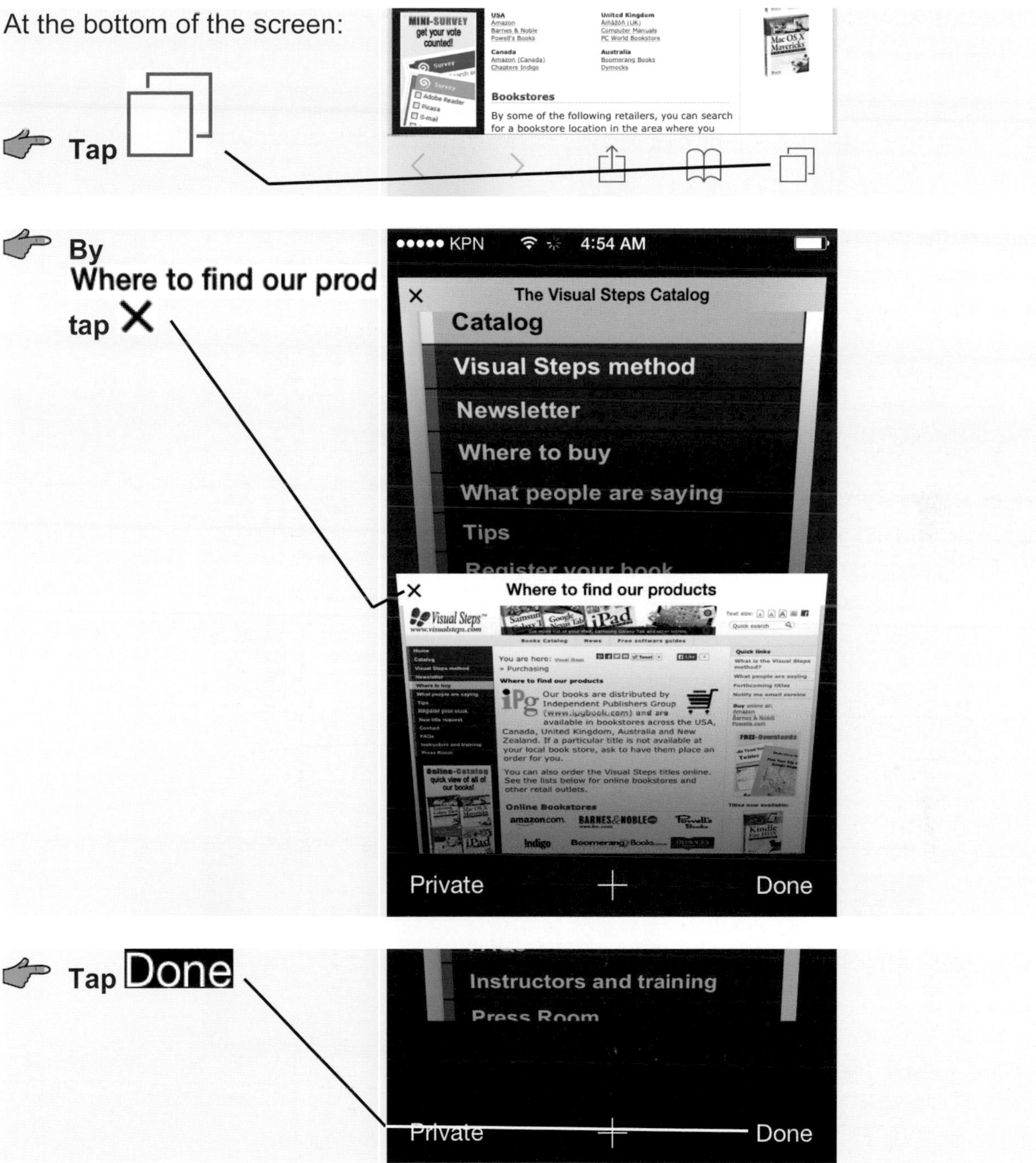

At the bottom of the screen:

Tap

By Where to find our prod tap ✕

Tap Done

You will see the menu again on the page with the Visual Steps catalog. To take a better look at the page:

Zoom out on the web page 54

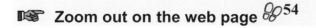

Tip

Type a new web address in the address bar

If you want to type a new address in the address bar, you can delete the address of the open web page first, like this:

 **Tap the address bar**

 **Tap**

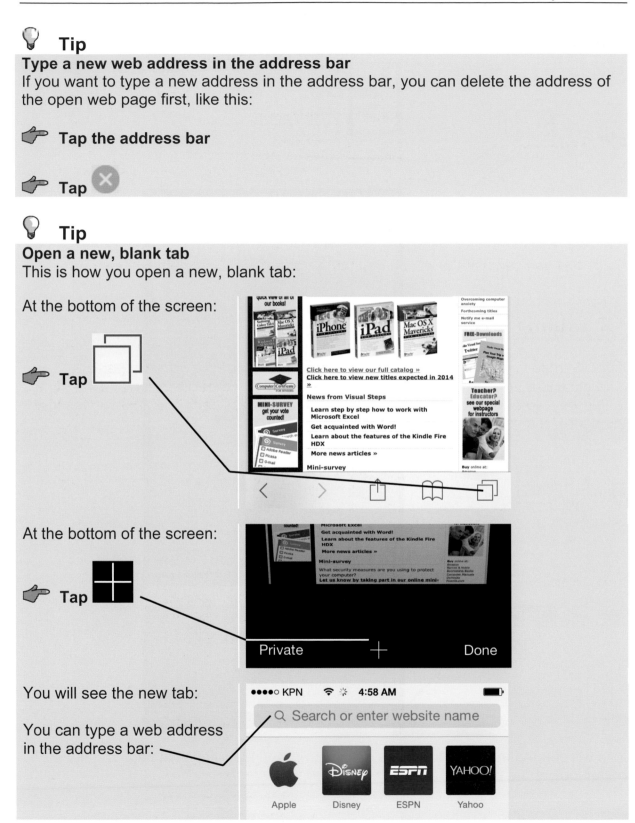

Tip

Open a new, blank tab

This is how you open a new, blank tab:

At the bottom of the screen:

Tap

At the bottom of the screen:

Tap

You will see the new tab:

You can type a web address in the address bar:

5.6 Go to Previous or Next Page

You can return to the web page you previously visited. Here is how to do that:

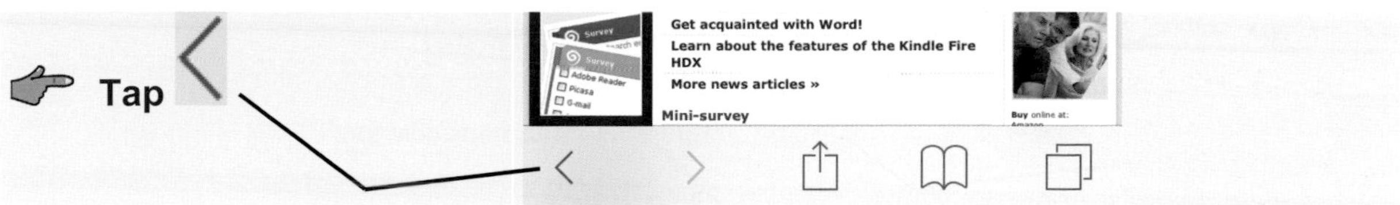

You will be back at the Visual Steps home page. You can also skip to the next page.

To do this you can use the > button, but for now this will not be necessary.

5.7 Adding a Bookmark

If you want to visit a page more often, you can add a bookmark for this page. A bookmark is a favorite website that you want to save, in order to visit it at a later time. In this way, you will not need to type the full web address each time you want to visit the page. Here is how to add a bookmark:

Tap

You will see a window:

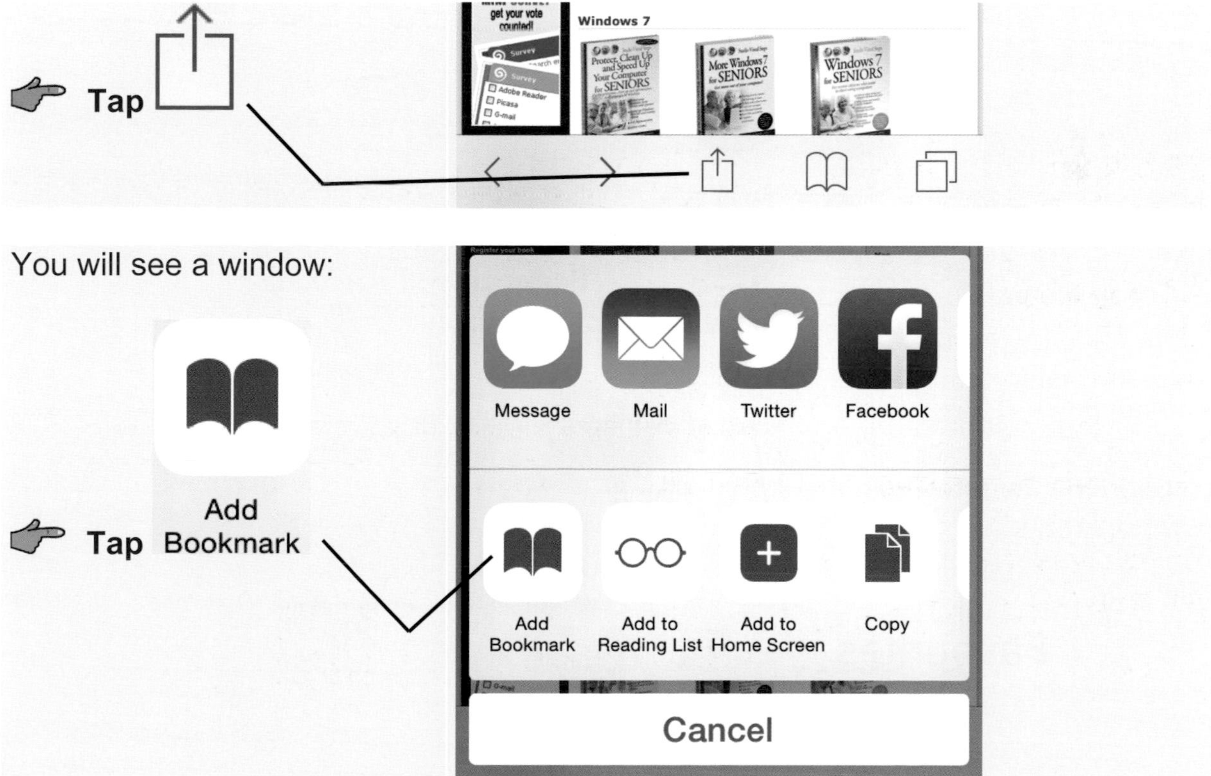

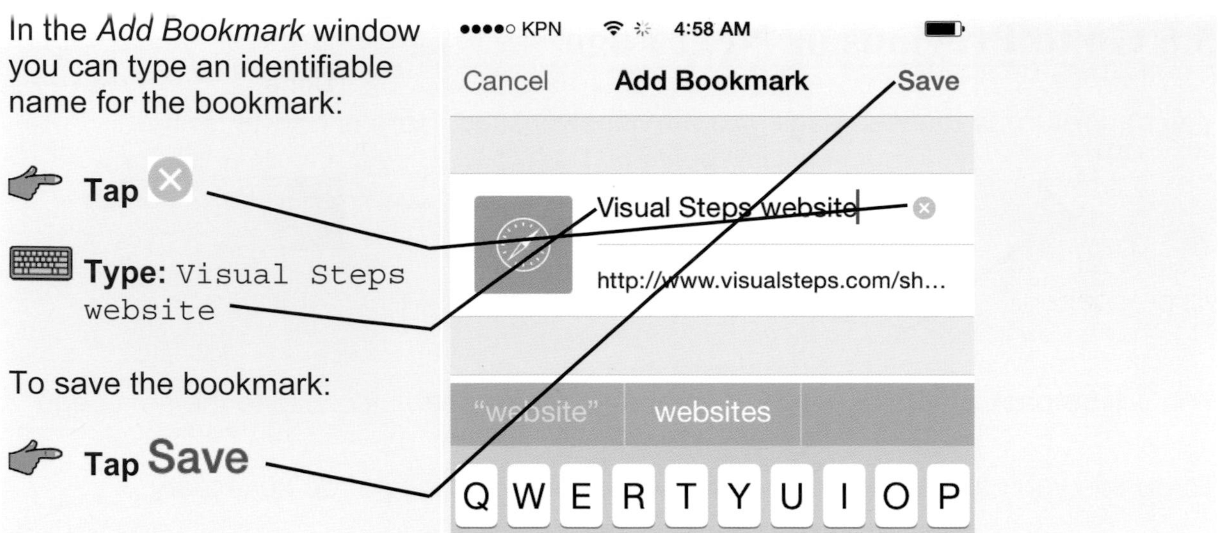

In the *Add Bookmark* window you can type an identifiable name for the bookmark:

Tap ⊗

Type: `Visual Steps website`

To save the bookmark:

Tap Save

The web page has been added to your bookmarks. You can verify this for yourself:

At the bottom of the screen:

Tap 📖

You will see the bookmarks list:

Apple adds by default a couple of handy bookmarks, such as a user guide:

To open the favorites with the new bookmark:

Tap ☆ Favourites

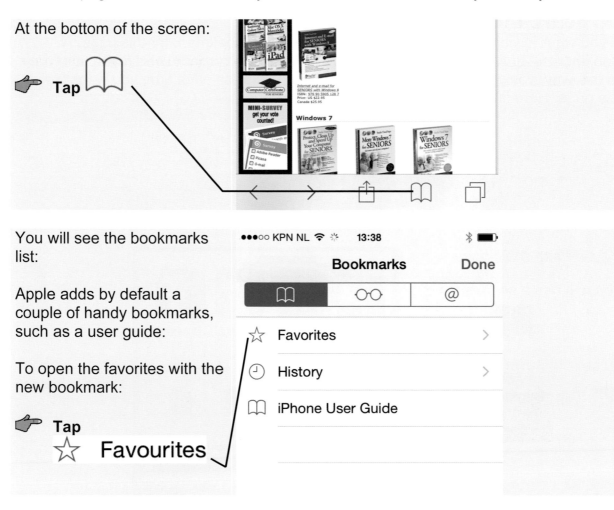

This is how you open the Visual Steps bookmark:

Tap
Visual Steps website

The Visual Steps web page will be opened.

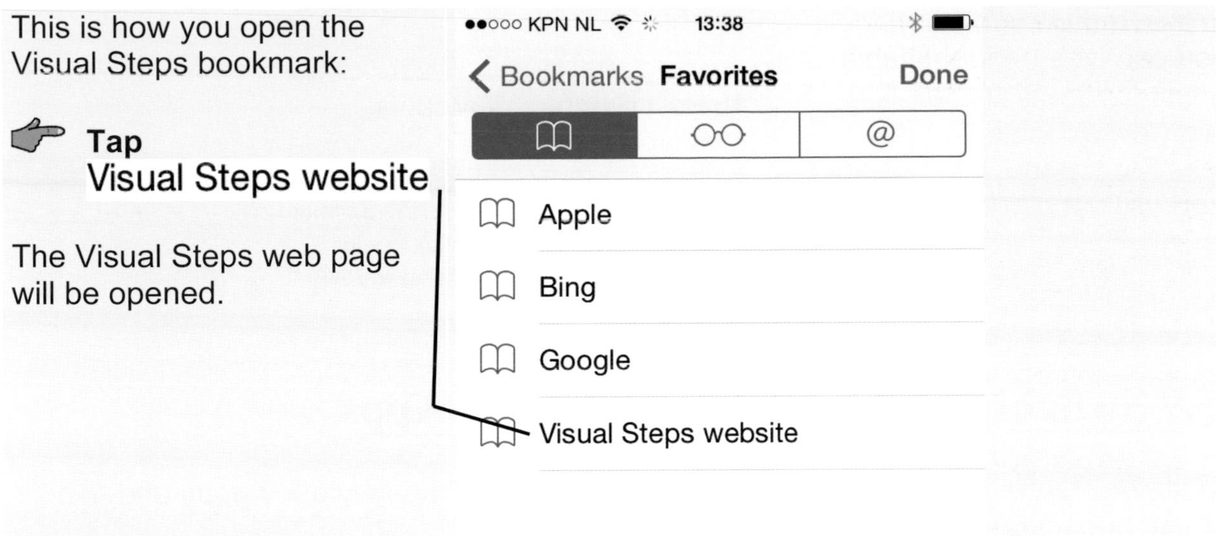

5.8 Searching

Google is the default search engine set up in *Safari*. To begin a search you can type the keywords in the address bar:

Tap the address bar

For example, type:
`iPhone holder`

Right away, you will see some suggestions for possible keywords:

You can use a suggestion by tapping it. For now, this will not be necessary.

To use your own keyword:

Tap Go

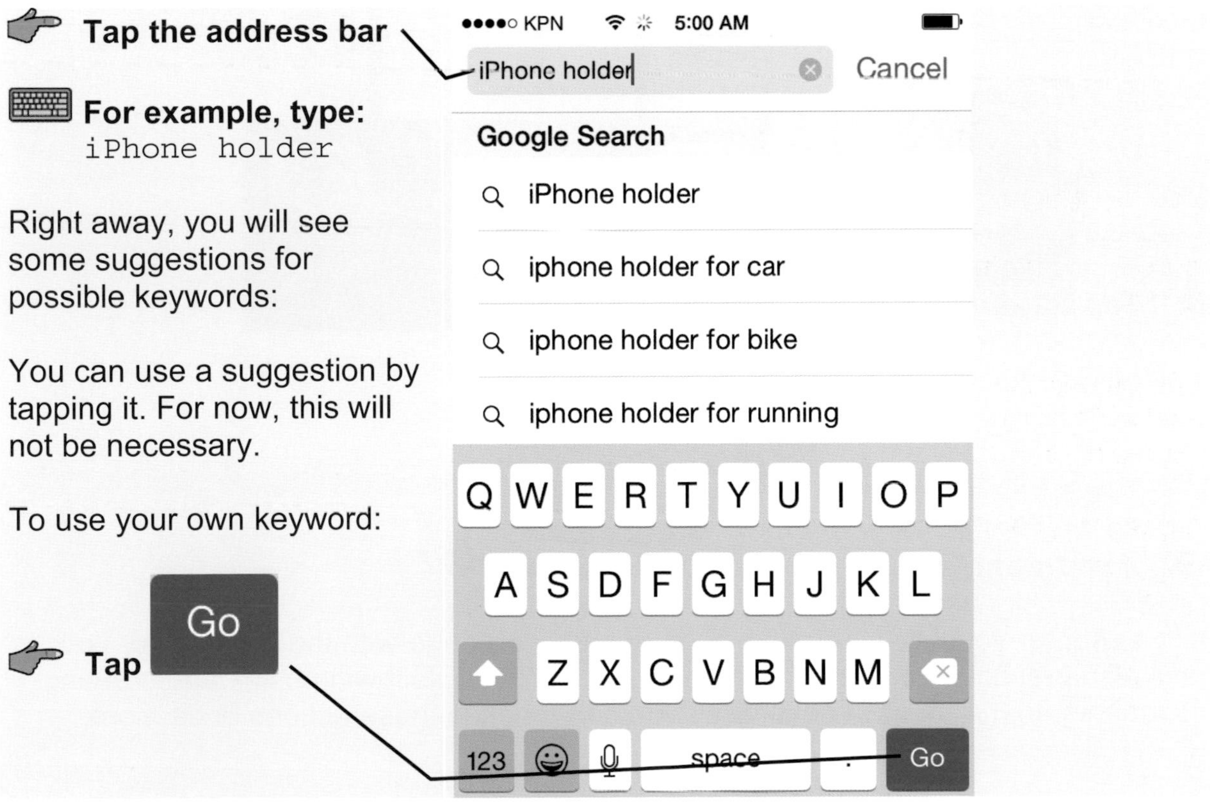

You will see the search results:

To view a result, you just need to tap the link. For now, this will not be necessary.

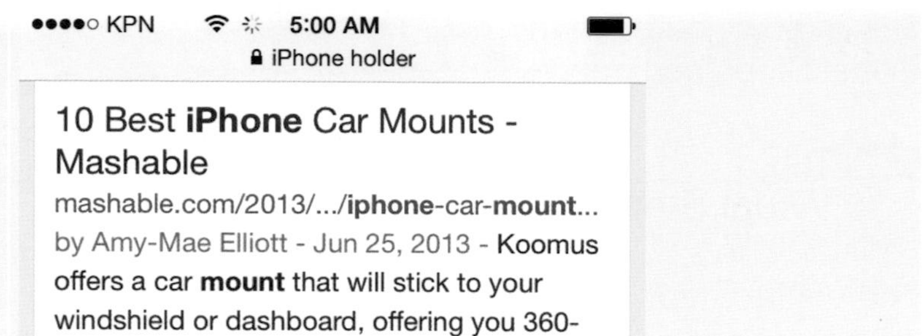

●●●●○ KPN 5:00 AM
iPhone holder
10 Best **iPhone** Car Mounts - Mashable
mashable.com/2013/.../**iphone**-car-**mount**...
by Amy-Mae Elliott - Jun 25, 2013 - Koomus offers a car **mount** that will stick to your windshield or dashboard, offering you 360-

5.9 Switching Between Recently Used Apps

With the Home button you can quickly switch between recently used apps and use these apps again. Just try it:

Press the Home button twice, in rapid succession

At the bottom of the screen you will see a bar containing the apps you have recently used:

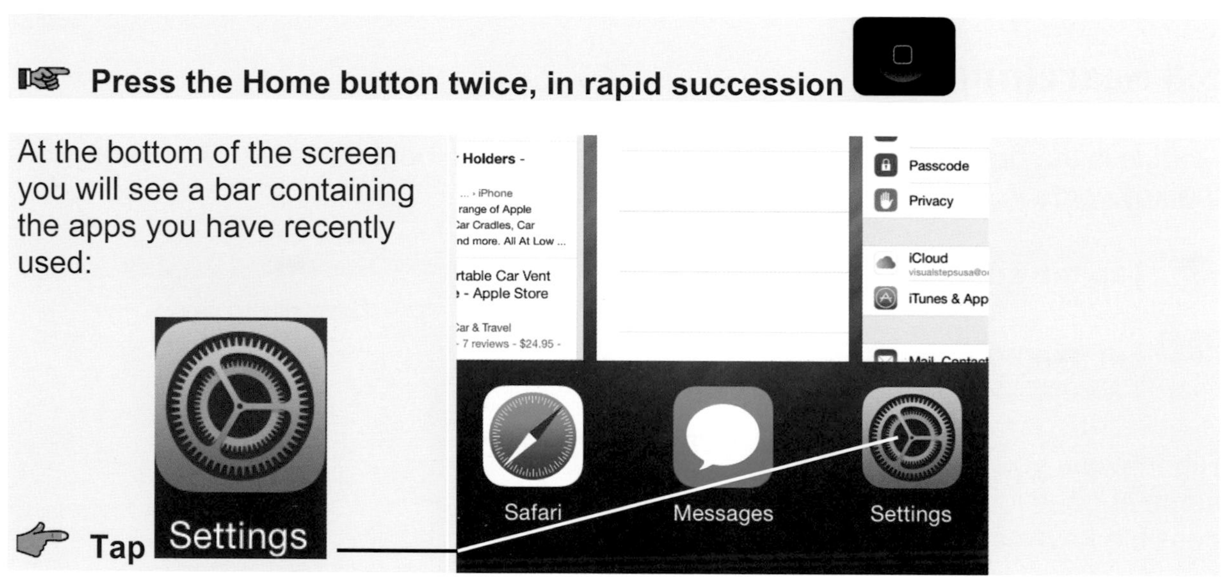

Tap Settings

You will see the *Settings* app again.

Go to the home screen [10]

If you want, put the iPhone into sleep mode [2]

In this chapter you have learned how to open a web page with the *Safari* app. You have also practiced zooming in, zooming out, scrolling, following a link and creating bookmarks. In the following exercises you can practice these actions once more.

5.10 Exercises

To be able to quickly apply the things you have learned, you can work through these exercises. Have you forgotten how to do something? Use the numbers next to the footsteps 1 to look up the item in the appendix *How Do I Do That Again?* This appendix can be found at the end of the book.

Exercise 1: Viewing a Web Page

In this exercise you are going to view a web page with *Safari*.

- If necessary, wake the iPhone up from sleep mode or turn it on. 1
- Open *Safari*. 3
- Open the website www.news.google.com 49
- Scroll downwards a bit. 50
- Quickly scroll all the way downwards. 51
- Return to the top of the page. 52
- Zoom in on the web page. 53
- Zoom out again. 54

Exercise 2: Adding a Bookmark

In this exercise you are going to add a bookmark.

- Add a bookmark for the current page. 55

Exercise 3: Opening a Link

In this exercise you are going to use different methods for opening a link to an interesting article in a new tab.

- Open a link to an article that interests you. [56]
- If possible, scroll downwards to the end of the article. [50]
- Open a link to a different article in a new tab. [57]

Exercise 4: Recently Used Apps

In this exercise you are going to switch between some recently used apps.

- View the recently used apps. [58]
- Switch to the *Settings* app. [59]
- View the recently used apps. [58]
- Open the *Safari* app. [59]
- Go to the home screen. [10]
- If you want, put the iPhone into sleep mode. [2]

5.11 Background Information

Dictionary

Bing	Search engine powered by *Microsoft*.
Bookmark	A reference to a web address, stored in a list, so you can easily retrieve the web page later on.
Google	Search engine.
Link	A link is a navigational tool on a web page that automatically leads the user to the information when it is tapped. A link may be a text, an image, a photo, a button or an icon. Also called hyperlink.
Reading list	In this list you can store links to websites you want to visit at a later time. The web addresses will be deleted from the list after you have visited the website.
Safari	The web browser made by Apple.
Scroll	Moving a web page upwards, downwards or to the left or right. On the iPhone scrolling is done with various touch actions such as pinching, swiping or dragging.
Yahoo!	Search engine.
Zoom in	Taking a closer look at an item. Letters and images become larger.
Zoom out	Viewing an item from a distance. Letters and images become smaller.

Source: User Guide iPhone, Wikipedia

Flash
One of the limitations of the iPhone is that it cannot display *Flash* content. *Flash* is a technique used to add animation and interactivity to websites. Some websites will not display properly on the iPhone if certain parts of the website require *Flash*.

5.12 Tips

Tip

Delete a bookmark

If you no longer want to use a bookmark, you can delete it. This is how you do that:

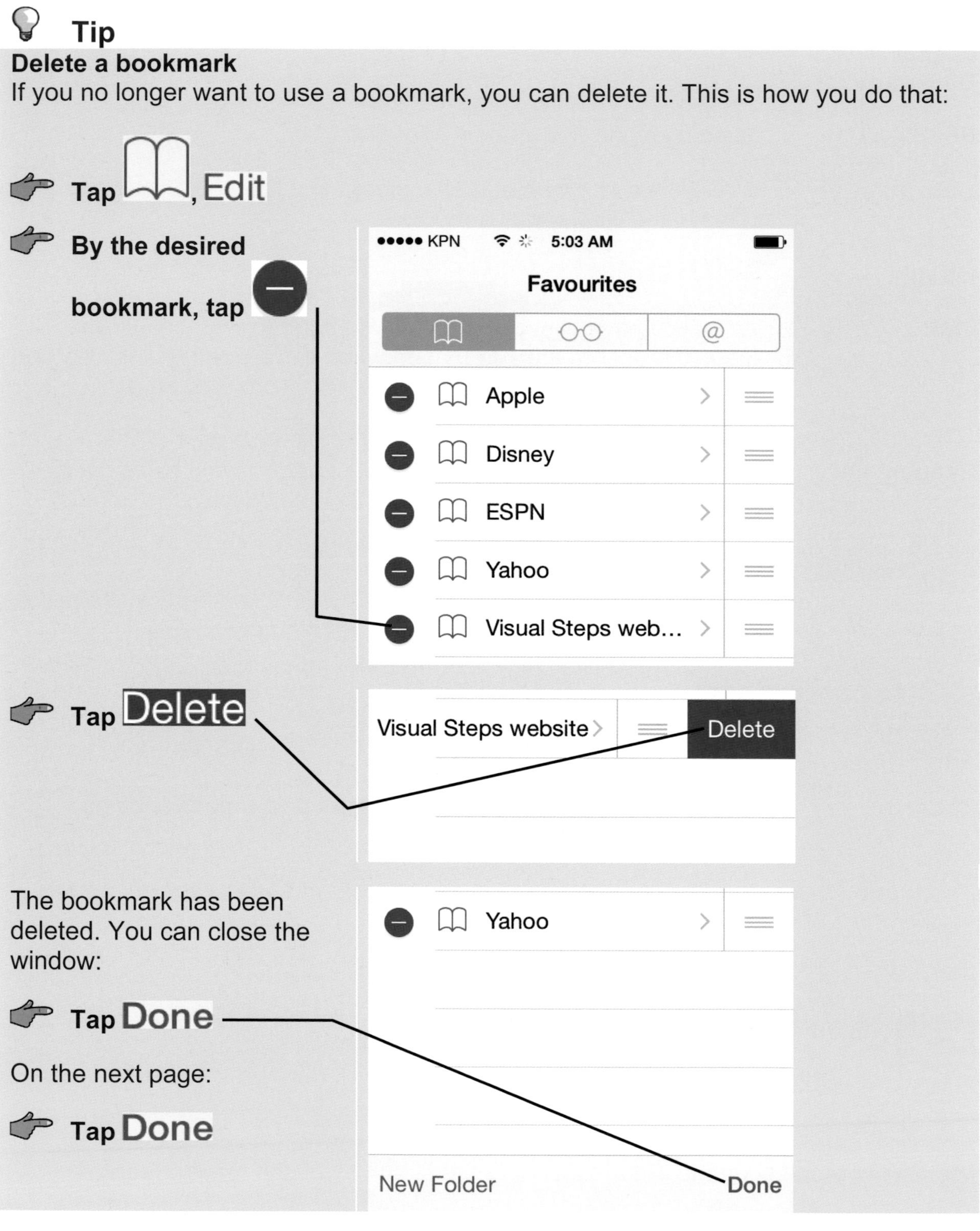

Tip

View and delete history

In the history, all the websites you have recently visited will be stored. To view your history:

Tap

If necessary, tap Bookmarks

Tap History

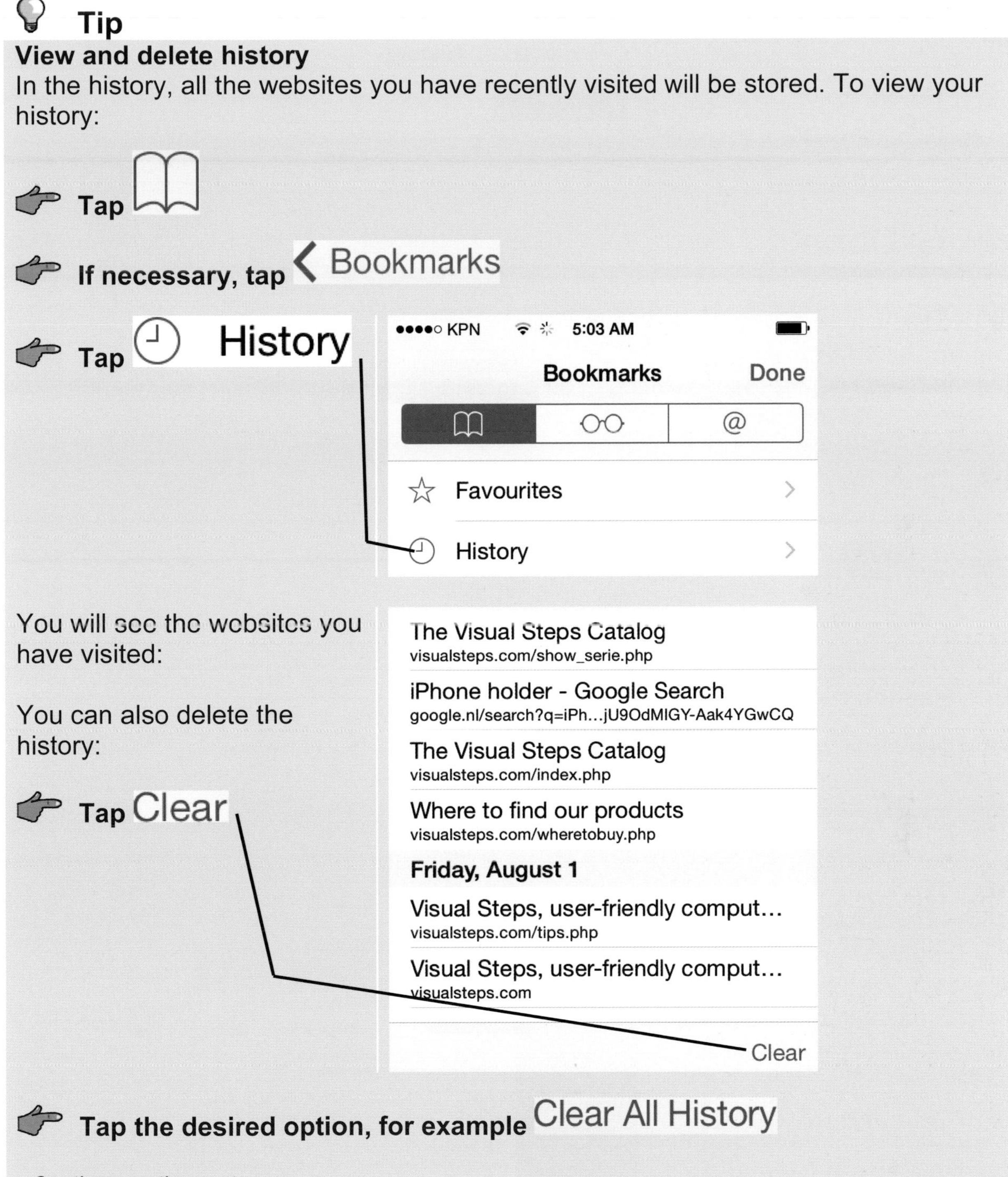

You will see the websites you have visited:

You can also delete the history:

Tap Clear

Tap the desired option, for example Clear All History

- Continue on the next page -

The history has been deleted:

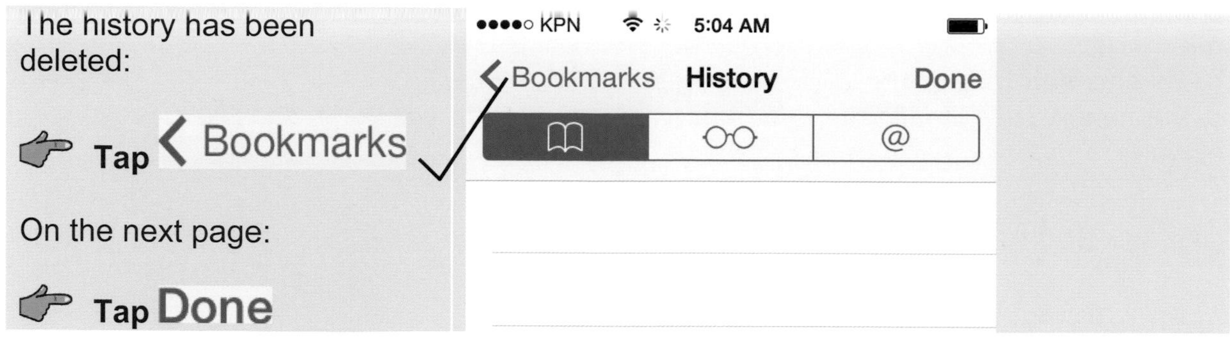

 Tap Bookmarks

On the next page:

Tap Done

Tip

Set up the search engine
On the page with the *Safari* settings you can select the search engine you want to use with the search box:

Open the *Settings* app 3

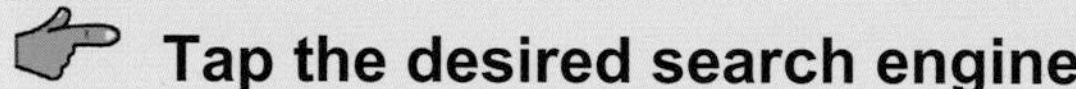

Tap Safari, Search Engine

You can choose between *Google, Yahoo*, *Bing* and *DuckDuckGo*:

Tap the desired search engine

After you have selected a search engine, you can save the changes:

 Tap Safari, Settings

Tip

iPhone in landscape orientation
If you rotate your iPhone sideways, so that it is horizontal, the contents of the web page will be enlarged and shown full screen:

If you tap the screen you will see the address bar and buttons again.

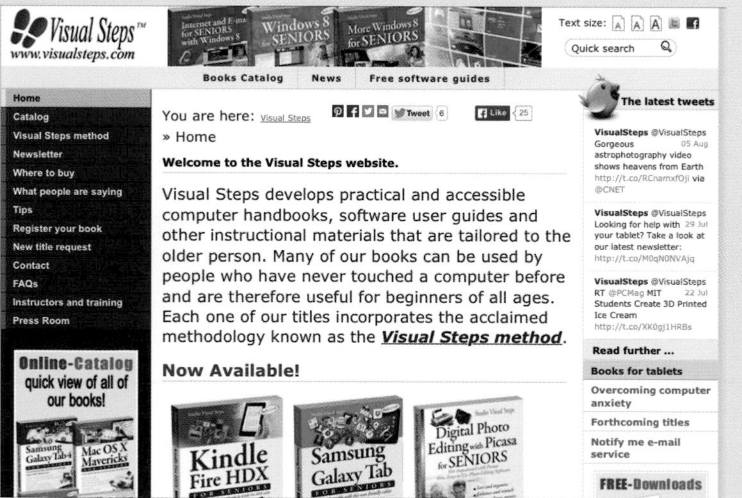

Tip

Synchronize bookmarks with Internet Explorer or Safari
If you have stored lots of favorite websites (bookmarks) on your computer, in *Internet Explorer* or *Safari*, you can synchronize them with your iPhone.

Open *iTunes* on the computer 11

Connect your iPhone to the computer

Click

Click Info

Drag the scroll bar downwards

By Other, check the box by Sync bookmarks with

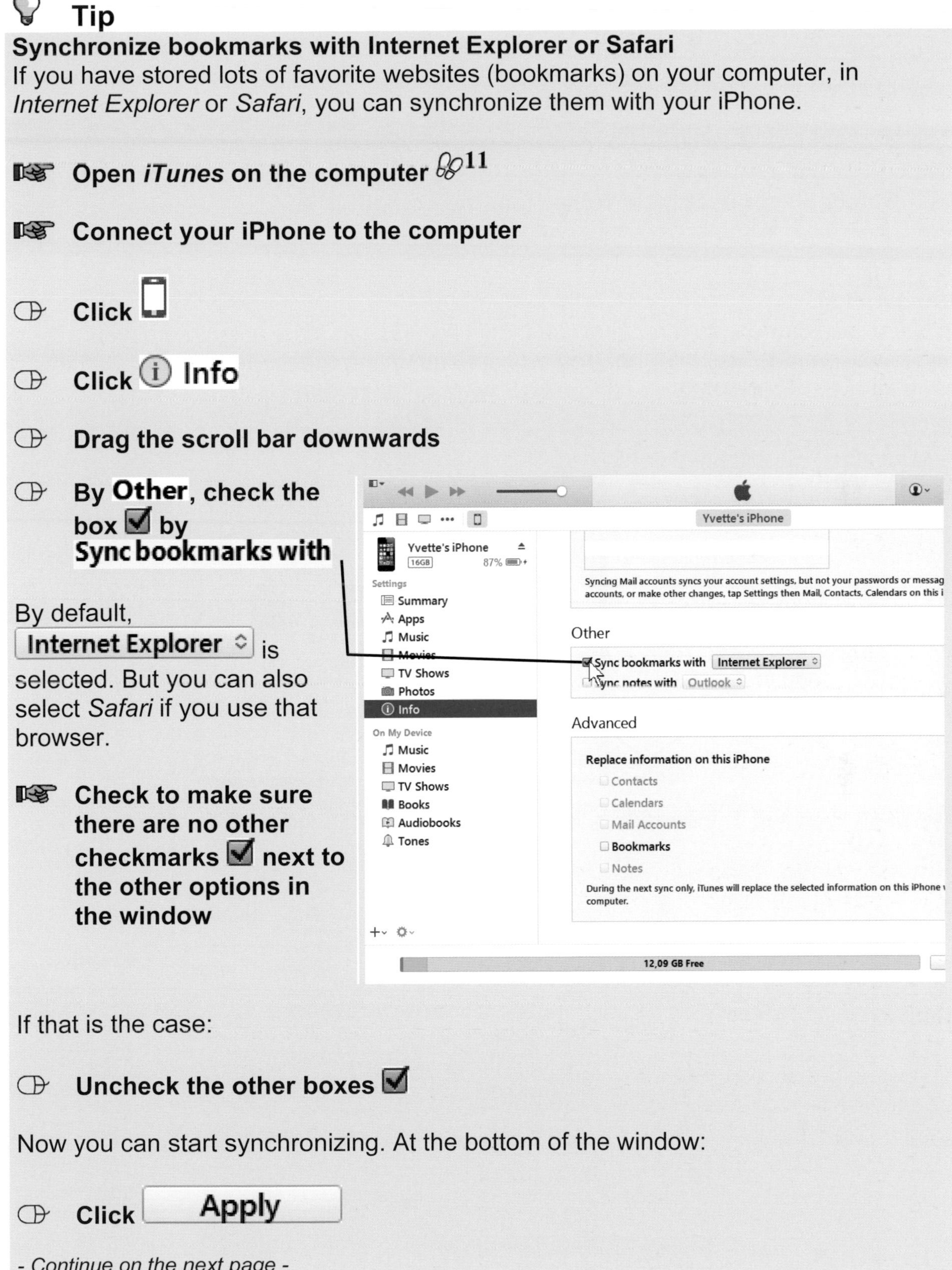

By default, Internet Explorer is selected. But you can also select *Safari* if you use that browser.

Check to make sure there are no other checkmarks next to the other options in the window

If that is the case:

Uncheck the other boxes

Now you can start synchronizing. At the bottom of the window:

Click Apply

- Continue on the next page -

First, a backup copy of your iPhone will be made, then the bookmarks will be synchronized:

Syncing "Yvette's iPhone"
Finishing sync

Now the bookmarks will also be available on your iPhone, in *Safari*.

Safely disconnect the iPhone from the computer 47

Tip

Reading list

In *Safari* you can create a reading list. In this list you can store links to the web pages you want to visit later on. You do not need an internet connection to read the page later on. This is how you add a web page to the reading list:

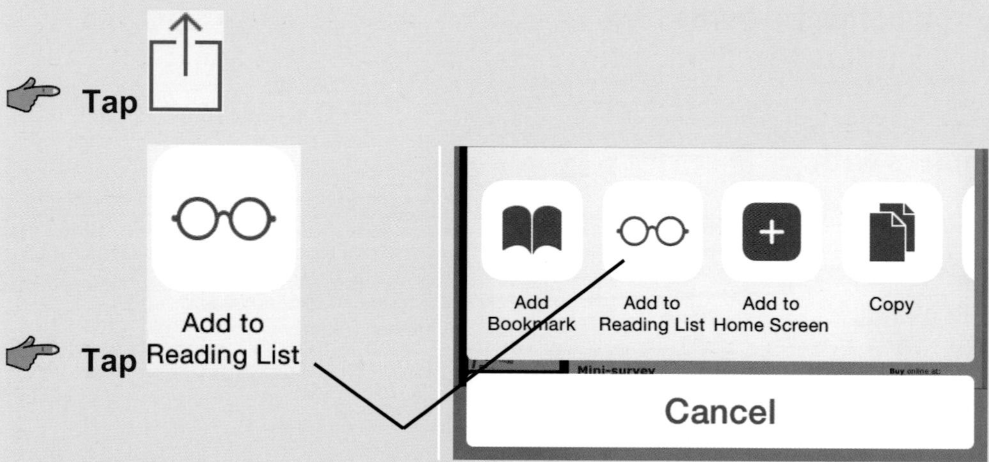

The page is added to the reading list. This is how you can view the contents of the reading list:

- Continue on the next page -

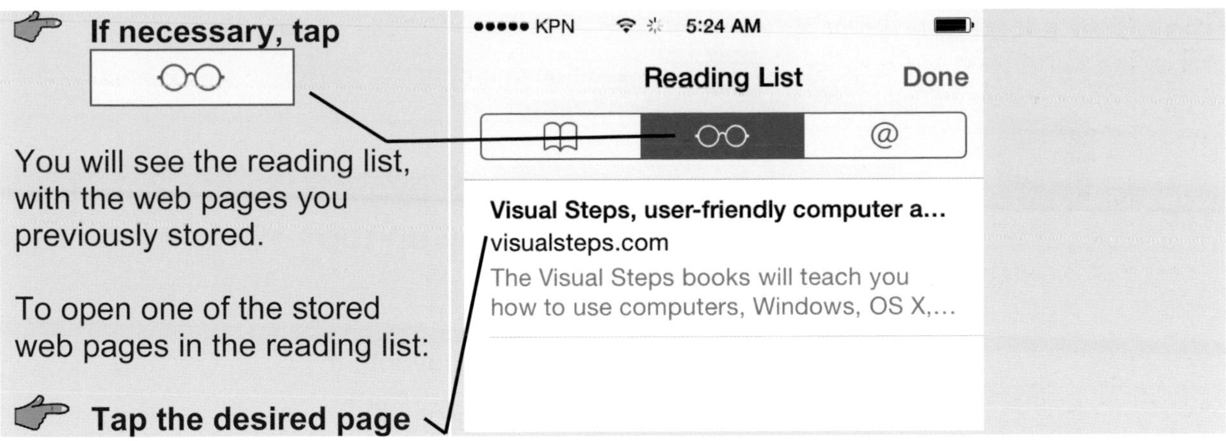

If necessary, tap

You will see the reading list, with the web pages you previously stored.

To open one of the stored web pages in the reading list:

Tap the desired page

Tip

Safari Reader

Safari Reader removes advertisements and other elements that can distract you while reading online articles. It is only available on web pages that contain articles.

In this example, the article is surrounded by all sorts of advertising banners and texts.

Safari has recognized an article on this web page. You can tell this by the button in the address bar:

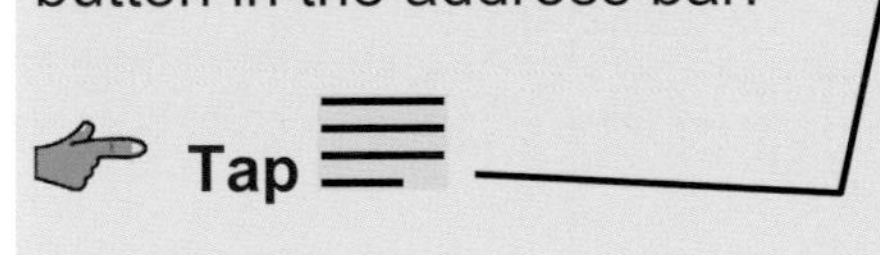

Tap

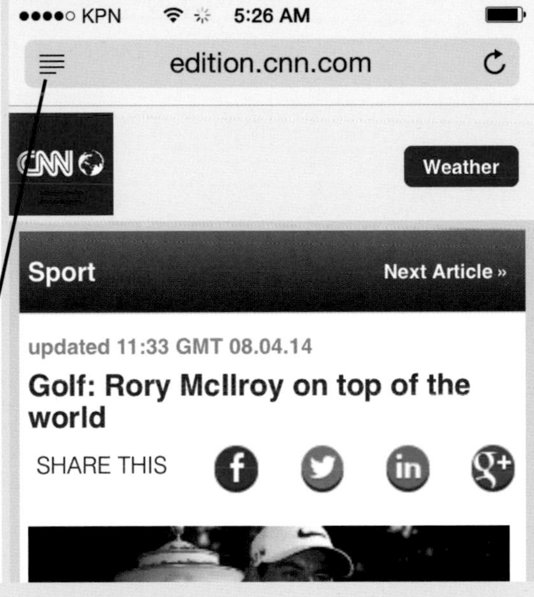

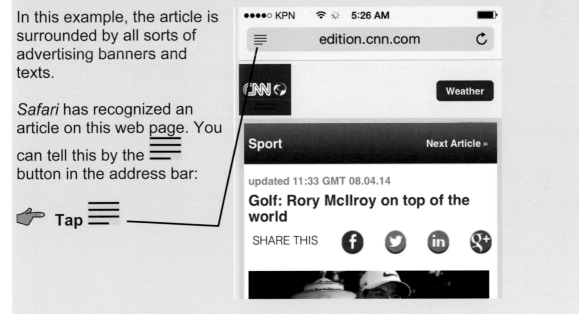

- Continue on the next page -

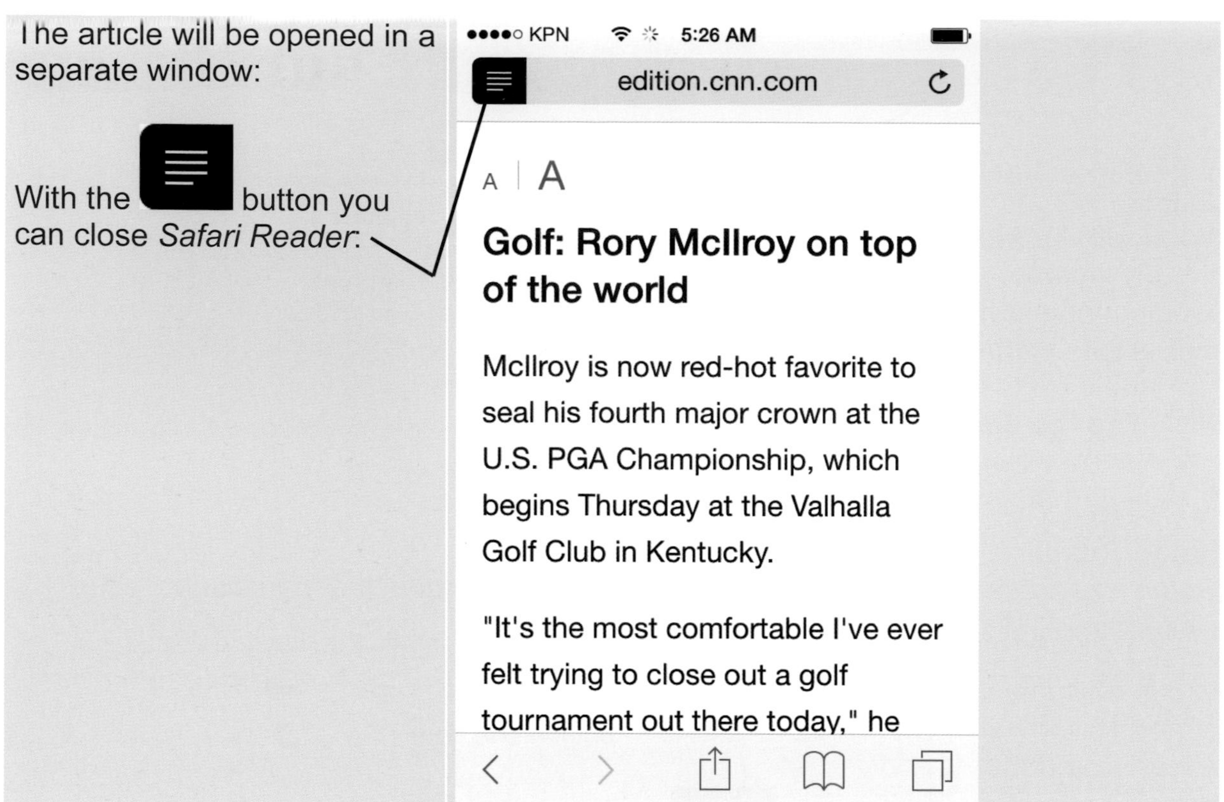
The article will be opened in a separate window:
With the button you can close *Safari Reader*:
●●●●○ KPN
5:26 AM
edition.cnn.com
A A
Golf: Rory McIlroy on top of the world
McIlroy is now red-hot favorite to seal his fourth major crown at the U.S. PGA Championship, which begins Thursday at the Valhalla Golf Club in Kentucky.
"It's the most comfortable I've ever felt trying to close out a golf tournament out there today," he

6. The Standard Apps on Your iPhone

Along with *Phone, Notes*, *Mail* and *Safari*, there are several other useful apps already installed on your iPhone. The *Calendar* app lets you keep track of your appointments and other activities. If you already have a calendar in *Outlook.com*, *Hotmail* or *Google Calendar*, you can show these calendars with your iPhone. In the *Tips* at the end of this chapter you can read how to do this.

The *Reminders* app lets you maintain a list of tasks. You can set up the app to display a reminder for each task, at any moment you like. This way, you will never again forget an important task or appointment.

In the *Maps* app you can look up addresses and well-known locations. Not only can you view these locations on a regular map, you can also see them on a satellite photo. After you have found the desired location, you can get directions for how to get there.

The *Weather* app lets you view a six-day weather forecast of your current location. You can also add other locations, for example, to monitor the weather conditions in your next vacation spot.

Spotlight is the iPhone's search utility. With this app you can search through the apps, files, activities and contacts stored on your iPhone.
There is also a central option with which you can neatly display all the messages you have received on your iPhone, such as new text messages and the notifications you have set on your iPhone. This is called the *Notification Center*.

In this chapter you will learn how to:

- add, edit and delete an activity in the *Calendar* app;
- add a reminder in the *Reminders* app;
- find your current location in the *Maps* app;
- change the view;
- search for a location;
- plan a route and get directions;
- search with *Spotlight*;
- view the weather forecast;
- add a location;
- use *Siri*;
- disable apps.

6.1 Calendar

With the *Calendar* app you can keep track of your appointments, upcoming activities, birthdays and more. Here is how to open the *Calendar* app:

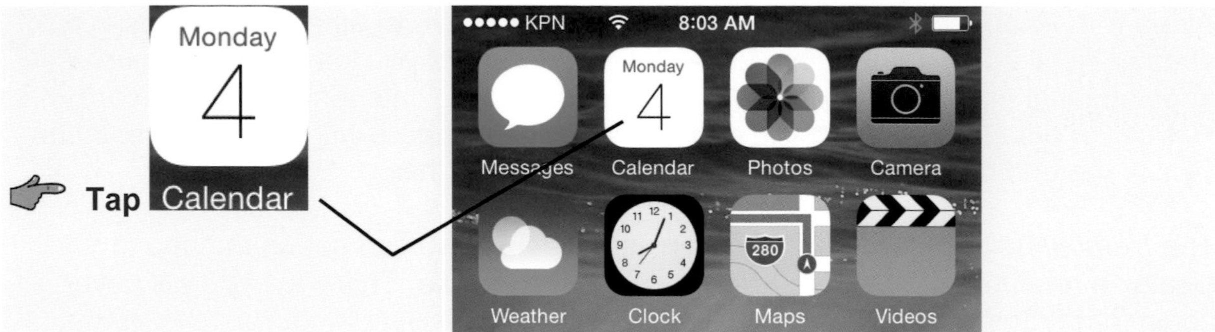

The calendar opens showing the current day of the week:

In the Day view you can select a different date:

If you have selected a different date from the current date, you can use the Today button to quickly return to your current appointments:

On the iPhone you can use different calendars. You can view these calendars with the Calendars button:

If you have not yet created or transferred any calendars, the iPhone's default calendar will be used.

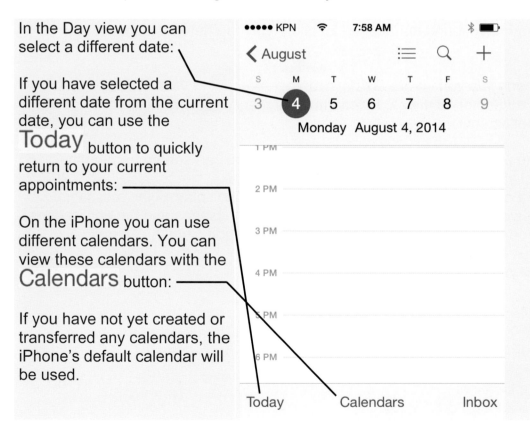

You can display the calendar view by day, week and month. Here is how to view the calendar by week:

☞ **Rotate the iPhone sideways**

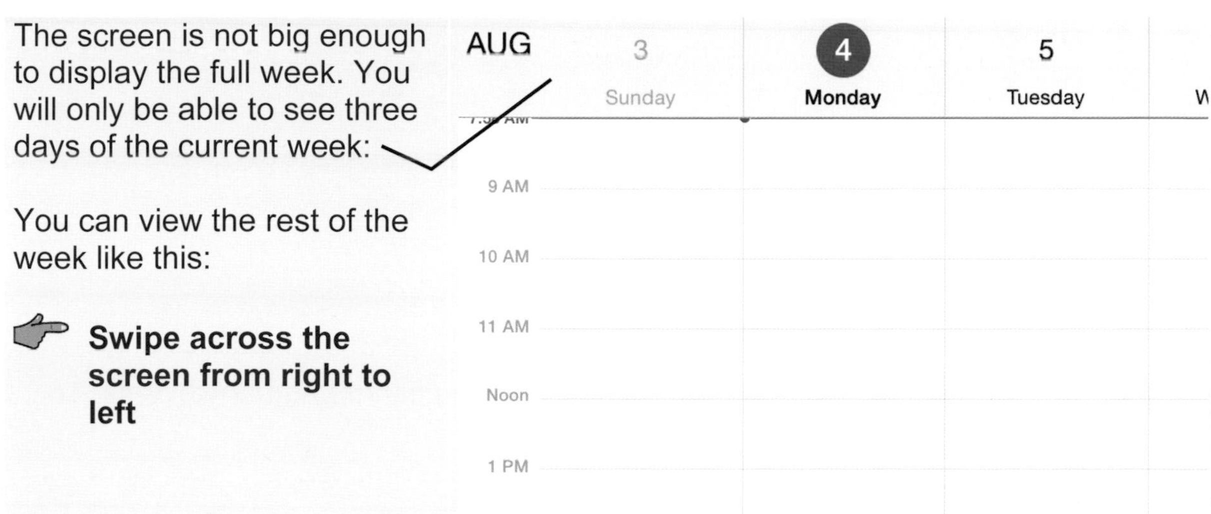

The screen is not big enough to display the full week. You will only be able to see three days of the current week:

You can view the rest of the week like this:

☞ **Swipe across the screen from right to left**

HELP! My screen does not rotate.

If your screen does not rotate when you turn your iPhone sideways, the portrait orientation mode on your iPhone is locked. You can unlock it like this:

☞ **Go to the home screen** 10

☞ **Swipe from bottom to top over the screen**

The *Control Center* appears:

☞ **Tap**

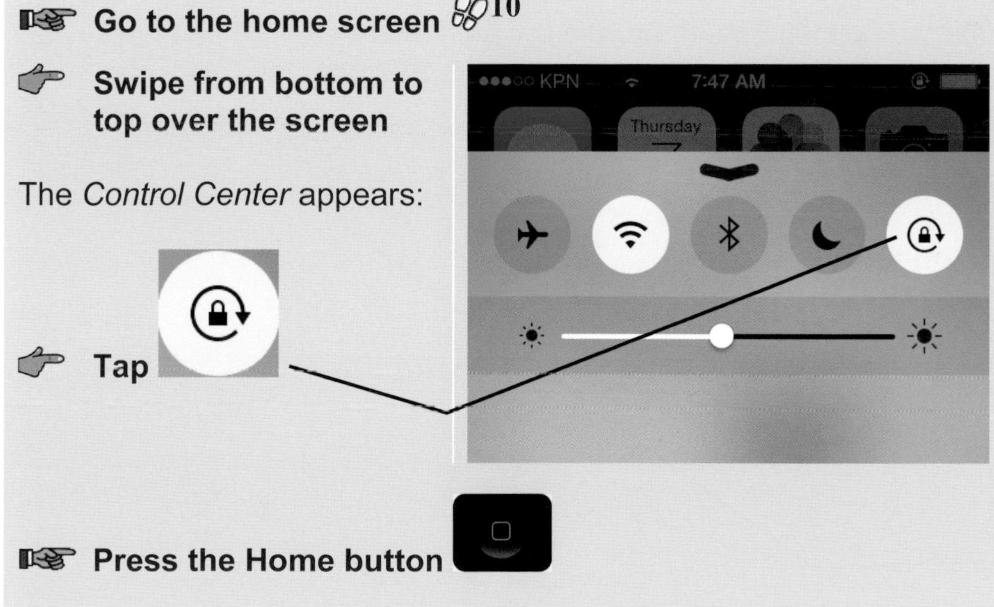

☞ **Press the Home button**

Now the screen will rotate when you turn the iPhone sideways.

You will see the other weekdays:

In the week view you can only look at the calendar. You cannot add any events. To add events, you need to open the day view:

☞ **Hold the iPhone upright again**

Once again, you will see the day view.

6.2 Adding an Event

In the *Calendar* app, an appointment or activity is called an *event*. You can easily add a new event to your calendar. First, you need to look up the right day:

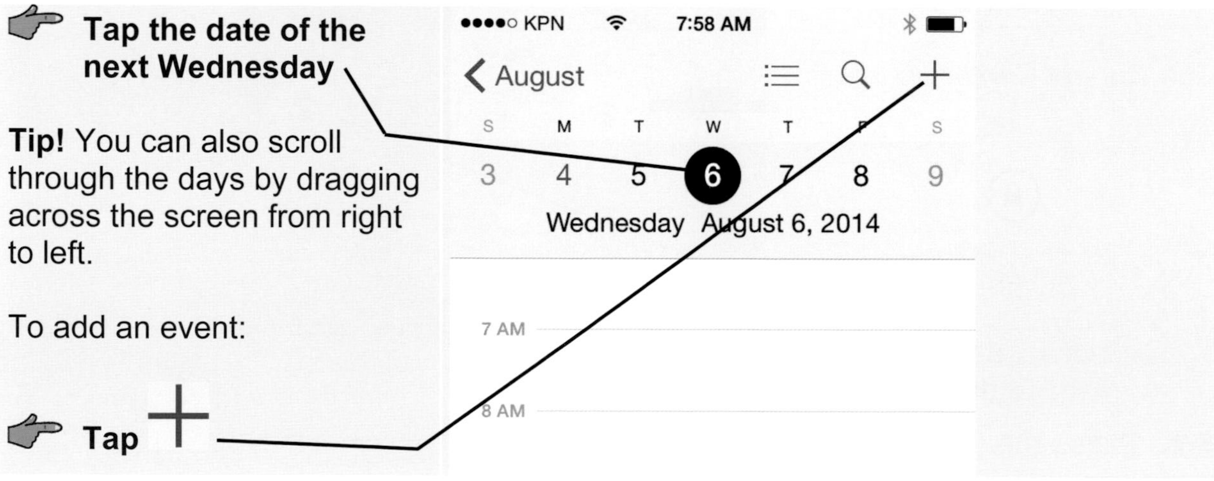

☞ **Tap the date of the next Wednesday**

Tip! You can also scroll through the days by dragging across the screen from right to left.

To add an event:

☞ **Tap +**

You can add a name and a location for the event:

Type a name, for example: `Tennis lessons`

Tap Location

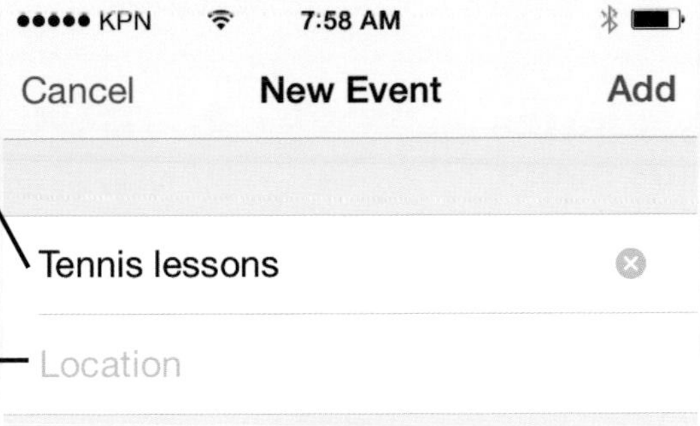

●●●●● KPN
7:58 AM
Cancel
New Event
Add
Tennis lessons
Location

You might see this window regarding using your location. For now, that is not necessary:

Don't Allow

Allow "Calendar" to access your location while you use the app?
Your location is used to estimate travel times to events and improve location searches.
Don't Allow
Allow

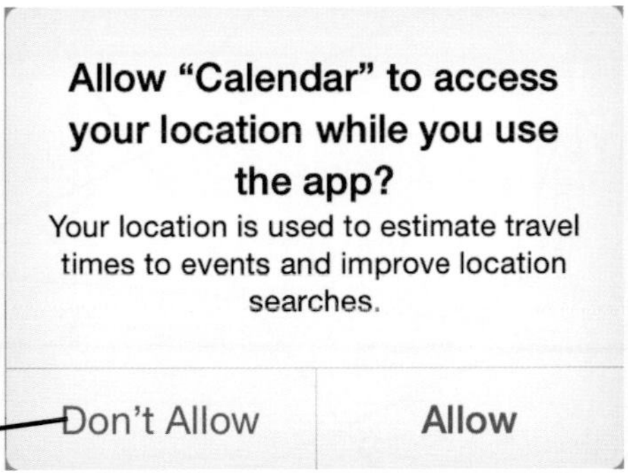

Type a location, for example: `Tennis court`

On the keyboard:

Tap Done

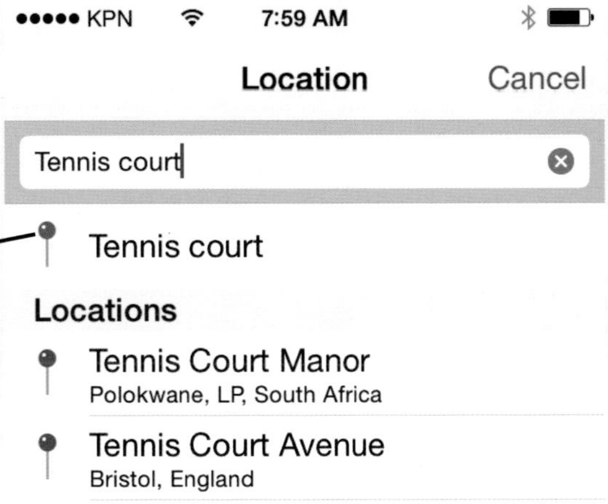

●●●●● KPN
7:59 AM
Location
Cancel
Tennis court
Tennis court
Locations
Tennis Court Manor
Polokwane, LP, South Africa
Tennis Court Avenue
Bristol, England

Now you can set the start and end time for the event:

If necessary, swipe upwards the screen a bit

Tap the start time, for example 7:00 AM

All-day
Starts
August 6, 2014
7:00 AM
Ends
8:00 AM
Repeat
Never

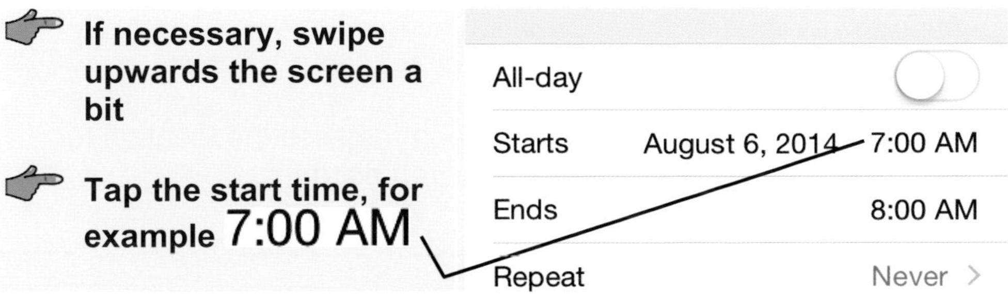

The date and time are displayed as three revolving wheels, a bit like a slot machine. You can change the time by turning the wheels. You need to touch the screen in a certain way:

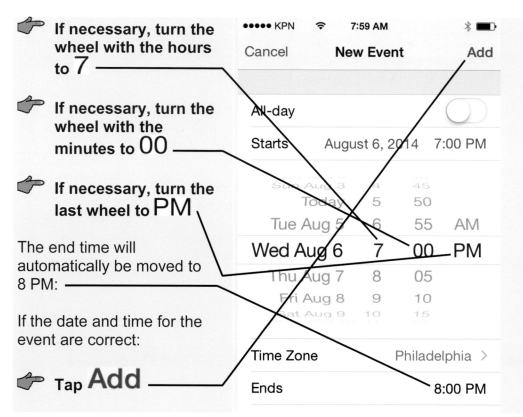

- **If necessary, turn the wheel with the hours to 7**

- **If necessary, turn the wheel with the minutes to 00**

- **If necessary, turn the last wheel to PM**

The end time will automatically be moved to 8 PM:

If the date and time for the event are correct:

- **Tap Add**

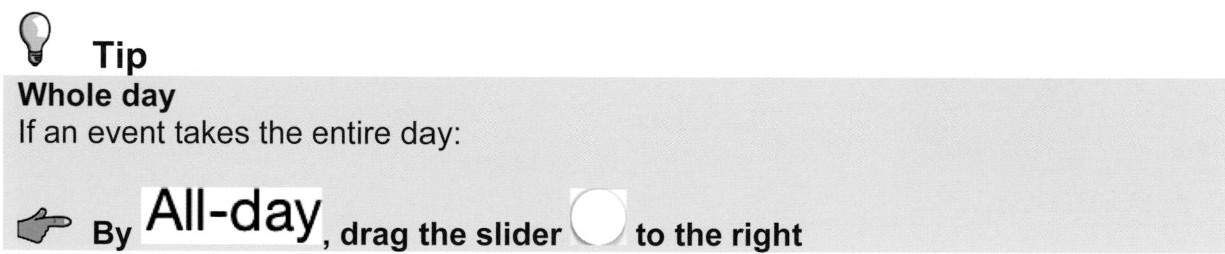

Tip

Whole day

If an event takes the entire day:

- **By All-day, drag the slider to the right**

The screen for adding events contains even more options:

Repeat	Here you can set the event to be repeated and select frequency for repeating the event. For instance, every week, or every month. By default, the Never option is selected.
Travel Time	Here you can add the travel time you need to get to the location for an event. Event alerts will take this time into account.

Alert	Here you can set an alert for the event. You can set the alert to go off a couple of minutes, hours, or even days before the event is due. By default, the None is selected.
Invitees	If you have a calendar associated with an email address such as *Yahoo!* or *Gmail* you can invite contacts to take part in the event. They will receive the invitation by email and can paste the event into their own calendars by tapping the attachment.
Calendar	If you have more than one calendar synced to your iPhone, you can use this option to select the calendar to which you want to add the event.

You will see the event in the calendar:

You can close the *Calendar* app:

☞ **Go to the home screen** 10

6.3 Reminders

You can use the *Reminders* app to store simple to-do lists or anything else you need to be reminded about. Reminders are organized by lists and tasks. You can create these lists yourself, including dates and locations. Just give it a try:

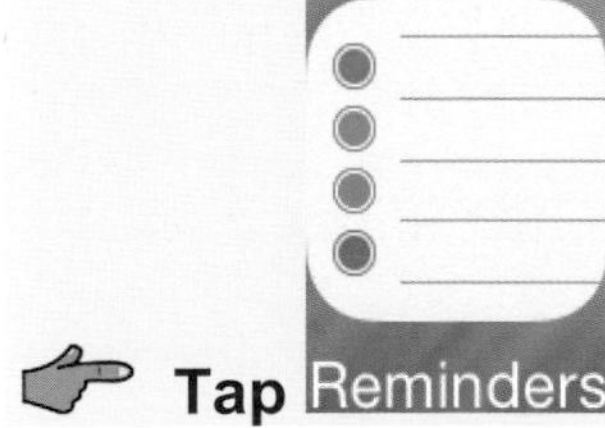

In this app you can manage various lists. For instance, a list for at home and one for at work. In this example you are going to make a list of your domestic tasks, and add a reminder to buy someone a present:

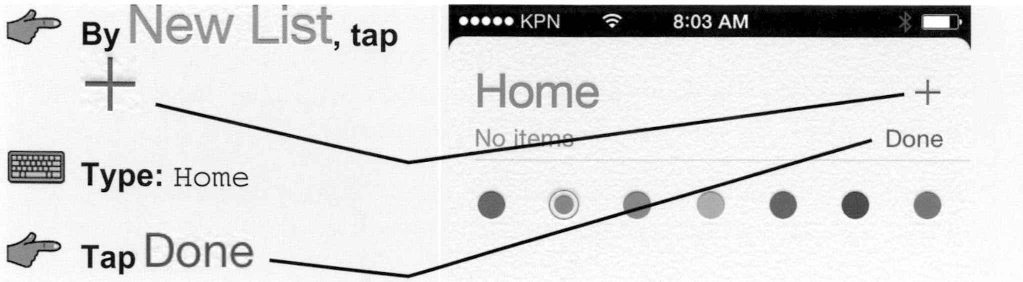

You will see an overview to which you can add a new task:

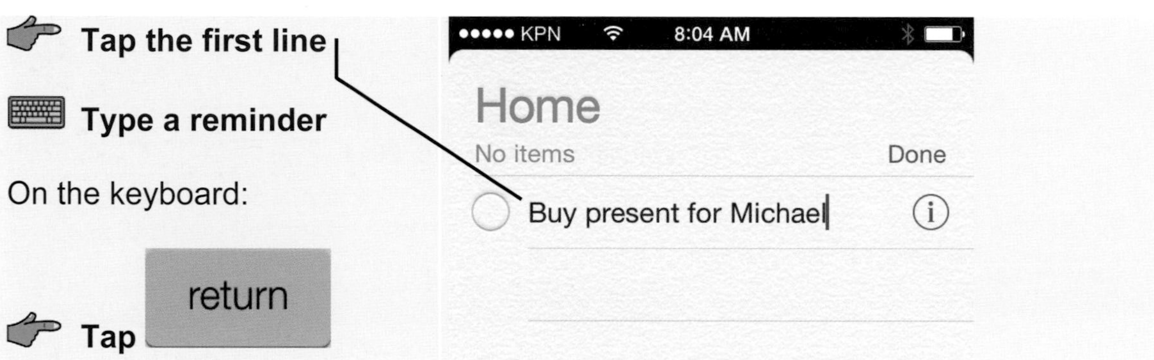

After you have added a reminder, you can add additional information:

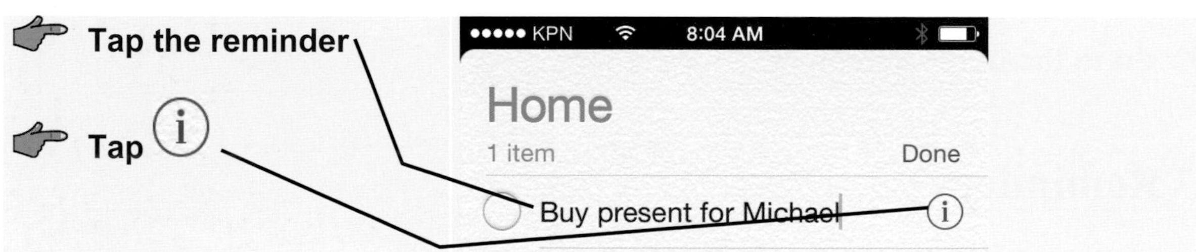

To set the date and time for the reminder to be triggered:

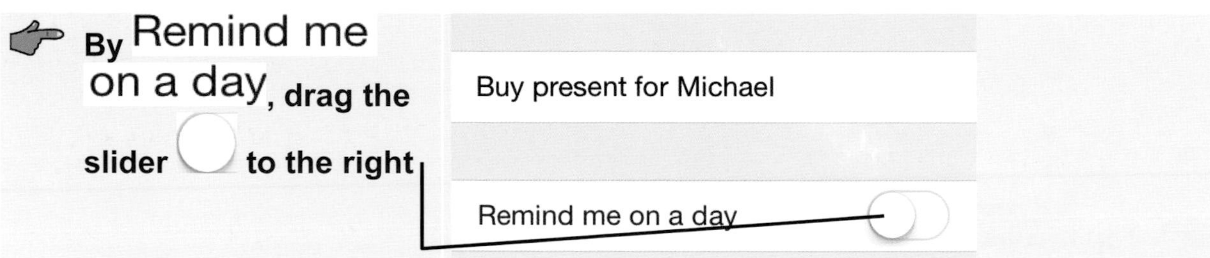

By Remind me on a day, drag the slider to the right
Buy present for Michael
Remind me on a day

Right away, a date will be suggested:

☞ **Tap the date**

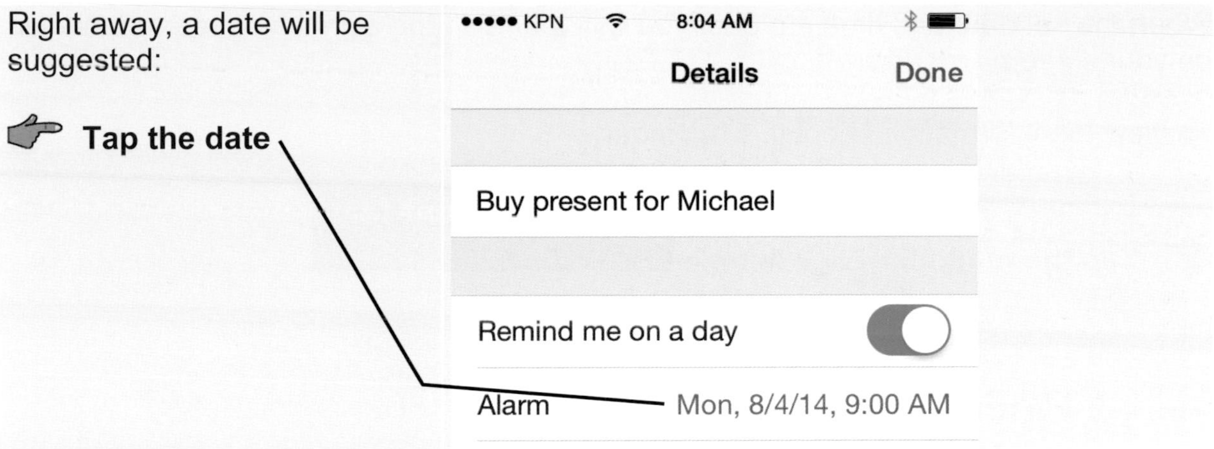

Set the desired date and time for the reminder to be triggered:

☞ **Turn the wheels to set the date and time**

After you have set the date and time:

☞ **Tap Done**

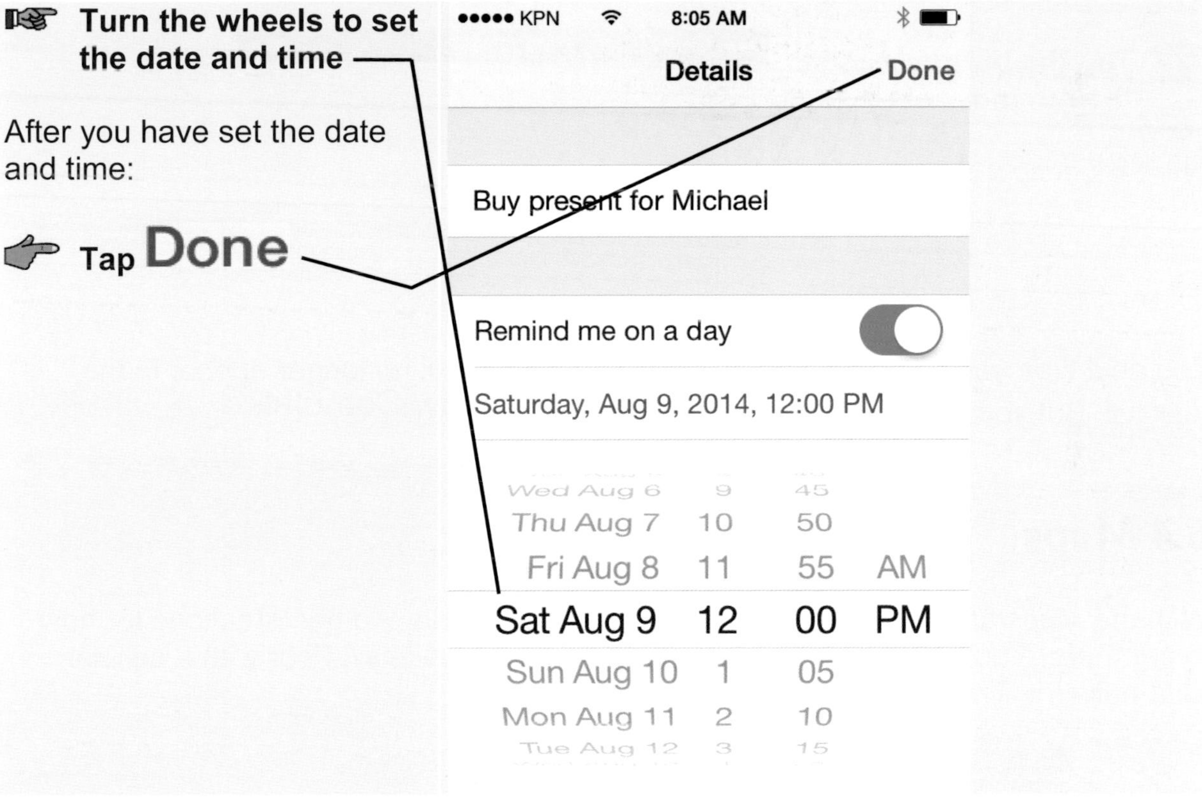

Now a time is set for this reminder and you will see the summary of the reminders.

☞ **Go to the home screen** 10

When the set date and time are due, you will hear a sound signal and see a reminder on your screen:

To view the information about this reminder:

Tap the reminder, for example

Or:

Tap Options, View

You will see the information in the *Reminders* app. The task will remain stored in the task list until you check off the task:

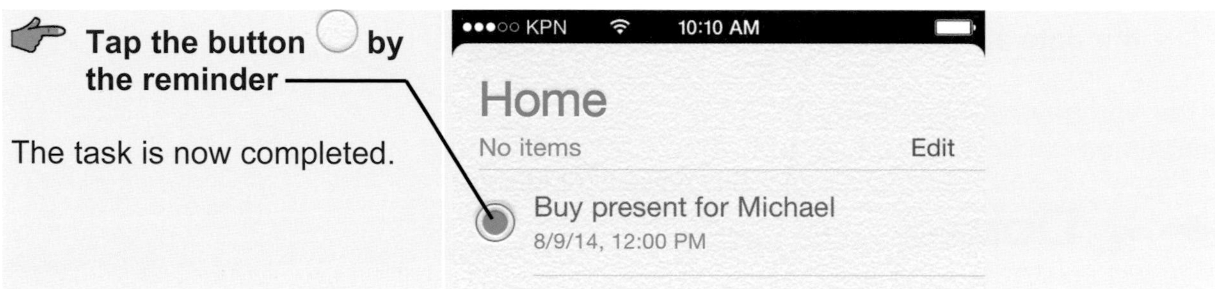

Tap the button ◯ by the reminder

The task is now completed.

The next time you open this app, the completed task will no longer appear in the task list. But you can still view the task by tapping Show Completed.

6.4 Maps

With the *Maps* app you can search for a specific location and get directions for how to get there. You need to be connected to the Internet with Wi-Fi or with a cellular data network. This is how you open the *Maps* app:

Tap

You will be asked for permission to use your current location:

Tap Allow

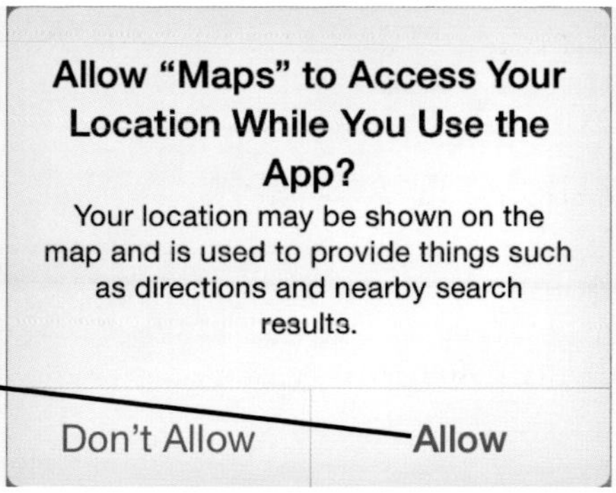

Allow "Maps" to Access Your Location While You Use the App?
Your location may be shown on the map and is used to provide things such as directions and nearby search results.
Don't Allow
Allow

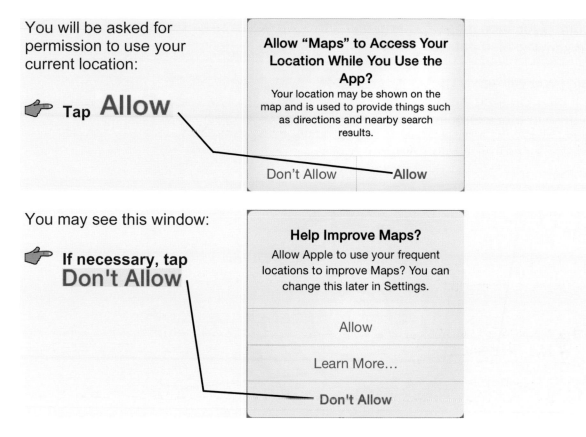

You may see this window:

If necessary, tap Don't Allow

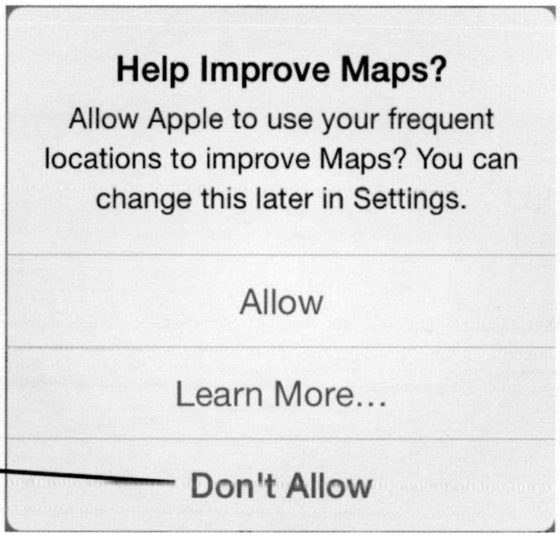

Help Improve Maps?
Allow Apple to use your frequent locations to improve Maps? You can change this later in Settings.
Allow
Learn More...
Don't Allow

You will see the map of the country where you are located. Now you need to establish your current location:

Tap

●●●○○ KPN
8:10 AM
Search or enter an address
NORTH AMERICA
Toronto
New York
Los Angeles
Mexico City
Bogotá
SOUTH AMERICA
Lima
La Paz
Brasília
Asuncion
Rio de J
Santiago

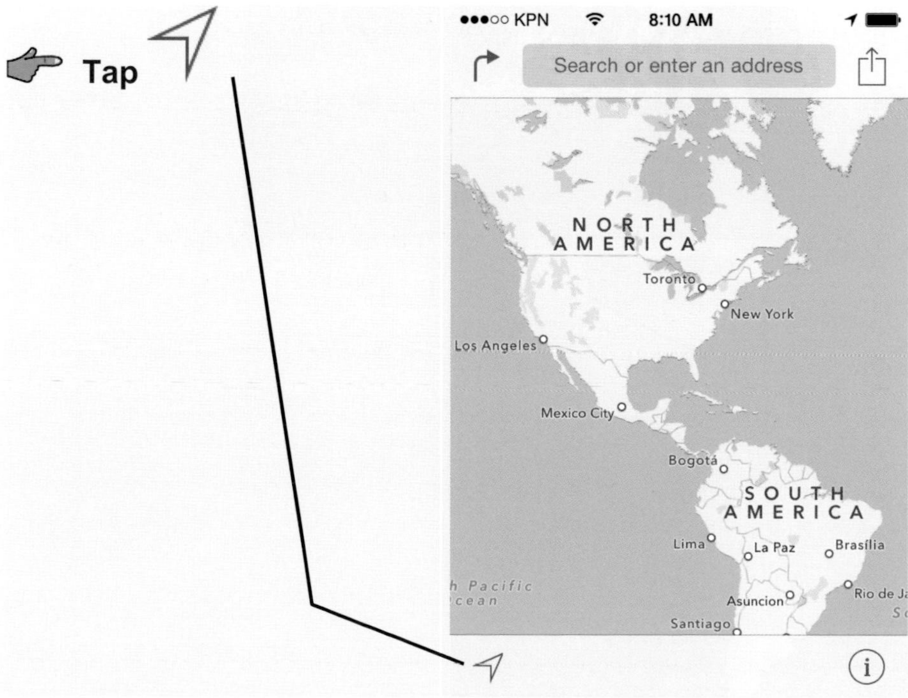

Your current location is indicated by the blue dot:

Naturally, you will see a different location than what is shown here in this example.

Here is how to change the view of the map:

Tap ⓘ

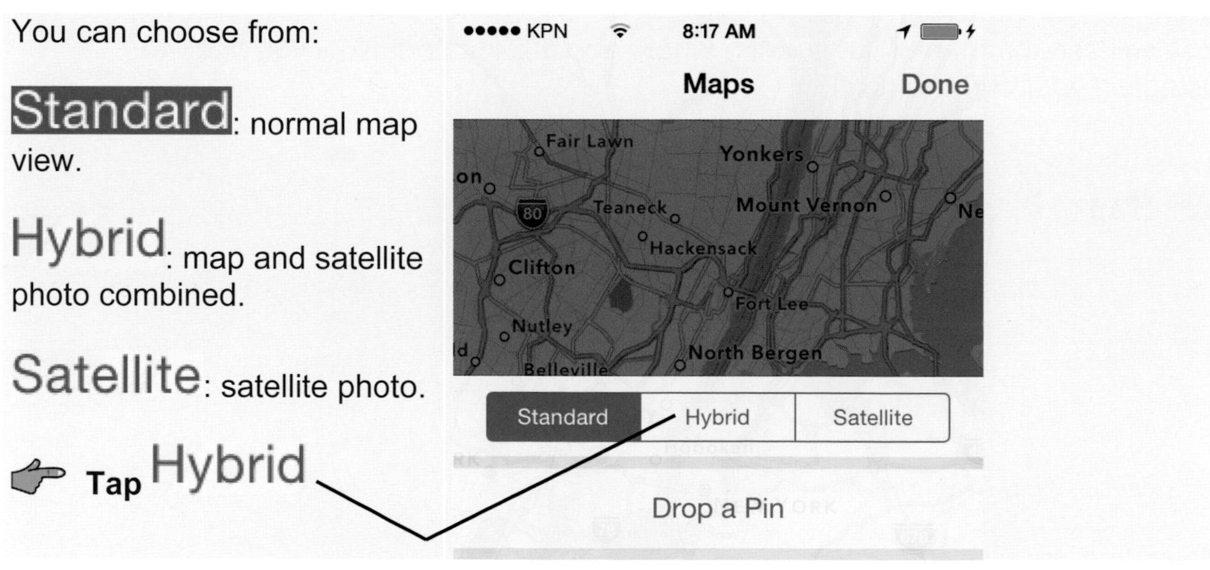

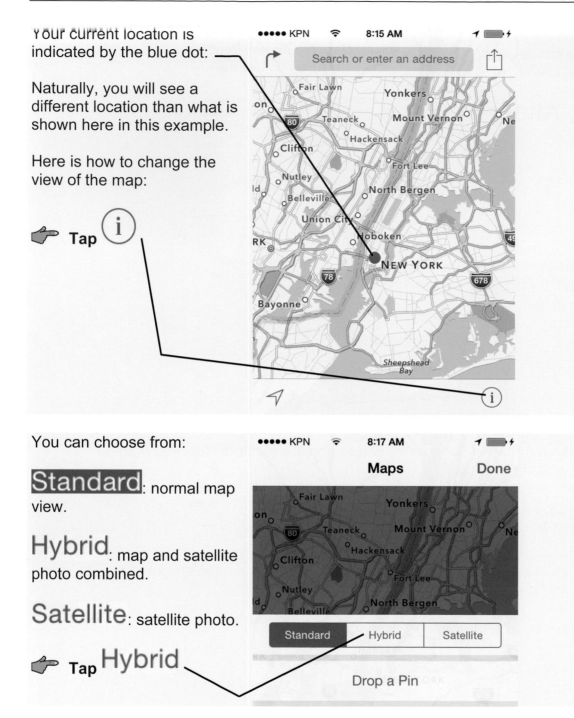

You can choose from:

Standard: normal map view.

Hybrid: map and satellite photo combined.

Satellite: satellite photo.

Tap **Hybrid**

You will see a combination of a map and a satellite photo of your current location:

 **Tip**

Zoom in and zoom out
Place two fingers gently on the screen and move them apart or towards each other, to zoom in or out.

6.5 Searching for a Location

You can use *Maps* to look for a specific location. You can search for a home address, a local business, famous public places or points of interest:

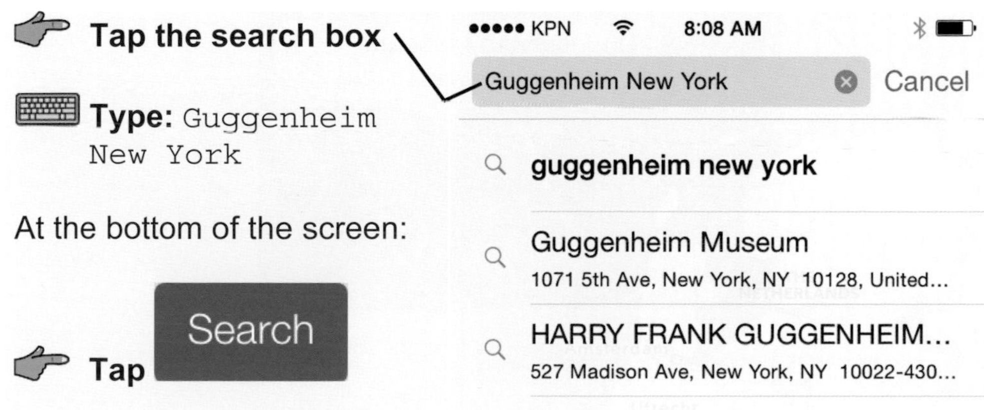

The location will be marked with a red pin on the map:

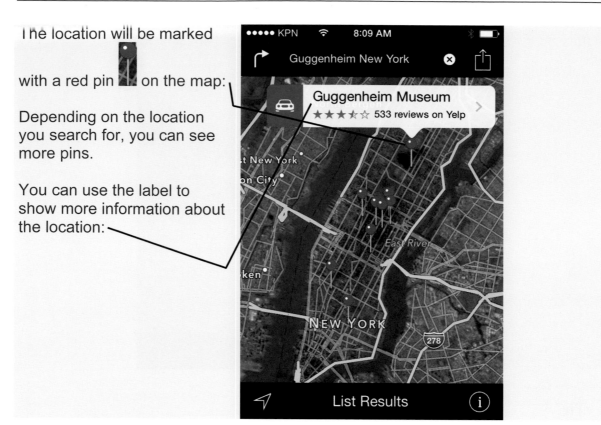

Depending on the location you search for, you can see more pins.

You can use the label to show more information about the location:

6.6 Map Out Your Trip

Once you have found the desired location, you can plan a route and get directions to it. Here is how to do that:

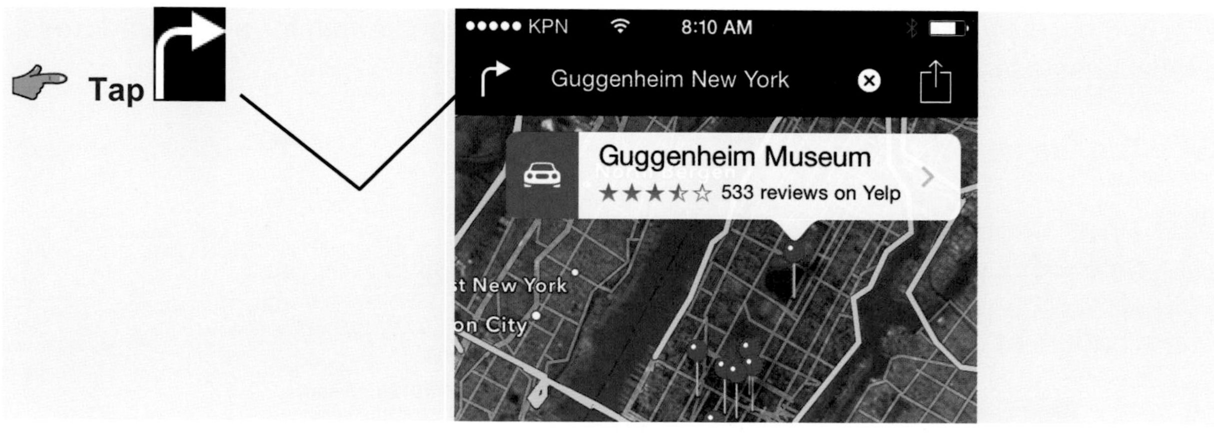

You may see a safety warning window:

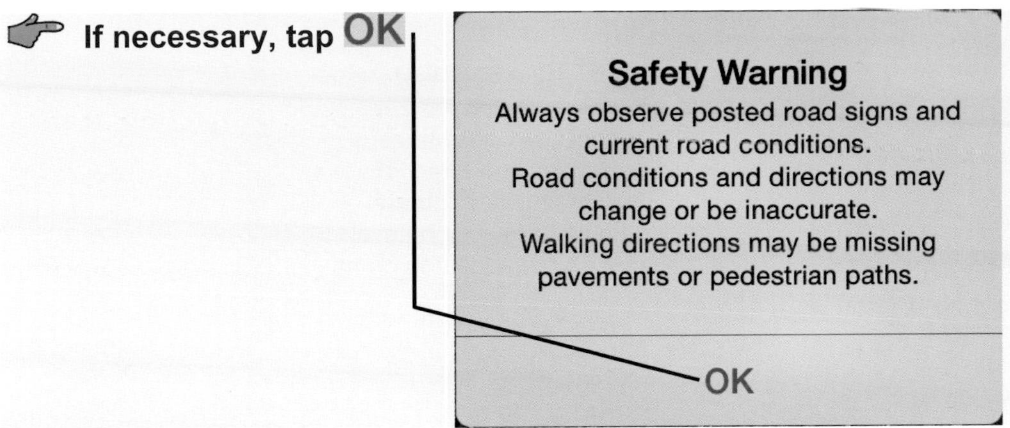

If necessary, tap OK
Safety Warning
Always observe posted road signs and current road conditions.
Road conditions and directions may change or be inaccurate.
Walking directions may be missing pavements or pedestrian paths.
OK

You are to change the starting point:

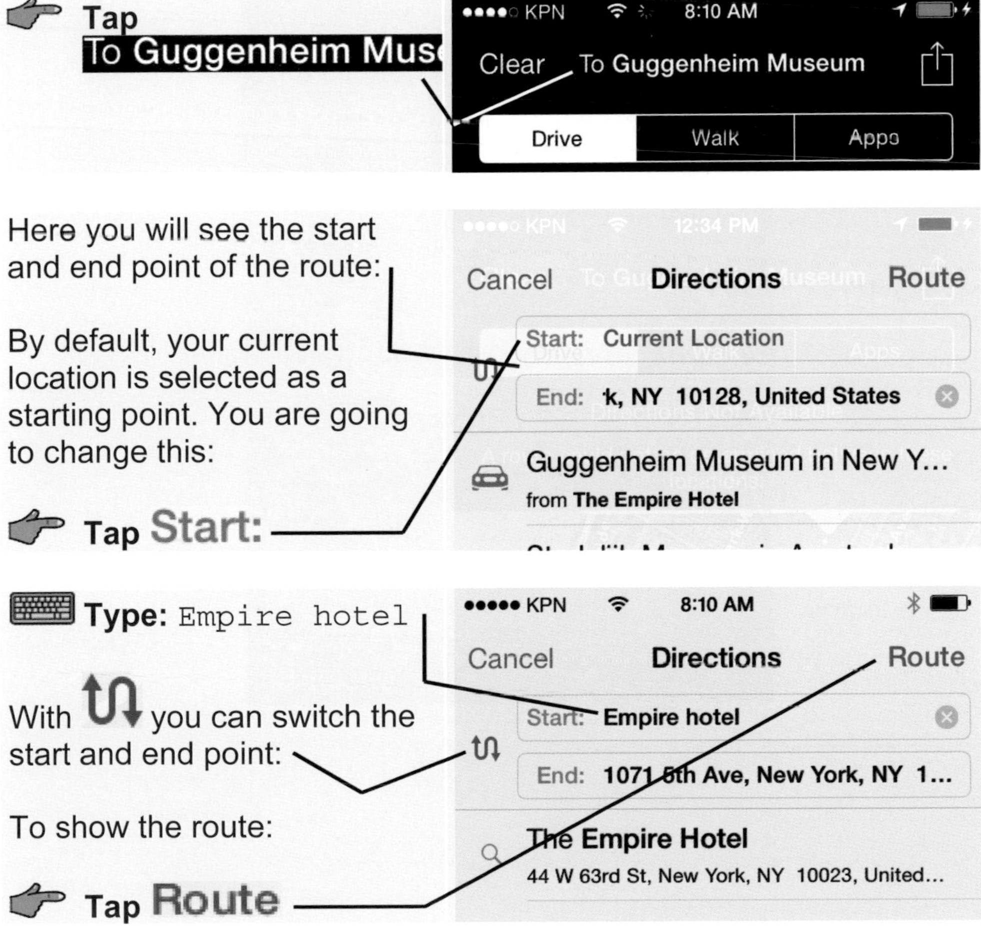

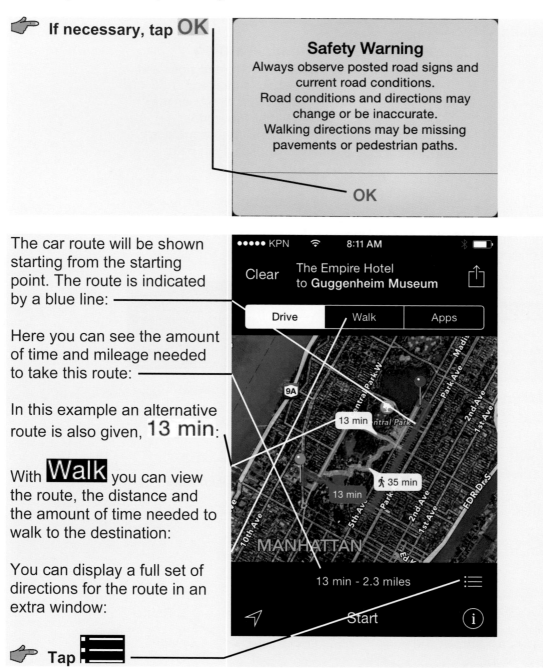

You may see a safety warning window:

 **If necessary, tap** OK

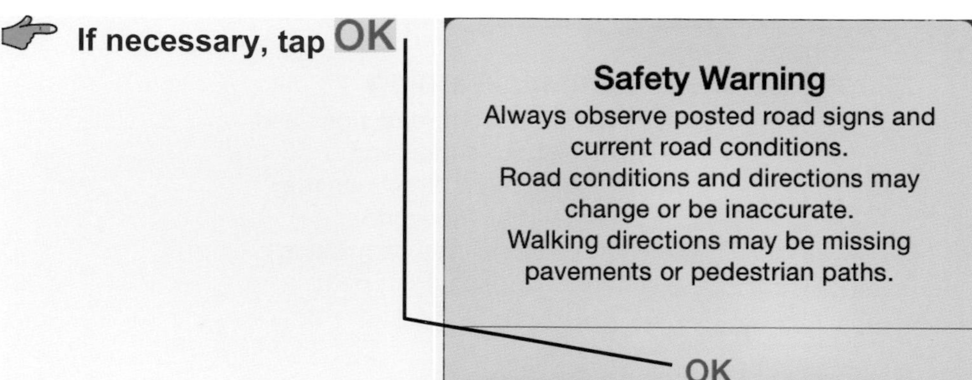

The car route will be shown starting from the starting point. The route is indicated by a blue line:

Here you can see the amount of time and mileage needed to take this route:

In this example an alternative route is also given, 13 min:

With Walk you can view the route, the distance and the amount of time needed to walk to the destination:

You can display a full set of directions for the route in an extra window:

Tap

Unfortunately you can't print the directions.

You can close the window with the directions:

Tap Done

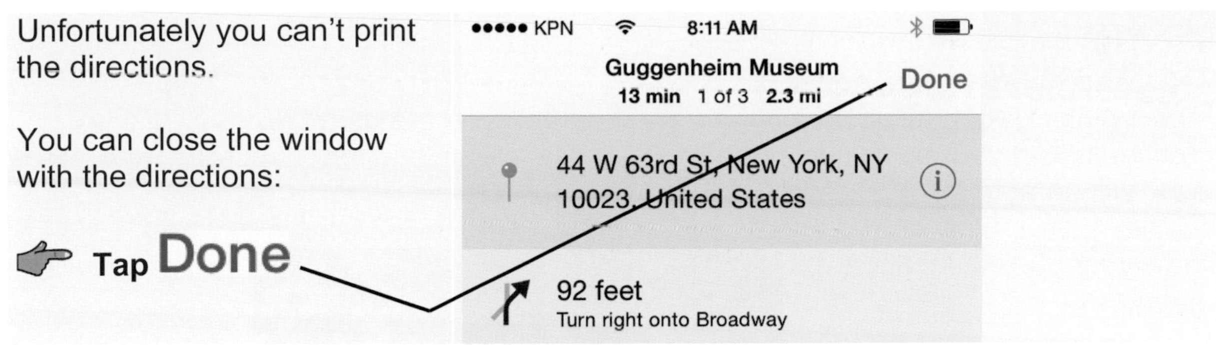

You can display the route step by step or one leg at a time:

At the bottom of the screen:

Tap Start

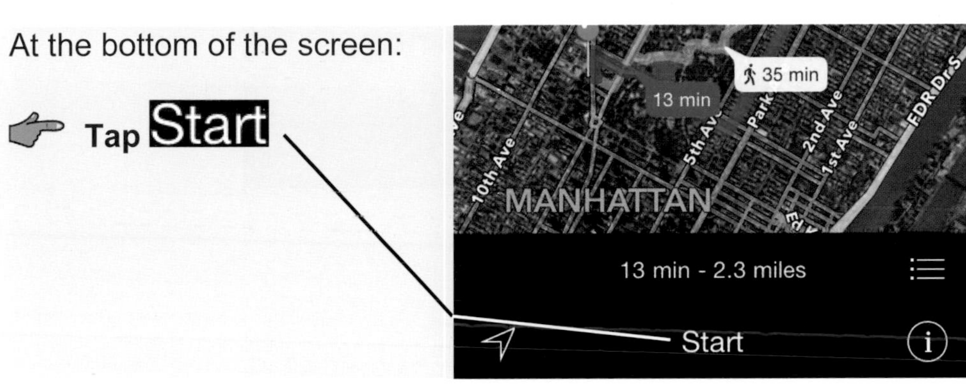

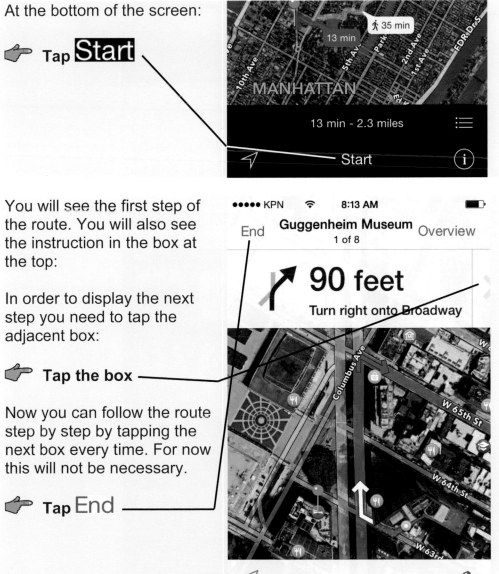

You will see the first step of the route. You will also see the instruction in the box at the top:

In order to display the next step you need to tap the adjacent box:

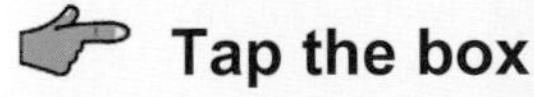

Now you can follow the route step by step by tapping the next box every time. For now this will not be necessary.

Tip

Maps and cellular data network

If the cellular data network has been turned on and you are using *Maps* to display directions from your current location, you will see a slightly different screen, and *Maps* will be able to supply live directions for your trip.

Show your current location again.

Tap

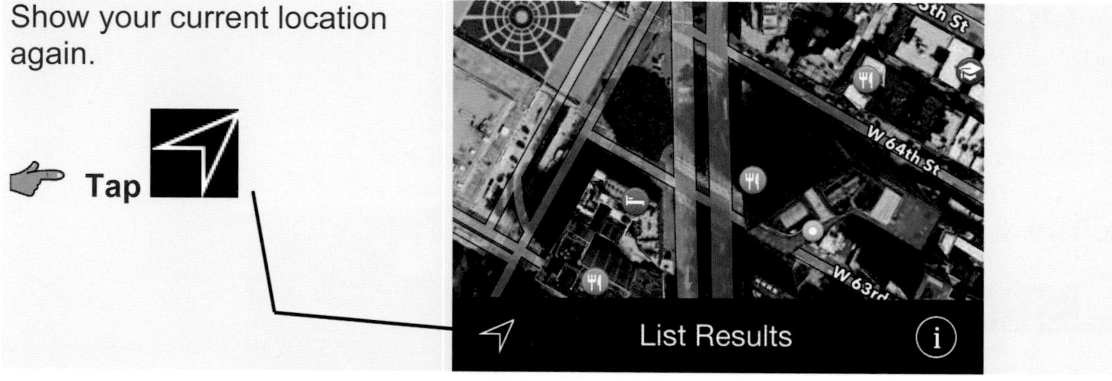

Go to the home screen 10

6.7 Spotlight

Spotlight is the iPhone's search utility. This is how you open *Spotlight*:

Swipe downwards across the screen a bit, halfway the screen

Spotlight will be opened. You can type your query right away. In this example we are searching for an event that has been previously entered in the *Calendar* app:

Type: `tennis lessons`

You will see the search results right away:

Tap Tennis lessons
Tennis court – 8/6/14 7:00 PM

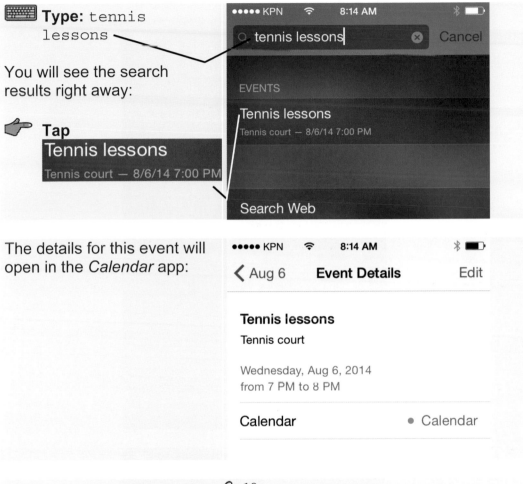

The details for this event will open in the *Calendar* app:

Go to the home screen 10

6.8 Weather

With the *Weather* app you can look up the current temperature and view a six-day weather forecast for a single city or for multiple cities all over the world. Here is how to open the *Weather* app:

The app may requests permission to use your current location:

If necessary, tap Allow

You will see the weather forecast for your current location:

By default, the temperature is rendered in Fahrenheit:

If you want, you can change this to Celsius:

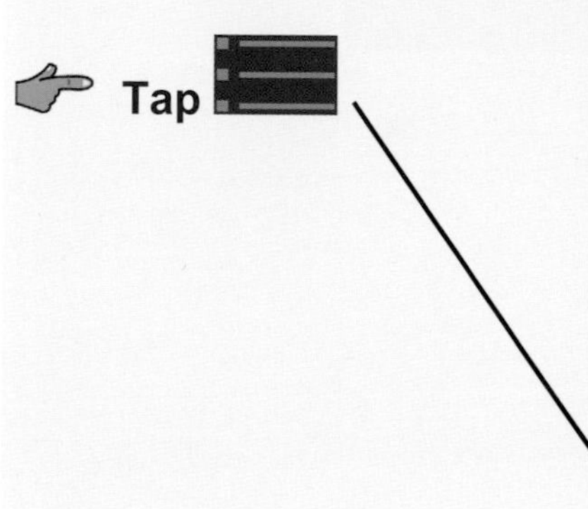

Tap

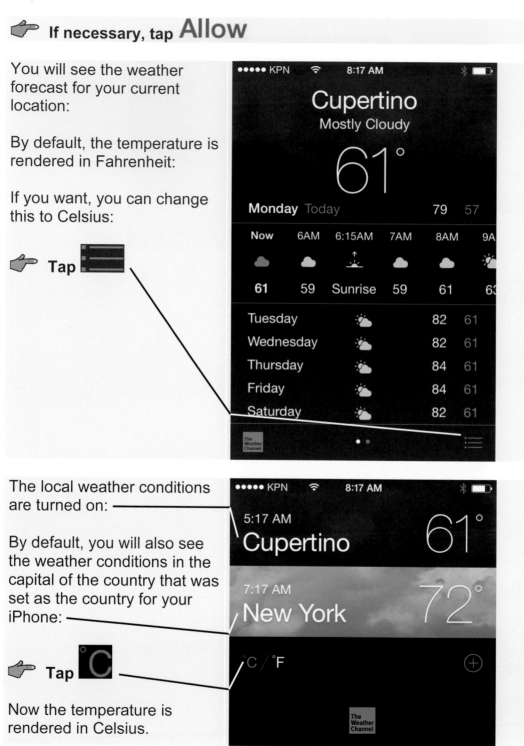

The local weather conditions are turned on:

By default, you will also see the weather conditions in the capital of the country that was set as the country for your iPhone:

Tap

Now the temperature is rendered in Celsius.

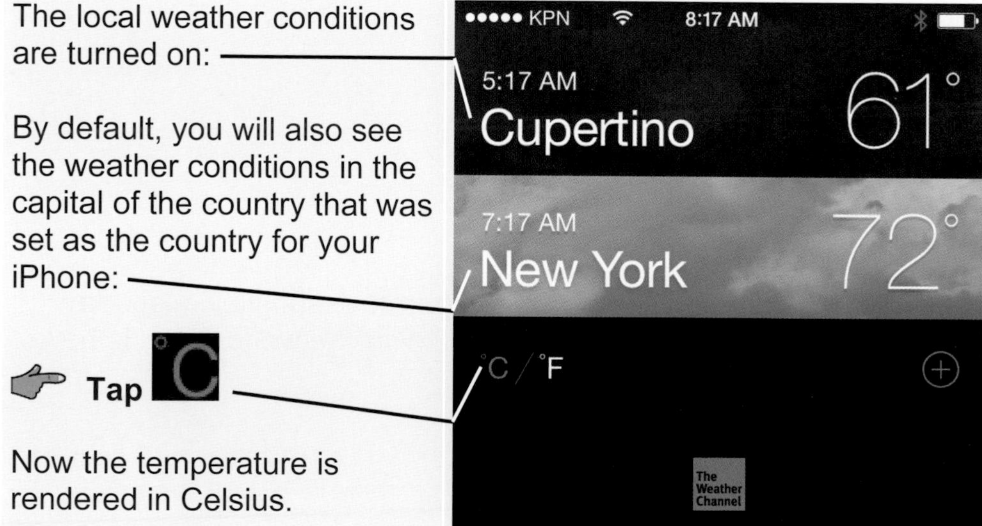

You can view the weather conditions in multiple locations. For example, the city that you are thinking about visiting on your next vacation:

Tap

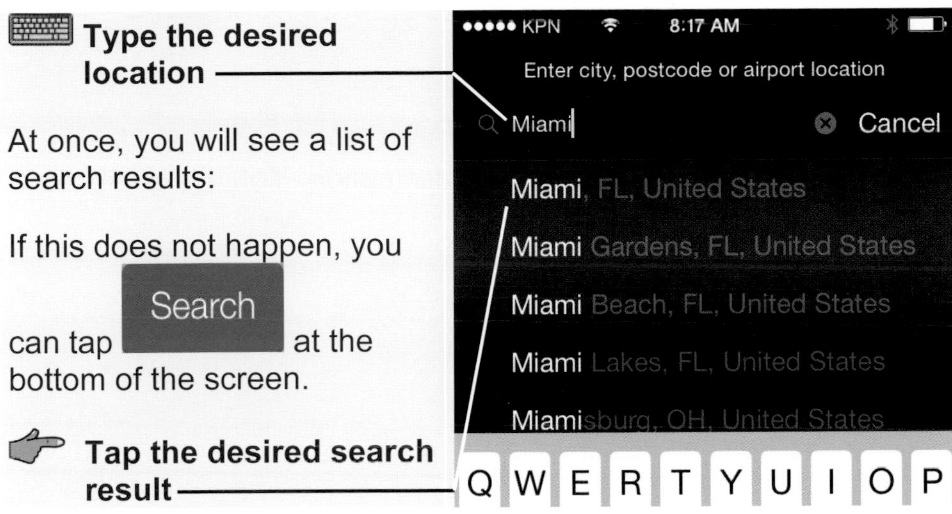

Type the desired location

At once, you will see a list of search results:

If this does not happen, you can tap Search at the bottom of the screen.

Tap the desired search result

In the next screen:

Tap Miami

You will see the current weather and the six-day forecast for the city you selected:

This is how you can leaf through the various cities you have selected:

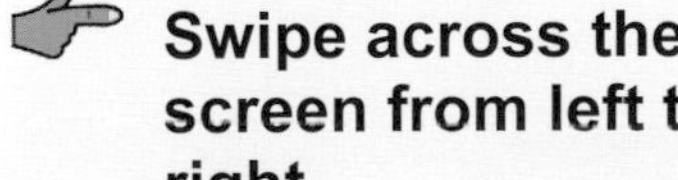

Swipe across the screen from left to right

You will see what the weather is like in the other city.

Swipe across the screen from left to right

Now you will see the weather conditions in one of the other selected cities. You can also swipe in the opposite direction to go back where you started.

Go to the home screen 10

6.9 Siri

The iPhone has a useful function with which you can give verbal instructions for the iPhone to execute, and you can also use it to ask for information. You are going to check if *Siri* has been turned on:

Open the *Settings* app 3

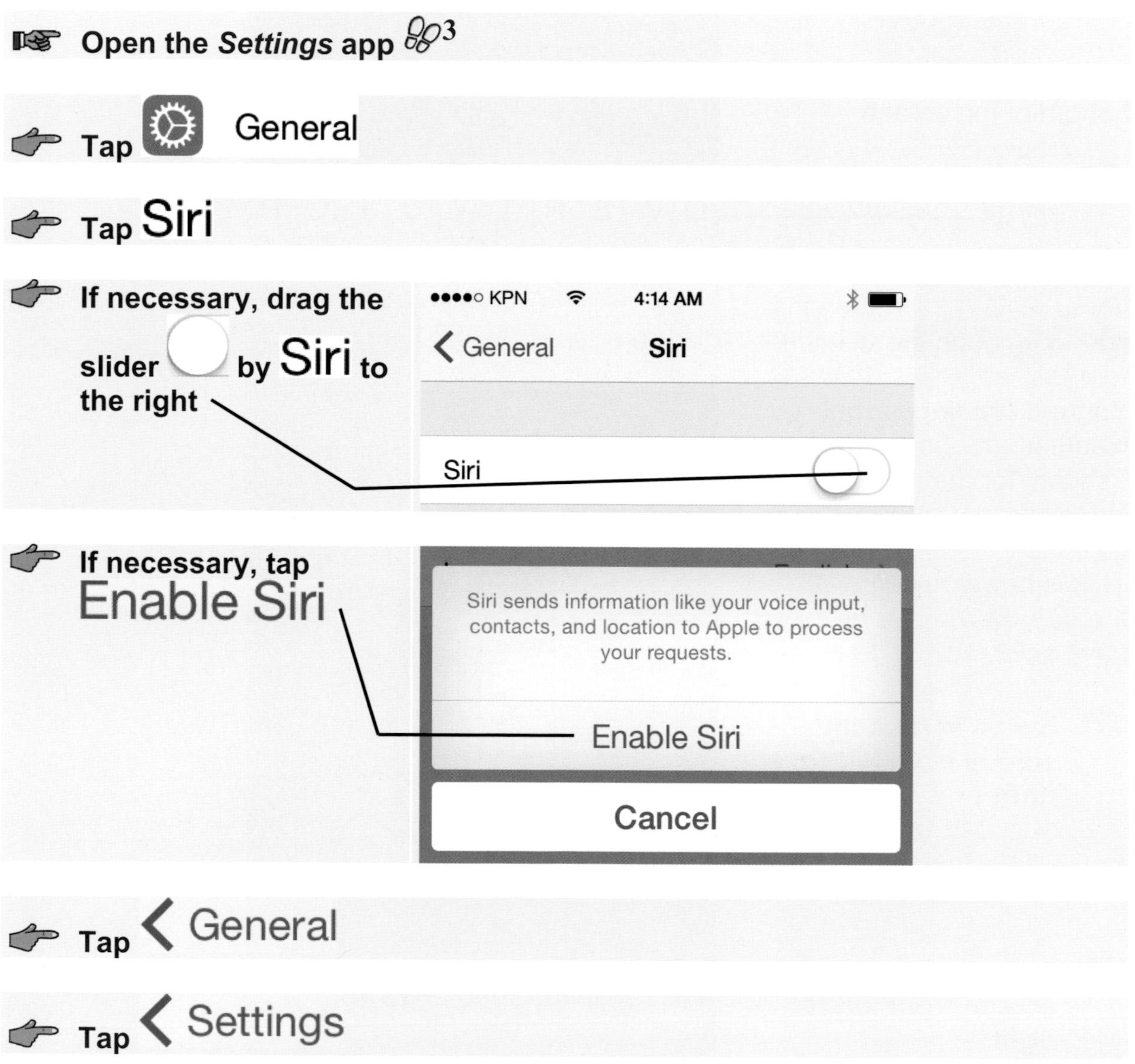

Tap General

Tap Siri

If necessary, drag the slider by Siri **to the right**

If necessary, tap Enable Siri

Tap < General

Tap < Settings

Go to the home screen 10

You open *Siri*:

Press and hold the Home button 

Siri opens and you can ask a question out loud:

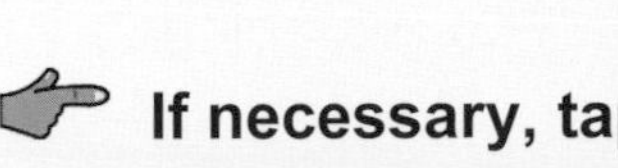

If necessary, tap

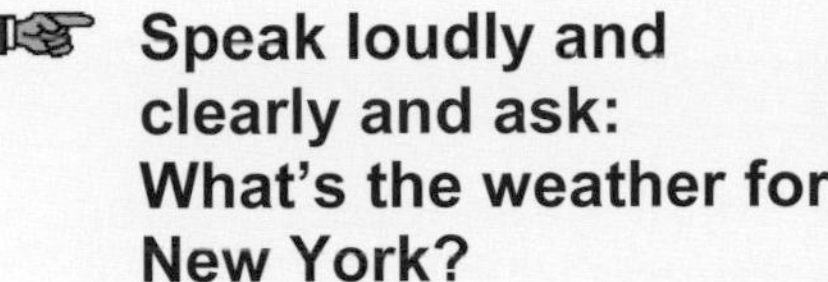

Speak loudly and clearly and ask: What's the weather for New York?

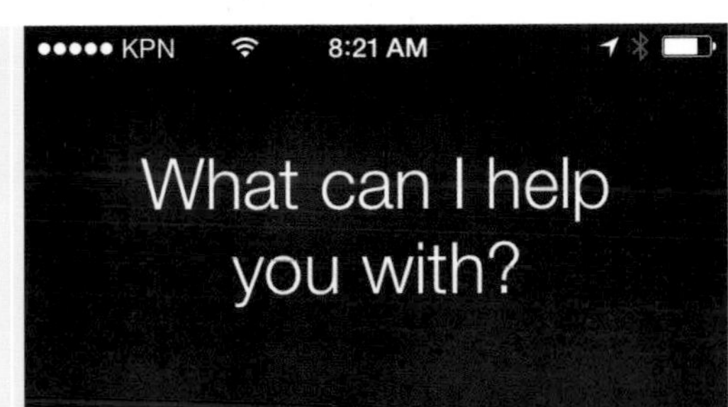

You will both see and hear the answer:

If you wish, you can tap the screen to open the weather forecast in the *Weather* app. For now this will not be necessary.

Pose another question:

Tap

Speak loudly and clearly and ask: Do I have any appointments today?

You will both see and hear the answer:

You can ask many more questions in the same way.

"Do I have any appointments today"
tap to edit
You don't have any appointments on your calendar for today.

 Go to the home screen 10

6.10 Notification Center

The messages you receive on your iPhone, such as new email messages or other messages set to be displayed on your iPhone, can all be viewed in the *Notification Center* in a neatly arranged list. This way, you can quickly see which messages you have recently received. This is how you open the *Notification Center*:

 **Swipe your finger across the screen, from top to bottom**

The *Notification Center* will be opened:

In this example, you can see the notification about a dinner on **Today** page:

You can also view all notifications or the missed notifications:

This is how you open a message:

Tap a message, for example, the event

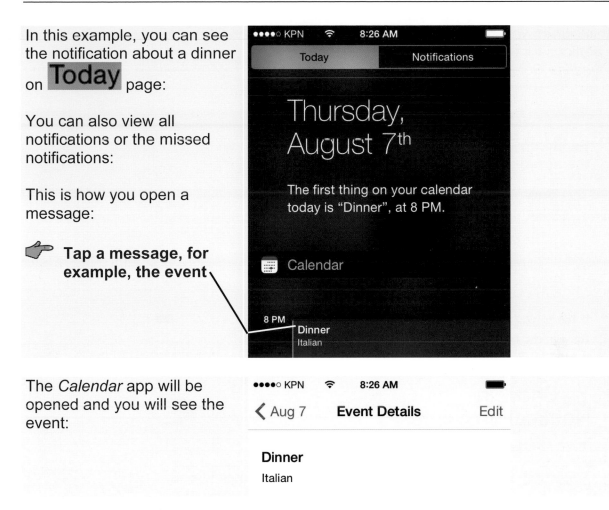

The *Calendar* app will be opened and you will see the event:

In this way you can view lots of things that are important for today.

Go to the home screen 10

Email messages will not be displayed in the *Notification Center* by default. You need to change the settings in the *Settings* app:

Open the *Settings* app 3

Swipe upwards over the screen

Tap Notifications

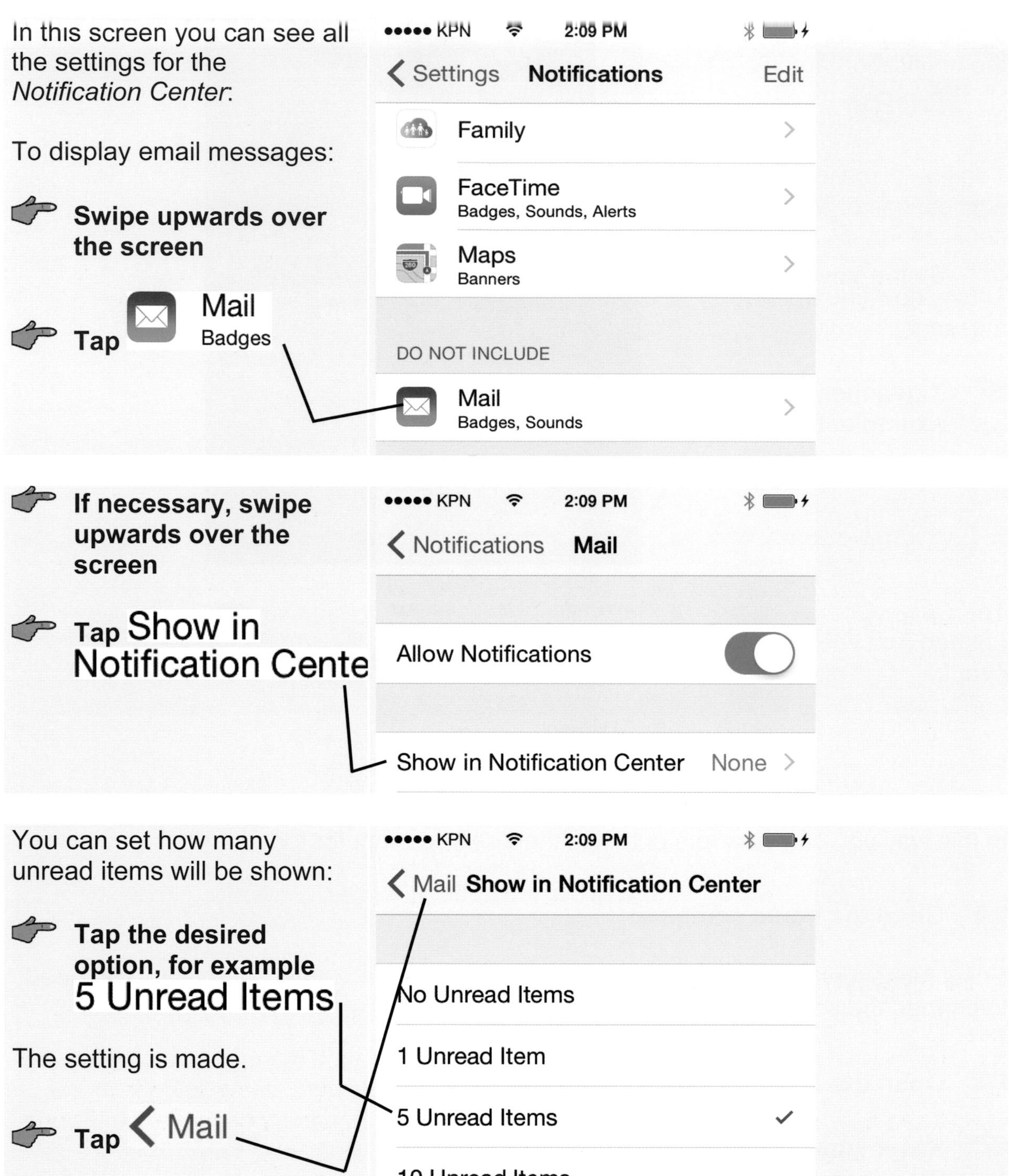

In this screen you can see all the settings for the *Notification Center*:

To display email messages:

- **Swipe upwards over the screen**
- **Tap** Mail Badges

- **If necessary, swipe upwards over the screen**
- **Tap** Show in Notification Cente

You can set how many unread items will be shown:

- **Tap the desired option, for example** 5 Unread Items

The setting is made.

- **Tap** Mail

Tap **< Notifications**

Tap **< Settings**

Go to the home screen 10

Swipe your finger across the screen, from top to bottom

The *Notification Center* will be opened:

Tap Notifications

In this example you will see a new email message has been received:

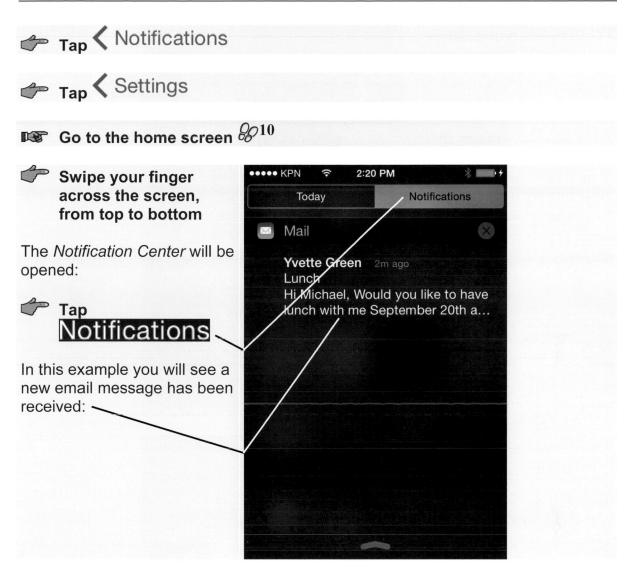

6.11 Disabling Apps

By now you have used a number of different apps on your iPhone. After using the app, you have always returned to the home screen. While you were doing this, the apps have not been closed. Actually, this is not really necessary because the iPhone hardly uses any power while it is locked. And it is very useful to be able to continue working where you left off when you unlock your iPhone again.

But if you want, you can close the apps. Here is how to do that:

Press the Home button twice

 **Drag the app window upwards**

The app will be closed.

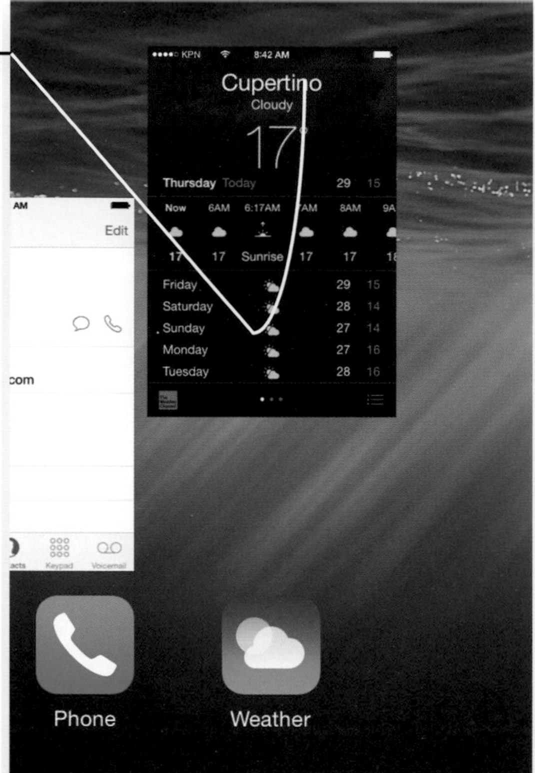

You will see the screen for the next app:

You can close the other apps in the same way:

Close the other apps too

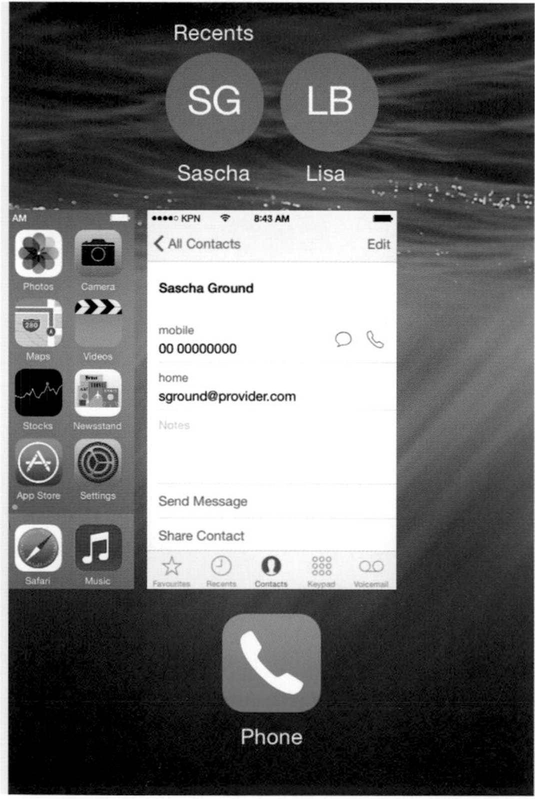

When all the apps have been closed:

Tap the screen

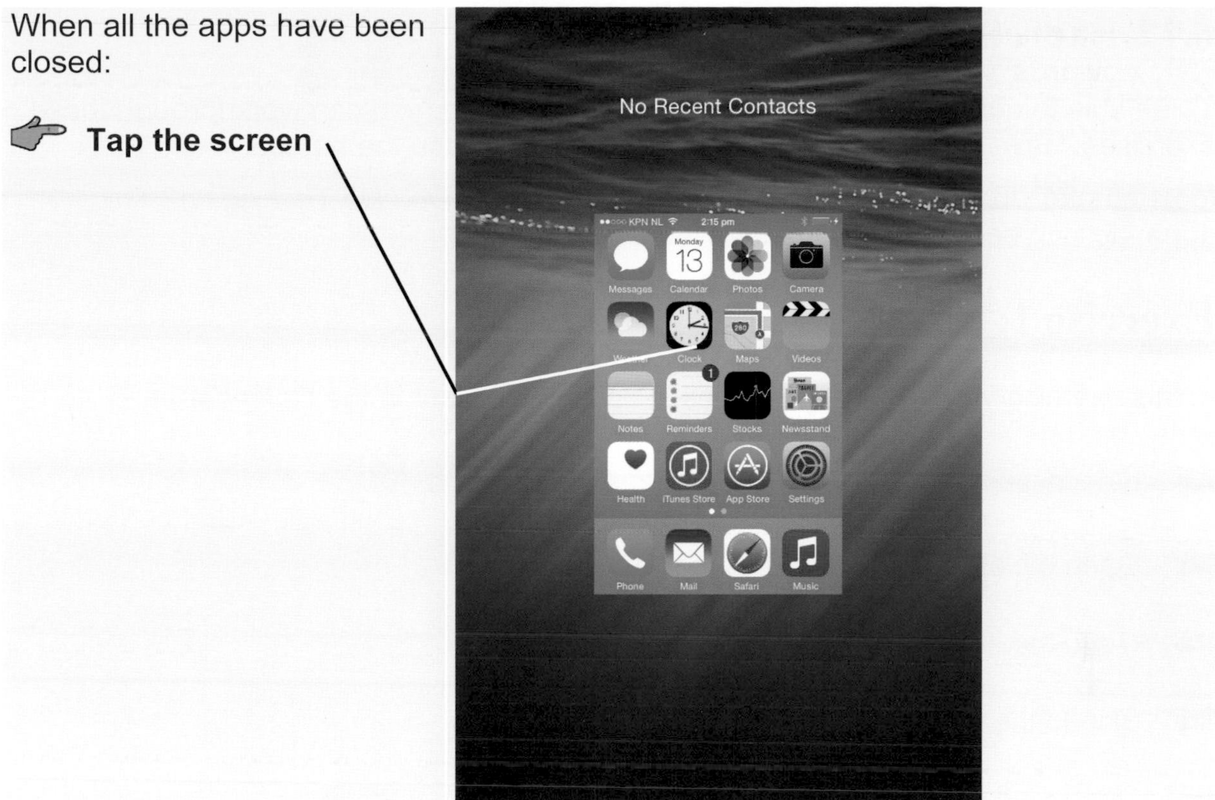

You will see the home screen again.

If you want, put the iPhone into sleep mode 2

In this chapter you have become acquainted with some of the standard apps installed on your iPhone. The following exercises will let you practice using these apps once more.

6.12 Exercises

To be able to quickly apply the things you have learned, you can work through these exercises. Have you forgotten how to do something? Use the numbers next to the footsteps 1 to look up the item in the appendix *How Do I Do That Again?* This appendix can be found at the end of the book.

Exercise 1: Calendar

In this exercise you are going to practice adding an event in the *Calendar* app.

- If necessary, wake the iPhone up from sleep mode. 1
- Open the *Calendar* app. 3
- Go to the current day. 62
- Skip to the day after tomorrow. 63
- Open a new event. 64
- Enter this information: 65
  name: `lunch`, location: `Lunchroom The Jolly Joker`.
- Adjust the time of the lunch. Start time: `12 p.m.`, end time `1.30 p.m.` 66
- Save the changes 67 and go to the home screen. 10

Exercise 2: Reminders

In this exercise you are going to practice adding a task and setting a reminder.

- Open the *Reminders* app. 3
- Add this task: `Call garage for appointment`. 69
- Set a reminder for this task for tomorrow morning at 11 a.m. 70
- Go to the home screen. 10

Exercise 3: Maps

In this exercise you are going to search for a location.

☞ Open the *Maps* app. [3]

☞ Establish your current location. [72]

☞ Change the view to Satellite. [73]

☞ Search for the Eiffel Tower, Paris. [74]

☞ Go to the home screen. [10]

Exercise 4: Spotlight

In this exercise you are going to practice searching with *Spotlight*.

☞ Open *Spotlight*. [78]

☞ Look for one of your contacts. [79]

☞ Tap the desired search result.

☞ Go to the home screen. [10]

☞ If you want, put the iPhone into sleep mode. [2]

6.13 Background Information

Dictionary	
Badge	A symbol that appears over an app, such as 1 indicating an alert, new message or other push notification.
Calendar	An app that lets you keep track of appointments and activities.
Contacts	An app for managing your contacts.
Event	An appointment in the *Calendar* app.
Facebook	Popular social network website.
Google Calendar	A service by *Google* which lets you maintain a calendar.
Google Contacts	A service by *Google* to manage contacts.
Maps	An app where you can look for locations and addresses, view satellite photos and plan routes.
Notification Center	An option that allows the display of push notifications on your iPhone. These are the messages sent to your device within certain approved apps even when they are not currently being used. In this way, you can quickly see, for example, the latest email messages you have received. You can change the frequency that your device scans for data to save battery life. You can open the *Notification Center* by dragging across the screen from top to bottom.
Reminders	In the *Reminders* app you can store things you need to remember and set the date and time for an alert to be triggered. You can create your own task lists, including dates and locations.
Siri	A function that lets you give verbal instructions for the iPhone to execute, and lets you ask the iPhone for information.
Spotlight	The search utility on the iPhone.
Synchronize	Literally this means: make even. You can synchronize your iPhone with the contents of your *iTunes Library* as well as your contacts.

- Continue on the next page -

Twitter	An Internet service with which users can publish short messages (tweets) of 140 characters or less. You can also add links to photos or websites in these messages.
Weather	An app for viewing current weather information as well as a six-day forecast. You can set it for your current location or any other location you want.

Source: User Guide iPhone, Wikipedia

Additional information

Many locations offer extra information; by tapping the > button you will see the address information, phone numbers and a link to the relevant website:

To close the window:

Tap < Map

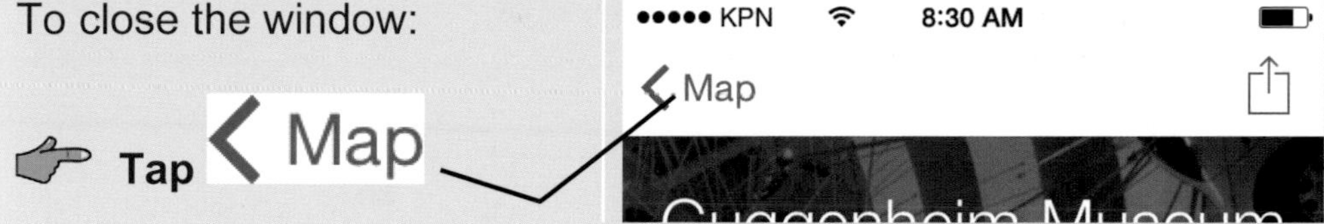

These are the function of the buttons of this window:

Directions to Here	Get directions to this location.
Directions from Here	Plan a route and get directions from this location to another location.
Create New Contact	Add this location to the *Contacts* list.
Add to Existing Contact	Add this location to a contact.
	Open a new message for the *Message* app, *Facebook*, *Twitter*, or an email containing information about this location.
Report a Problem	Use this button to report an incorrect listing, such as a wrong address or when a certain location is closed.

6.14 Tips

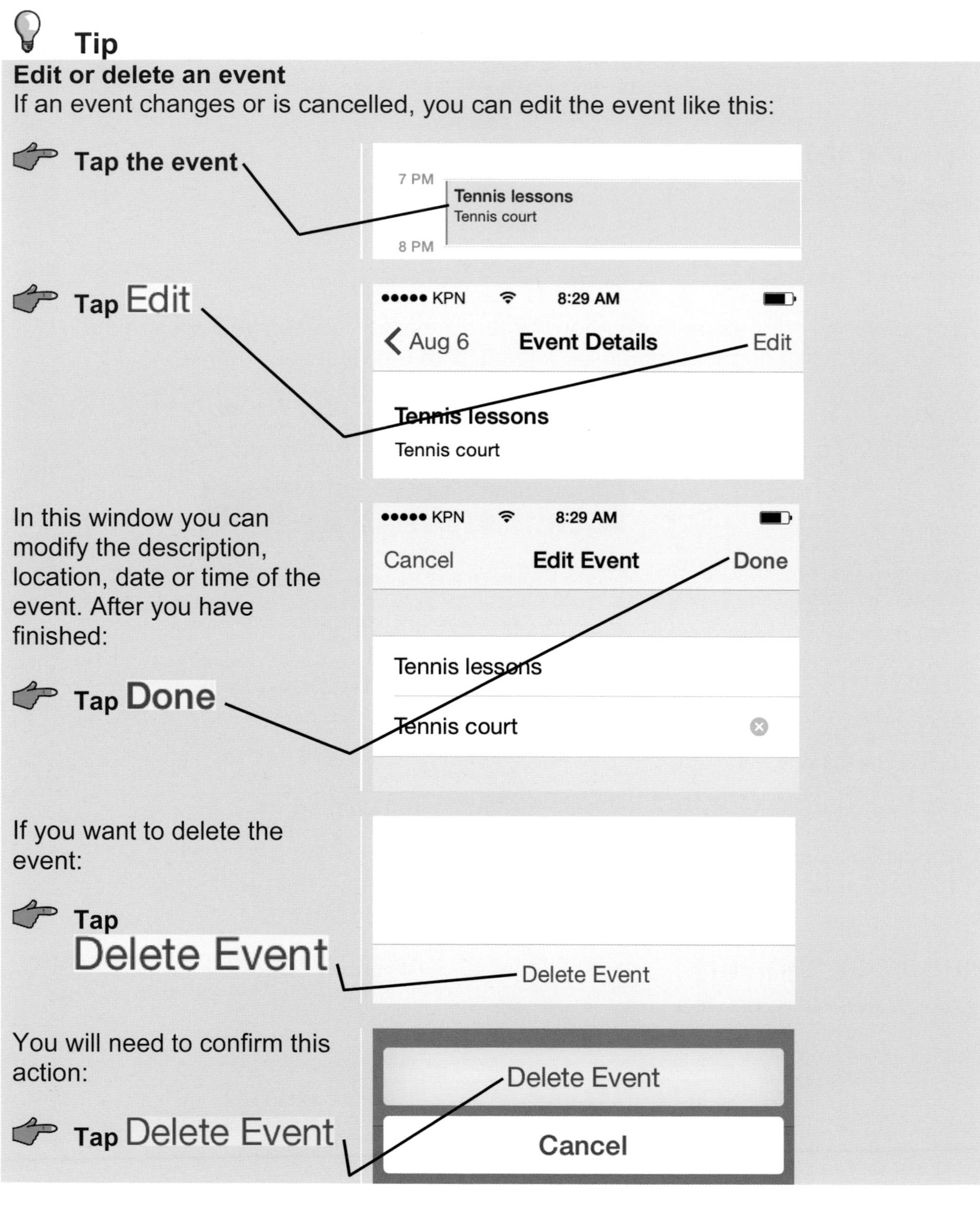

Tip

Edit or delete an event

If an event changes or is cancelled, you can edit the event like this:

- **Tap the event**
- **Tap** Edit

In this window you can modify the description, location, date or time of the event. After you have finished:

- **Tap** Done

If you want to delete the event:

- **Tap** Delete Event

You will need to confirm this action:

- **Tap** Delete Event

Tip

Add an event from an email message

Mail will recognize dates in email messages and will link them to your calendar. When a date has been identified, you can quickly add an event to your calendar:

- **Tap the date, for example** September 20th 12.30

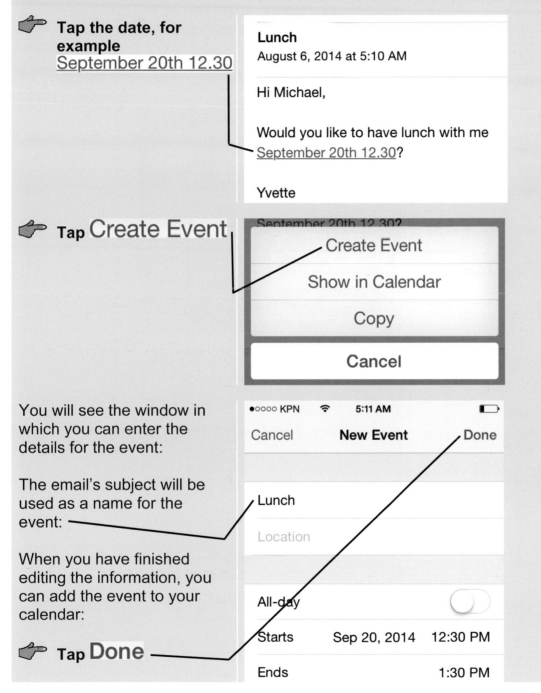

Lunch
August 6, 2014 at 5:10 AM
Hi Michael,
Would you like to have lunch with me September 20th 12.30?
Yvette

- **Tap** Create Event

You will see the window in which you can enter the details for the event:

The email's subject will be used as a name for the event:

When you have finished editing the information, you can add the event to your calendar:

- **Tap** Done

Tip

The Contacts app

In *Chapter 2 Making and Receiving Calls* you learned how to add and edit contacts with the *Phone* app. There is however, another standard app on your iPhone for managing contacts, called the *Contacts* app. Here you will see all the contacts on your iPhone, including the people you added if you have worked through the previous chapter:

 **Swipe across the home screen from right to left**

You will see a second page with app icons:

Tap Extras

You will see the contents of the *Extras* folder:

Tap Contacts

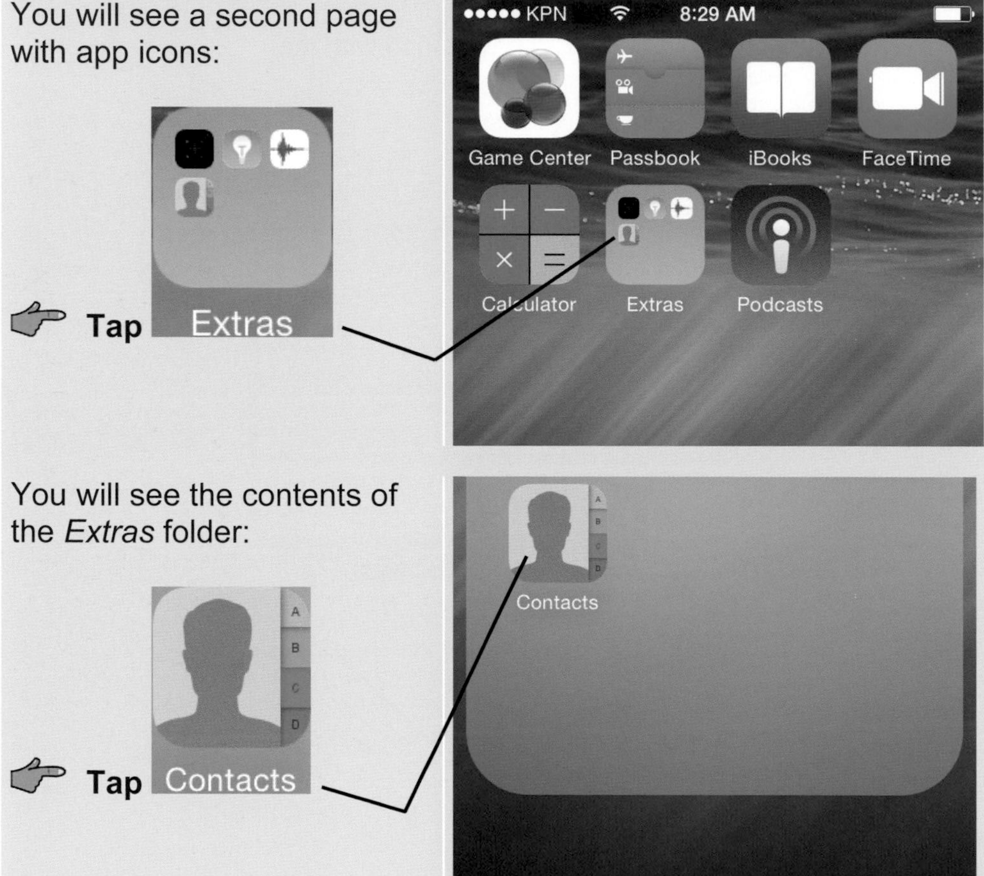

You will see your contacts. In the *Contacts* app you can add, edit and delete contacts in the same way as in the *Phone* app.

Tip

Display traffic information

You can display the traffic conditions on the main roads and highways on the map:

Tap , Show Traffic

You will see the traffic information marked by the red line:

To see information about the road work, you can tap :

Please note: you are not able to see traffic information when you are viewing the map in Satellite.

 **Tip**

Display Google, Hotmail, Outlook.com or Yahoo! calendar and contacts

Do you use *Google*, *Hotmail, Outlook.com* or *Yahoo! Calendar* to keep track of appointments and activities? Or do you manage your contacts in one of these accounts? If you have set up your *Gmail, Hotmail, Outlook.com* or *Yahoo!* account on the iPhone, you can set your account to display your calendar or contacts on the iPhone too:

Open the *Settings* app 3

Swipe upwards the screen

Tap Mail, Contacts, Calendars

In this example an *Outlook* account is chosen to display the calendar:

To open the account settings:

Tap Outlook Mail

By Calendars, **drag the slider to the left**

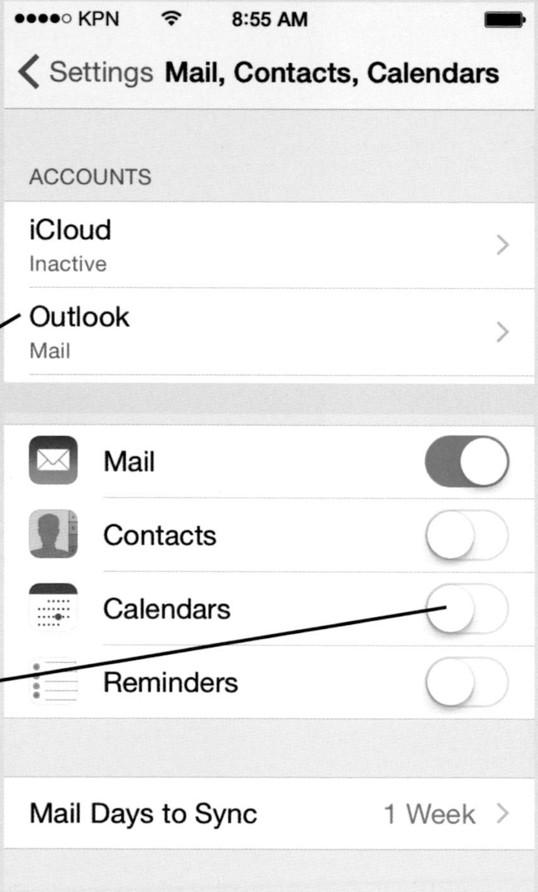

●●●●○ KPN 8:55 AM
Settings **Mail, Contacts, Calendars**

ACCOUNTS

iCloud
Inactive

Outlook
Mail

Mail
Contacts
Calendars
Reminders

Mail Days to Sync 1 Week

- Continue on the next page -

You may see this message:

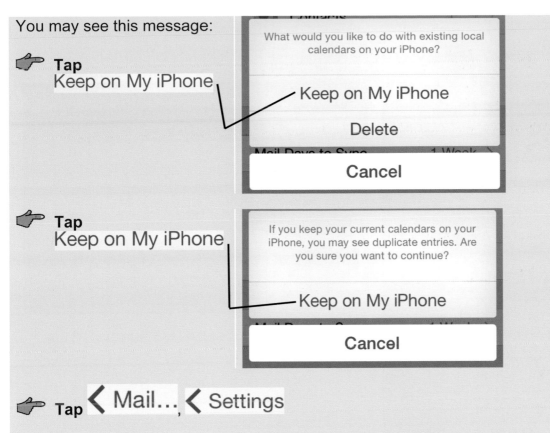

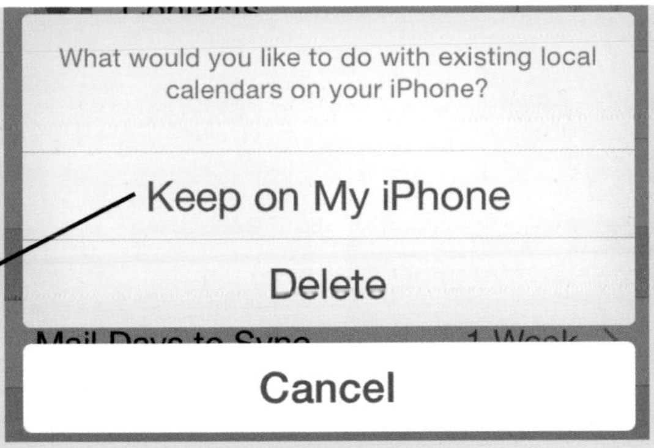

Tap Keep on My iPhone

What would you like to do with existing local calendars on your iPhone?

Keep on My iPhone

Delete

Cancel

Tap Keep on My iPhone

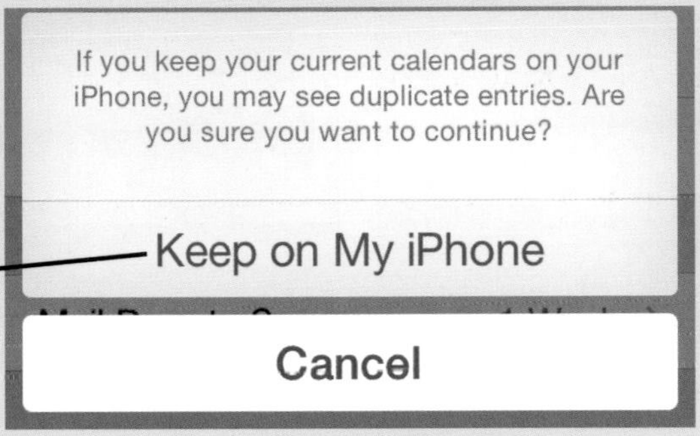

If you keep your current calendars on your iPhone, you may see duplicate entries. Are you sure you want to continue?

Keep on My iPhone

Cancel

Tap < Mail..., < Settings

Now the events from the calendar will be displayed in the *Calendar* app on your iPhone.

Tip

Calculator

There is bound to be a time when a calculator can come in handy. This is one of the standard apps on your iPhone. This is how you open the *Calculator* app:

Swipe across the home screen from right to left

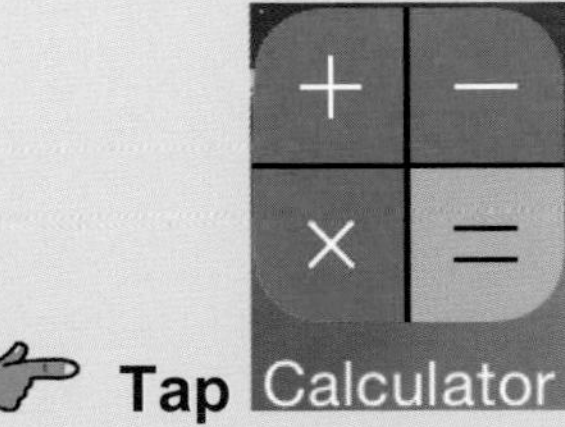

Tap

You will see the calculator in the upright position. This calculator works the same way as a regular calculator.

- Continue on the next page -

You can also turn it into a scientific calculator:

Turn the iPhone sideways

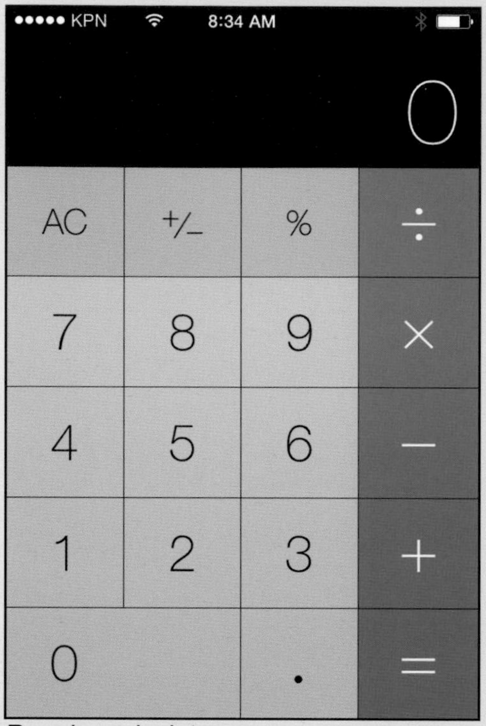

Regular calculator

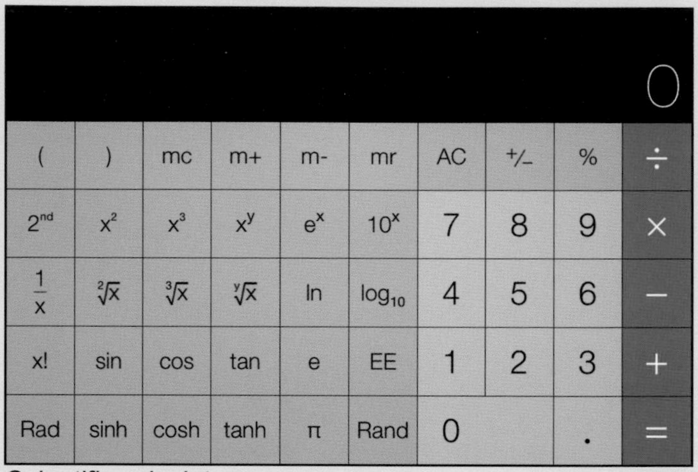

Scientific calculator

You can close the *Calculator* app:

Go to the home screen 10

Tip

Twitter and Facebook
If you use *Twitter* or *Facebook*, you can also set up your account on your iPhone. In this example *Twitter* is used:

Open the *Settings* app 3

Swipe upwards over the screen

Tap 

- Continue on the next page -

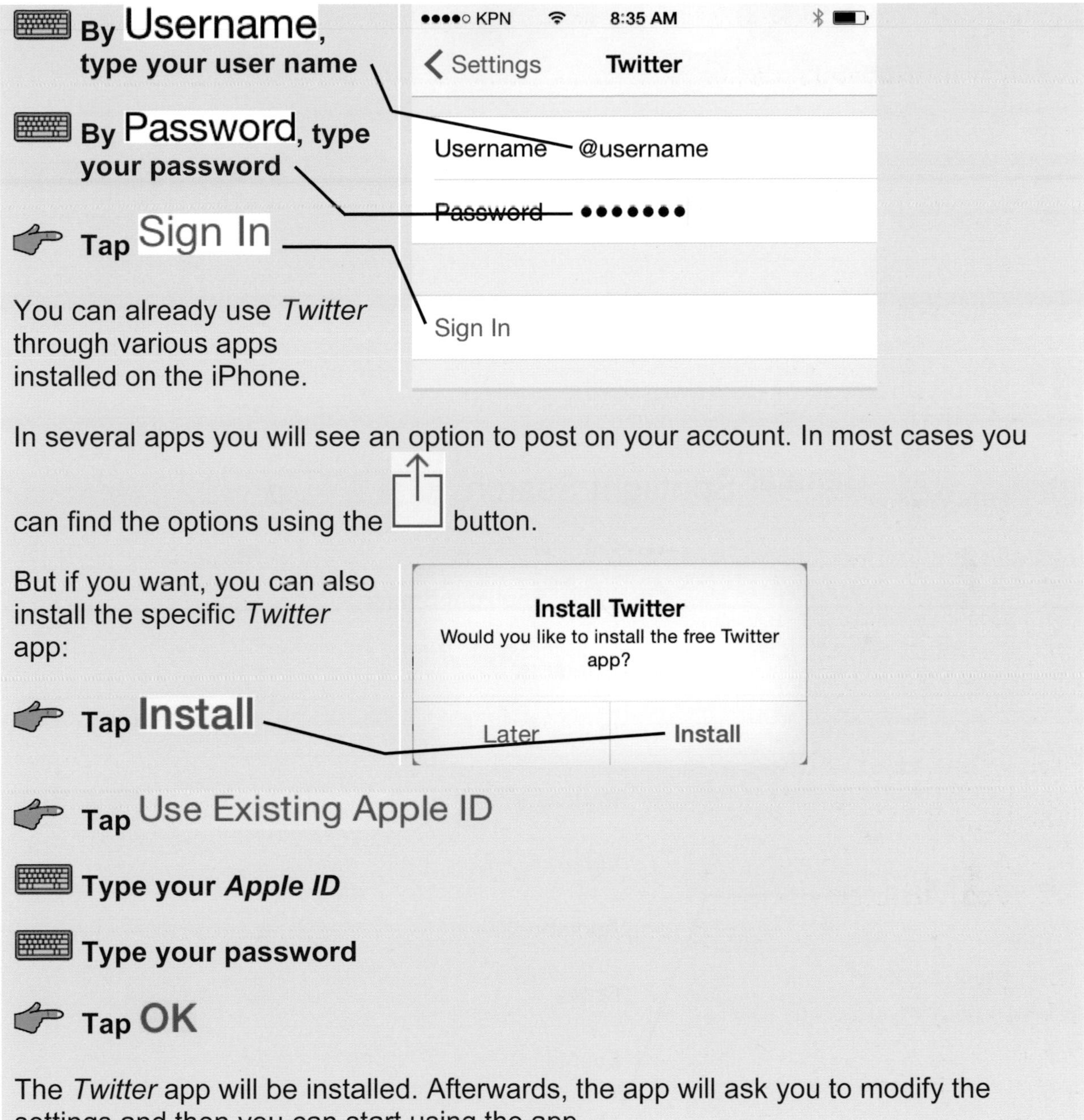

By Username**, type your user name**

By Password**, type your password**

Tap Sign In

You can already use *Twitter* through various apps installed on the iPhone.

In several apps you will see an option to post on your account. In most cases you can find the options using the button.

But if you want, you can also install the specific *Twitter* app:

Tap Install

Tap Use Existing Apple ID

Type your *Apple ID*

Type your password

Tap OK

The *Twitter* app will be installed. Afterwards, the app will ask you to modify the settings and then you can start using the app.

Tip

Settings for Spotlight

By default, *Spotlight* will search all items on the iPhone. If you want, you can adjust the settings for *Spotlight*:

Open the *Settings* app 3

If necessary, tap Settings

Swipe upwards or downwards the screen

Tap General, Spotlight Search

You will see the standard items that are searched by *Spotlight*. For example, if you do not want to search your email messages:

If necessary, swipe upwards over the screen

Tap Mail

The checkmark will disappear:

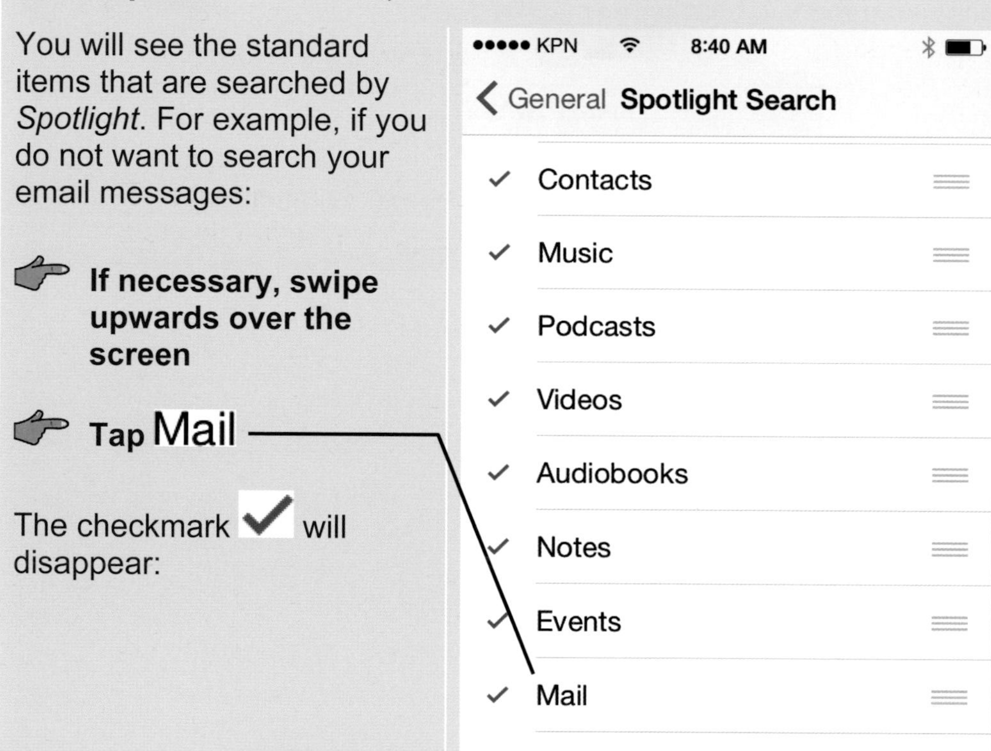

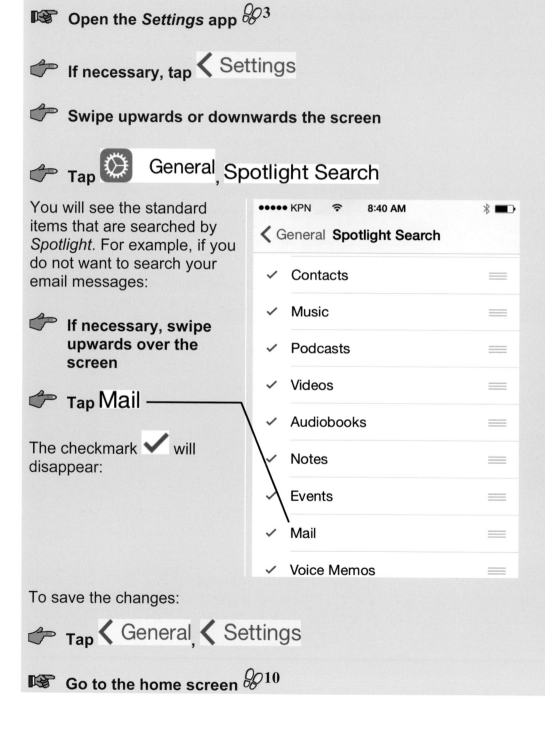

To save the changes:

Tap General, Settings

Go to the home screen 10

7. Downloading and Managing Apps

In the previous chapters you have become acquainted with a number of the standard apps installed on your iPhone. But that is just the beginning, there's so much more to your iPhone than the basics. In the *App Store* you will find thousands of apps, free of charge or for a small fee, which you can download and install.

There are too many apps to list them all in this chapter. Apps for news, magazines, games, recipes, photo editing, sports results: you name it, there is bound to be an app available that interests you!

In this chapter you will learn how to download free apps in the *App Store*. If you want to download apps that charge a fee, you can pay for them safely with an *iTunes Gift Card*. This is a prepaid card available in a variety of different venues. You can also link a credit card to your *Apple ID*.

As soon as your apps are installed, you can arrange them on your iPhone in any way you want. You can also create space-saving folders that can hold up to a dozen similar apps. If you are no longer happy with a particular app, you can delete it.

In this chapter you will learn how to:

- open the *App Store*;
- download and install a free app;
- redeem an *iTunes Gift Card*;
- buy and install an app;
- sign out from the *App Store*;
- move apps;
- store apps in a folder;
- delete apps.

Please note:

To follow the examples in this chapter you will need to have an *Apple ID*. If you have not created an *Apple ID* when you started to use your iPhone, you can learn how to do that in the *Bonus Chapter Creating an Apple ID*. In *Appendix B Opening Bonus Chapters* you can read how to open a bonus chapter.

7.1 Downloading and Installing a Free App

In the *App Store* you will find thousands of apps that can be used on your iPhone. This is how you open the *App Store*:

☞ **Wake the iPhone up from sleep mode** 𝒪𝒪1

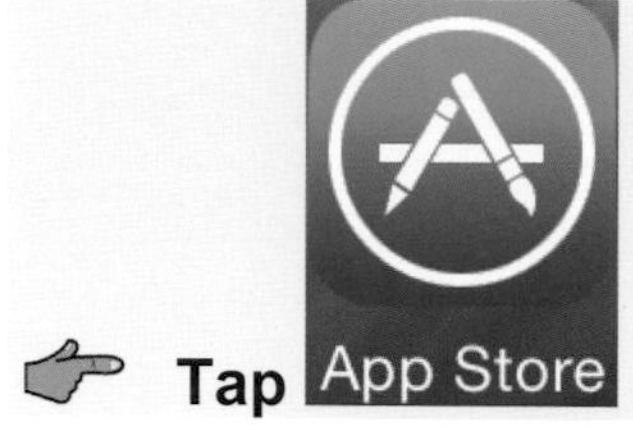

☛ **Tap** App Store

You will see the Featured page, where attention is paid to a number of new apps.

You can use the search function to look for a popular free app:

At the bottom of the screen:

☛ **Tap** Search

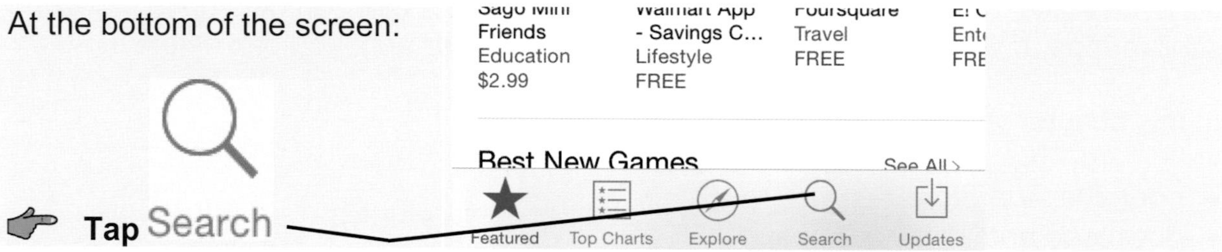

Maybe a screen about *Apple Apps* appears. You can ignore the screen for now:

☛ **If necessary, tap** Not Now

☛ **Tap the search box**

⌨ **Type:** `the weather channel`

Right away, you will see a few suggestions:

☛ **Tap** the weather channel and weather.c...

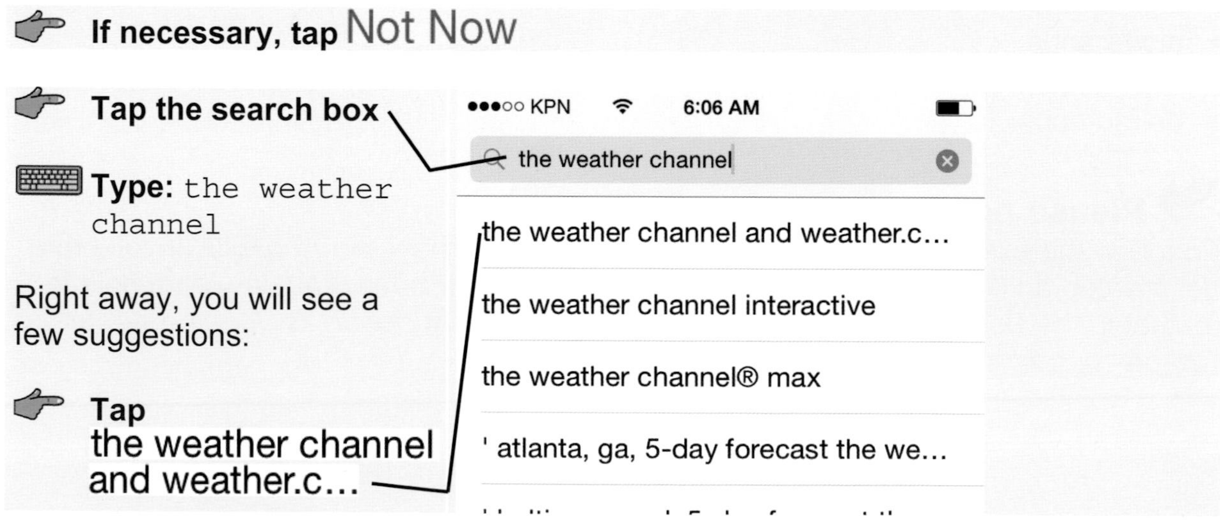

The page with the app is now shown:

If you prefer, you can show a page with additional information about the app first by tapping the image.

This is how you download the app:

☞ **Tap** FREE

☞ **Tap** INSTALL

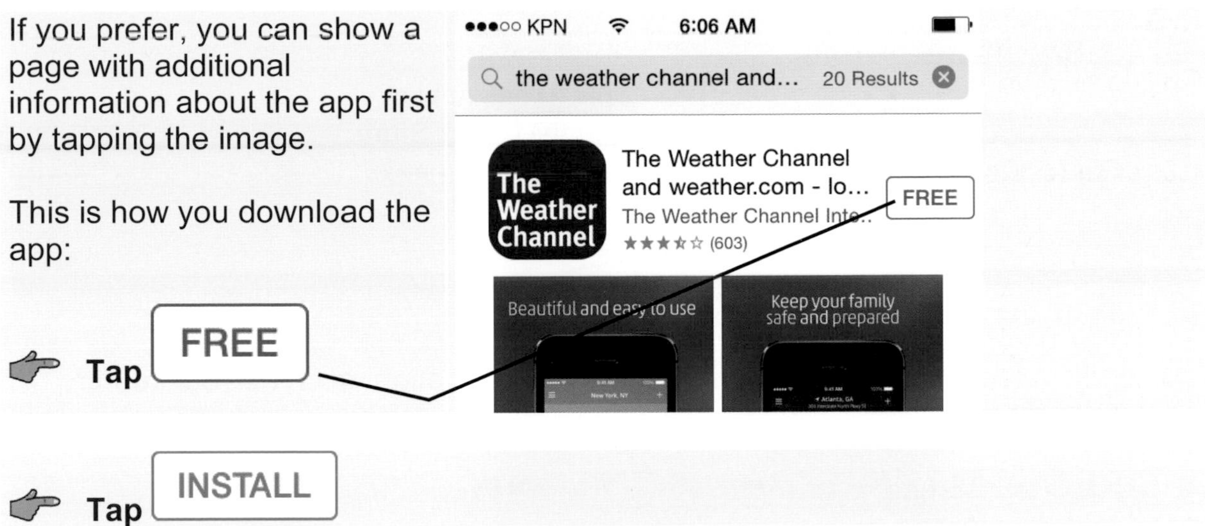

You need to sign in with your *Apple ID* in order to install the app. If you signed out, you will see this window:

☞ **If necessary, tap** Use Existing Apple ID

⌨ **Type your *Apple ID***

⌨ **Type your password**

☞ **Tap** OK

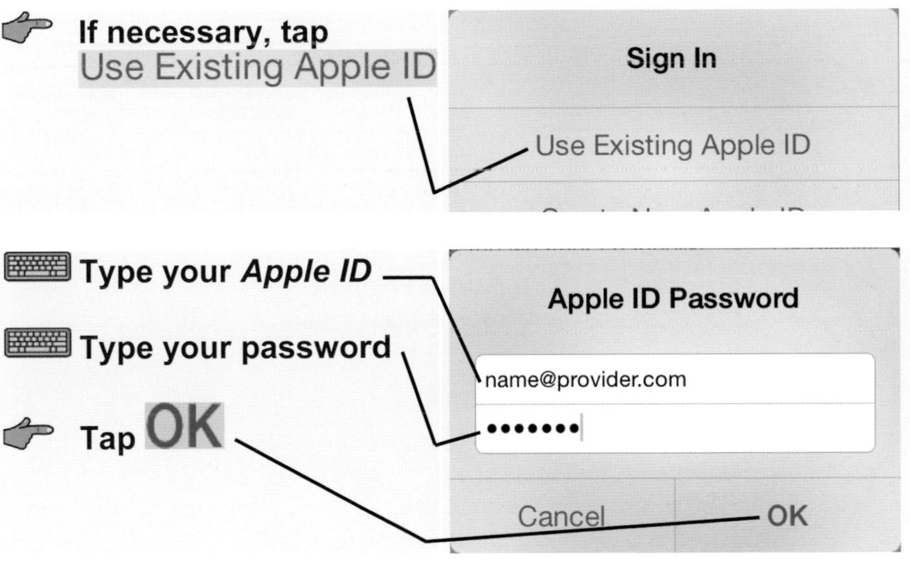

If you have already used the *App Store* you can continue on page 224. If you have not yet downloaded an app in the *App Store* previously, you will see a message:

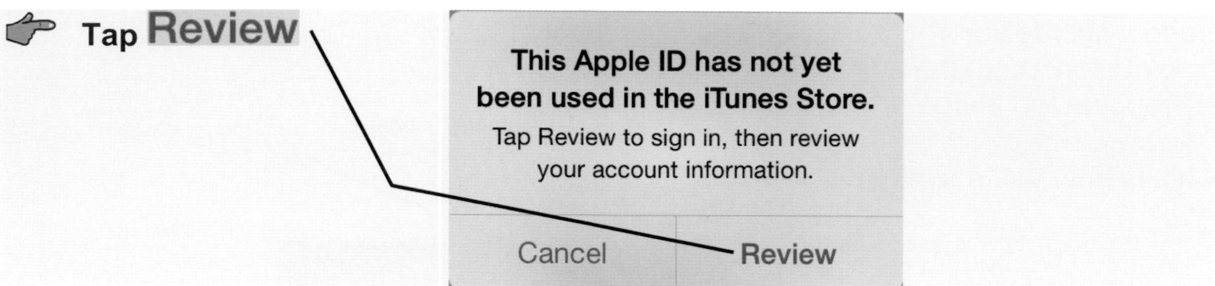

Your *Apple ID* needs to be completed with extra information, such as your country and your home address:

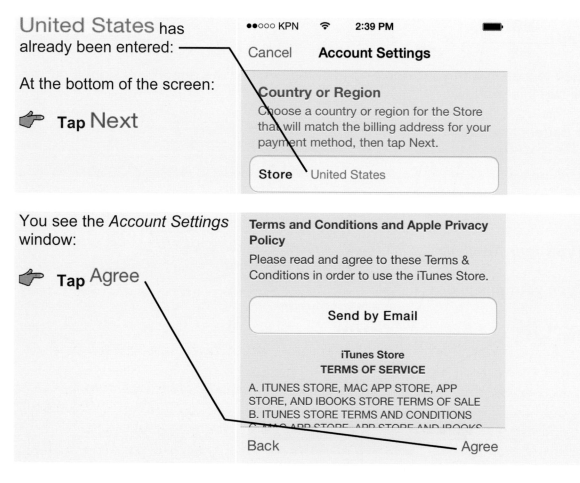

United States has already been entered:

At the bottom of the screen:

Tap Next

You see the *Account Settings* window:

Tap Agree

Once more, you need to confirm that you agree to the general terms and conditions:

Tap Agree

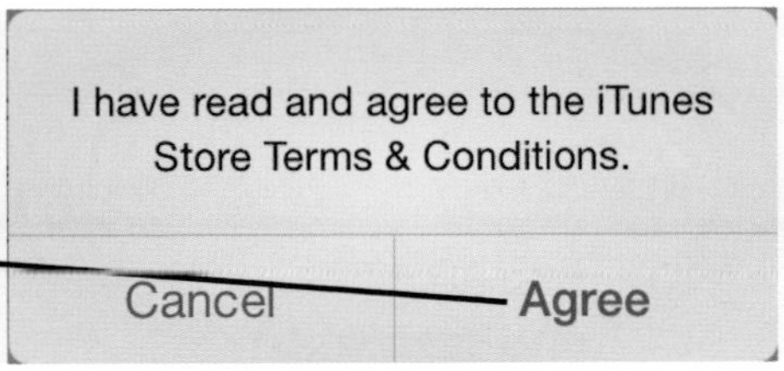

Type the necessary information

Tap Next

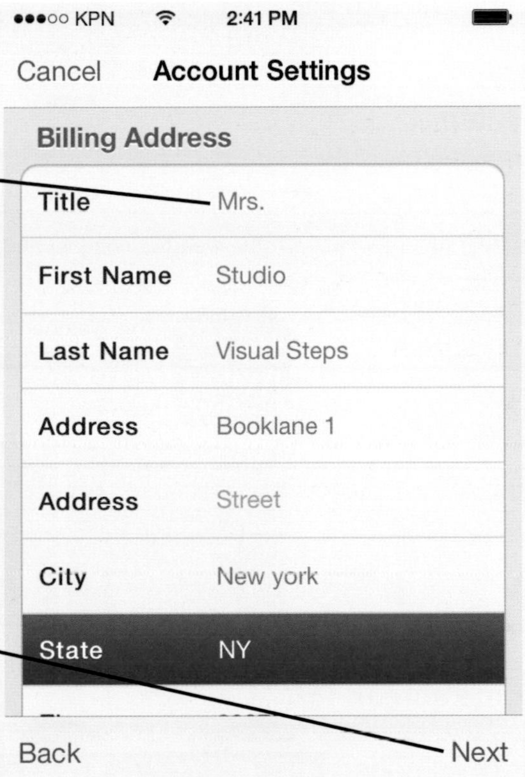

HELP! I am asked to enter payment information and I do not want to do that.

Apple would like you to link your payment method to your *Apple ID*. If you do not want to this, you can select **None** at the top of the window, by **Billing Information**. If you cannot select this option and you do not want to enter any credit card information, you can link an *iTunes Gift Card* to your *Apple ID*. You can fill in the gift card code by **iTunes Gift Cards and iTunes Gifts**. We will tell you more about this subject in the next section.

Your *Apple ID* is ready:

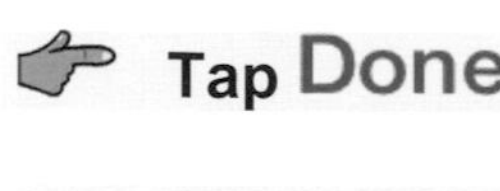

Tap Done

If necessary, tap FREE

The FREE button will turn into INSTALL.

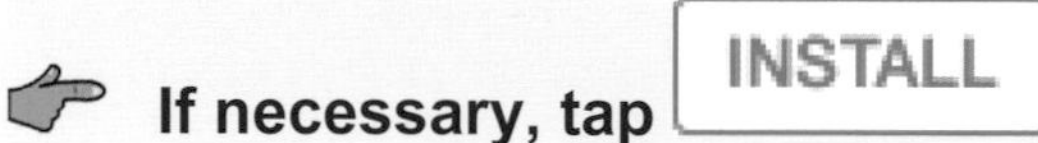

If necessary, tap INSTALL

The app is installed when you see the button OPEN. You do not need to open the app right now.

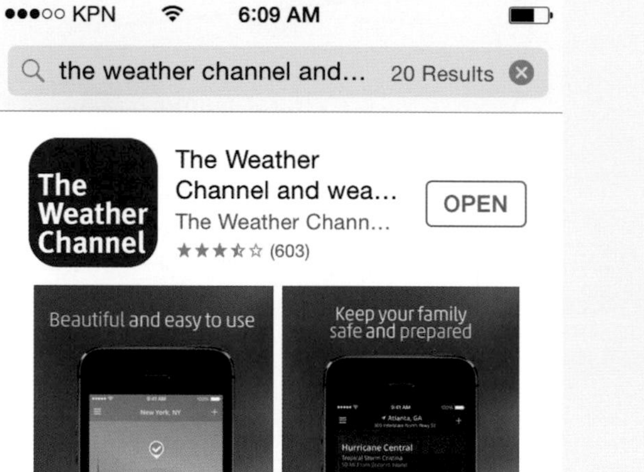

Go to the home screen 10

You will see the second page with the app:

You can go back to the home page:

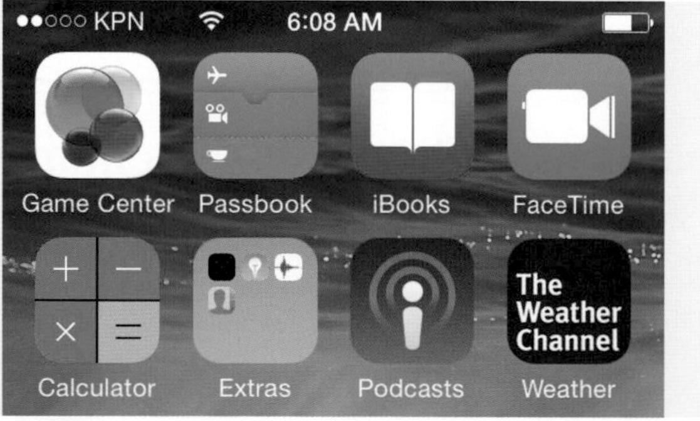

Press the Home button 

7.2 The iTunes Gift Card

The *iTunes Gift Card* is a prepaid card with which you can buy items in the *App Store.* This means you will not need a credit card to buy things.

 **Tip**

iTunes Gift Card

You can get an *iTunes Gift Card* with various denominations, starting at $15. You can purchase these cards at the *Apple Online Store*, at your *Apple* retailer, but also at thousands of other retailers across the USA, the UK and Australia. You can also get the *iTunes Gift Card* at www.instantitunescodes.com.

This web store allows you to pay online and you will receive the code for the card by email instantly. *iTunes Gift Cards* purchased at this store are only valid in the US *iTunes Store*.

 **Please note:**

To be able to follow the examples in the next section, you need to have an *iTunes Gift Card* available. If you do not (yet) have such a card, you can just read the text.

☞ **Open the *App Store*** 80

At the bottom of the page you will find the link for redeeming an *iTunes Gift Card*:

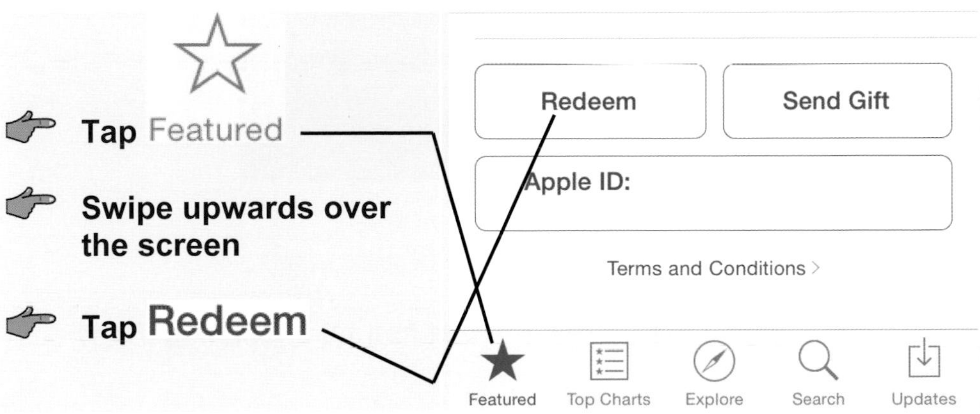

Before you can redeem the code, you need to sign in with your *Apple ID*:

☞ **Sign in with your *Apple ID*** 87

Now you will see a window where you can enter the code for your *iTunes Gift Card*.

You will find the code under the scratch layer on the back of the card:

☞ **Carefully remove the scratch layer**

👉 **Tap** You can also enter yo

Now you will see a code composed of 16 digits and letters, which you can enter:

⌨ **Type the code**

Although the code on the *iTunes Gift Card* contains capital letters, you can just type lower-case letters.

👉 **Tap** Redeem

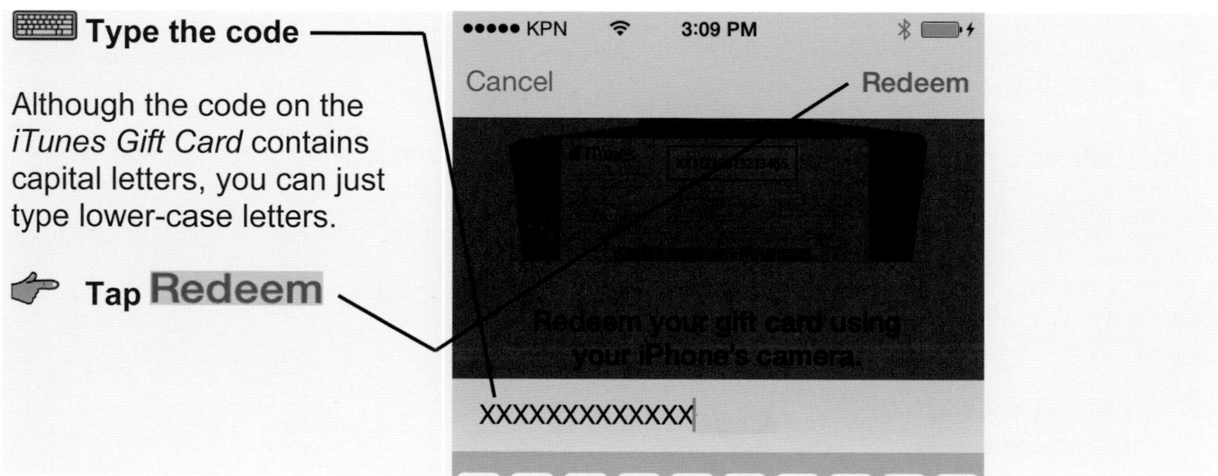

You will see a confirmation and the amount of the credit that has been added to your *Apple ID*.

7.3 Buying and Installing an App

Now that you have purchased prepaid credit for your *Apple ID*, you will be able to buy apps in the *App Store*. Previously, you used the search box to look for an app. But you can also view the most popular apps:

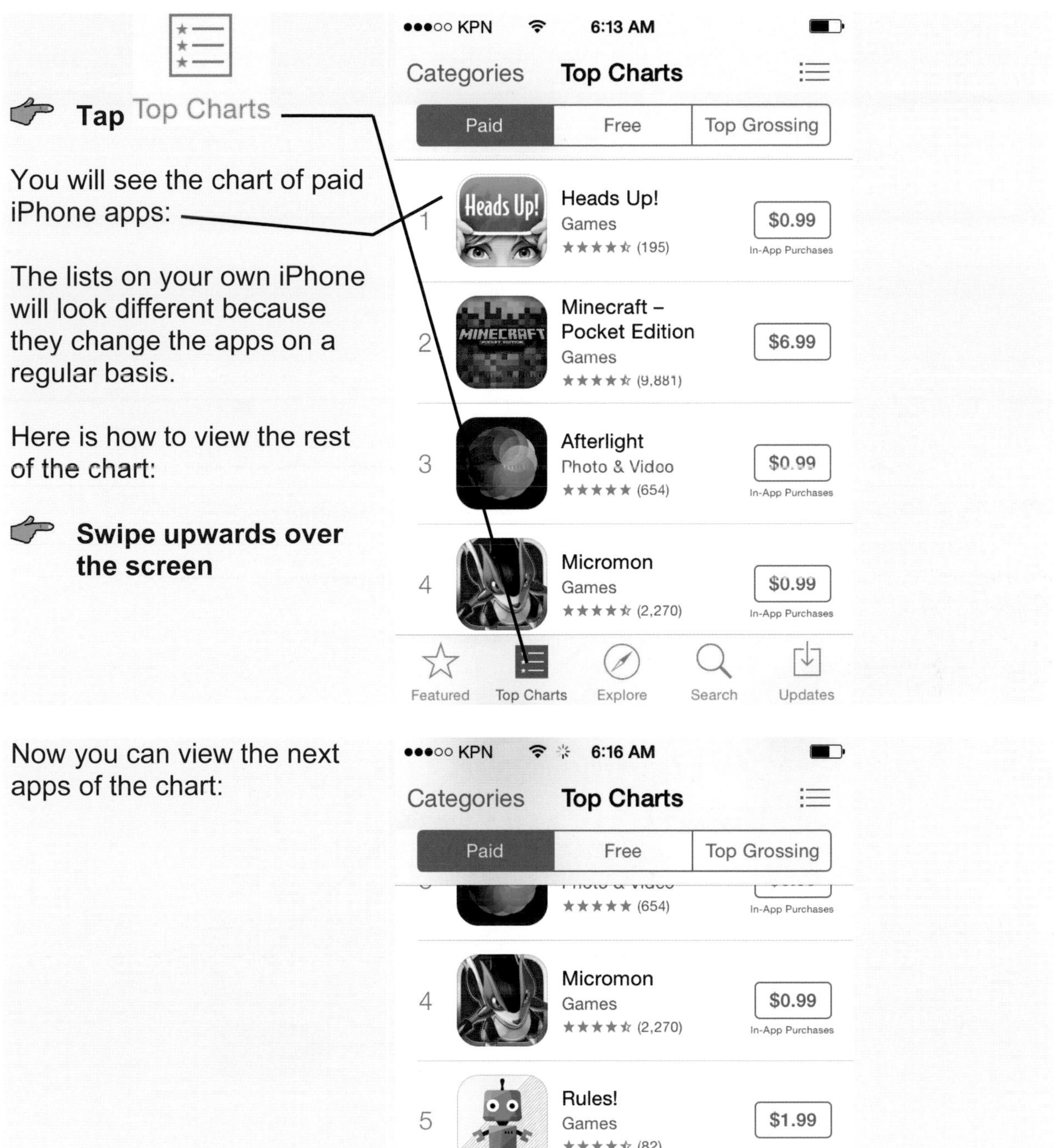

☞ **Tap** Top Charts

You will see the chart of paid iPhone apps:

The lists on your own iPhone will look different because they change the apps on a regular basis.

Here is how to view the rest of the chart:

☞ **Swipe upwards over the screen**

Now you can view the next apps of the chart:

Please note:

In the following example we go through the steps of actually purchasing an app. You will need to have redeemed an *iTunes Gift Card* or have a credit card linked to your *Apple ID*. You can decide for yourself whether you actually want to purchase this app now or simply read the instructions so you will be able to purchase an app later on when you are ready.

In this example we will purchase the *Weather+* app. First we will search for this app:

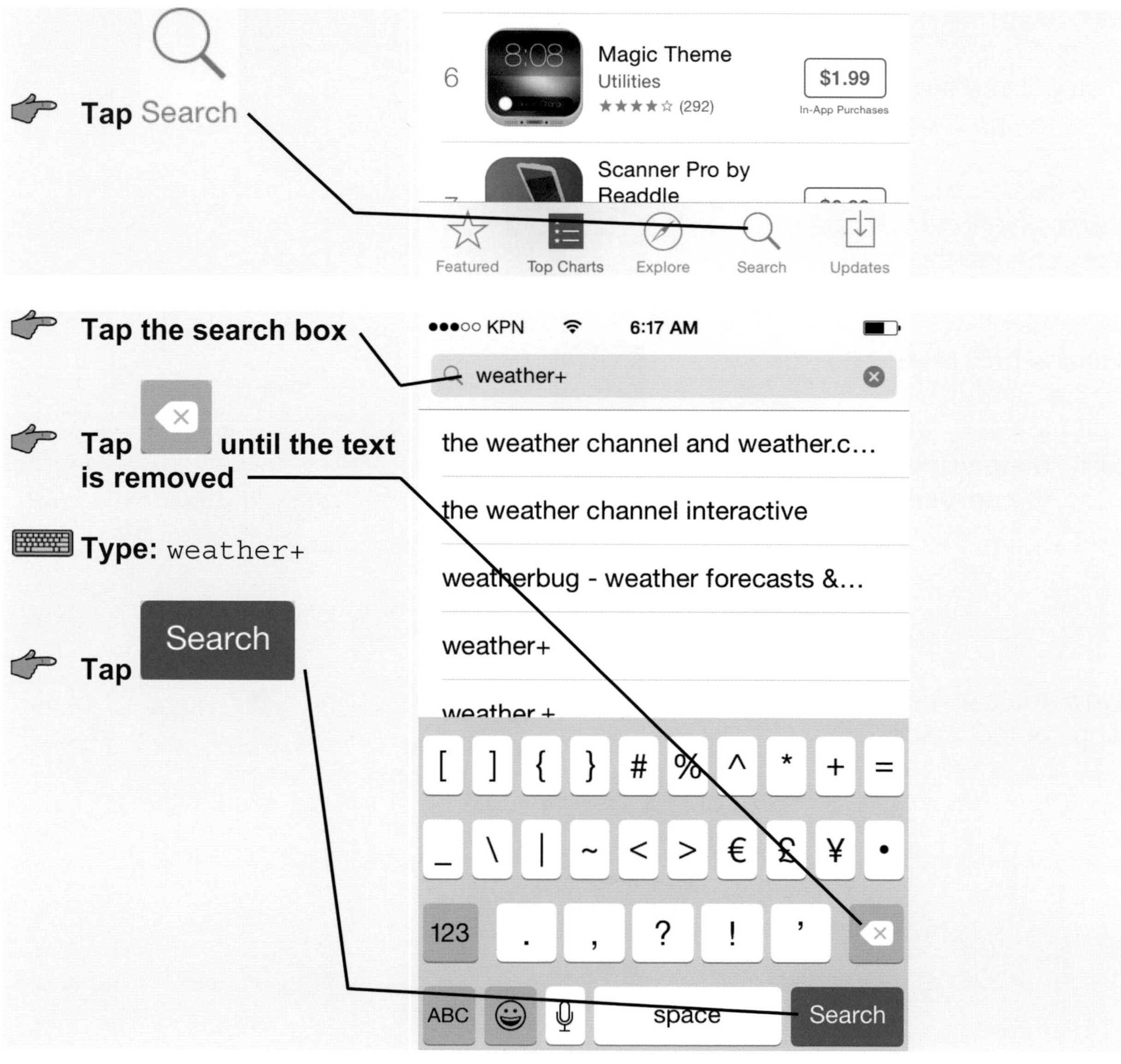

You will see the app:

Please note: choose the paid version with $0.99. Not the free version.

If you want to buy the app:

Tap $0.99

The $0.99 button will turn into BUY.

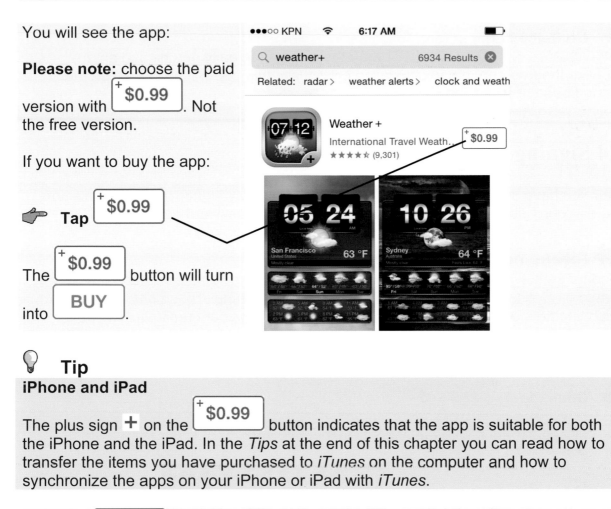

Tip

iPhone and iPad

The plus sign + on the $0.99 button indicates that the app is suitable for both the iPhone and the iPad. In the *Tips* at the end of this chapter you can read how to transfer the items you have purchased to *iTunes* on the computer and how to synchronize the apps on your iPhone or iPad with *iTunes*.

Tap BUY

Before you can buy the app, you may have to sign in again with your *Apple ID*. This is a security measure, to prevent someone else from using your credit card to buy things, in case you have lent your iPhone to someone else, for instance.

Sign in with your *Apple ID* 87

After a while, the app is ready for use:

You do not need to open the app right now.

Go to the home screen 10

Just like the free app that you installed previously, this app will be placed on the second page of your iPhone.

7.4 Signing Out from the App Store

After you have signed in with your *Apple ID*, you will stay signed in. During this time you can purchase items without having to enter your password again.

Please note:

In some games apps, such as the popular game *Smurfs Village*, you can buy fake money or credits during the game and use it for bargaining. These *smurfberries* are paid with the money from your remaining credit or from your credit card. If you let your children or grandchildren play such a game, they can purchase items without having to enter your password. So, it is better to sign out.

Open the *App Store* 80

You will see the page with the app you just purchased:

Tap Featured

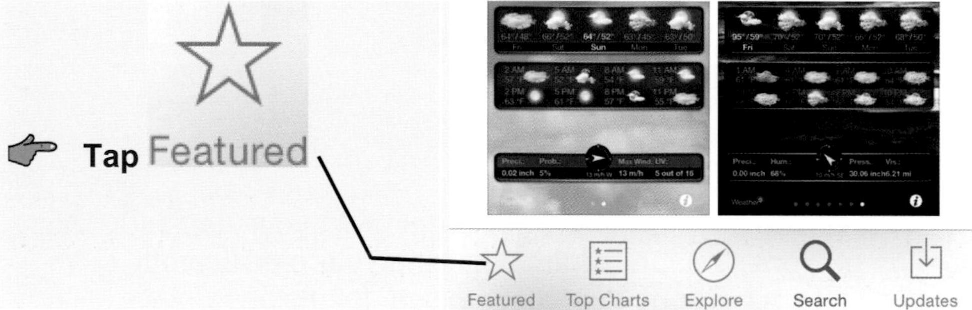

You need to go to the bottom of the screen:

Swipe upwards over the screen

To sign out:

Tap Apple ID:

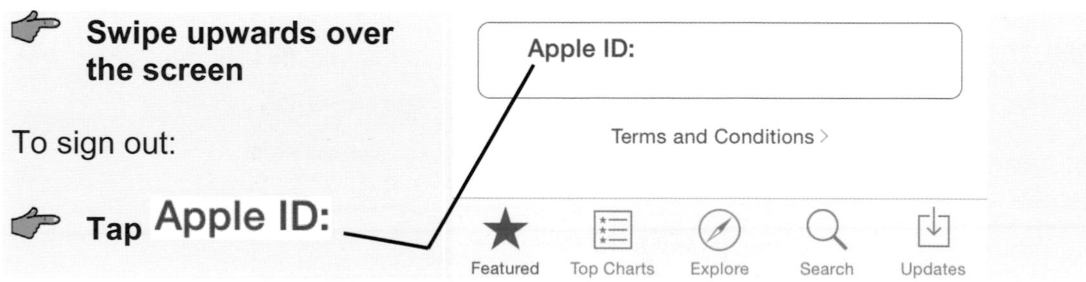

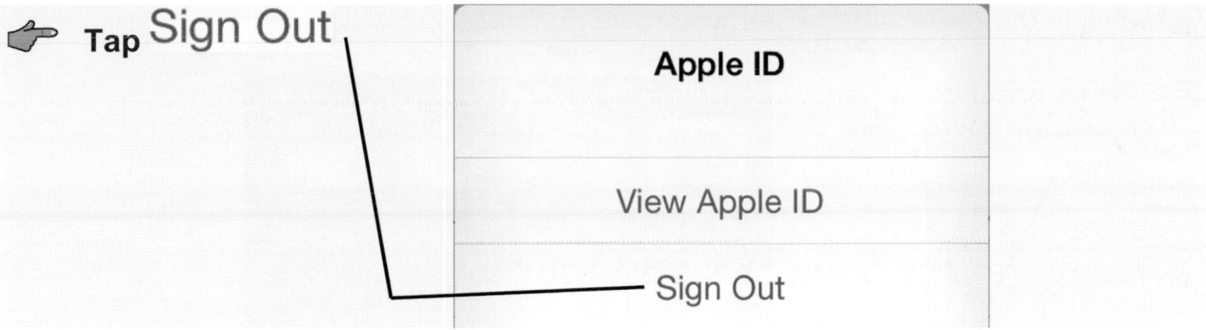

You will see the *Featured* page again:

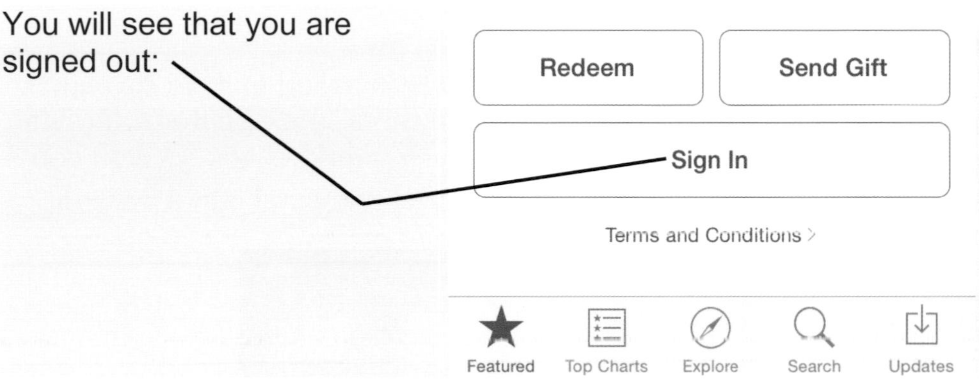

Go to the home screen 10

7.5 Managing Apps

The order of the apps on your iPhone is entirely up to you, you can arrange the apps according to your own taste by moving them between pages. This is how you scroll to the second page where you will find the apps you just purchased:

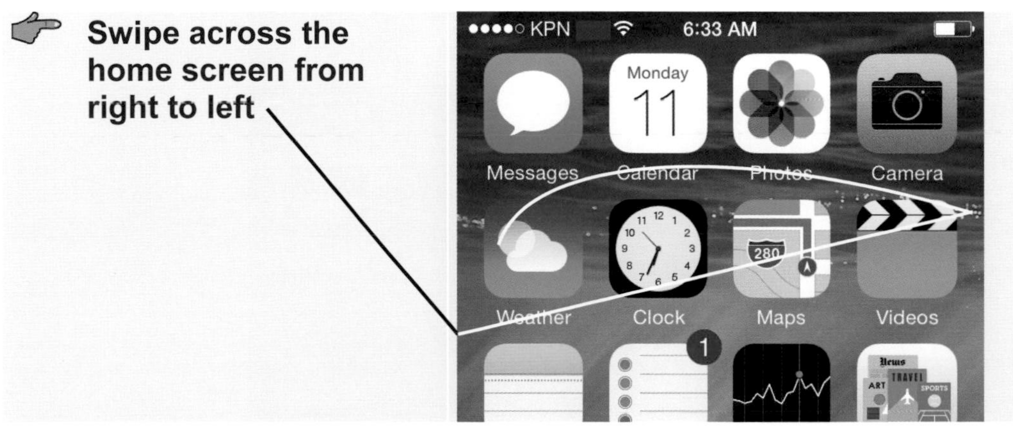

You will see the page with the app you have purchased:

Press and hold your finger on one of the apps

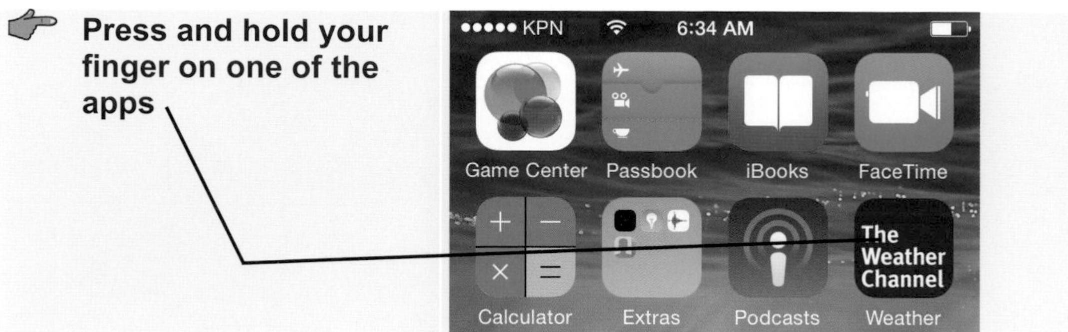

Please note:

In order to carry out the next few steps, you need to have installed at least two apps. If you have not purchased an app, you can download another free app that interests you, as described in *section 7.1 Downloading and Installing a Free App*. Or you can use other apps to perform the steps in this section.

The apps will start to jiggle, and a badge  will be shown. Now they can be moved:

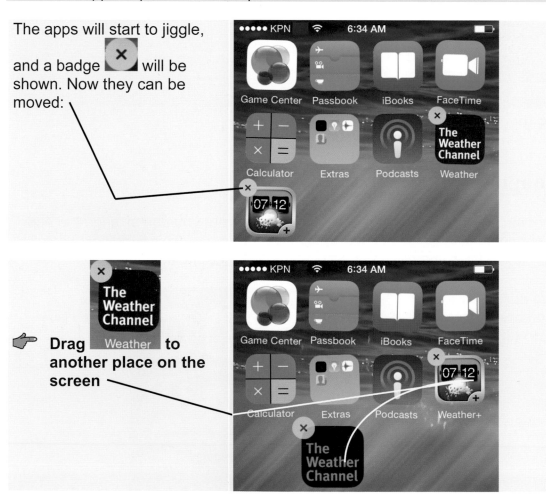

Drag Weather to another place on the screen

Now the apps have changed place:

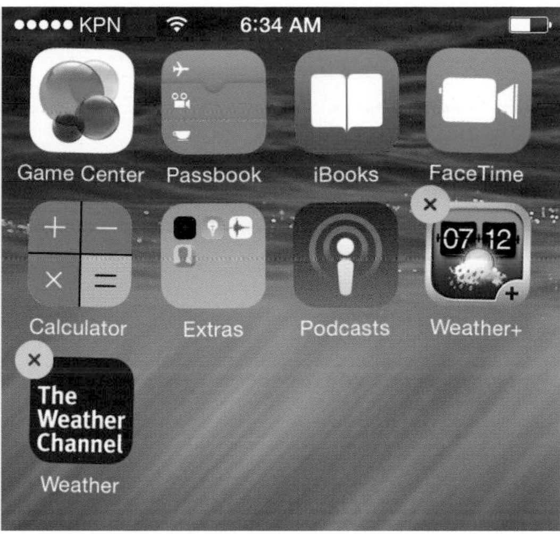

You can also move an app to a different page. This is how you move an app to the home screen:

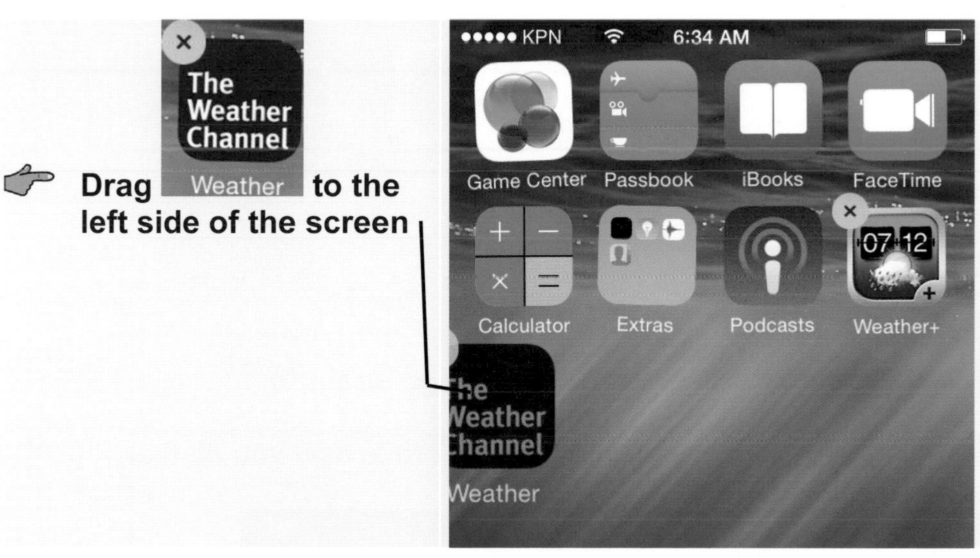

Drag Weather **to the left side of the screen**

When you see the home screen:

Release Weather

Now the app has been placed between the other apps on the home screen:

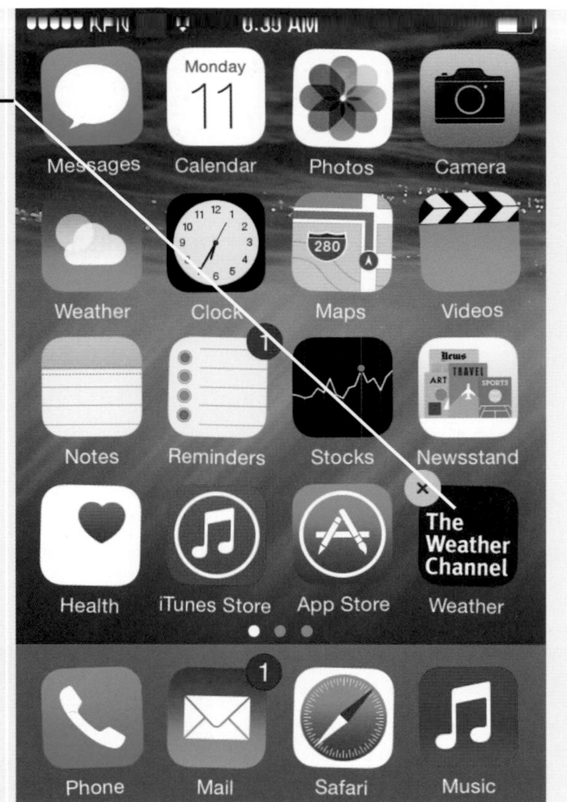

If you want, you can also change the order of the apps on this page. For now, this will not be necessary.

Now the Settings app has been moved to the second page, to create space for the new app:

Move the The Weather Channel Weather app back to the second page again 82

You can also store related apps in a separate folder. Here is how you do that:

Drag The Weather Channel Weather **on top of** Weather+

A suitable name will be suggested for the new folder. You can change this name:

If you wish, tap the name

If you wish, type the desired name

If you are satisfied with the name of the new folder:

Tap Done

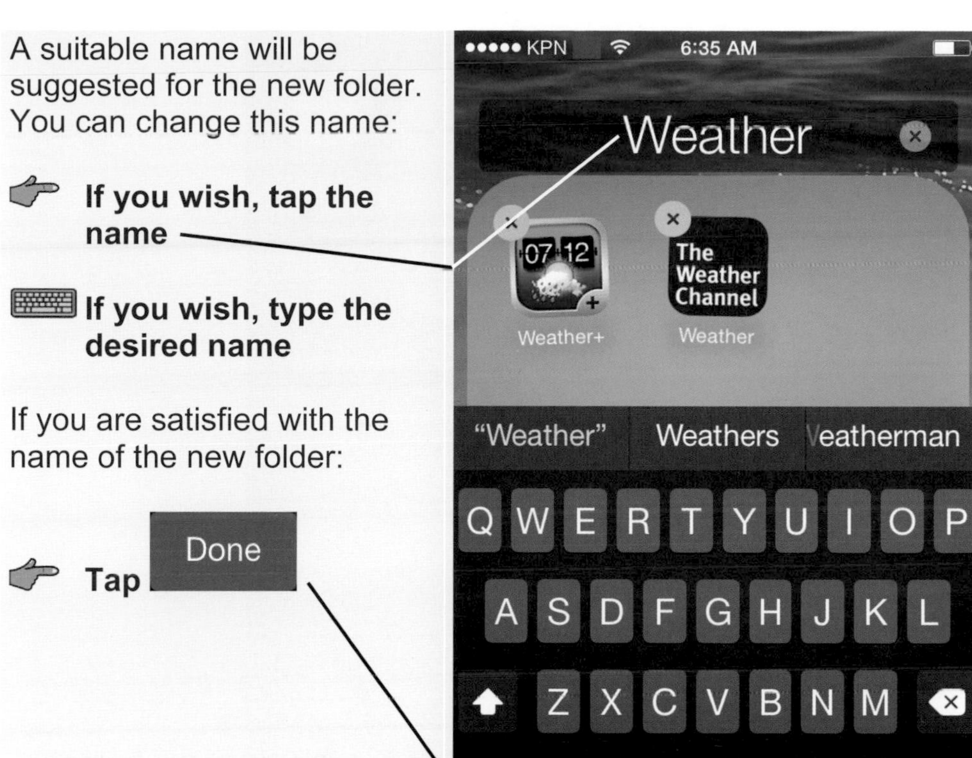

Tap below the folder

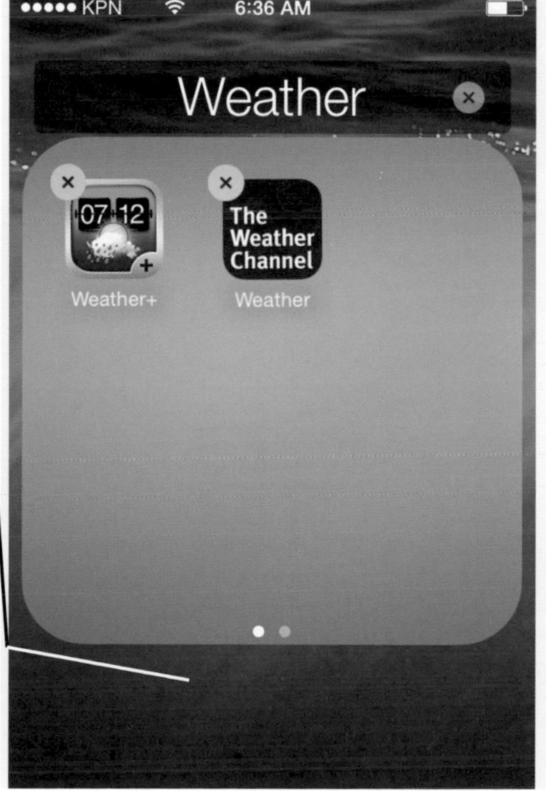

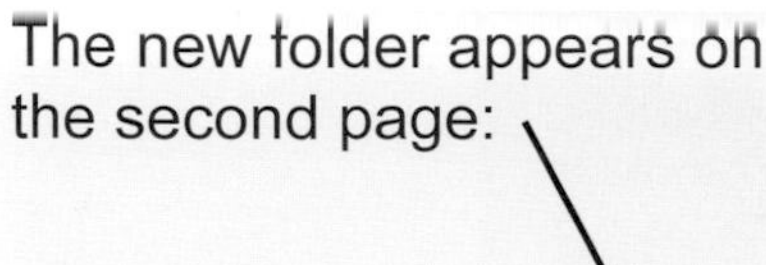
The new folder appears on the second page:

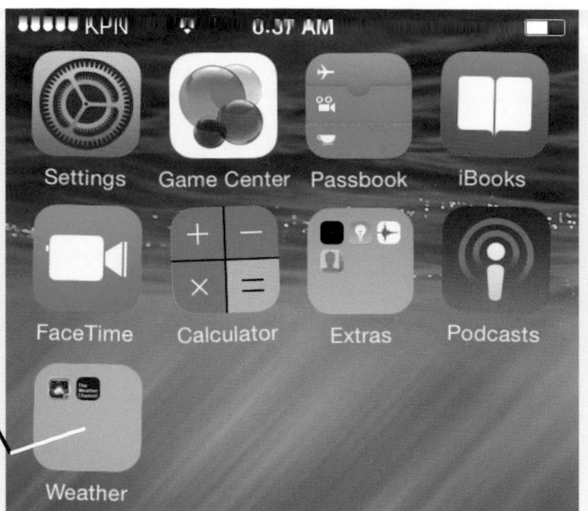

This is how to stop the apps from jiggling:

Press the Home button

Now the apps have stopped moving. This is how to view the contents of the folder:

Tap Weather

You will see both the apps in the folder:

You can always decide later to remove the app from the folder. You do that like this:

Make the apps jiggle 83

Drag the app away from the folder

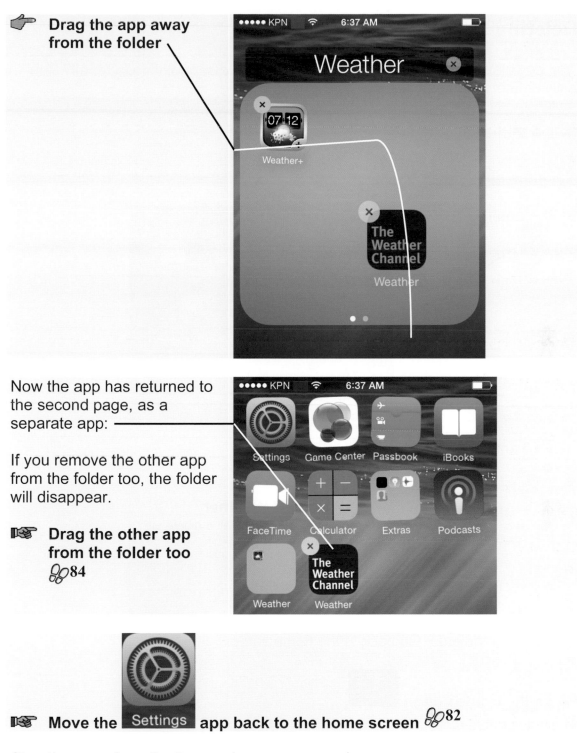

Now the app has returned to the second page, as a separate app:

If you remove the other app from the folder too, the folder will disappear.

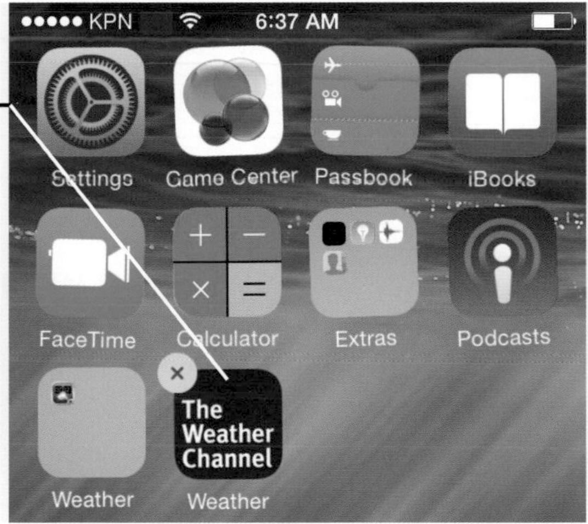

Drag the other app from the folder too 84

Move the 

app back to the home screen 82

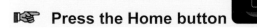

Stop the apps from jiggling again:

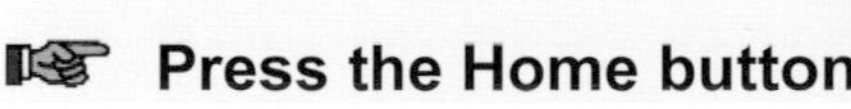

Press the Home button 

7.6 Deleting an App

Have you downloaded an app that turns out to be a bit disappointing, after all? You can easily delete such an app.

Swipe to the second page 81

Make the apps jiggle 83

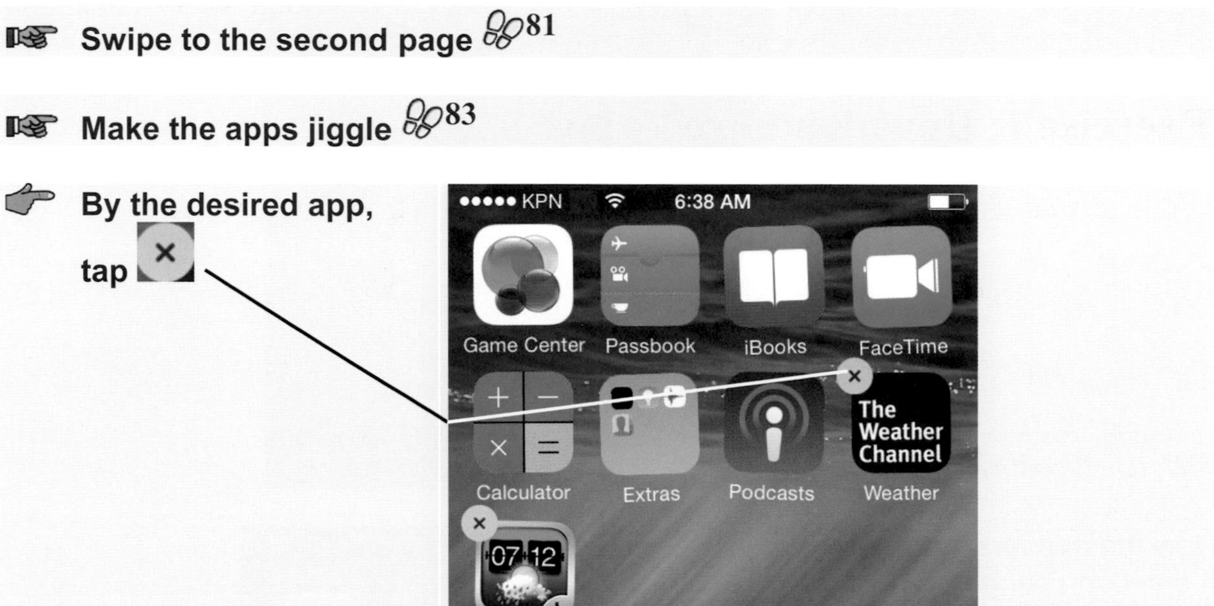

If you really want to delete the app:

Tap Delete
Delete " Weather "
Deleting " Weather " will also delete all of its data.
Delete
Cancel

The app has been deleted. Go back to the home screen:

If you want, put the iPhone into sleep mode 2

In this chapter you have learned how to download free and paid apps from the *App Store*. If you want, you can practice using the *Weather+* app to view the weather and temperature forecast for your favorite city.

7.7 Exercises

To be able to quickly apply the things you have learned, you can work through these exercises. Have you forgotten how to do something? Use the numbers next to the footsteps [1] to look up the item in the appendix *How Do I Do That Again?* This appendix can be found at the end of the book.

Exercise 1: Download Free Apps

In this exercise you are going to download two free apps from the *App Store*.

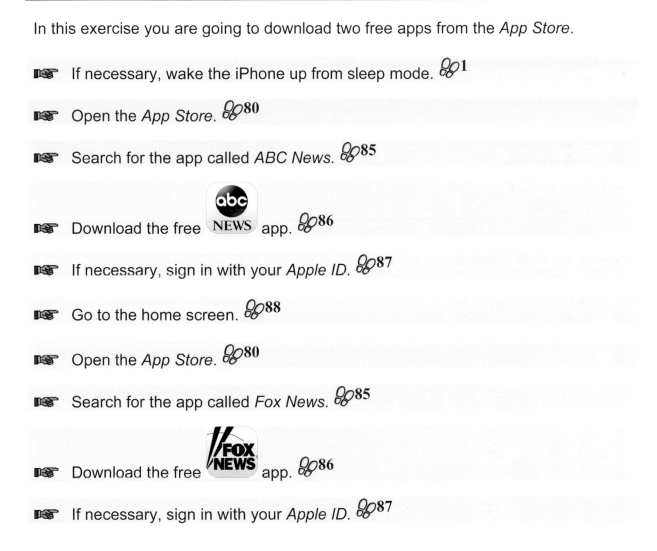

- If necessary, wake the iPhone up from sleep mode. [1]
- Open the *App Store*. [80]
- Search for the app called *ABC News*. [85]
- Download the free  app. [86]
- If necessary, sign in with your *Apple ID*. [87]
- Go to the home screen. [88]
- Open the *App Store*. [80]
- Search for the app called *Fox News*. [85]
- Download the free app. [86]
- If necessary, sign in with your *Apple ID*. [87]

Exercise 2: Manage Apps

In this exercise you are going to change the order of the apps on your iPhone.

- Make the apps jiggle. 83
- Move NEWS to the right-hand side of NEWS. 89
- Move NEWS to the home screen. 82
- Swipe to the second page. 81
- Move NEWS to the home screen. 82
- Put NEWS and NEWS together in a folder 90 and close the folder. 91
- Stop the apps from jiggling. 92
- Make the apps jiggle. 83
- Open the *News* folder. 93
- Remove NEWS and NEWS from the folder. 84
- Delete NEWS and NEWS altogether. 94
- Stop the apps from jiggling. 92
- If you want, put the iPhone into sleep mode. 2

7.8 Background Information

Dictionary

App	Short for *application*, a program for the iPhone.
App Store	Online store where you can buy and download apps. You can also download many apps for free.
Apple ID	Combination of an email address and a password, also called *iTunes App Store Account*. You need to have an *Apple ID* in order to download apps from the *App Store*.
Authorize	Allow a computer to store apps or play music purchased from the *App Store* and *iTunes Store*. You can authorize up to a maximum of five computers at any one time.
Chart	Overview of the most popular free and paid apps in the *App Store*.
iBooks	App with which you can read and manage digital books in PDF or ePub file format.
iTunes Gift Card	A prepaid card that can be used to purchase items in the *App Store*.

Source: User Guide iPhone

7.9 Tips

Tip

Update Apps

After a while, the apps you have installed on your iPhone will be updated for free. These updates may be necessary in order to solve existing problems. But an update may also add new functionalities, such as a new game level.
If desired, apps can update themselves automatically. But you can check for updates manually as well. This is how you can check for updates:

Open the *App Store* 80

Tap

If you see this window, you can choose to update automatically:

Tap the desired option

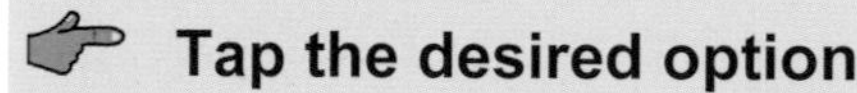

If you wish to update manually, you can use the UPDATE button next to the app or the Update All options at the top of the screen.

Tip

Download a paid app once again

If you have deleted a paid app, you will be able to download it again, free of charge. Although you need to use the same *Apple ID* as the first time.

If you are still signed in with the *App Store*, you will see the button instead of the price:

Tap

If necessary, sign in with your *Apple ID* 87

The app will be downloaded and installed. You will not be charged for downloading it a second time.

Tip

Transfer purchases to iTunes

In *iTunes* you can copy the apps you have purchased to your computer. This way, you will have a backup copy of the apps you bought and you will also be able to synchronize these with other devices, such as an iPad or iPod touch. This is how you transfer your purchases:

Open the *iTunes* program on your computer 11

Connect your iPhone to the computer

Click

To show the menu bar:

If necessary, click

If necessary, click Show Menu Bar

First, you need to authorize your computer to use the content you have downloaded with your iPhone:

Click

Click iTunes Store

Click Authorize This Computer

By Apple ID**, type your email address**

By Password**, type your password**

Click Authorize

- *Continue on the next page* -

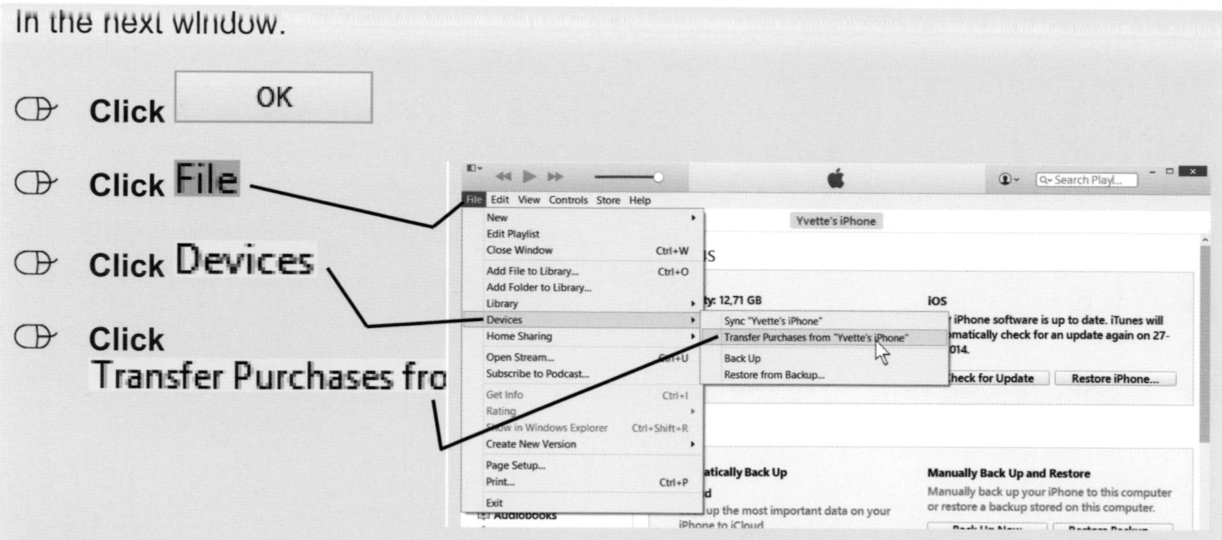

You will see the progress of the transfer process. After that, at the left side of the window:

You will see your iPhone apps.

If you download music to your iPhone, like described in *Chapter 9 Music*, you can transfer the music to *iTunes* in the same way.

Tip

Downloading a Book with the iBooks App

The *iBooks* app will turn your iPhone into an e-reader with which you can read digital books.

Open the *iBooks* app 3

You may will be asked whether you want to synchronize the content of *iBooks* with various other devices:

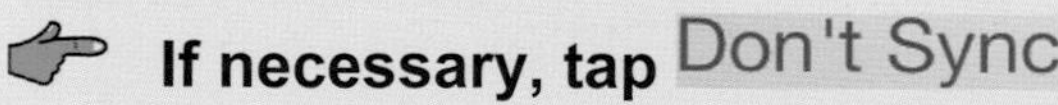

- Continue on the next page -

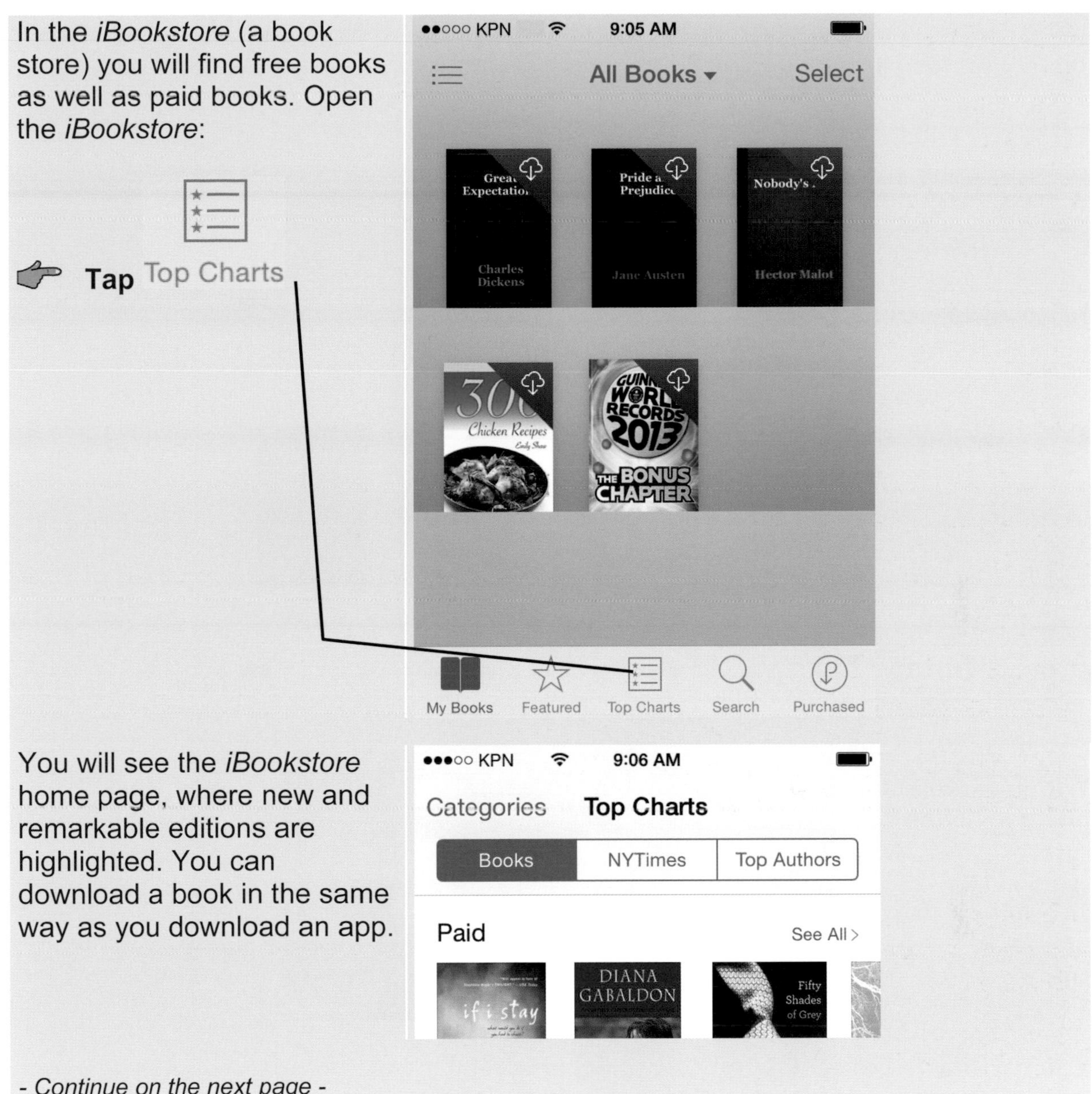

In the *iBookstore* (a book store) you will find free books as well as paid books. Open the *iBookstore*:

Tap Top Charts

You will see the *iBookstore* home page, where new and remarkable editions are highlighted. You can download a book in the same way as you download an app.

- *Continue on the next page* -

Many classic books are no longer subject to copyright, which means they can now be offered as a free e-book. In this example the book 'The Choice' is downloaded:

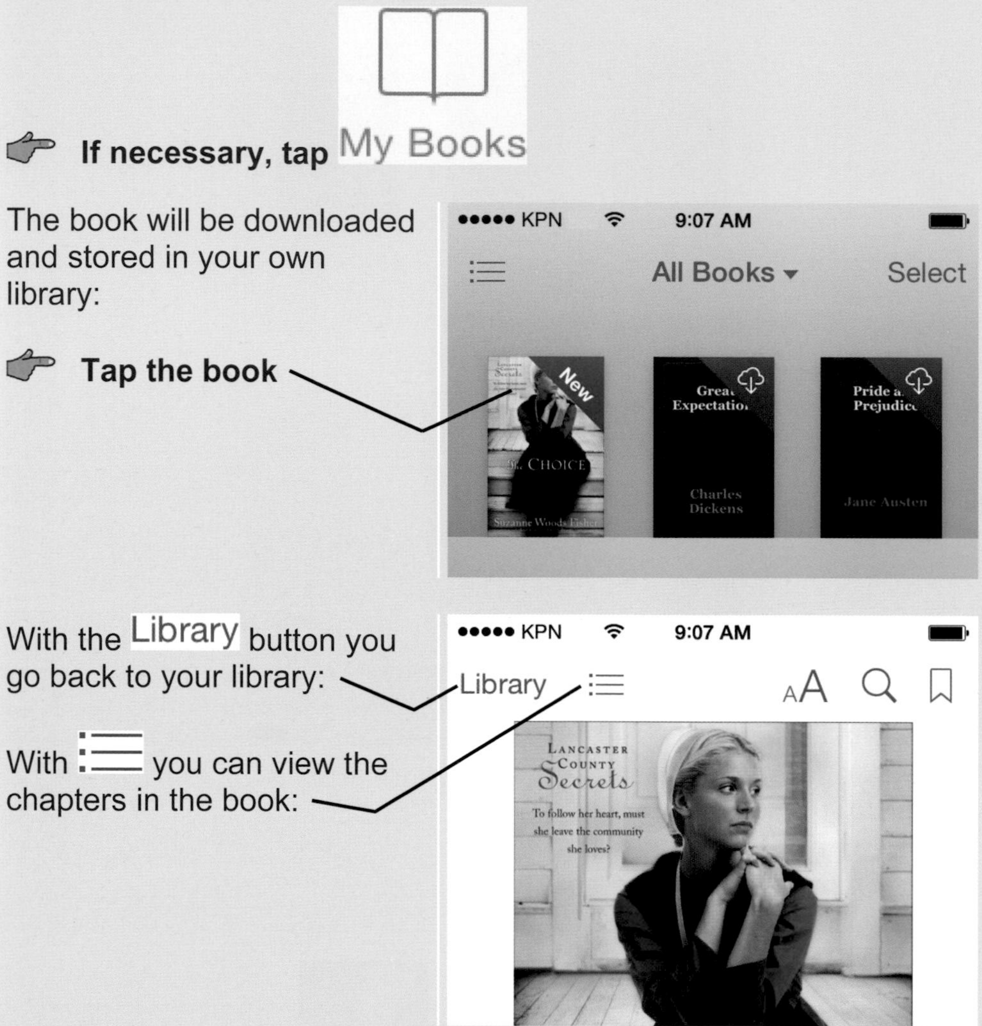

If necessary, tap My Books

The book will be downloaded and stored in your own library:

Tap the book

With the Library button you go back to your library:

With ☰ you can view the chapters in the book:

You can leaf to the next page, by swiping from right to left over the screen. And you can also leaf through the pages more quickly, by tapping the right-hand margin of the page.

You can easily change the *iBooks* settings. If the toolbars have disappeared, this is how you can display them again, by tapping the middle of the page.

- Continue on the next page -

Tap AA

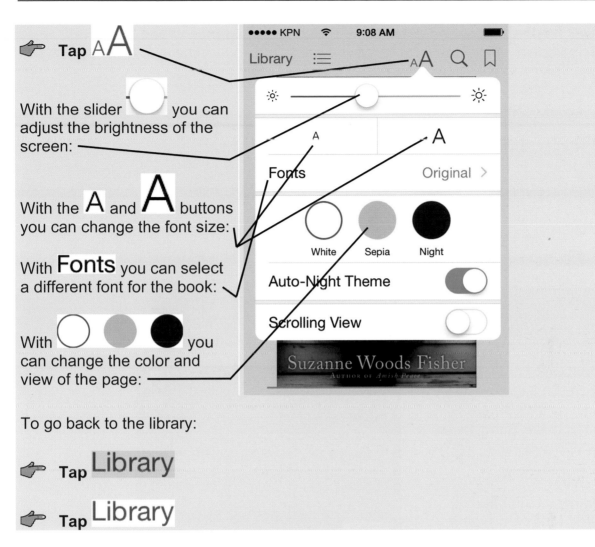

With the slider you can adjust the brightness of the screen:

With the A and A buttons you can change the font size:

With **Fonts** you can select a different font for the book:

With you can change the color and view of the page:

To go back to the library:

Tap Library

Tap Library

Your subscriptions in the Newsstand app
In the *Newsstand* app you can manage your subscriptions to papers and magazines, and also the single copies you have purchased.

Tap Newsstand, Store

- Continue on the next page -

You will see the *Newsstand* apps of the newspapers and magazines that offer subscriptions or single copies. The apps are free but you will have to pay for most copies. Take a look at one of the examples:

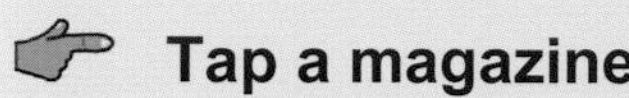

Tap a magazine

Download the app of the magazine 85, 86

If necessary, sign in with your *Apple ID* 87

Tap OPEN

You might see a message about push notifications:

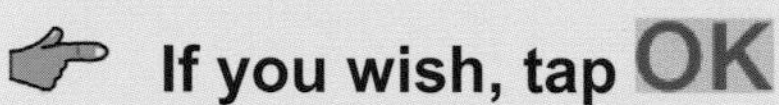

If you wish, tap OK

You will see the home screen of the magazine's app:

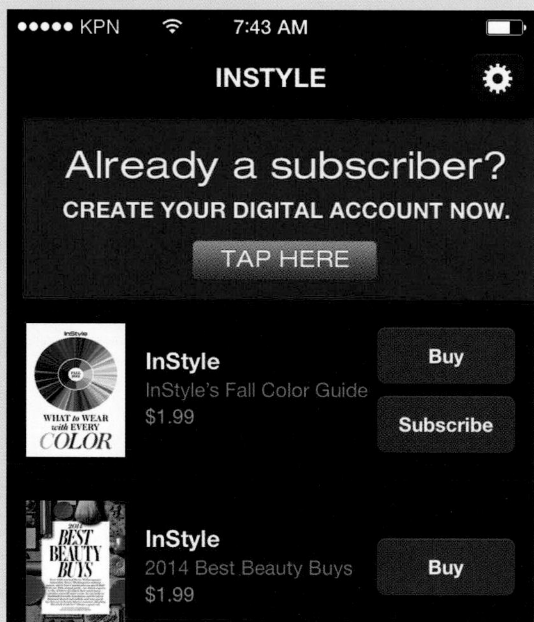

The magazine can also ask you some questions, like if you want to subscribe.

To go back to the home screen of the *Newsstand* app:

Press the Home button

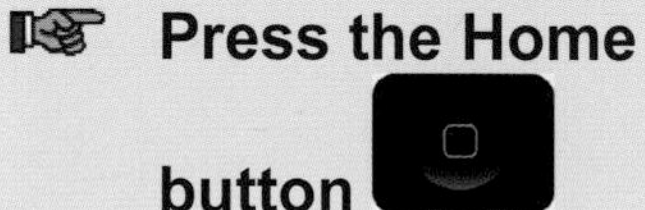

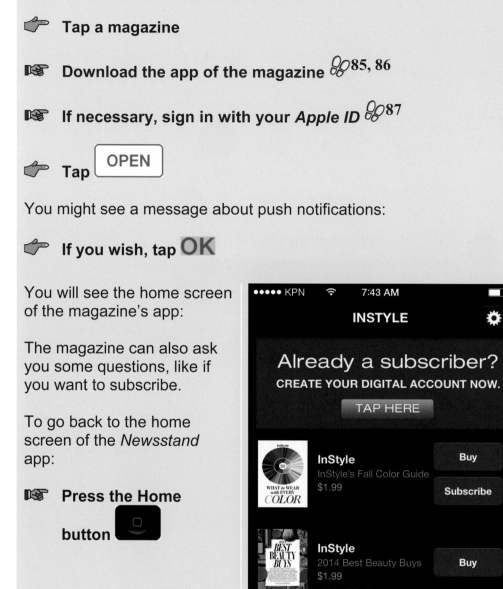

The magazine is stored in your kiosk. You can open the app by tapping it. Each *Newsstand* app offered by a paper or magazine may look different. You can purchase single copies with your *iTunes* credit and download them. Many newspapers also offer digital subscriptions, or free access to the digital edition if you have subscribed to the regular newspaper. In the app, you can enter your login information for the digital edition. This means new editions will be downloaded automatically.

8. Photos and Video

With the *Camera* app you can use the camera on the back of the iPhone to take a picture or shoot a video. You can also focus and zoom in or zoom out. The iPhone has an extra camera on the front. You can use that to make your own self-portrait.

You can use the *Photos* app to view your photos and videos. This app will even help you create a slide show with background music and nice transitions or edit your photos.

You can copy the pictures you have taken with your iPhone to your computer. In this chapter you can read how to do that. It works the other way round, too. Using the *iTunes* program, you can also transfer photos from your computer to your iPhone.

In this chapter you will learn how to:

- take pictures with your iPhone;
- use the tap to focus feature;
- zoom in and zoom out;
- make a video with your iPhone;
- view photos;
- zoom in and zoom out on the photos you took;
- view a slideshow;
- play the video you recorded;
- copy photos and video to the computer;
- copy photos and video to your iPhone;
- automatically enhance a photo;
- crop a photo;
- use filters;
- send a photo by email;
- print a photo.

8.1 Taking Pictures

You can use the *Camera* app to take pictures. In this section, you will be using the camera on the back of the iPhone. This is how you open the *Camera* app:

If necessary, wake the iPhone up from sleep mode [1]

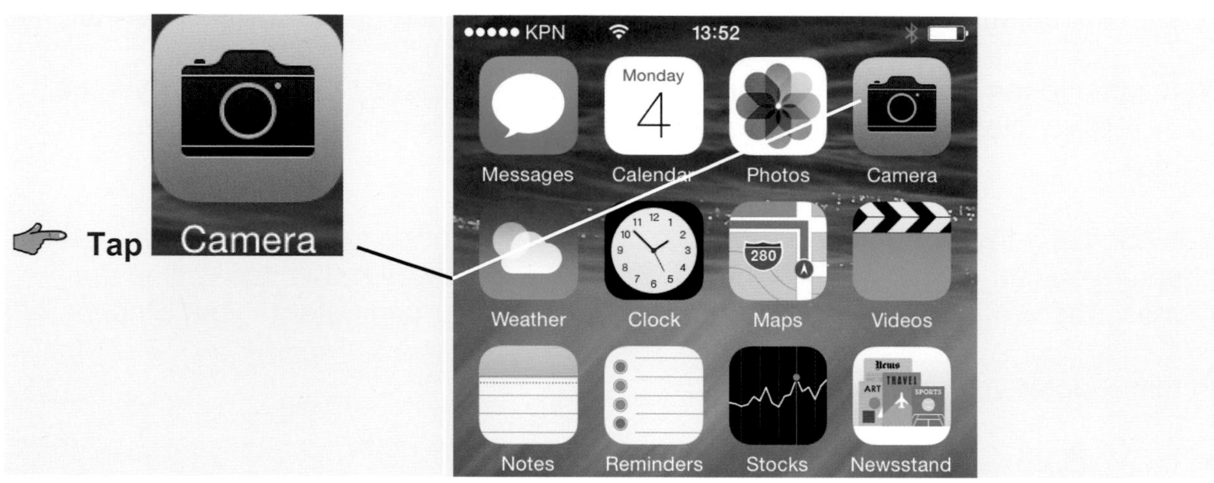

When this app is opened, you will be asked for permission to use your current location. This information is used to indicate the location where the picture has been taken.

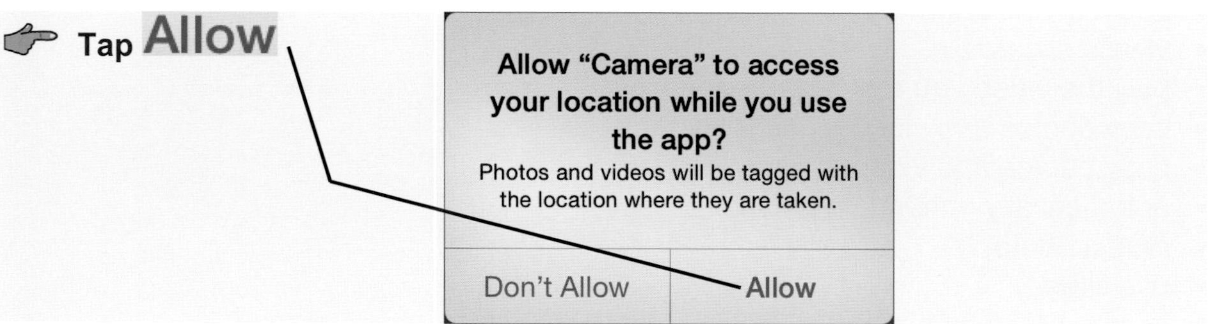

Now you will see the image that is recorded by the camera on the back of the iPhone.

Point the camera towards the object you want to photograph

This is how you take the photo:

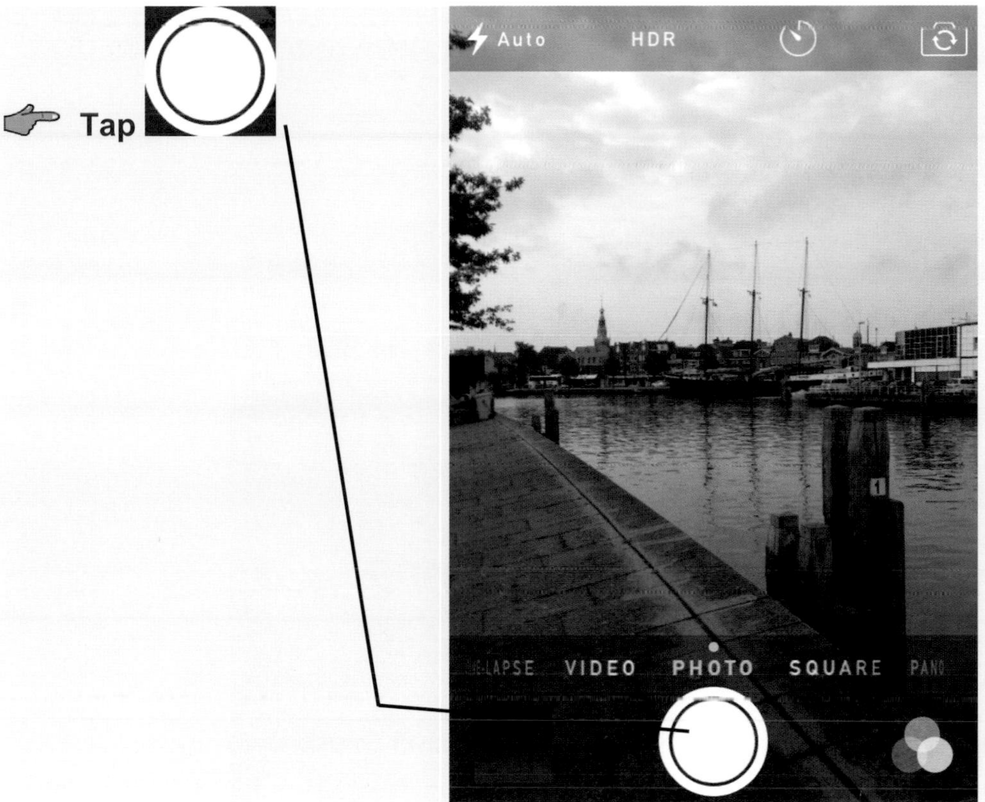

The photo will be saved on your iPhone.

Although the iPhone's camera features auto-focus, you can also choose what to focus on using the *Tap to Focus* feature. You can shift the focus to a specific object:

Tap the part of the object you want to use

For a moment, the image will become blurred while the camera is re-focusing.

The lighting will be adapted to the object you selected. If you tap a darker part of the object you will see the image lighten up.

If the image becomes too light, you can tap a lighter part of the object.

Take another photo:

Tap 

Tip

Taking square or panorama pictures

You can also take square or panorama pictures. This is how you do it:

 **Swipe SQUARE or PANO to the point**

In case of the SQUARE photo, now you see a square image and you can take the picture, as you have just learned previously.
If you wish to use the PANO option, you need to move the iPhone continuously when you take the photo.

With the digital zoom you can zoom in on an object. You can only do this with the camera on the back of the iPhone. This is how you zoom in:

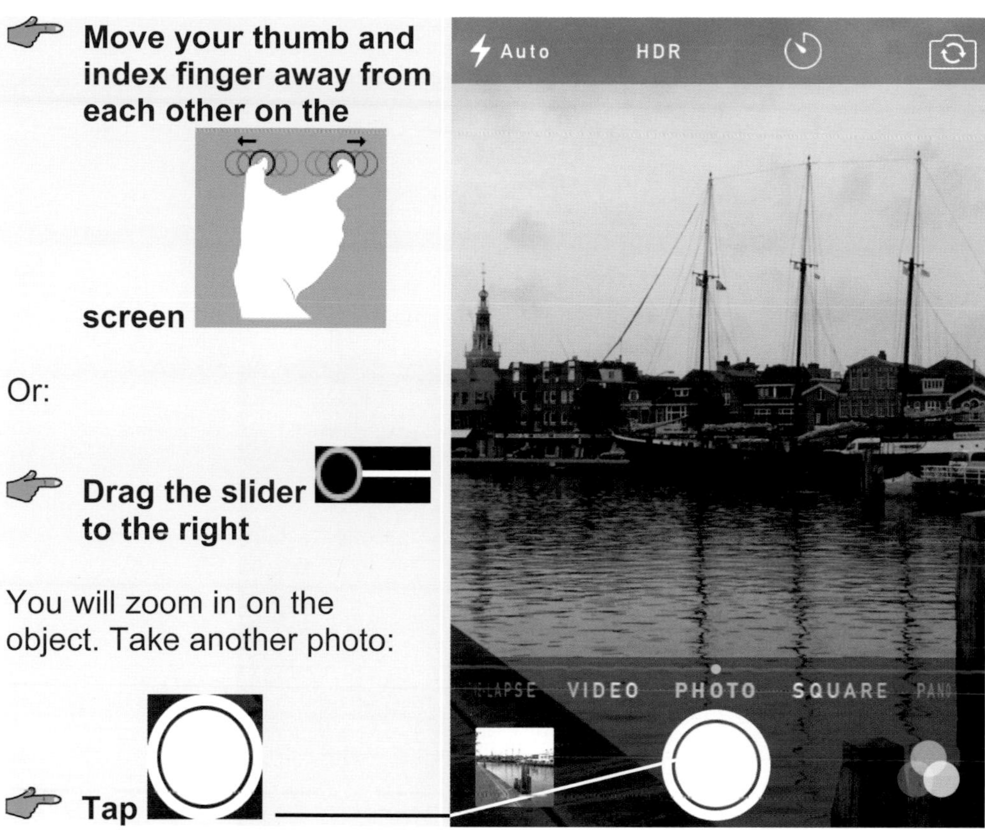

Move your thumb and index finger away from each other on the screen

Or:

Drag the slider to the right

You will zoom in on the object. Take another photo:

Tap

This is how you zoom out again:

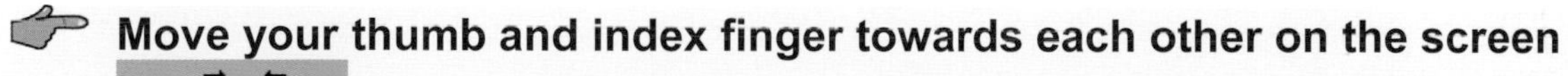

Move your thumb and index finger towards each other on the screen

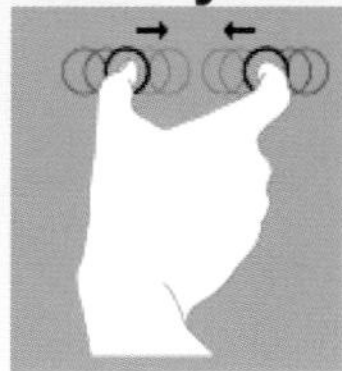

Or:

Drag the slider to the left

8.2 Making Movies

You can also use the iPhone's camera to record a video:

Swipe VIDEO to the point

The button will turn into:

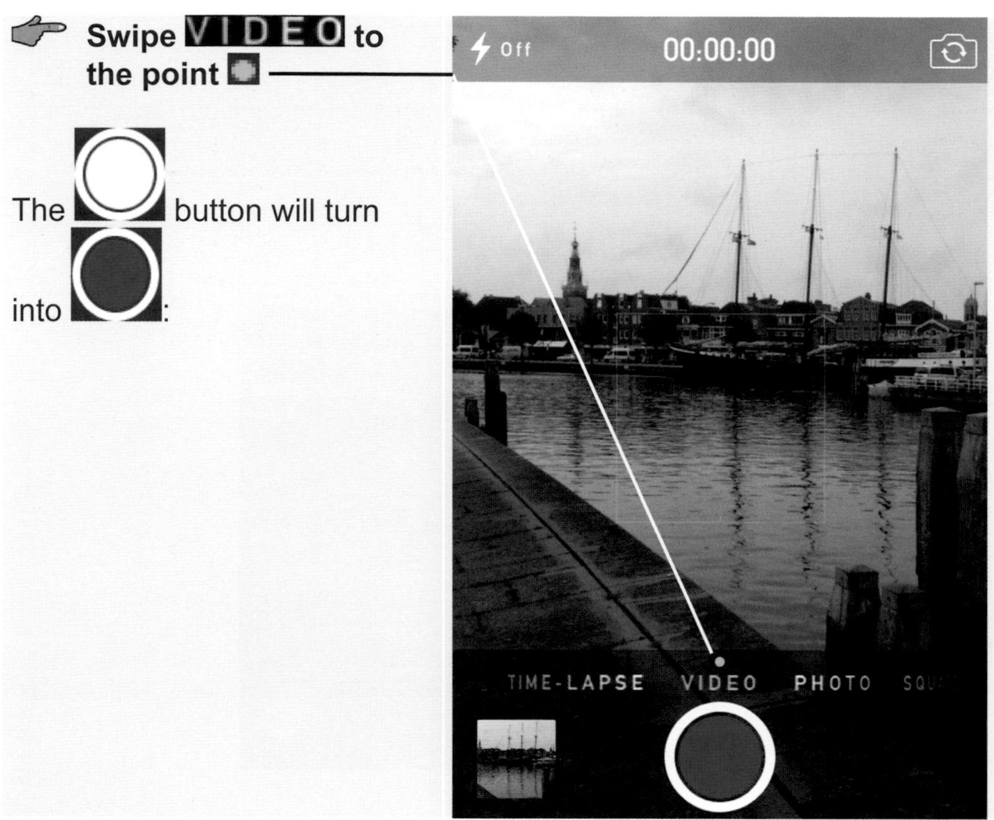

Tip

Sideways

If you want to play the video on your television or on a larger screen later, then rotate your iPhone sideways. This way, you will get a nice, full-screen image. You do not need to lock the screen to do this.

If you want, rotate the iPhone sideways, in a horizontal position

This is how you start filming:

Tap

While you are recording, the red light on the button will blink.

This is how you stop recording:

Tap

You can set up the *Camera* app to take photos again:

Swipe PHOTO to the point

Hold the iPhone upright, in a vertical position

Go to the home screen 10

Tip

Focus

Before you start recording a video and during the recording itself, you can zoom in and out on an object just like you do when taking photos.

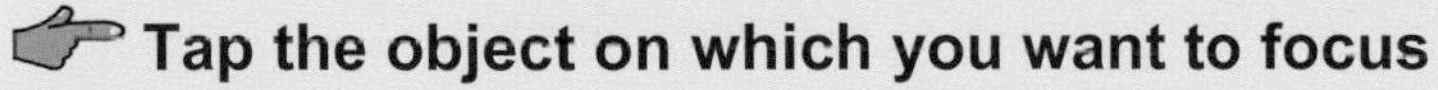

Tap the object on which you want to focus

The lighting will be adapted to the selected object. If you tap a darker part of the object, the image will lighten up. If the image is becoming too light, then tap a lighter part of the object.

8.3 Viewing Photos

You have taken a few photos with your iPhone. You can view these photos with the *Photos* app. This is how you open the app:

Tap Photos

You might see a message about *iCloud Photo Library*:

If necessary, tap Skip

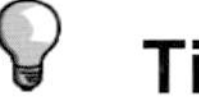

Tip

Transfer photos to the iPhone through iTunes
If you have some nice pictures stored on your computer, you can transfer these to your iPhone with *iTunes*. This might be a great idea if you want to show your favorite photos to others. In *section 8.6 Copy Photos and Videos to Your iPhone Through iTunes* you can read how to do this.

You will see the collections of your pictures, grouped by location:

You may see a different screen, because the groups may be arranged differently.

You are going to the screen where the albums have been arranged in a more orderly way:

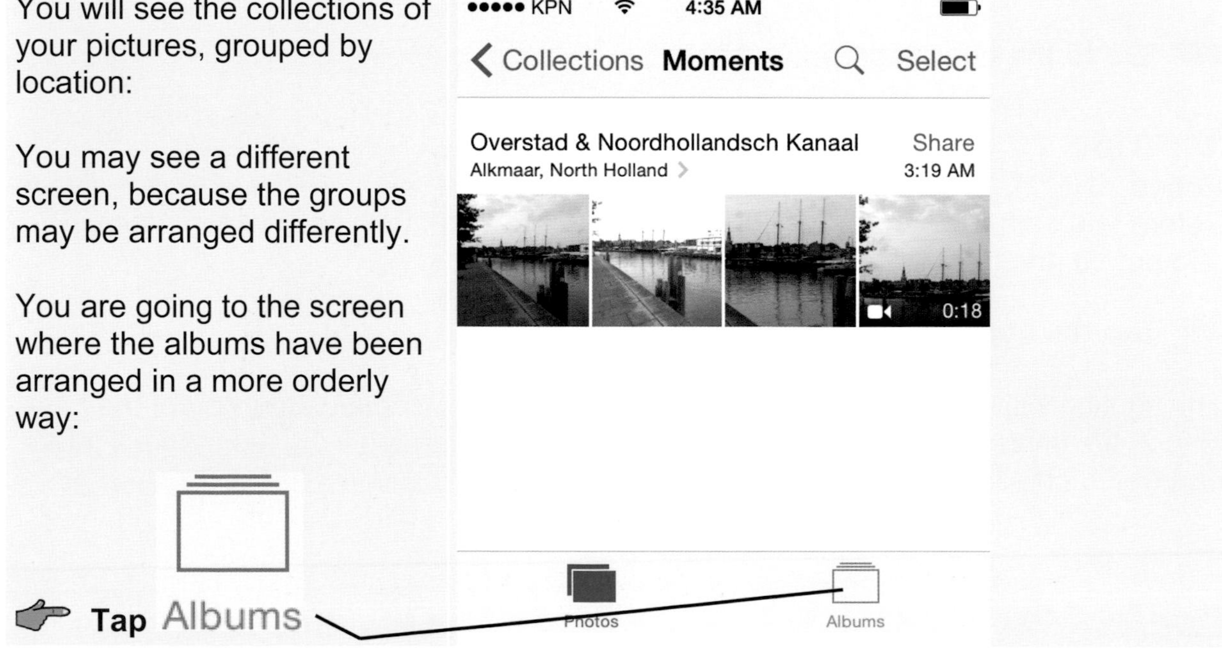

Tap Albums

In the *Albums* view, the photos have been arranged into piles:

Tap Camera Roll

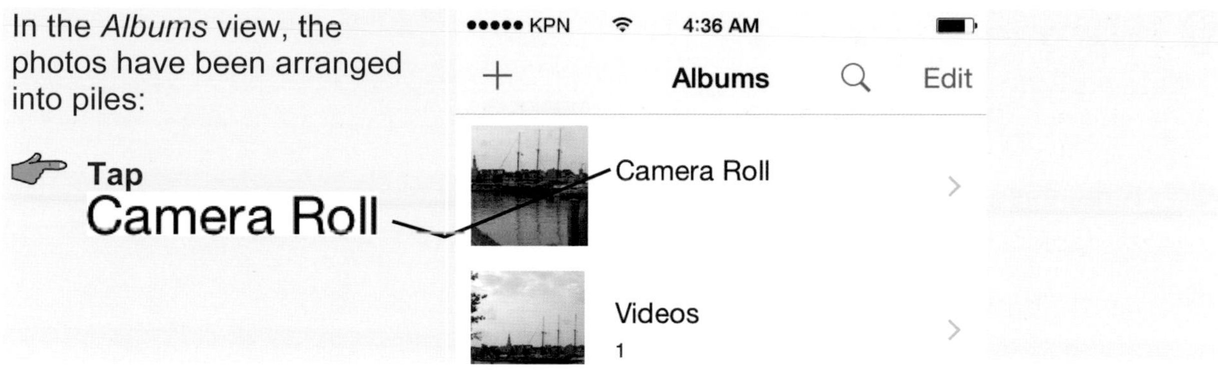

You will see the thumbnails of the pictures and the video you have taken:

Tap the first photo

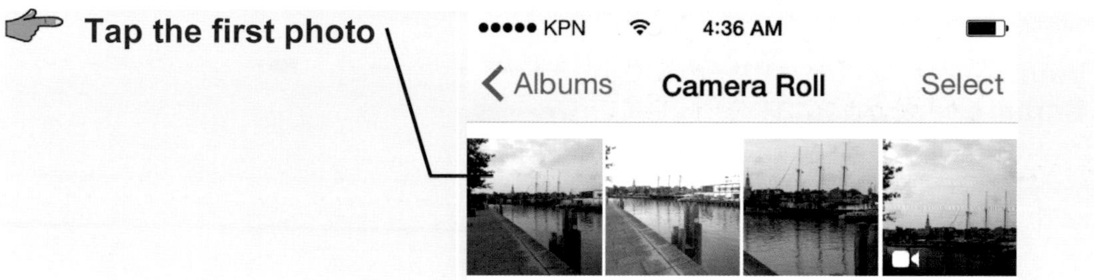

The photo will be displayed on a full screen. This is how you scroll to the next photo:

Swipe across the photo, from right to left

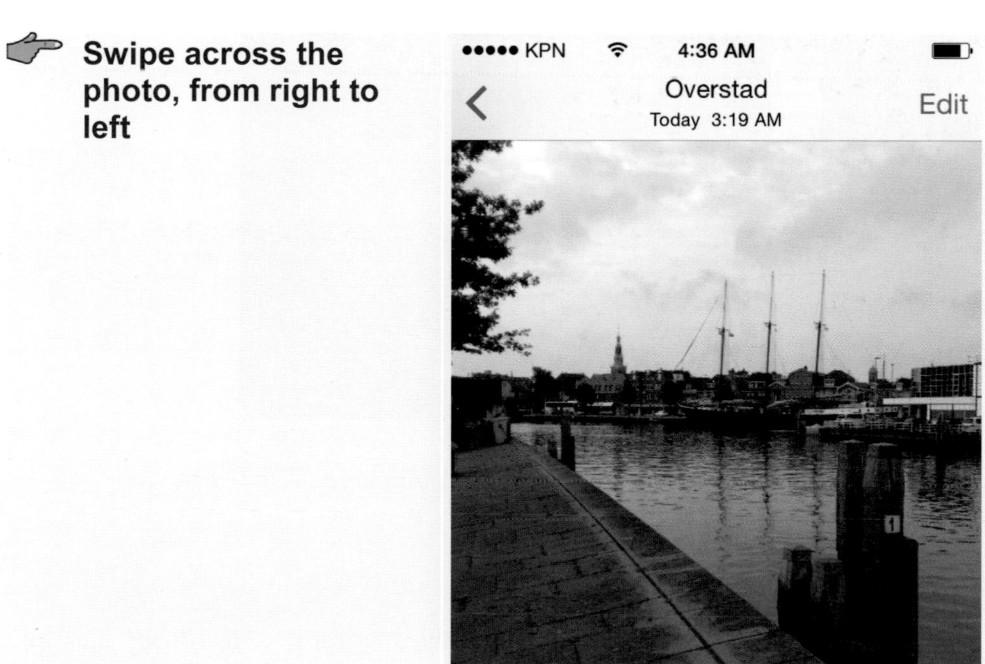

You will see the next photo. You can go back to the previous photo:

Swipe across the photo, from left to right

Tip

Delete a photo

You can easily delete a photo taken with your iPhone:

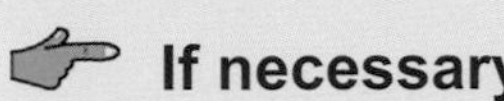

If necessary, tap the photo

At the bottom right, tap 

Tap 

You can also zoom in on a photo:

Move your thumb and index finger apart, on the screen

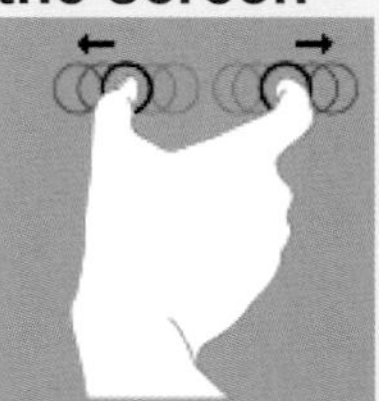

You will zoom in on the photo:

Please note: the picture might become a bit blurry when you zoom in.

Tip

Move away

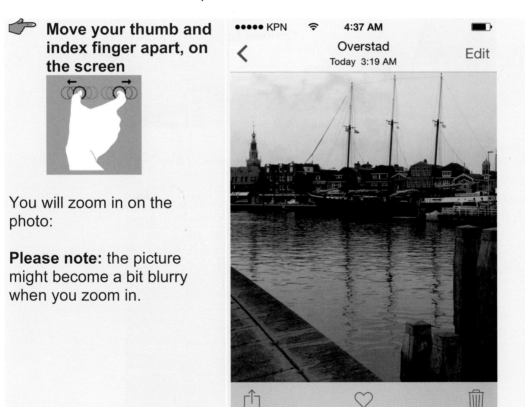

You can move the photo you have just zoomed in on, by dragging your finger across the screen.

This is how you zoom out again:

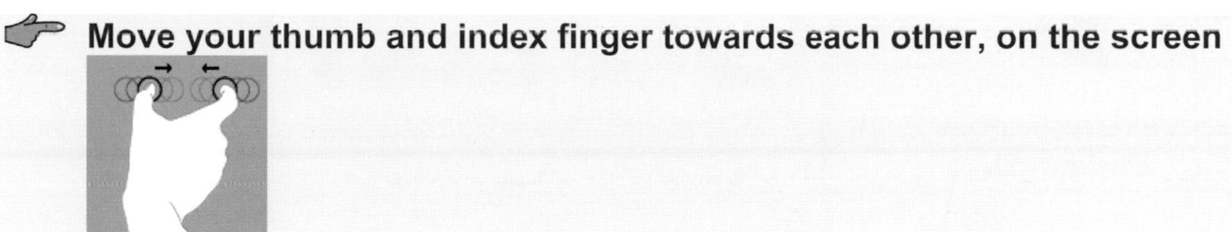

Move your thumb and index finger towards each other, on the screen

You will again see the regular view of the photo. You can also view a slideshow of all the pictures on your iPhone. Here is how to do that:

If necessary, tap the photo

Tap

Tap Next

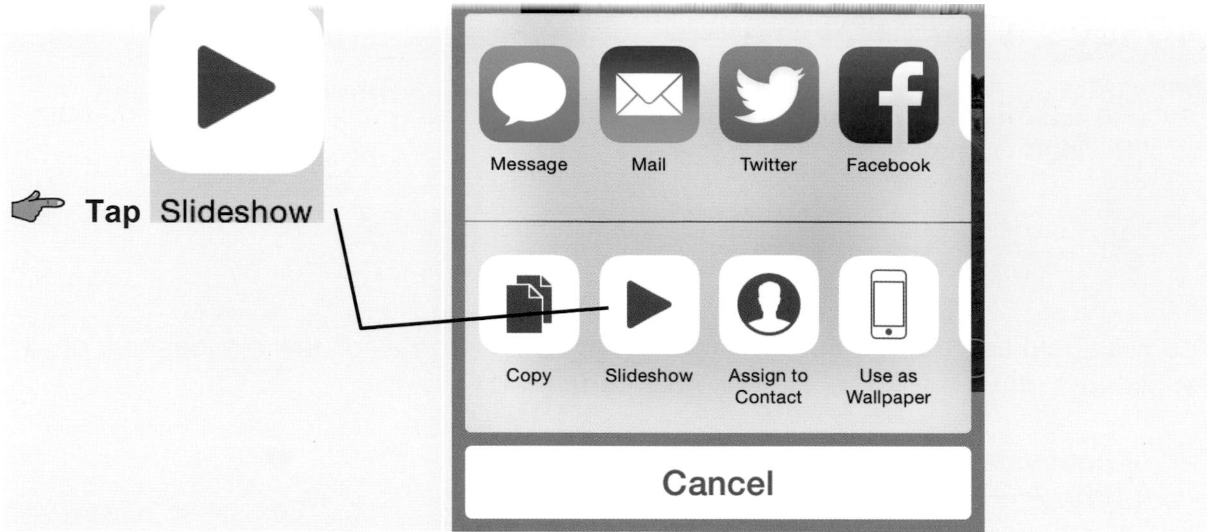

Tap Slideshow

Before the slideshow starts, you can set various options:

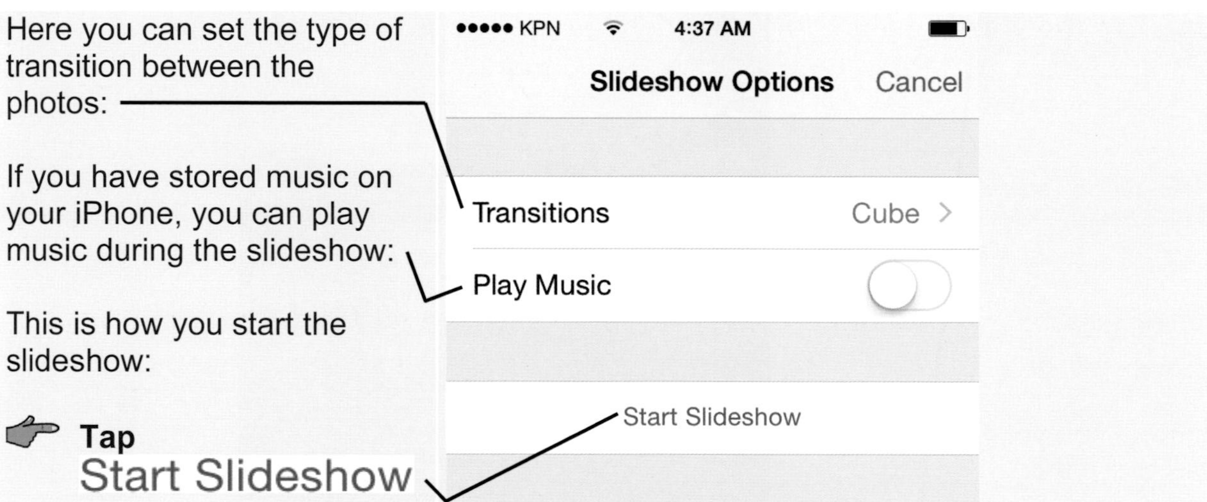

Here you can set the type of transition between the photos:

If you have stored music on your iPhone, you can play music during the slideshow:

This is how you start the slideshow:

Tap Start Slideshow

You will see the slideshow. If you have also made a video, this will be played during the slideshow. This is how you stop the slideshow:

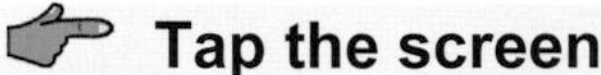

Tap the screen

The last photo that was displayed during the slideshow will freeze and remain on screen.

Tap <

Tap < Albums

8.4 Play a Video Recording

In *section 8.2 Making Movies* you have shot a short video with your iPhone. You can view this video with the *Photos* app as well:

Tap Videos

Tap the video

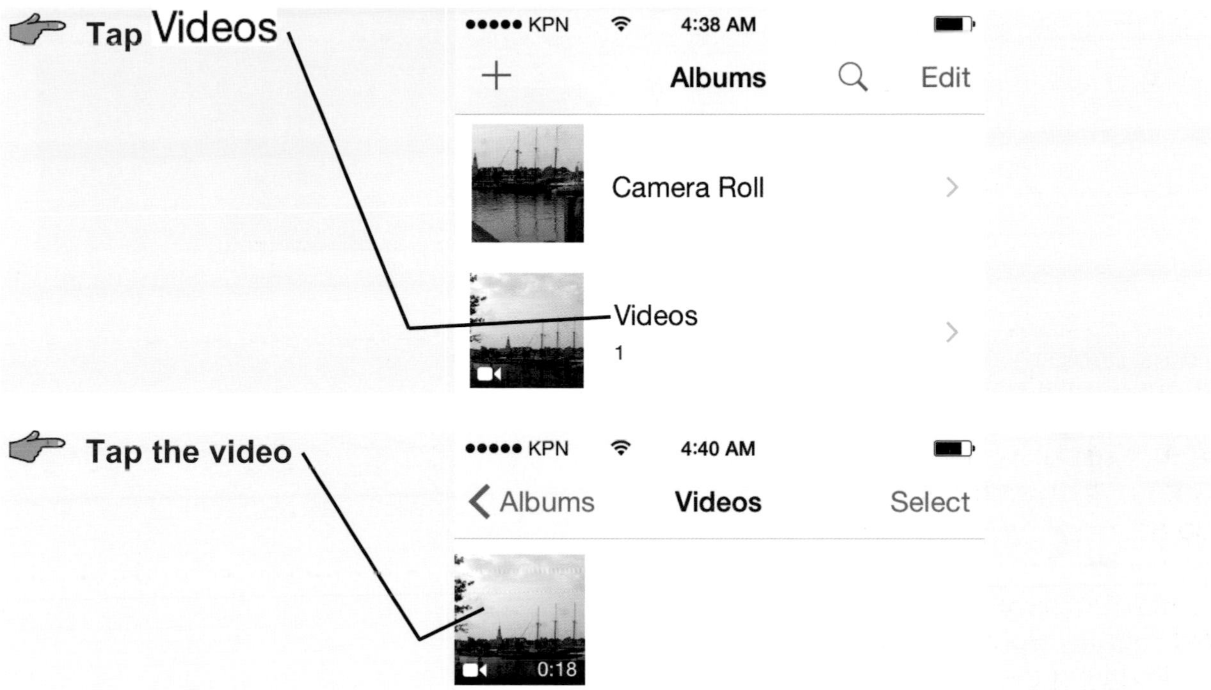

If necessary, turn your iPhone a quarter turn, so it is in the horizontal position

You will see your video. To play the video:

Tap

The video will fill the screen:

Tap the screen

You can see a pause button:

With this slider, you can fast forward or rewind the video:

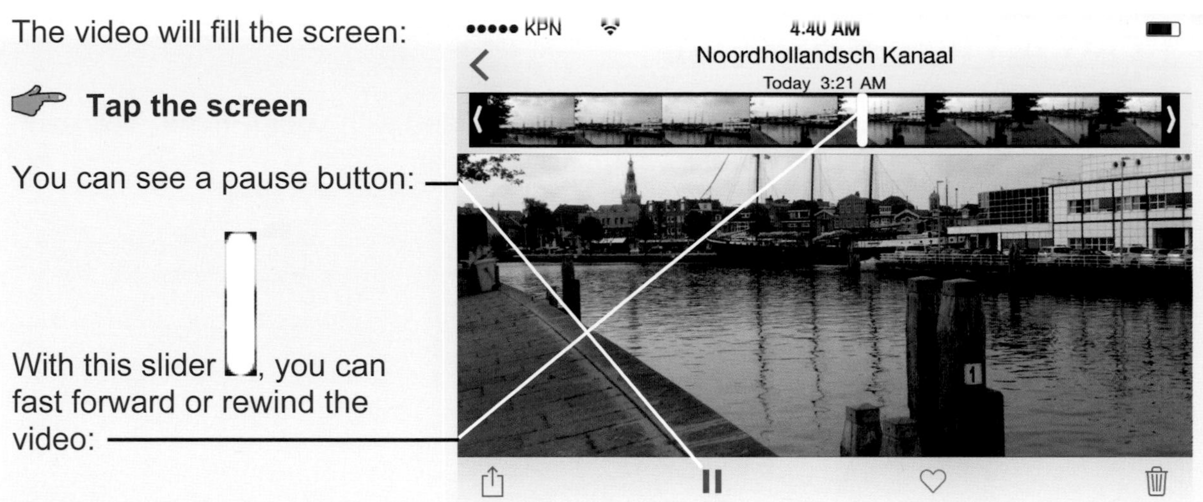

To go back:

Tap <

Tap < Albums

Go to the home screen 10

Turn the iPhone a quarter turn until it is in upright position again

8.5 Copying Photos and Video to the Computer

You can use *File Explorer* to copy the photos and videos you have made with your iPhone. This is how you do that:

Connect the iPhone to the computer

If necessary, close the *AutoPlay* window 5

You can open *File Explorer* from the desktop:

Click 

Your iPhone will be recognized by *Windows* as a portable storage device:

Click the name of your iPhone, for example Yvette's iPhone

Naturally, your own iPhone will have a different name than shown here.

Double-click Internal Storage

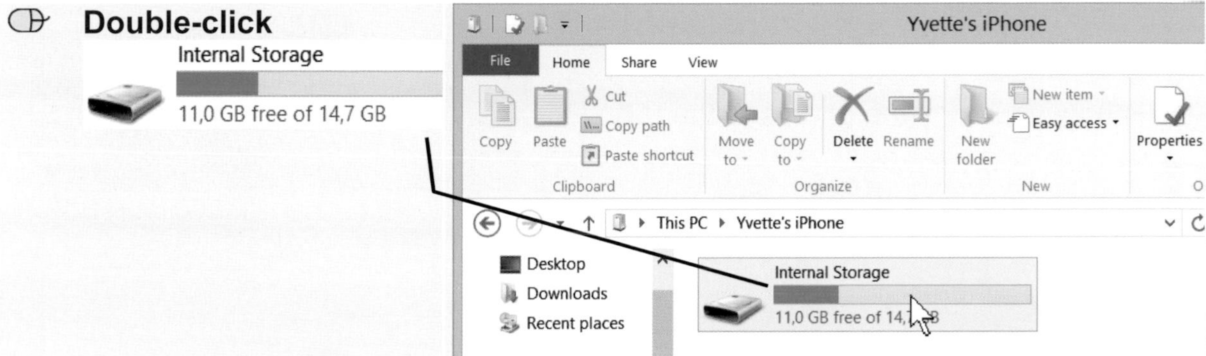

The photos and video(s) are stored in a folder called *DCIM*:

Double-click DCIM

Double-click 860OKMZO

Please note: this folder may have a different name on your own iPhone and it may contain more subfolders.

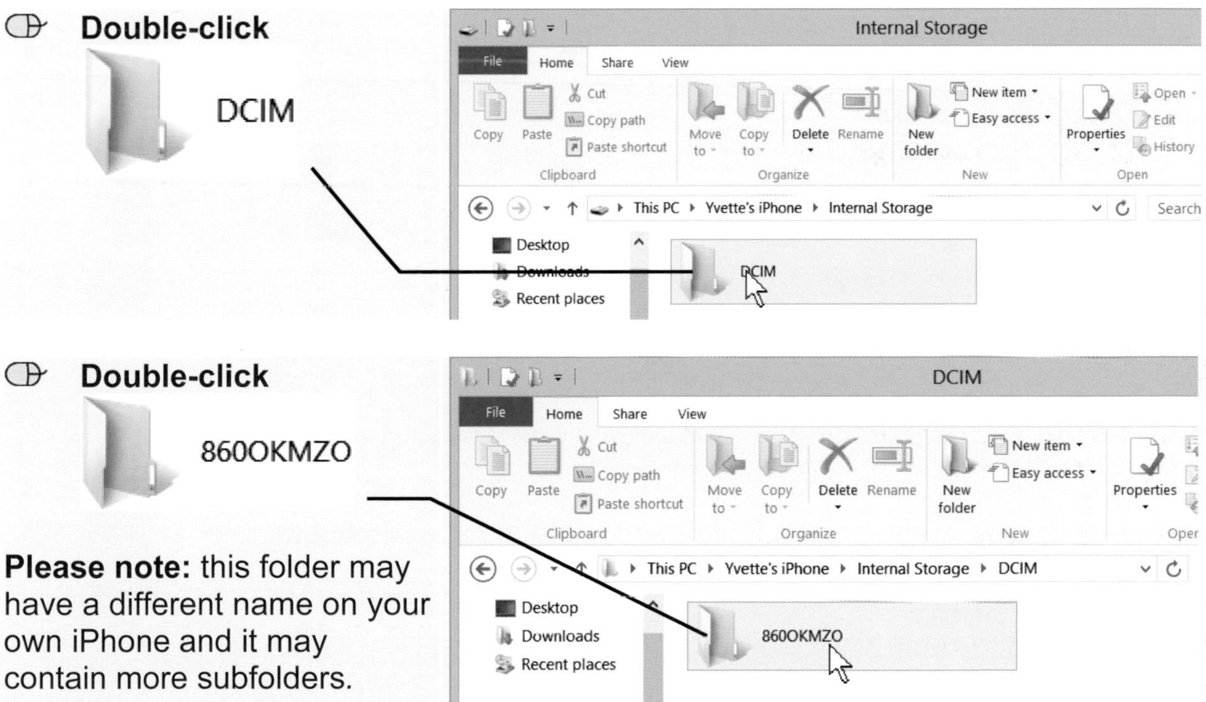

You will see all the photos and videos stored on your iPhone:

This is how you copy the photos to the (*My*) *Pictures* folder on your computer:

Simultaneously press Ctrl and A

This will select all of the photos and the video at once:

When you drag the photos and video to a folder on the computer, they will be copied:

Drag the files to a folder, for example Pictures

When you see the message Copy to Pictures.

Release the mouse button

Now the pictures and the video have been copied to your computer.

Please note:

This will only work while copying photos and video from your iPhone to your computer. You cannot use this method the other way around, to copy photos and video from your computer to your iPhone. In the next section you can read how to do this using *iTunes*.

Close *File Explorer* 5

Safely disconnect the iPhone from the computer 47

8.6 Copy Photos and Videos to Your iPhone Through iTunes

Your iPhone is a useful tool for showing your favorite photos and videos to others. Actually, you can also use the photos and videos on your computer. This is done by synchronizing the folder containing the photos and videos with your iPhone, through *iTunes*.

Open *iTunes* on your computer 11

Connect the iPhone to your computer

Click

Click **Photos**

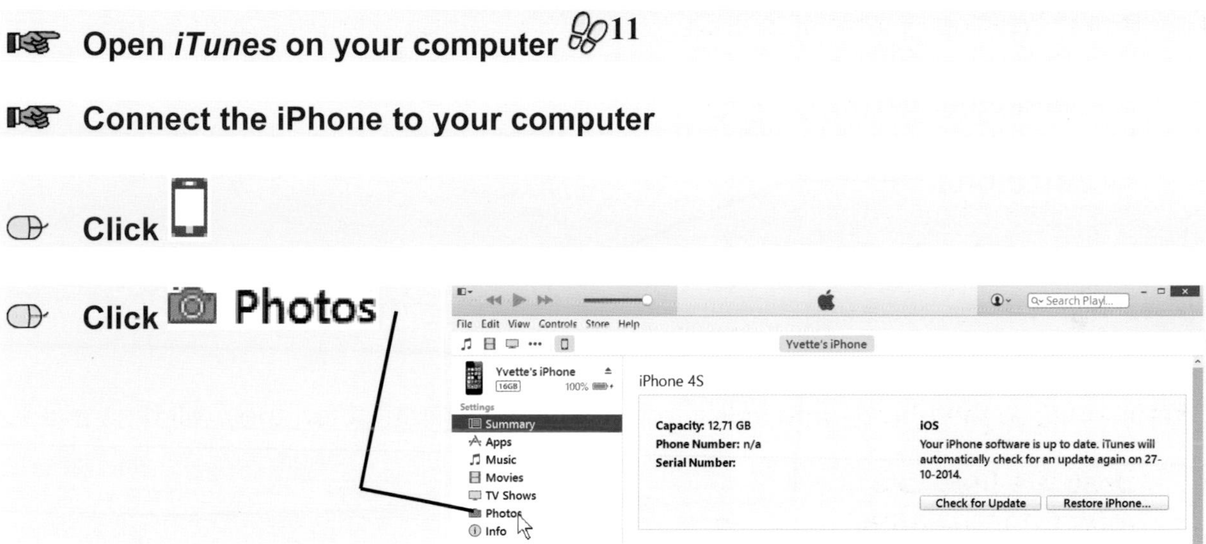

In this example, the photos from the (*My*) *Pictures* folder will be synchronized. You will select a folder with your own pictures:

Check the box ☑ by Sync Photos from

The Pictures folder has already been selected:

In this example we will synchronize all the subfolders of the *(My) Pictures* folder:

Check the radio button ◉ by Selected folders

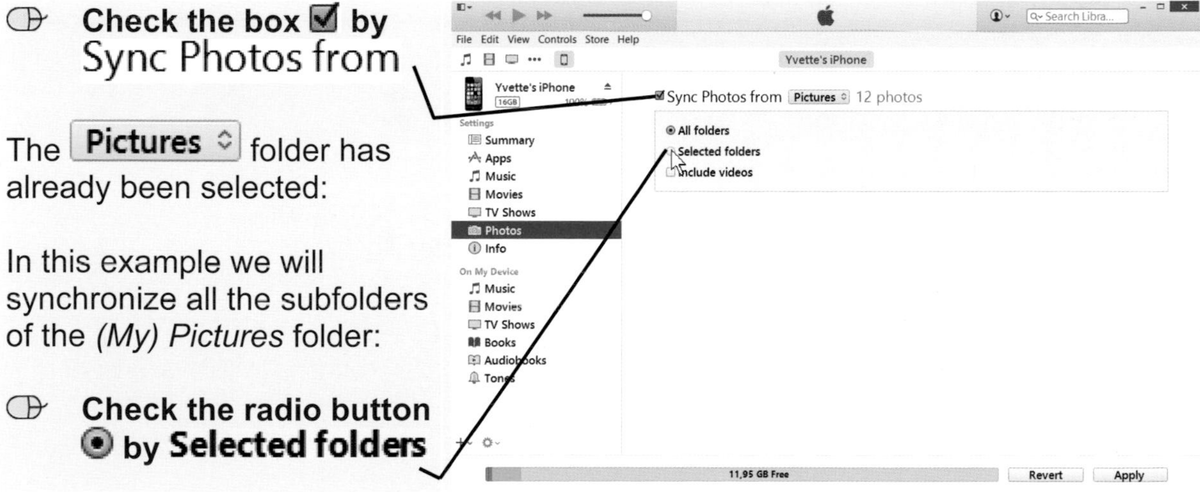

Tip

Videos

If you also want to synchronize the videos stored in this folder:

Check the box ☑ by Include videos

Select the folder(s) you want to synchronize with your iPhone. You will see different folders from the ones in this example, of course:

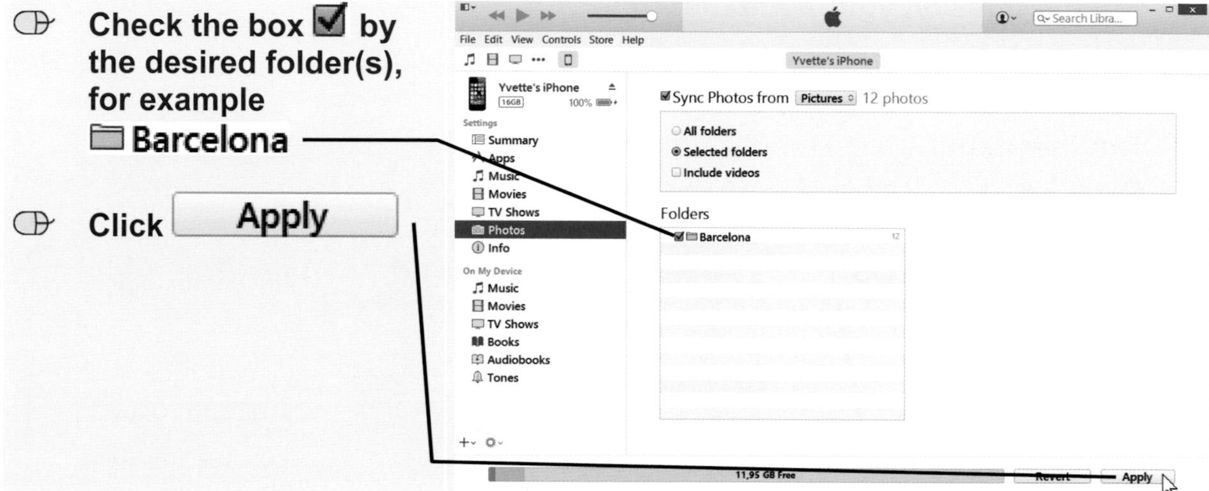

The synchronization is started:

You will see the progress of the synchronization:

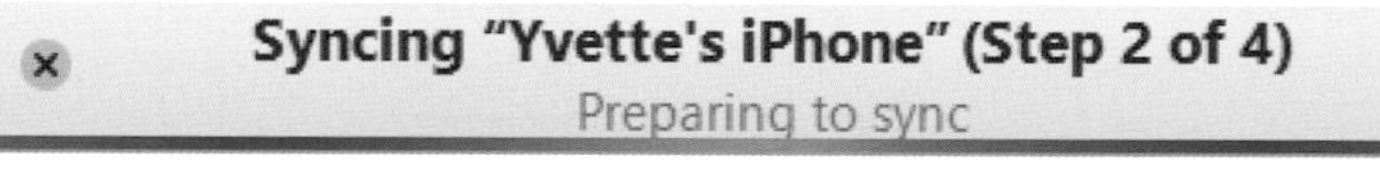

When you see the Apple logo the synchronization operation has finished:

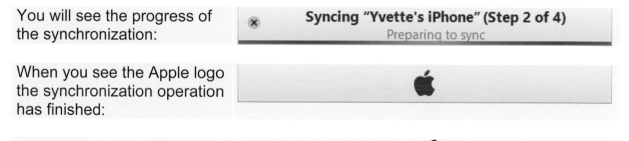

Safely disconnect the iPhone from the computer 47

Close *iTunes* 5

The photos are transferred to your iPhone.

Open the *Photos* app 3

At the bottom of the screen

If necessary, tap Albums

The pile with the synchronized photos has been given the same name as the folder on your computer:

Tap the album

The pictures are shown:

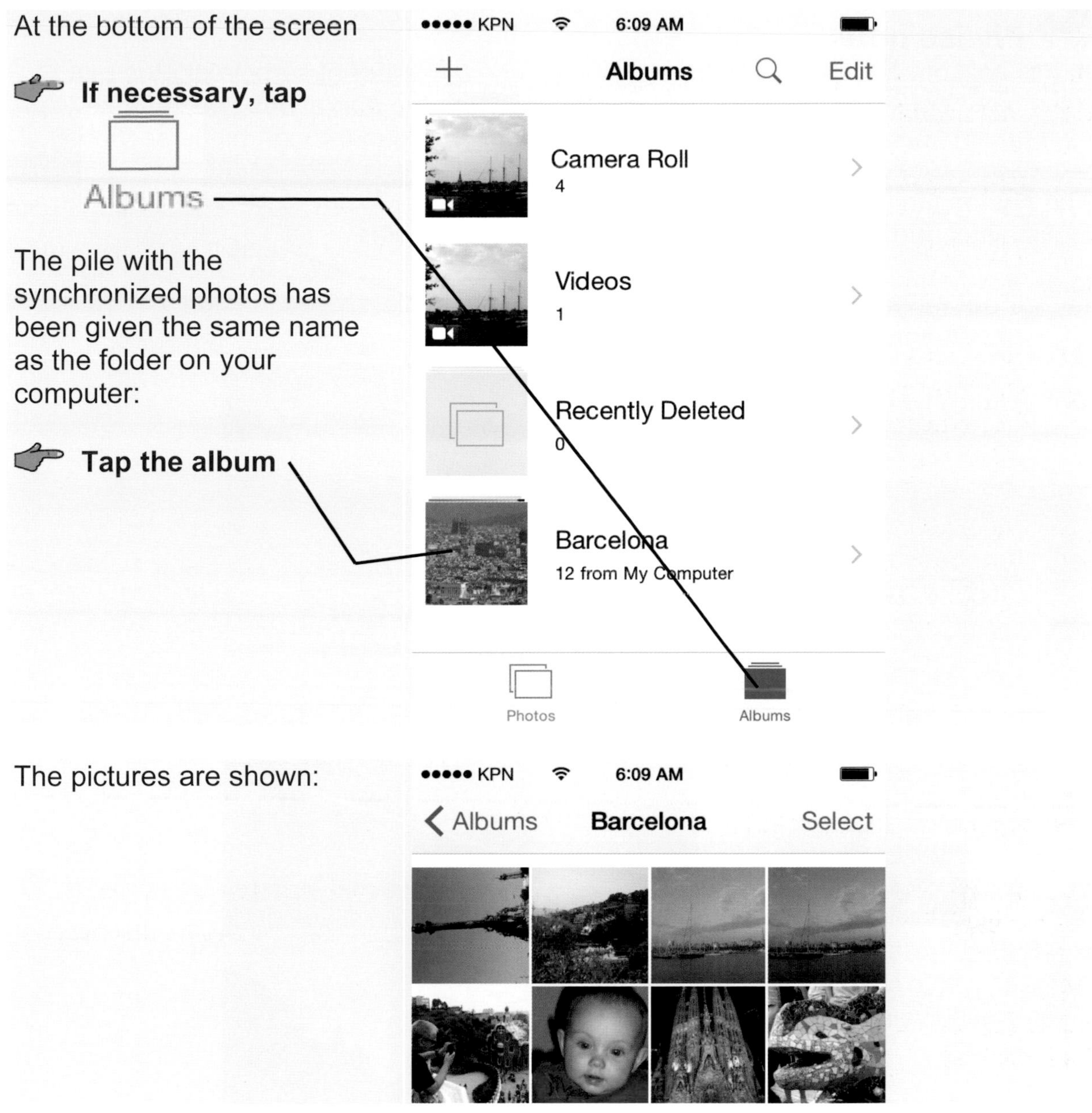

8.7 Automatically Enhance a Photo

Sometimes, a photo can be too dark or too light. The auto-enhance function will let you make a ‘ruined’ photo look better in just a short while. This function adjusts the exposure and saturation of the photo. Just try it:

Open a photo 96

Please note:

In this section, and the next sections, we will use a number of sample photos that have been copied to the iPhone. In order to execute the operations you can use your own photos, take a few more pictures yourself or just read through these sections.

The photo in this example looks bleak and blurred:

- **If necessary, tap the photo**
- **Tap** Edit

You may see this window:

- **If necessary, tap** Duplicate and Edit

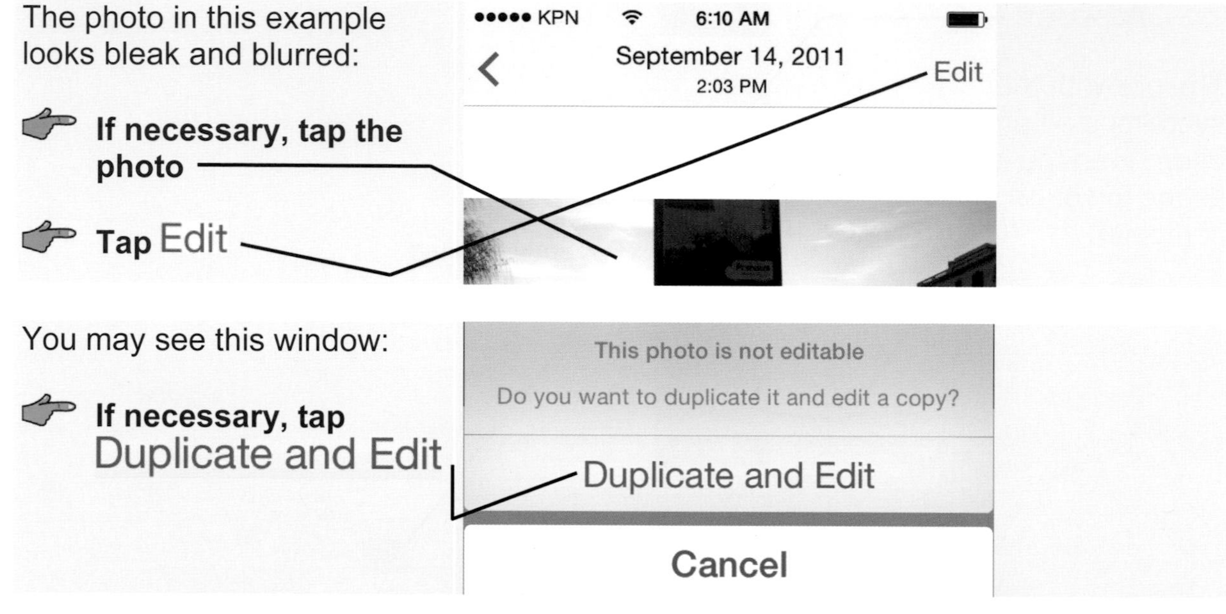

To automatically enhance the photo:

- **Tap**

Now the photo looks a bit clearer and livelier:

You will briefly see the Enhancing Photo message:

This means you have used this function.

If you tap , you will see the original photo again.

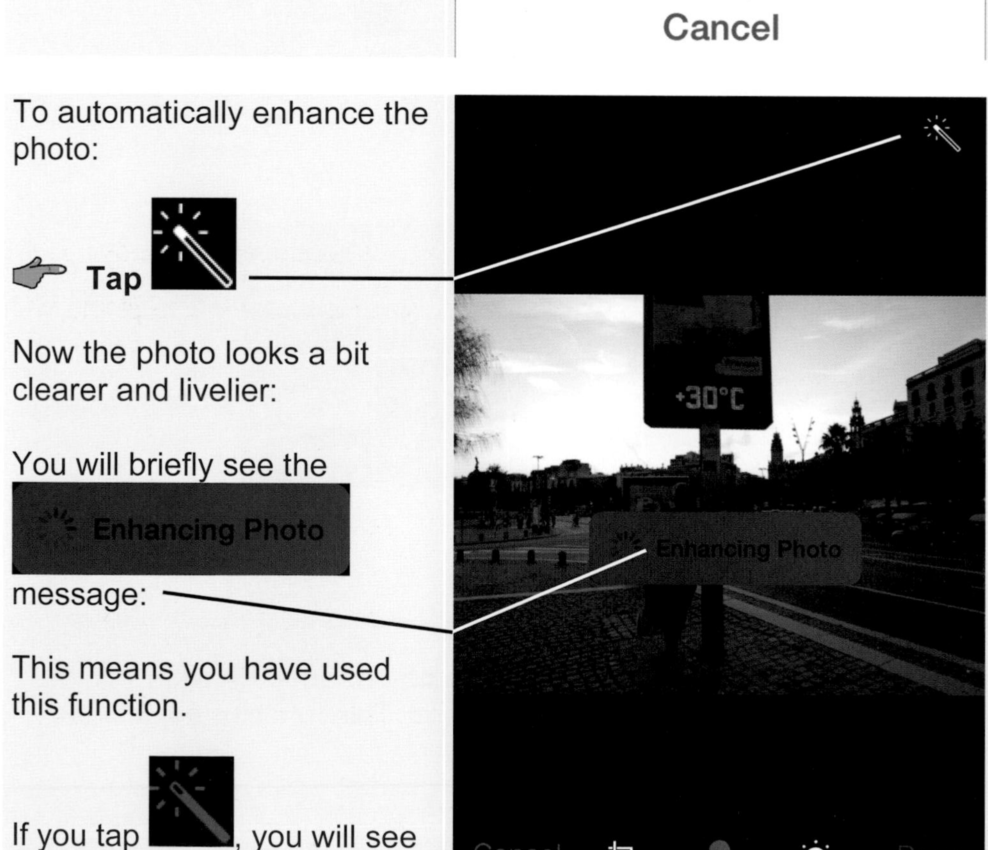

To save the photo:

At the bottom of the screen:

Tap Done

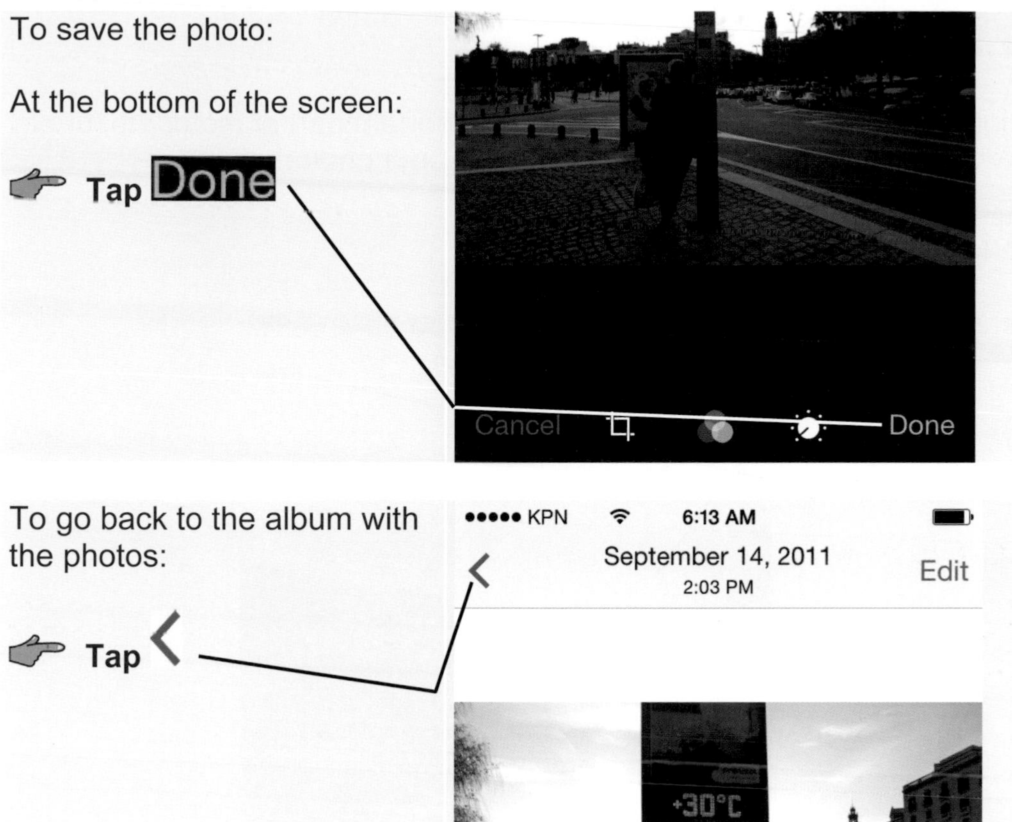

To go back to the album with the photos:

Tap <

The photo is saved.

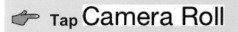

Please note:

If you have transferred photos from your computer to your iPhone you need to tap Duplicate and Edit before you can edit the photo. Then a copy of the photo will be saved on your iPhone.

If you want to view the picture you have saved, you do this:

Tap <

Tap < Albums

Tap Camera Roll

You will see the edited photo.

8.8 Crop a Photo

By cropping photos you can bring forward the most important part of the photo, or get rid of less pretty parts of the photo. You are going to crop a photo:

Open a photo 96

If necessary, tap the photo

Tap Edit

You may see this window:

If necessary, tap Duplicate and Edit

At the bottom of the screen:

Tap

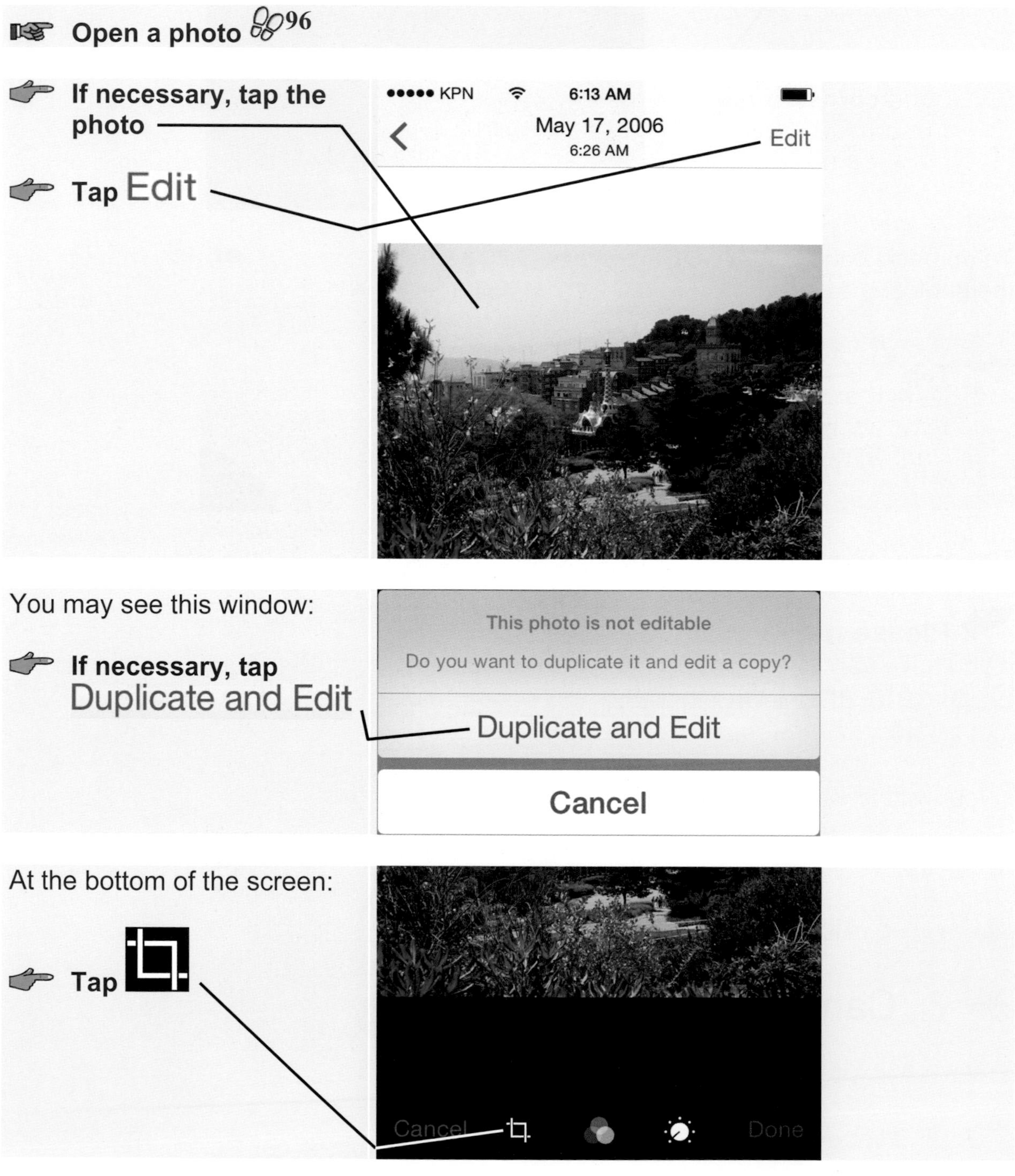

In this example we will crop a building:

You will see a frame across the photo:

You can move this frame:

Drag the top right-hand corner to the bottom left-hand corner a bit

You will see that the view of the photo is immediately adjusted to the frame.

Drag the bottom left-hand corner to the top right-hand corner a bit

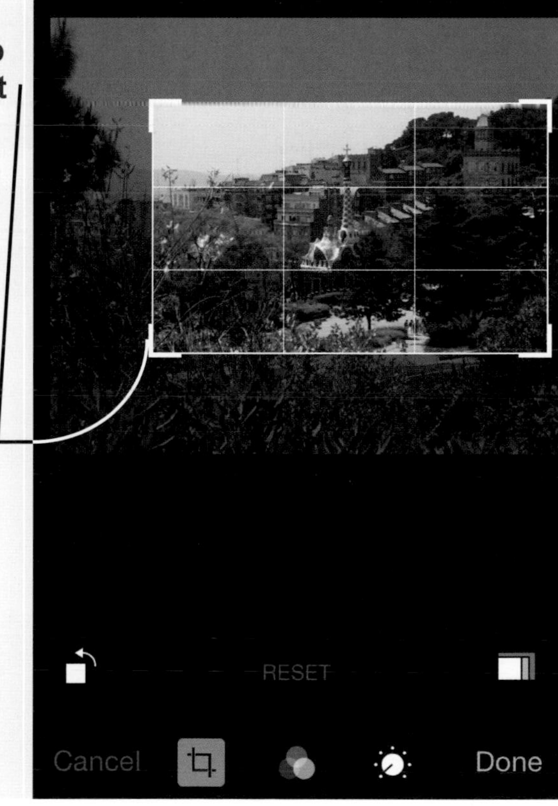

Now the height/width ratio of the photo is no longer correct. Select the desired ratio:

Tap

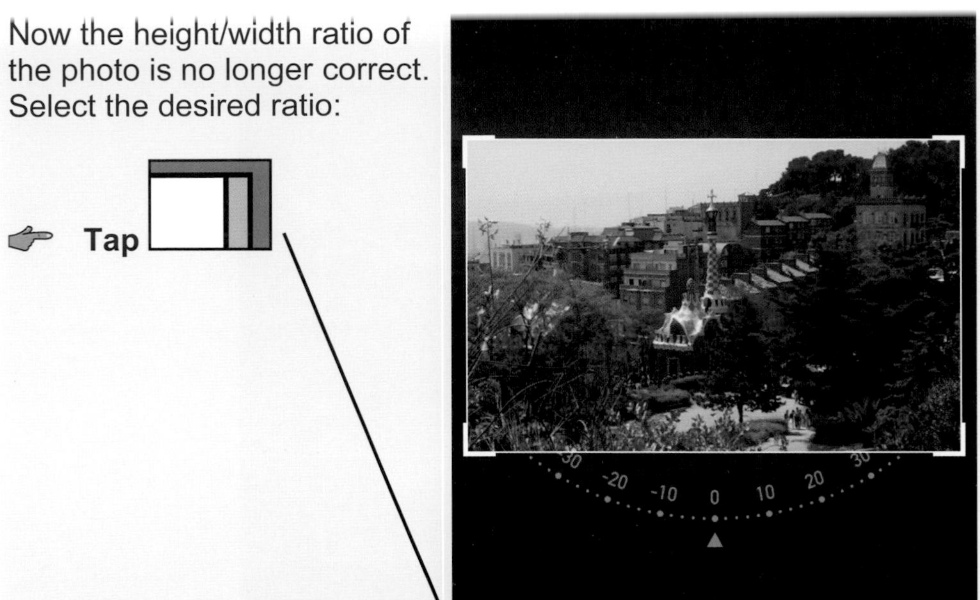

The iPhones screen has a 4:3 ratio:

Tap 4:3

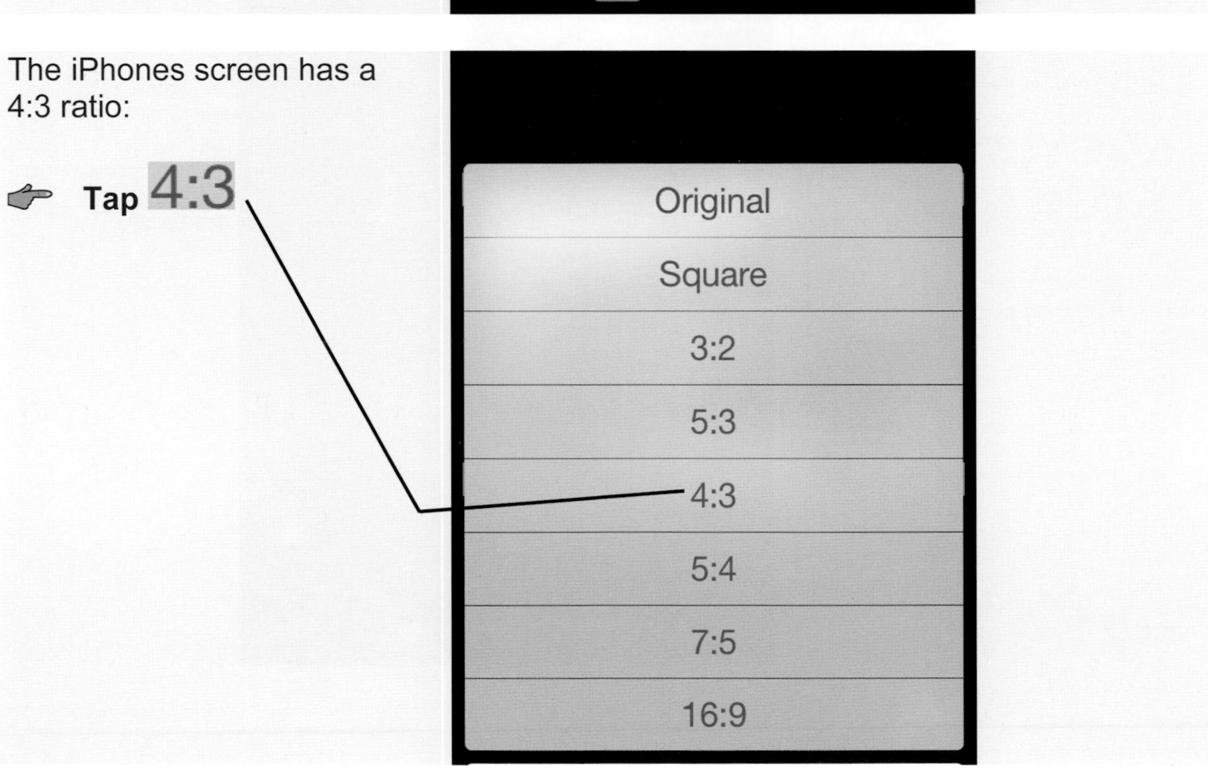

The cropped photo has been adjusted to the selected image ratio:

If necessary you can still move the photo, so the desired object is placed in the frame on the right spot.

With the Cancel button you can restore the photo:

You may need to practice a bit in order to crop the photo as it should be.

To save the photo:

Tap Done

You are going back to the album with the photos. In the top left-hand corner of the screen:

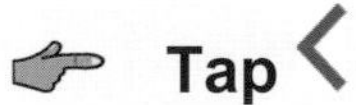

Tap <

8.9 Use Filters

You can also apply a filter to a photo. This will often produce a creative effect. Just try it:

Open a photo 96

Tap Edit

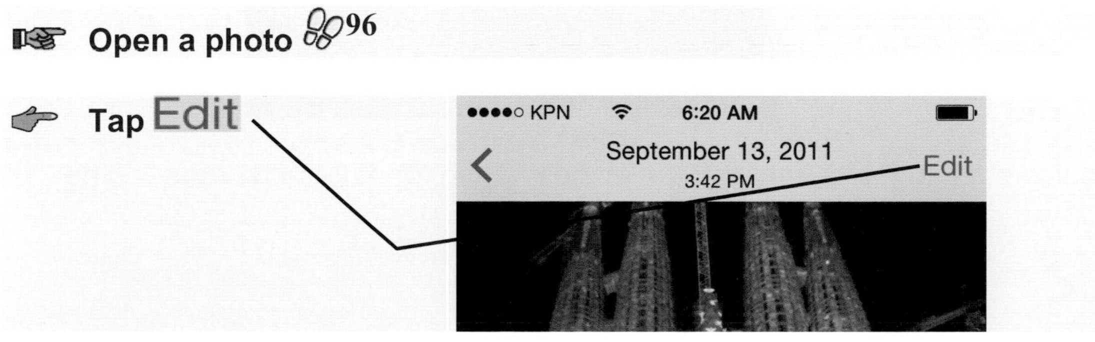

You may see this window:

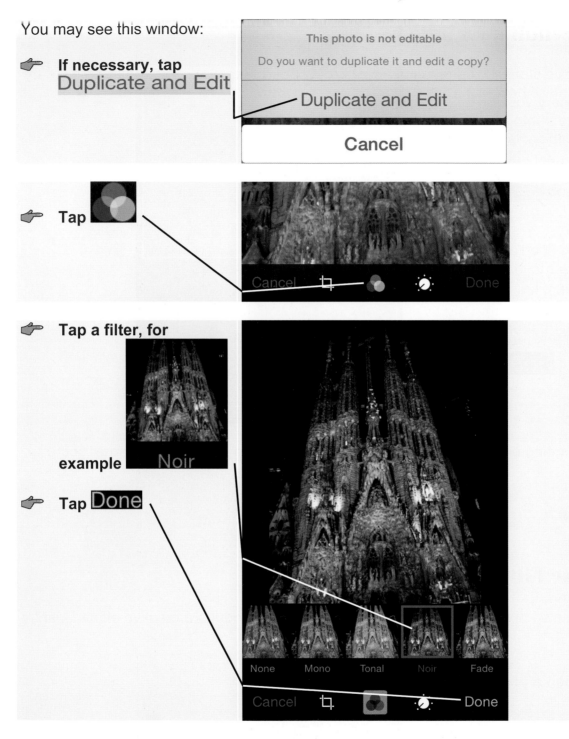

- **If necessary, tap** Duplicate and Edit

- **Tap**

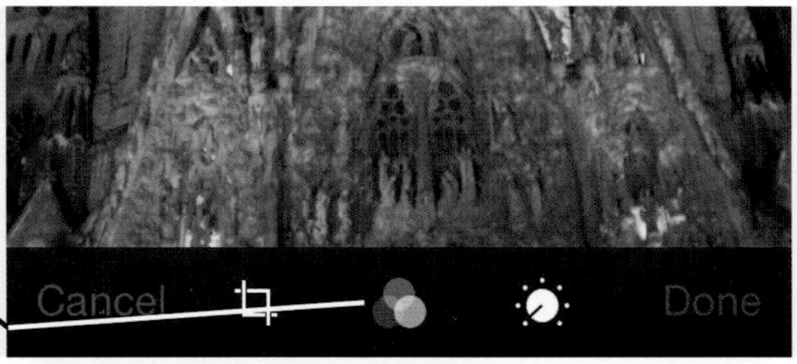

- **Tap a filter, for example** Noir

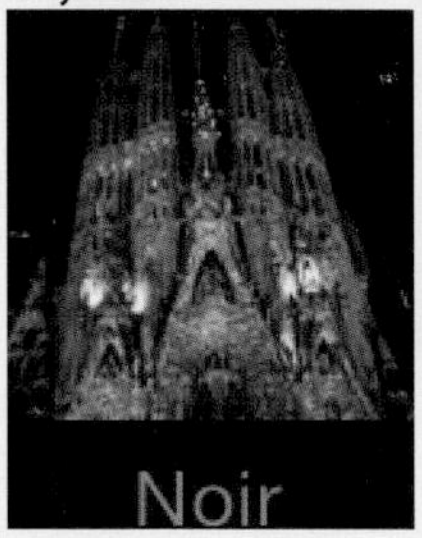

- **Tap** Done

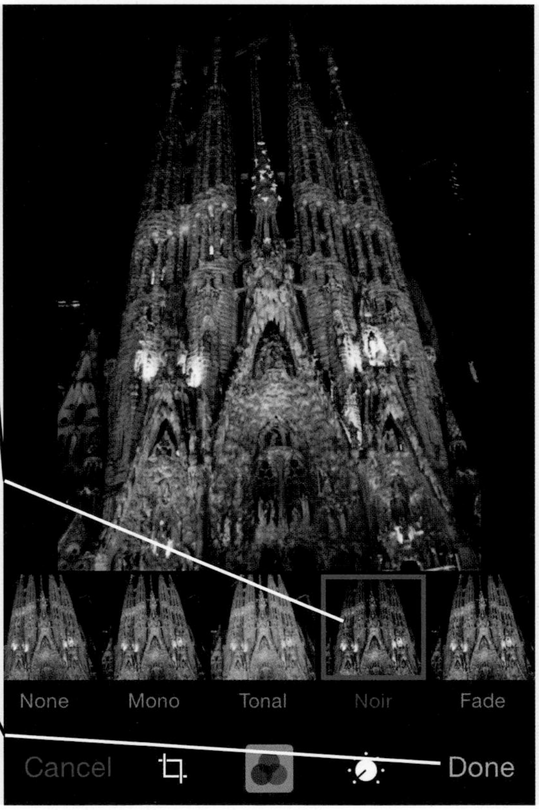

You are going back to the album with the photos. In the top left-hand corner of the screen:

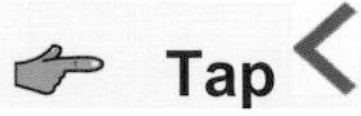

- **Tap** <

8.10 Sending a Photo by Email

If you have stored or taken a nice photo on your iPhone, you can send this picture by email. This is how you do it:

If necessary, open a photo 96

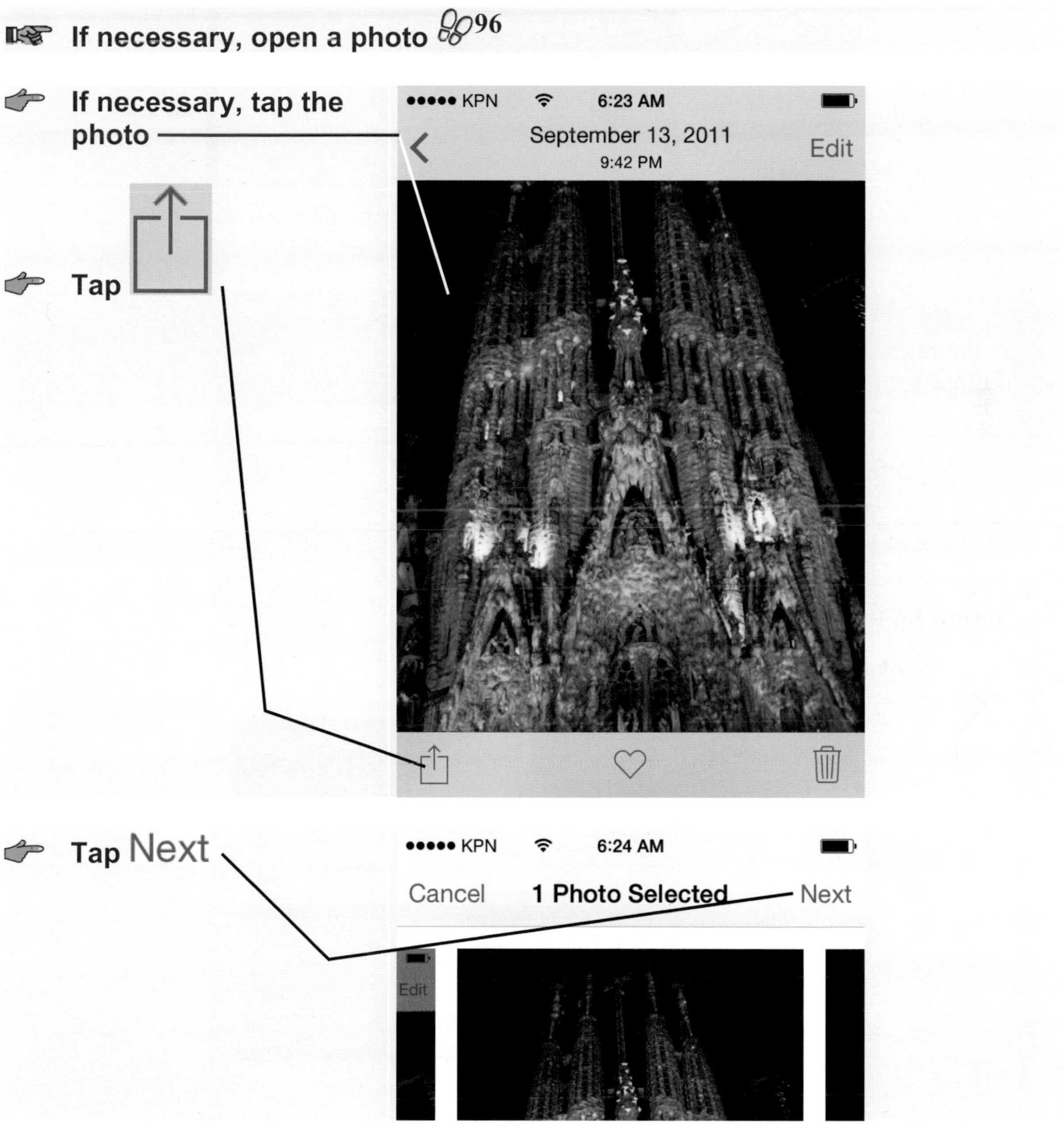

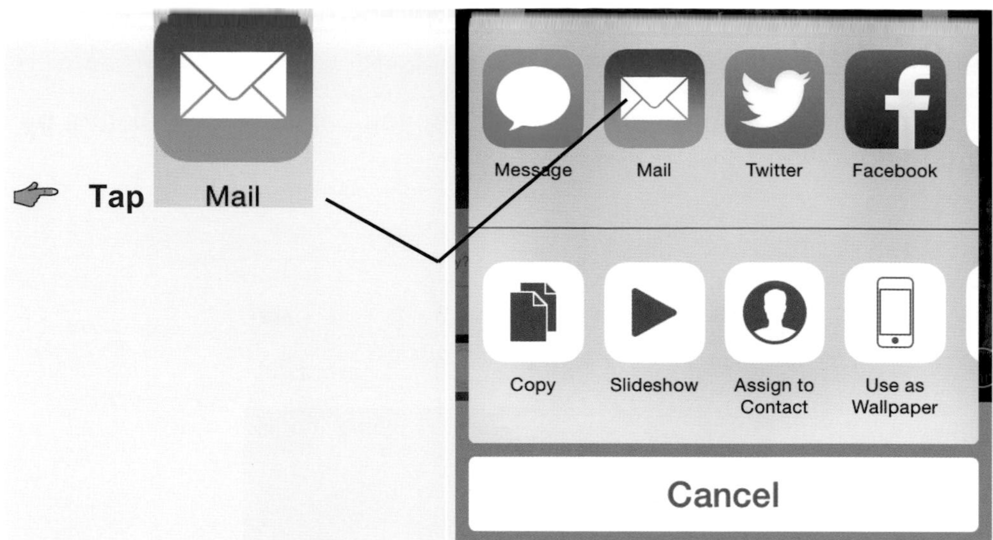

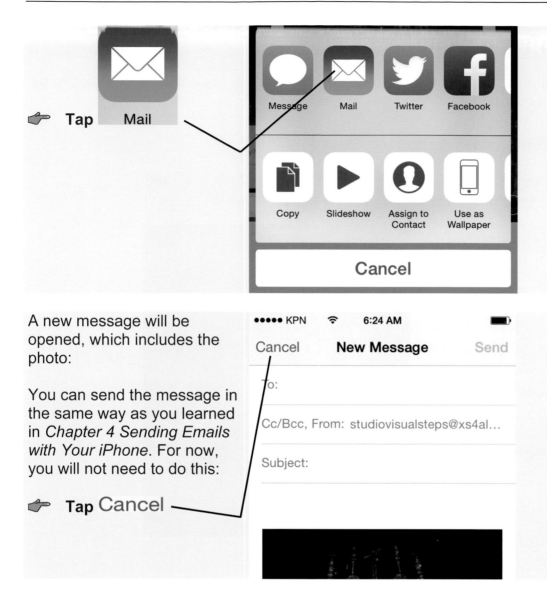

A new message will be opened, which includes the photo:

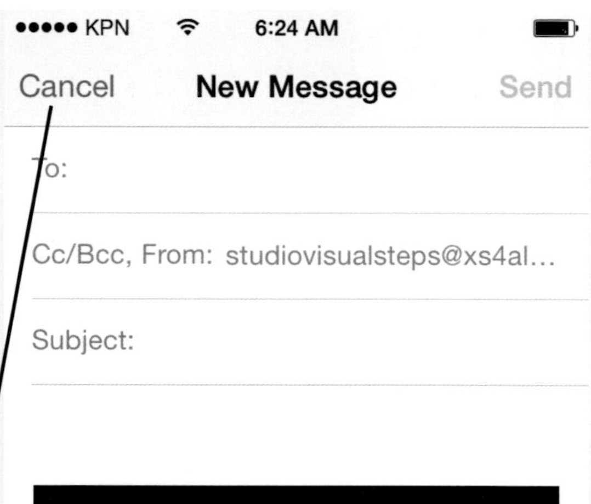

You can send the message in the same way as you learned in *Chapter 4 Sending Emails with Your iPhone*. For now, you will not need to do this:

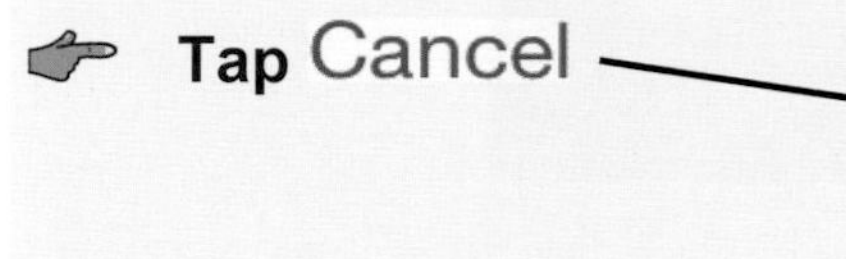

You will be asked if you want to save the draft:

You will see the photo again.

8.11 Printing a Photo

If you have a printer that supports the *AirPrint* function, you can use the wireless print function on the iPhone.

This is how you print a photo with your iPhone:

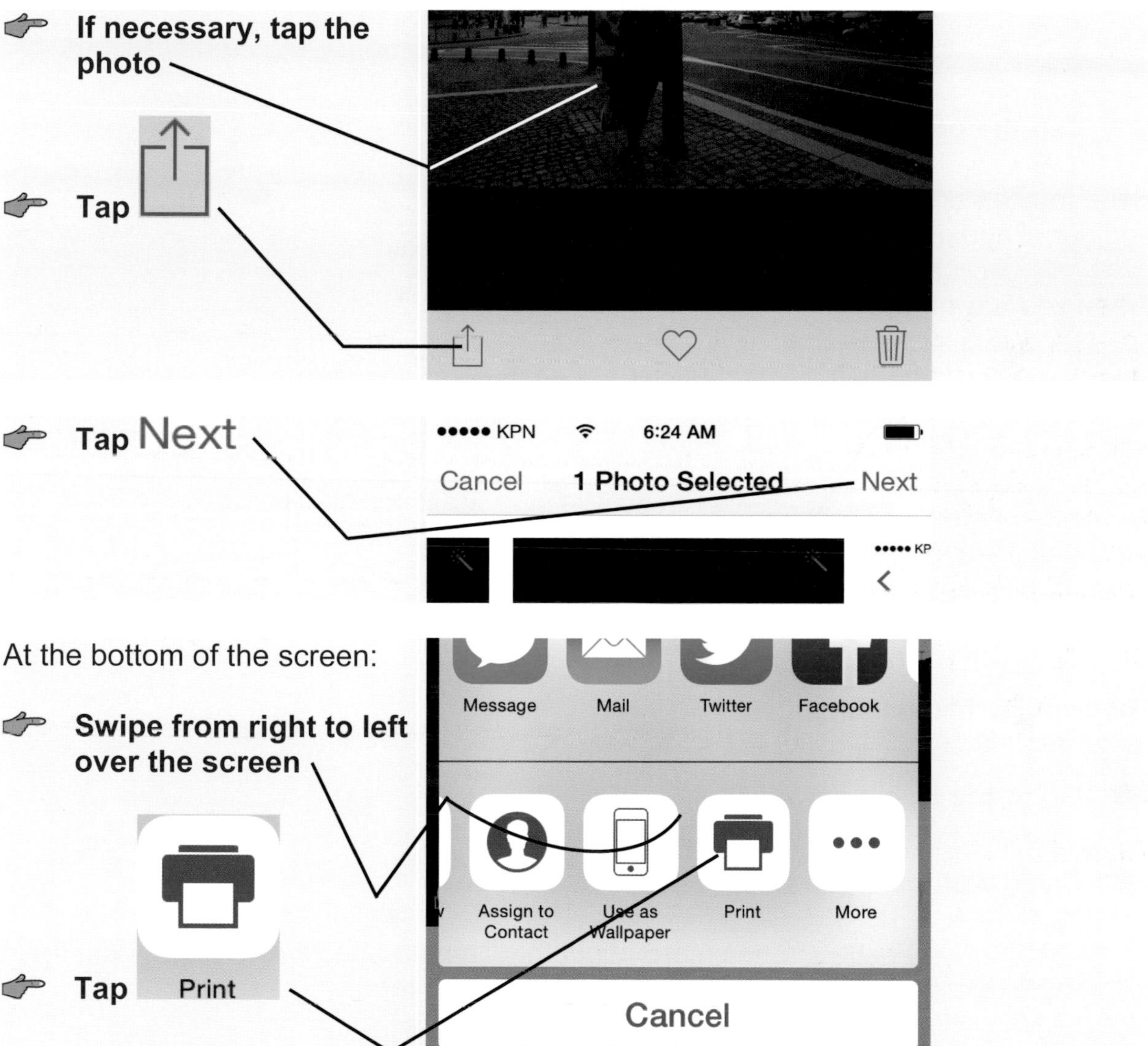

If necessary, tap the photo

Tap [share icon]

Tap Next

At the bottom of the screen:

Swipe from right to left over the screen

Tap Print

Select the correct printer:

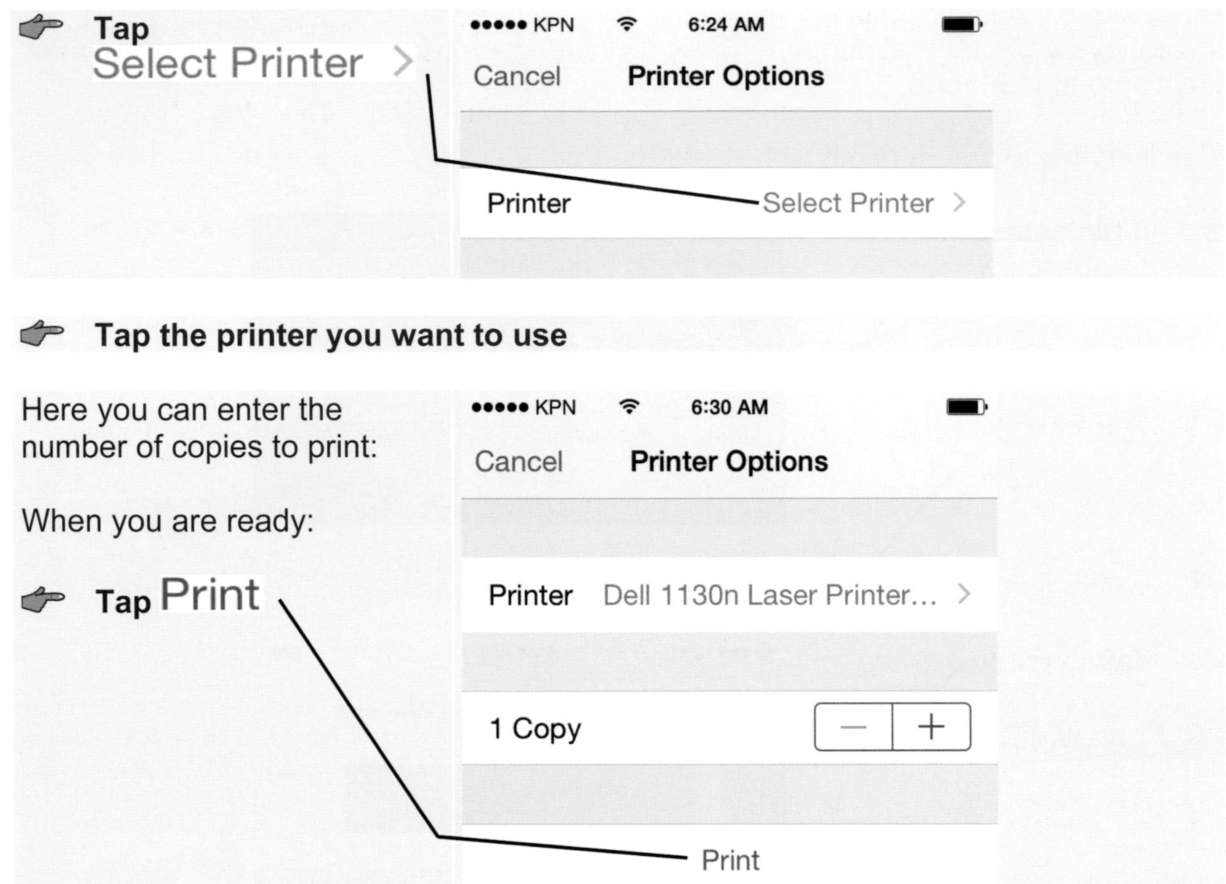

Tap Select Printer >

Tap the printer you want to use

Here you can enter the number of copies to print:

When you are ready:

Tap Print

The photo will be printed.

Go to the home screen 10

If you want, put the iPhone into sleep mode 2

In this chapter you have learned more about the *Camera* and *Photos* apps. With the following exercises you can practice what you have learned.

8.12 Exercises

To be able to quickly apply the things you have learned, you can work through these exercises. Have you forgotten how to do something? Use the numbers next to the footsteps 1 to look up the item in the appendix *How Do I Do That Again?* This appendix can be found at the end of the book.

Exercise 1: Taking Photos

In this exercise you are going to take photos with the *Camera* app.

- If necessary, wake the iPhone up from sleep mode. 1
- Open the *Camera* app 3 and choose an object or a person for your photo.
- Focus on a part of the object 99 and take a photo. 100
- Zoom in on the object 98 and take a photo. 100
- Switch to the camera on the front. 97
- Take a picture of yourself. 100
- Go to the home screen. 10

Exercise 2: View Photos

In this exercise you are going to look at the pictures stored on your iPhone.

- Open the *Photos* app 3 and open a photo. 96
- Flip to the next photo 95 and flip back to the previous photo. 77
- Start the slideshow and select the transition called *Origami*. 76
- Stop the slide show. 75
- Zoom in on the photo currently on your screen 53 and zoom out again. 54
- Go to the home screen. 10
- If you want, put the iPhone into sleep mode. 2

8.13 Background Information

Dictionary

AirPrint	An iPhone function that allows you to print on a printer that supports *AirPrint* via a wireless connection.
Camera	An app for taking pictures and shooting film. You can use both the front and back cameras on the iPhone.
Camera Roll	The name of the photo folder where the photos on your iPhone are stored. This can include the photos you made with your iPhone, or those downloaded from an attachment or a website.
Digital zoom	A digital zoom function enlarges a small part of the original picture. You will not see any additional details; all it does is make the pixels bigger. That is why the photo quality will diminish.
Family Sharing	This option lets families of up to six people share their *iTunes* purchases. You can also share family photos, a family calendar, locations and more.
Photos	An app that lets you view the photos on the iPhone.
Slideshow	Automatic display of a collection of pictures.
Transition	An animated effect that is displayed when browsing through the photos in a slideshow.
Zooming	Take a closer look or view from a distance.

Source: User Guide iPhone, Wikipedia

8.14 Tips

Tip

Flash

You can set the LED-flash on the iPhone as follows:

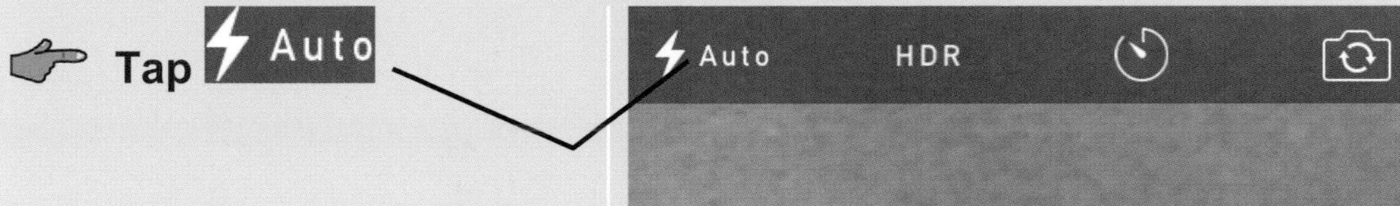

Now you can select Auto (auto flash), On (always flash), and Off (never flash).

Tip

Self-portrait

On the iPhone you can also use the front-facing camera. For instance, to take a picture of yourself. This is how you switch to the camera on the front:

At the top right, tap

Now you will see the image of the camera on the front:

You can take a photo in the same way as you have previously done with the camera on the back. Only, the front-facing camera does not have a digital zoom.

This is how you switch back to the camera on the back:

At the top right, tap 

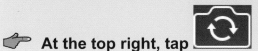

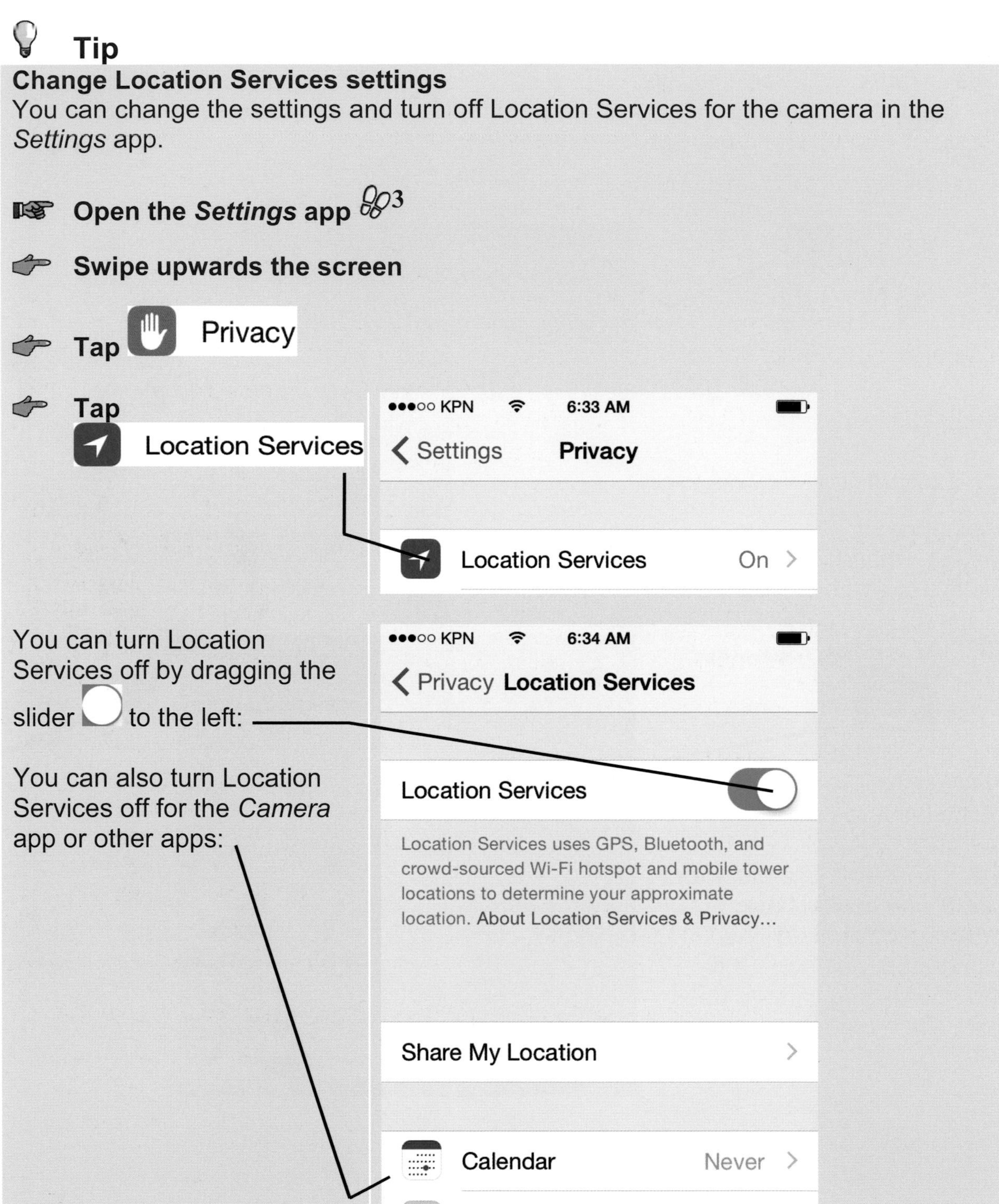

Tip

Change Location Services settings

You can change the settings and turn off Location Services for the camera in the *Settings* app.

- **Open the *Settings* app** 3
- **Swipe upwards the screen**
- **Tap** Privacy
- **Tap** Location Services

You can turn Location Services off by dragging the slider to the left:

You can also turn Location Services off for the *Camera* app or other apps:

 **Tip**

Use a photo in different ways

In this chapter you have learned how to send a photo by email and how to print a photo. But you can do many other things with your photos:

A selection of the options:

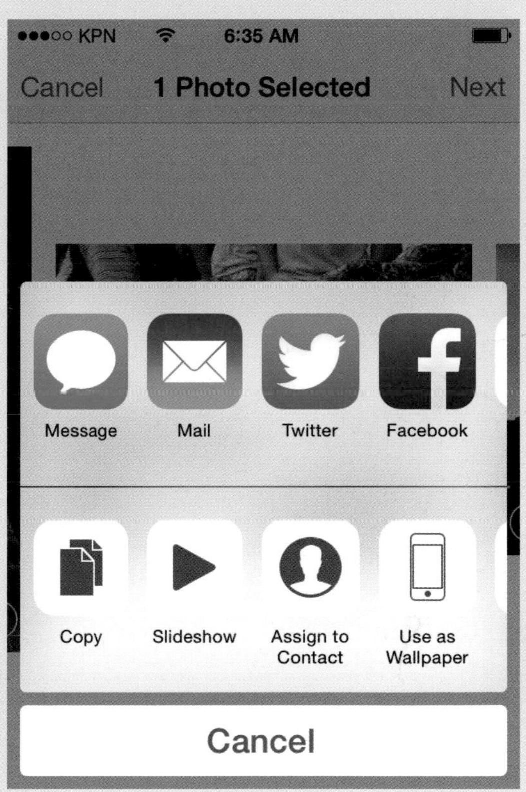

Message: a new text (SMS) message or *iMessage* message will be opened with the photo attached to the message.

Assign to Contact : the contacts list will be opened, so you can select the person in the photo and add it to the contact. You can also move, enlarge or shrink the photo.

Use as Wallpaper: you can use your own photo as a background for the Lock screen or the home screen.

Twitter: if you have linked your *Twitter* account to your iPhone, you can open a new tweet which contains a link to the photo.

You can show all the options by swiping from right to left over the lower part of the screen.

Tip

Delete multiple photos at once

On your iPhone, you can delete your photos one by one. But if you want to delete a lot of photos, it is better to do it like this:

Please note: you can only do this photos that have been made on your iPhone.

Tap Select

Tap the desired photos

On the selected photos, a checkmark will appear :

Tap

Instead of deleting them, you can also share the selected photos (by email, message, or print), copy them or add them to an album:

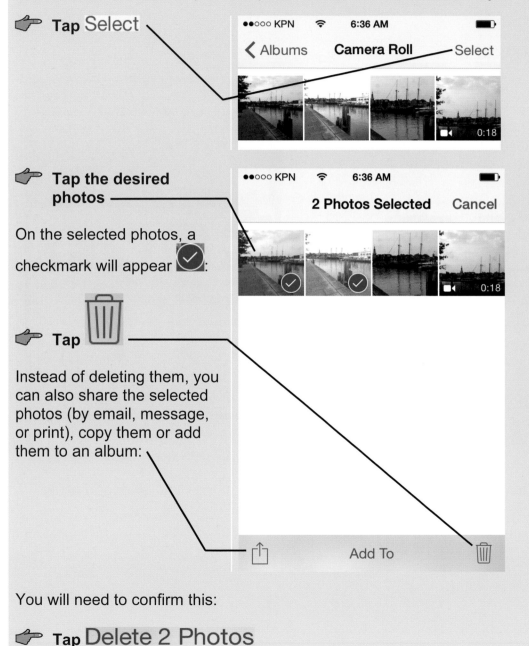

You will need to confirm this:

Tap Delete 2 Photos

Tip

Different displays in Photos app

In the *Photos* app you can display your photos in various ways:

Open the *Photos* app 3

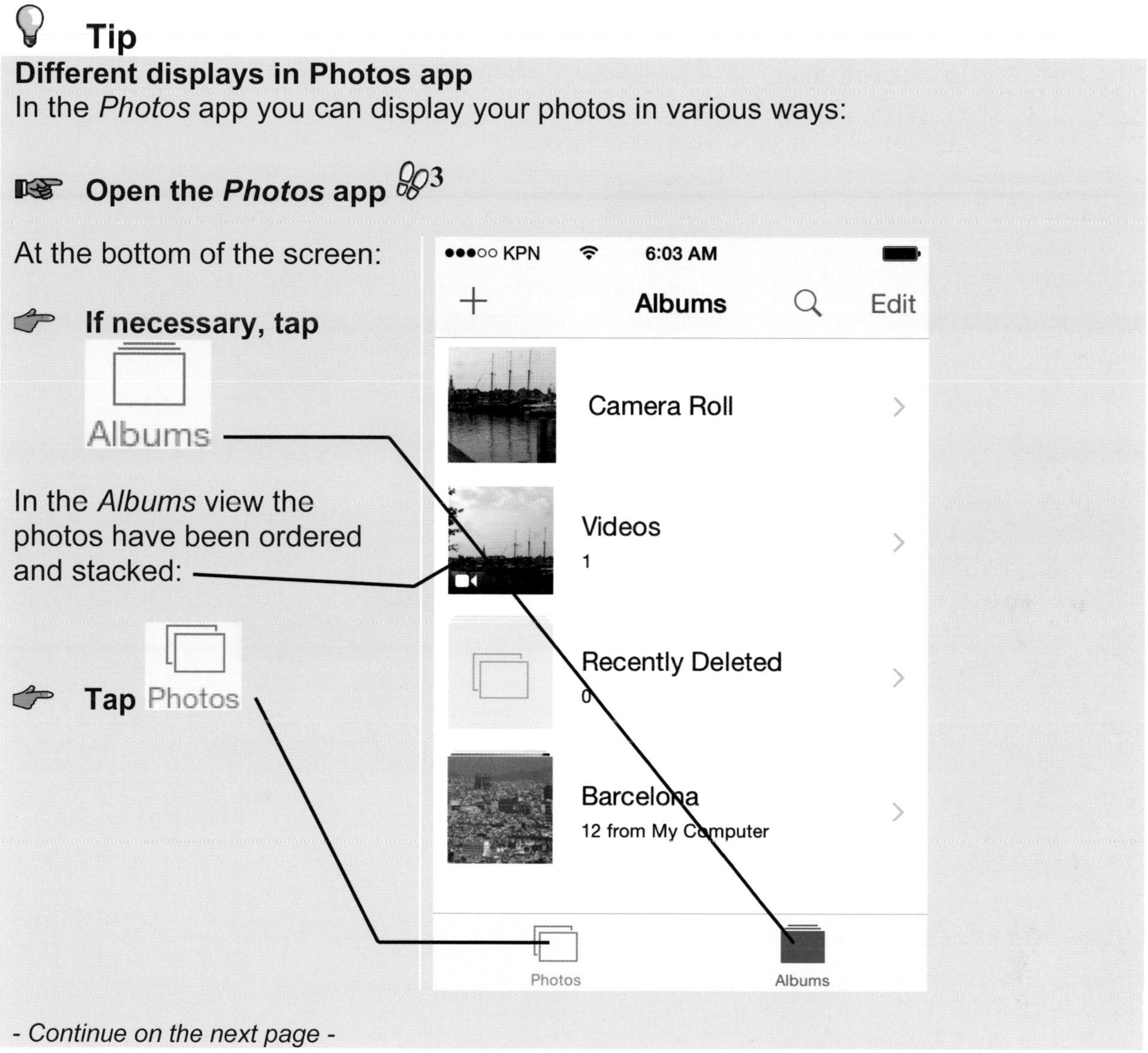

- *Continue on the next page* -

In the *Moments* view you will see all the photos, below and next to each other, sorted by date and location:

By tapping < Collections the view will become a bit more compacted. And in the next view, the < Years, view, it will become even more compacted:

You can view the pictures that were taken with the Location Services turned on and look at them on the map:

👉 **Tap a location**

In this view you will see a map showing the locations where the photos were taken:

To go back to the recent view:

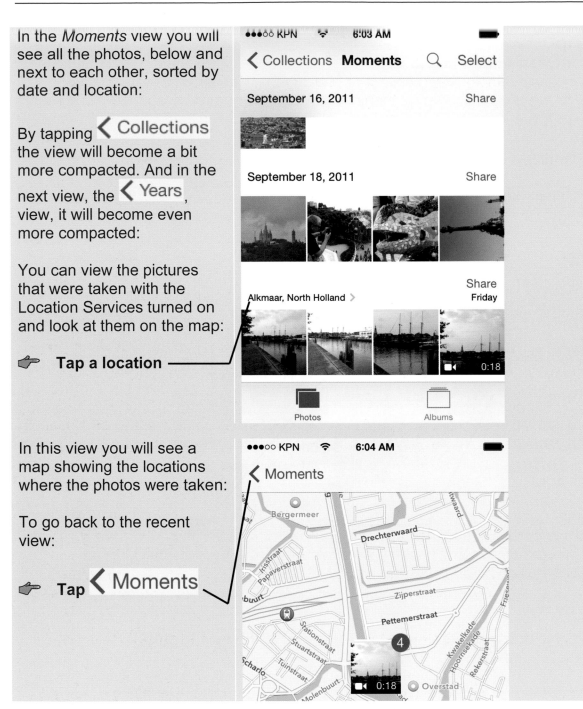

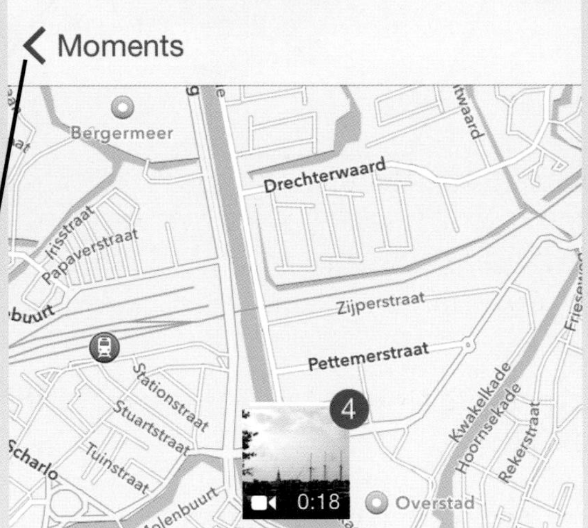

 **Tip**

Make a screenshot
It is very easy to make a screenshot of your iPhone. For instance, you can take a picture of a high game score, a funny message or an error message on your screen:

☞ **Simultaneously press the Home button** 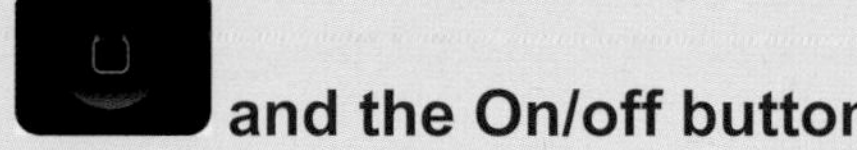 **and the On/off button**

You will hear the clicking sound of the camera and the screenshot will be added to your iPhone. You can view the screenshot in the *Photos* app.

 **Tip**

Different video formats
The iPhone supports a limited number of video formats: .M4V, .MP4, and .MOV. Perhaps you have video files on your computer that have a different file format, such as .MPG or .AVI. In that case you can do two things.
First, you can convert the video to another file format. You can use the free *WinFF* program to do this, if you want. The downside of this conversion is that it takes a lot of time.

But you can also download an app that is capable of playing different types of video formats, such as the *Movie Player* (free app) or the *GoodPlayer* app ($2.99 August 2014).

 **Tip**

Delete synchronized photos and videos
If you have second thoughts and you do not want to save one or multiple synchronized photos on your iPhone you will need to delete these through *iTunes*. You can do this in several ways. If you want to delete just a few pictures, this is what you need to do:

☞ **Delete or move the unwanted photos from the synchronized folder on your computer**

☞ **Synchronize the folder with your iPhone once more, just like you have done in the previous section**

Synchronizing means that the content of the iPhone folder will be made equal to the content of the folder on your computer. The photos that have been deleted or moved will also disappear from the iPhone. You can also delete one or more synchronized folders:

- Continue on the next page -

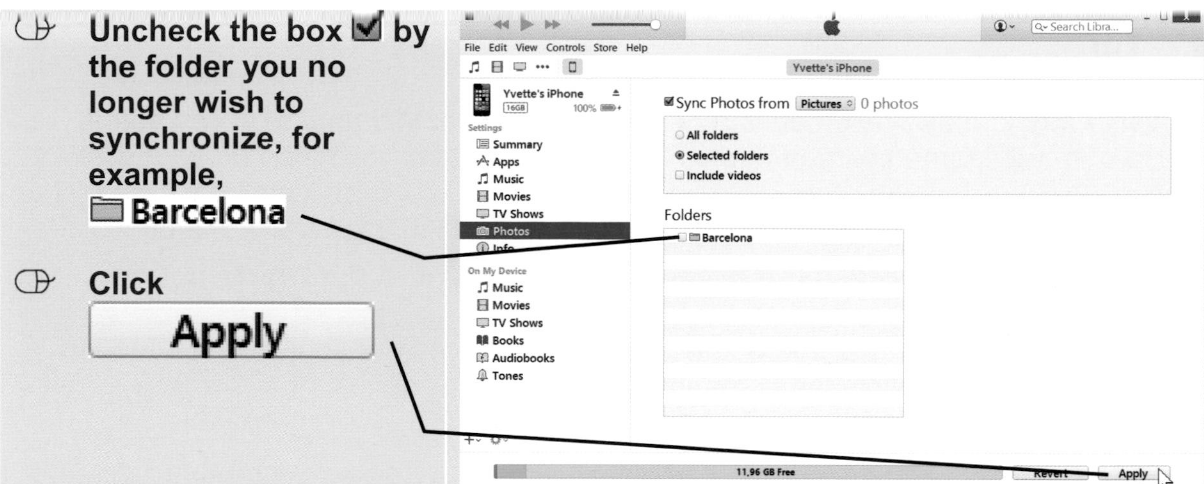

- **Uncheck the box ☑ by the folder you no longer wish to synchronize, for example, Barcelona**
- **Click** Apply

The synchronization operation is started and the folder is deleted from your iPhone.

If you do not want to synchronize any photos at all with your iPhone, you can delete all the photos, like this:

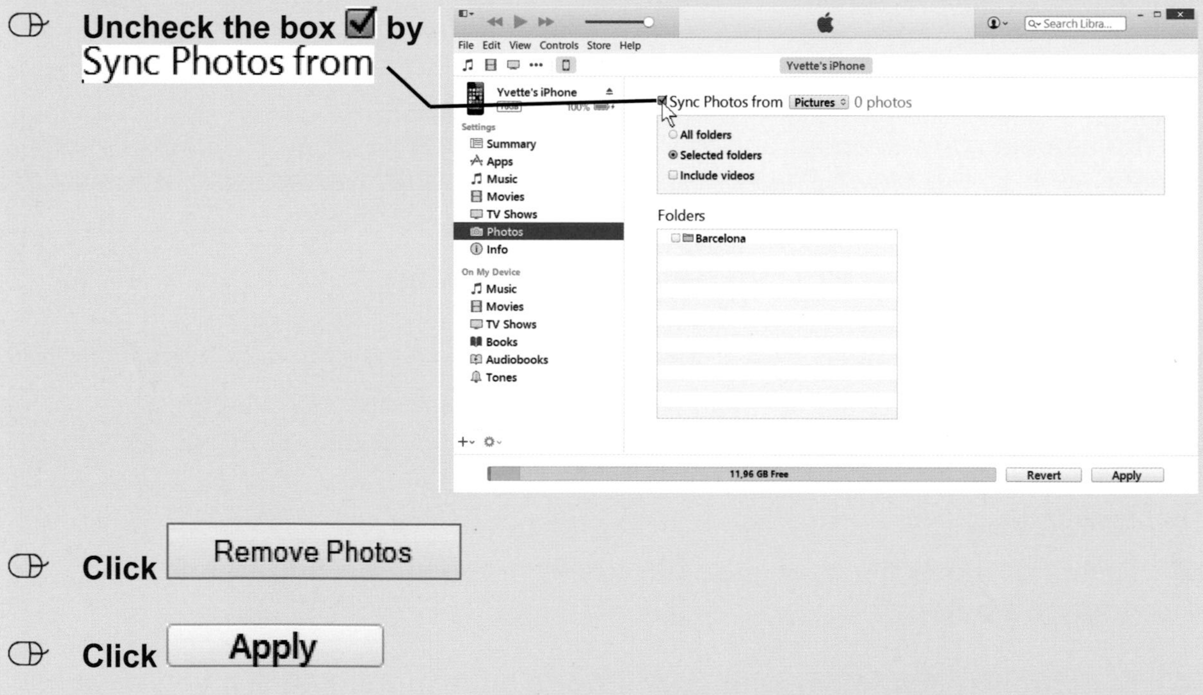

- **Uncheck the box ☑ by** Sync Photos from
- **Click** Remove Photos
- **Click** Apply

The synchronization operation is started and all synchronized photos will be deleted.

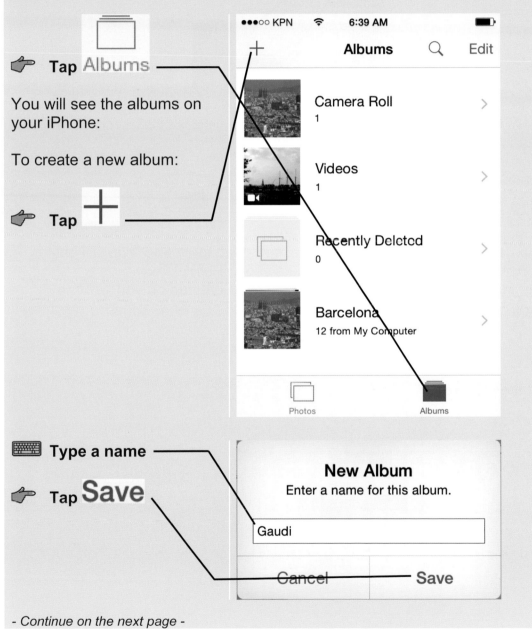

Tip

Organize your photos in albums

You can create albums for your photos directly on your iPhone. When you add a photo to a new album, you are actually adding a link to the photo from the original album to the new one. By sorting your photos into albums, it makes it easier to find a series of photos about a specific subject later on. You can create a new album like this:

Tap Albums

You will see the albums on your iPhone:

To create a new album:

Tap +

Type a name

Tap Save

- Continue on the next page -

- **Tap the desired photos**
- **Tap** Done

The new album is created:

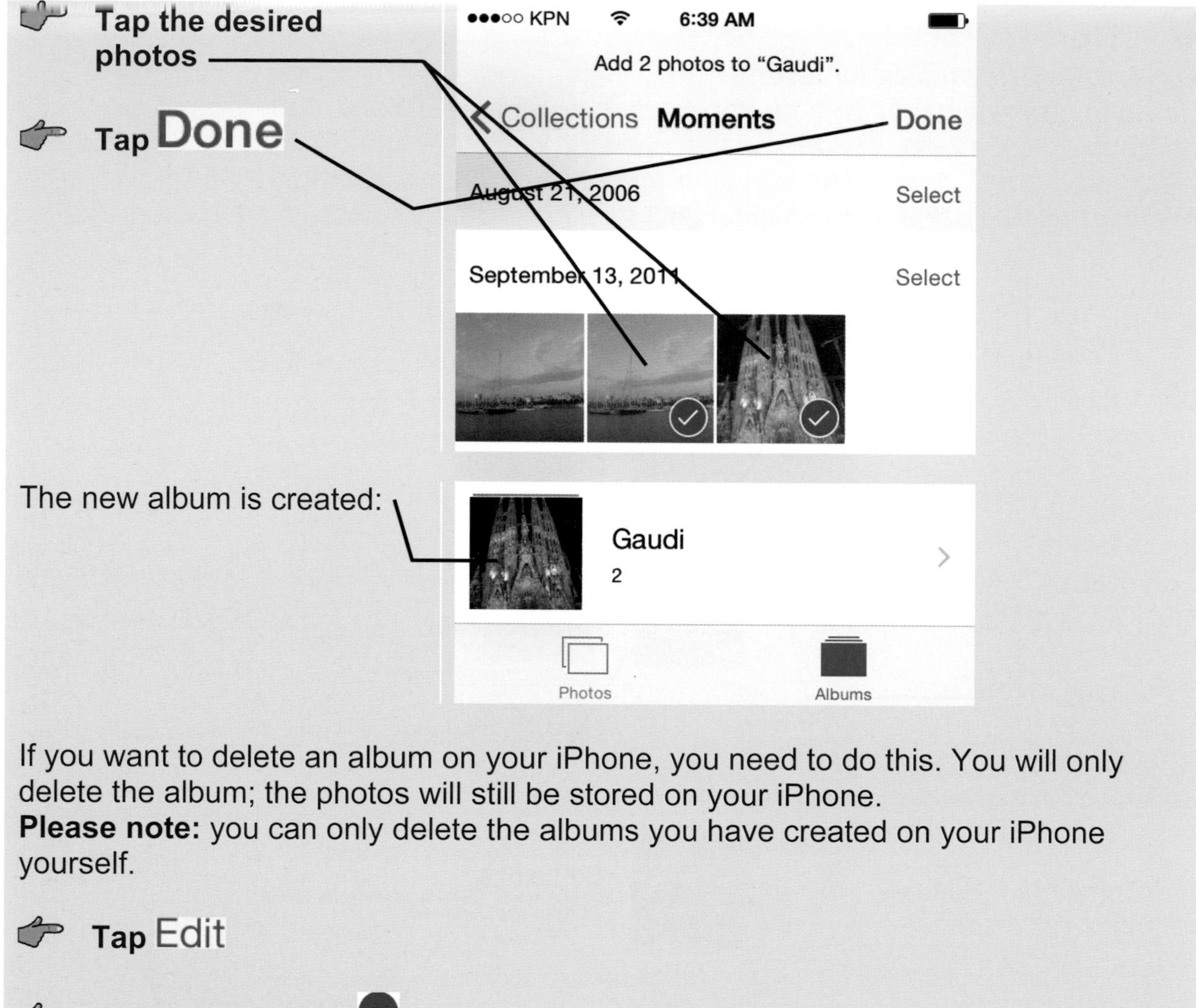

If you want to delete an album on your iPhone, you need to do this. You will only delete the album; the photos will still be stored on your iPhone.
Please note: you can only delete the albums you have created on your iPhone yourself.

- **Tap** Edit
- **By the album, tap** ⊖
- **Tap** Delete
- **Tap** Delete Album

Tip

Upload a video to YouTube

You can also upload a video directly from your iPhone to *YouTube*. Here is how you do that:

Open the video

Tap

Tap Next

Tap YouTube

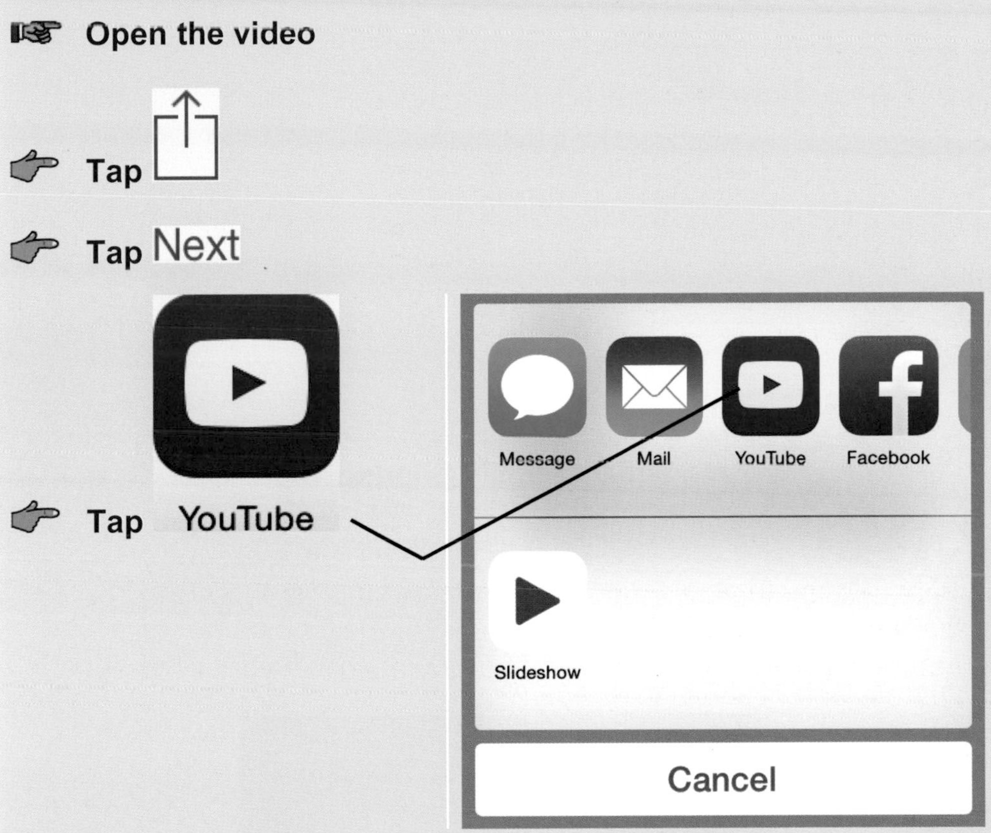

Note that you can also send a video through email or as a message. This is done in the same way as with photos. But keep in mind that videos take up a lot of space and will sometimes be too big to send along with an email or a message.

If you want to upload to *YouTube* you need to sign in with your *YouTube* account. Next, you can enter the information about the video on the screen. If you do not yet have a *YouTube* account, you can create one at www.youtube.com

Tip! *YouTube* also has its own app. With this app you can easily view all sorts of videos on *YouTube* and create playlists of your favorite videos. You can find this app on the iPhone's home screen.

Tip

Rent or purchase a movie on your iPhone

In the *iTunes Store* you can buy much more than just music. You can rent or buy movies and view them on your iPhone. The movies are arranged in various categories or genres, such as children's movies, action films, and comedies.

Open the app *iTunes Store* 3

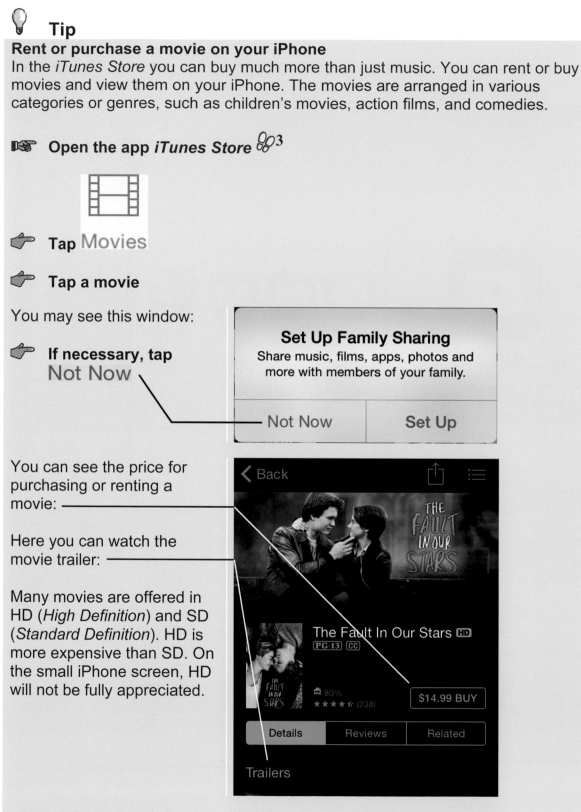

Tap Movies

Tap a movie

You may see this window:

If necessary, tap Not Now

Set Up Family Sharing
Share music, films, apps, photos and more with members of your family.

Not Now | Set Up

You can see the price for purchasing or renting a movie:

Here you can watch the movie trailer:

Many movies are offered in HD (*High Definition*) and SD (*Standard Definition*). HD is more expensive than SD. On the small iPhone screen, HD will not be fully appreciated.

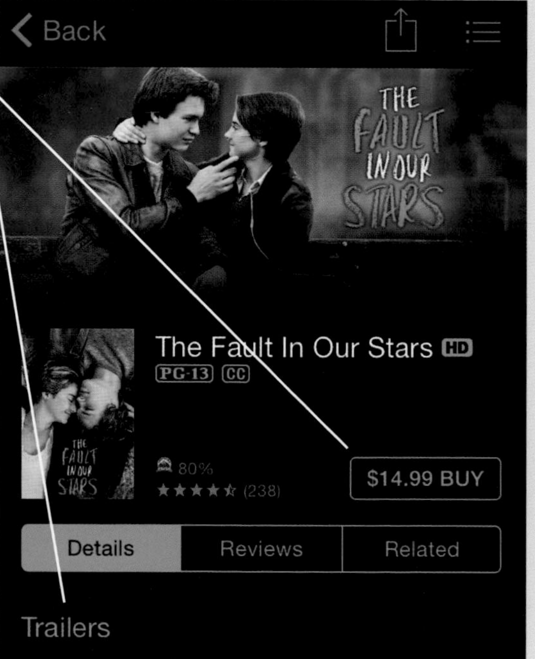

- *Continue on the next page* -

If you purchase a movie for your iPhone it will be yours to view as often as you like. If you rent a movie you will need to watch it within 30 days. Also, after you have started watching the movie you will need to watch the entire movie within 48 hours. Within these 48 hours you are allowed to watch the movie several times. After that period the movie will be automatically removed from your iPhone. If you do not start the movie within 30 days, the movie will be removed as well.
When you buy or rent a movie for your iPhone you will not be able to transfer this movie to other devices, such as your computer, iPad, iPod touch, or Apple TV. This will only be possible if you purchase or download the movie through *iTunes*, on your computer.

Buying or renting a movie is similar to buying music, for instance:

☞ **Buy or rent the movie, if you wish**

You can watch the rented movie in the Videos app that is one of the standard apps installed to your iPhone. The screen of this app can be compared to the screen you see when you watch a video in the *Photos* app. The playback sliders are very similar too.

Through the *iTunes Store* you can also purchase TV Shows or Audiobooks. This works much the same way.

Tip

Photostream, AirDrop and Family Sharing
If you use *iCloud* you can use *Photostream* to share your photos on your iPhone, computer (Mac or *Windows*), or on other devices, such as your iPad or iPod touch.

Photostream will automatically send copies (through Wi-Fi) of the photos on your iPhone to other devices on which *iCloud* has been set up, and on which *Photostream* has been activated.

The photos that are added to *Photostream* from an iPhone will include all the photos taken with your iPhone, the photos that have been downloaded from email, text, or *iMessage* messages, and the screen prints you have made. With *Photostream* you can exchange up to 1000 of your most recent pictures with your iPhone, iPad, iPod touch, and computer.

Through *Photostream* you can easily share photos as well. The friends who use *iCloud* on a device where *iOS 6* or higher is installed, or on a Mac computer with *OS X Mountain Lion* or higher will be able to see the photos right away, in the *Photos* app or in *iPhoto*. Anyone who does not use an Apple device but a *Windows* computer, for instance, will be able to view the shared photos on the Internet. Your friends can also comment on your photos.

Another useful function is *AirDrop*. This function lets you quickly and easily share photos and other files with others next to you using Wi-Fi or Bluetooth. It is also possible to share photos directly with family members. You can do this with *Family Sharing*.

Do you want to know more about *iCloud*, *Photostream*, *AirDrop* and *Family Sharing*? Then download the free *Bonus Chapter iCloud* from the website accompanying this book. In *Appendix B Opening Bonus Chapters* you can read how to do this.

9. Music

Your iPhone contains a very extensive music player, the *Music* app. If you have stored music files on your computer, you can use the *iTunes* program to transfer these files to your iPhone. You can also purchase individual songs or entire CDs in the *iTunes Store*.

In this chapter you will learn how to:

- add music to the *iTunes Library*;
- copy music to your iPhone;
- purchase music for your iPhone;
- play music on your iPhone.

9.1 Adding Music to iTunes

Your iPhone is equipped with an extensive music player, called the *Music* app. If you have stored any music on your computer, you can use *iTunes* to transfer these audio files to your iPhone.

Open *iTunes* on your computer 11

You will see the *iTunes* window. First you have to show the menu bar:

If necessary, click

If necessary, click Show Menu Bar

This is how you add a folder with music files to the *Library*:

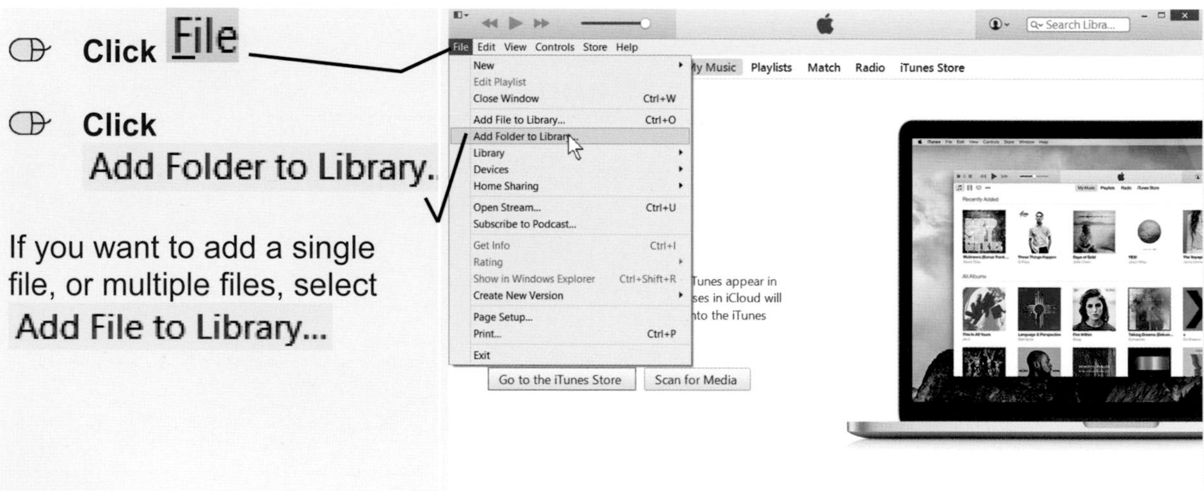

Click File

Click Add Folder to Library.

If you want to add a single file, or multiple files, select Add File to Library...

In this example we have chosen the *Windows* folder with sample files. But you can use your own music files if you want:

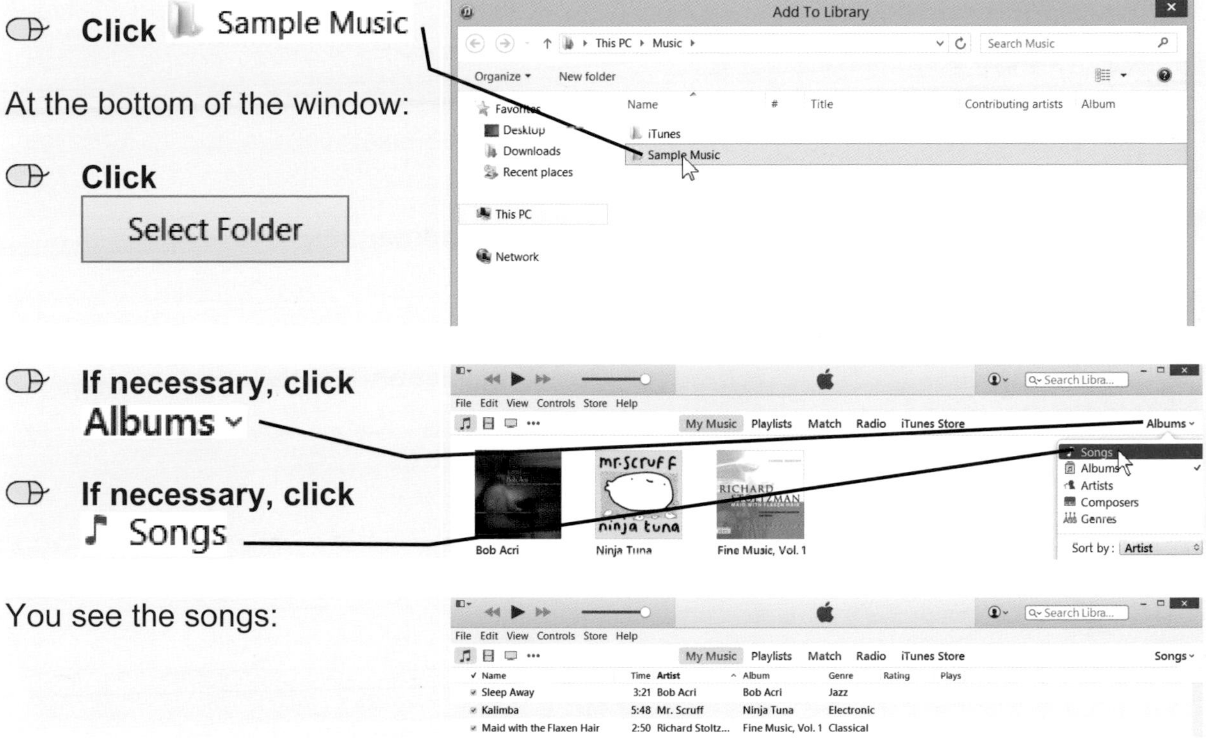

Click Sample Music

At the bottom of the window:

Click Select Folder

If necessary, click Albums

If necessary, click Songs

You see the songs:

9.2 Copying Music to Your iPhone

Once the songs have been included in *iTunes*, it is very easy to add them to your iPhone.

Connect your iPhone to the computer

The iPhone will appear in *iTunes*. Now you can select the songs you want to transfer:

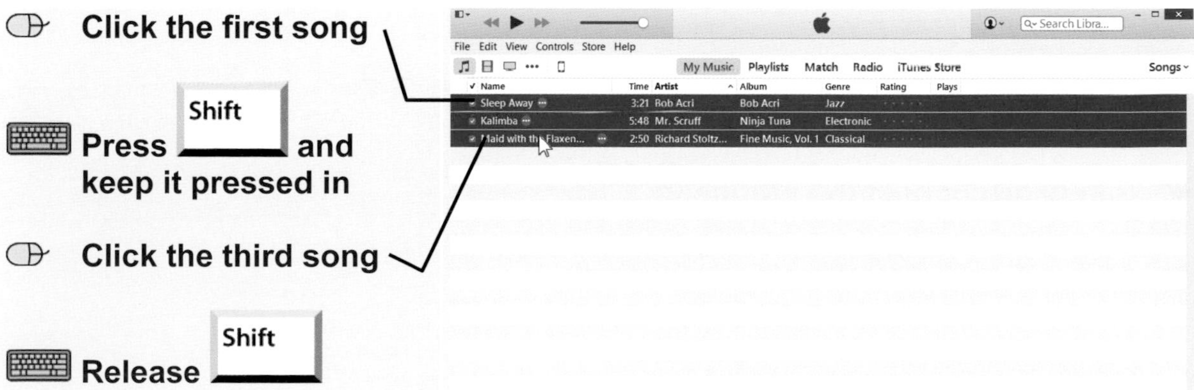

Click the first song

Press Shift **and keep it pressed in**

Click the third song

Release Shift

The songs have been selected. Now you can copy the songs to your iPhone:

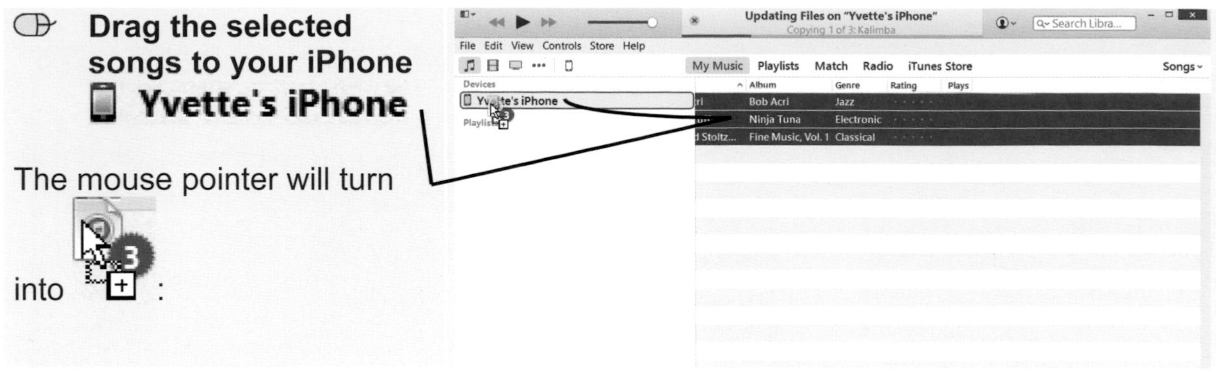

Drag the selected songs to your iPhone Yvette's iPhone

The mouse pointer will turn into :

The copying process is indicated at the top of the window:

Now you can take a look at the contents of the iPhone:

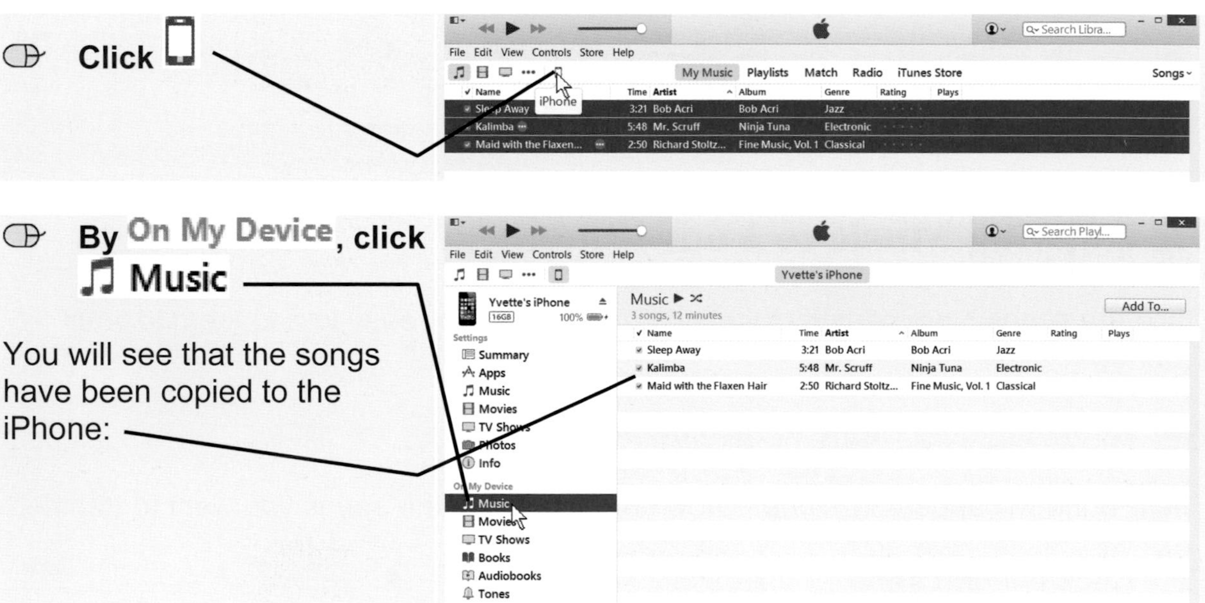

Click

By On My Device, click Music

You will see that the songs have been copied to the iPhone:

You can disconnect the iPhone and close *iTunes*:

Safely disconnect the iPhone 47

Close *iTunes* 5

9.3 Purchase Music for Your iPhone

You can also transfer music directly to your iPhone by purchasing songs in the *iTunes Store*.

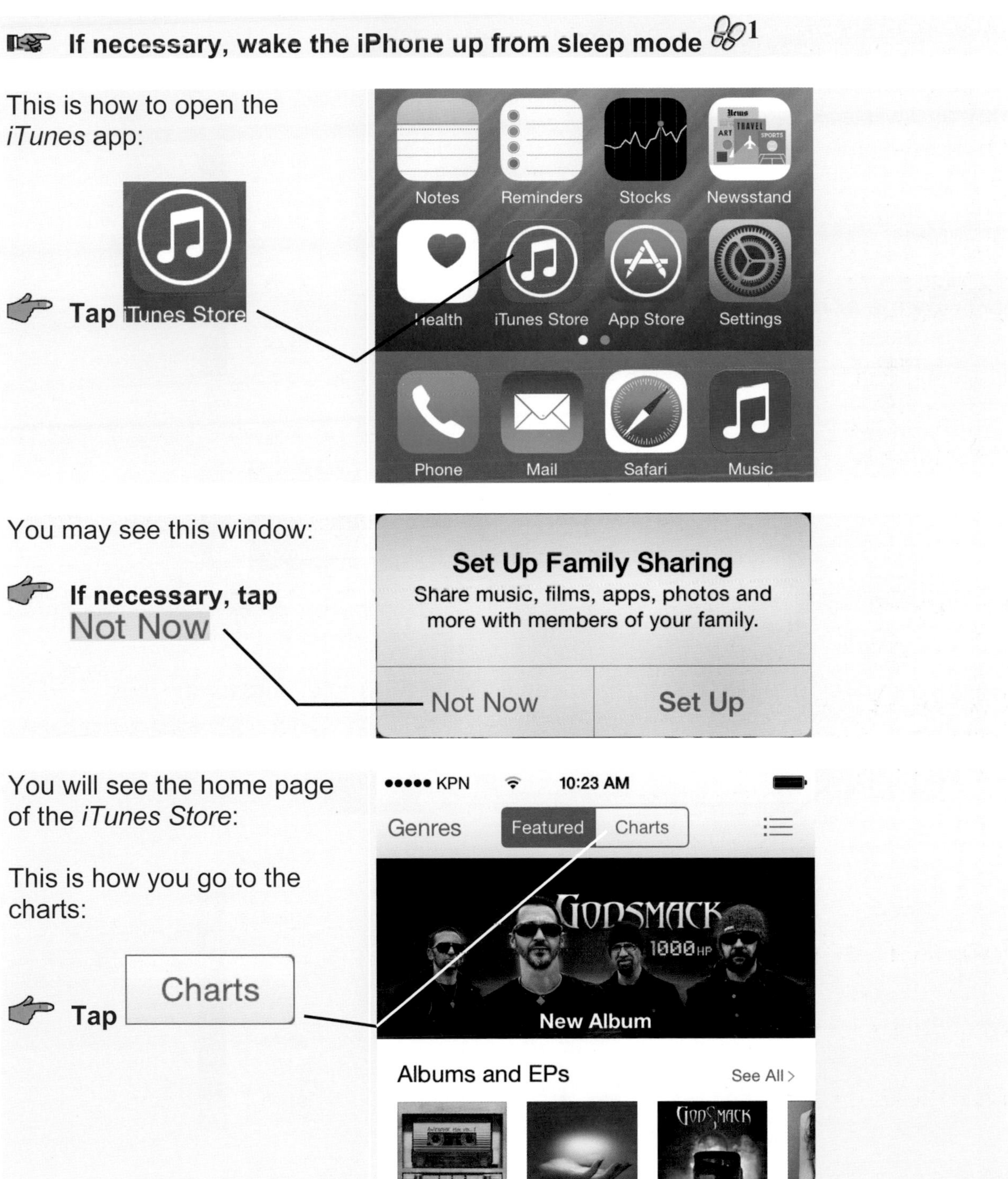

If necessary, wake the iPhone up from sleep mode 1
This is how to open the *iTunes* app:
Tap iTunes Store
Notes
Reminders
Stocks
Newsstand
Health
iTunes Store
App Store
Settings
Phone
Mail
Safari
Music
You may see this window:
If necessary, tap Not Now
Set Up Family Sharing
Share music, films, apps, photos and more with members of your family.
Not Now
Set Up
You will see the home page of the *iTunes Store*:
This is how you go to the charts:
Tap Charts
KPN
10:23 AM
Genres
Featured
Charts
GODSMACK
1000HP
New Album
Albums and EPs
See All >

Please note:

The *iTunes Store* changes almost daily. The home page and the current artist or album selection will be different from the screenshots shown in this book.

You will see the most purchased songs:

These charts change every day and will look different on your own screen.

This is how to view the rest of the chart:

Swipe across the screen from right to left

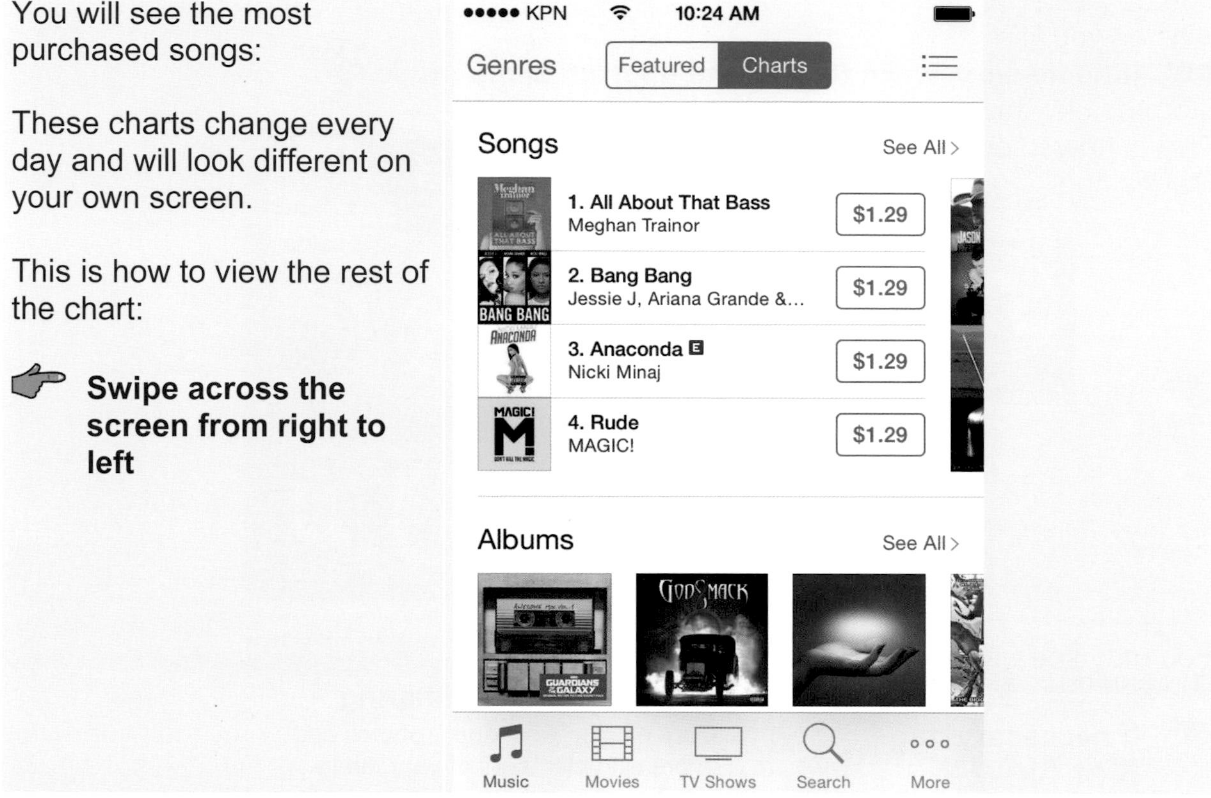

Before you decide to buy a song, you can listen to a sample. Just try it:

Tap the picture next to the song

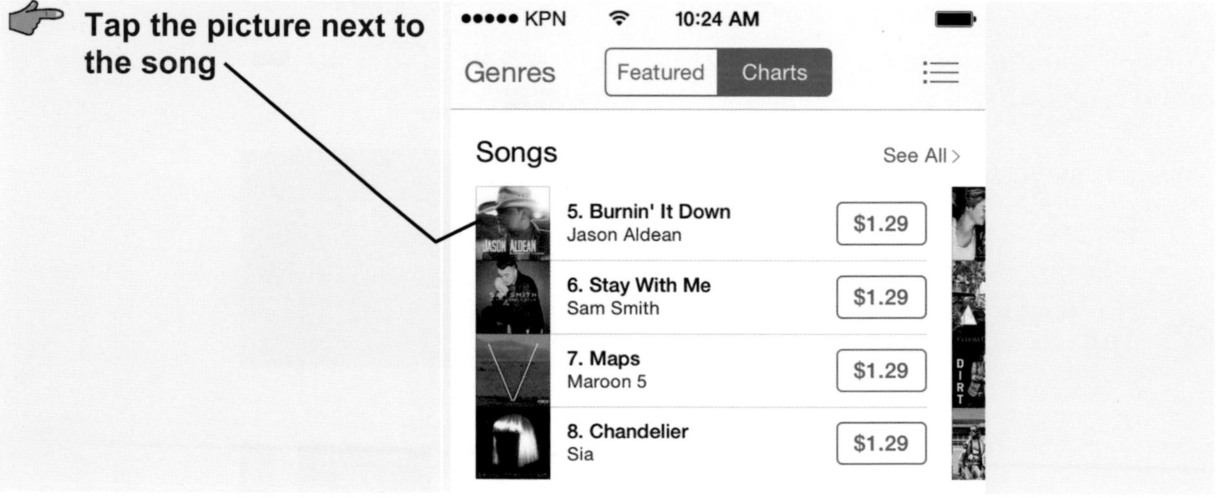

The clip will be played. Here you can see that playback of the song is in process:

You can listen to as many clips as you like.

Stop the playback:

Tap

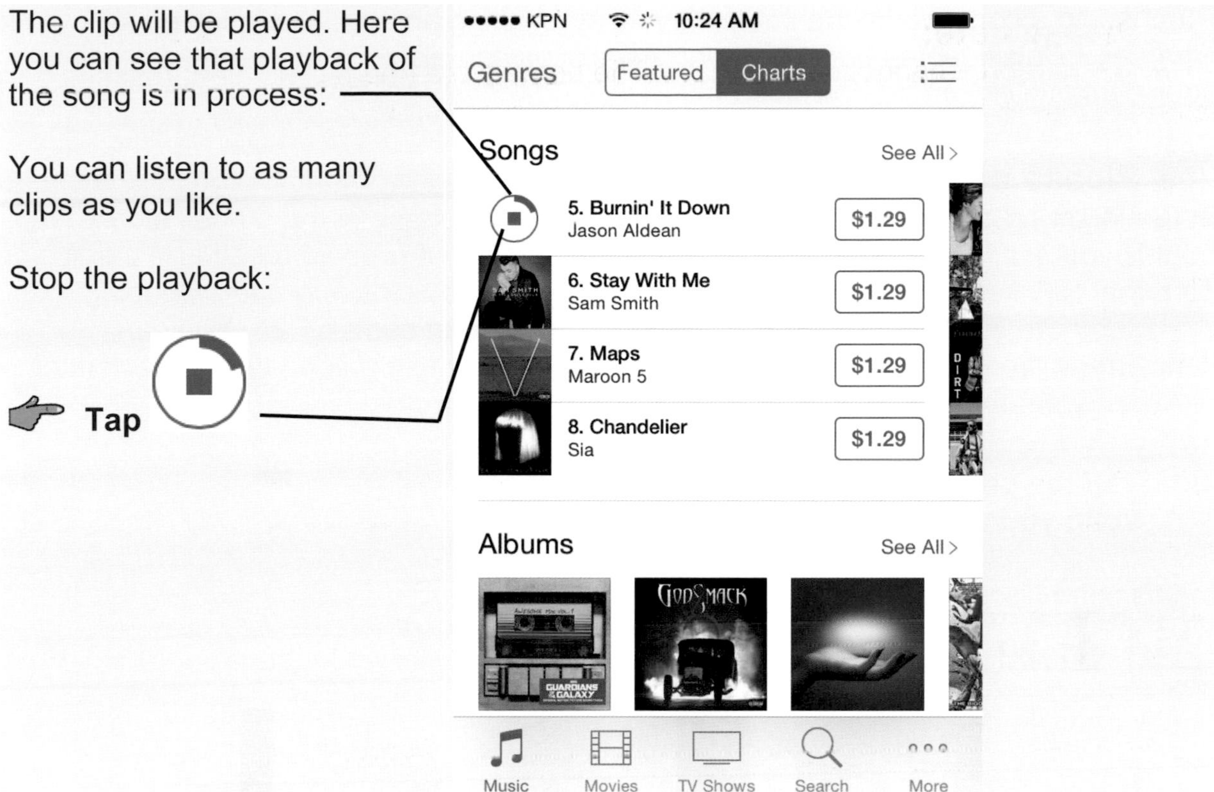

You can also search for a song:

At the bottom of the screen:

Tap Search

Type the name of an artist

Tap the artist

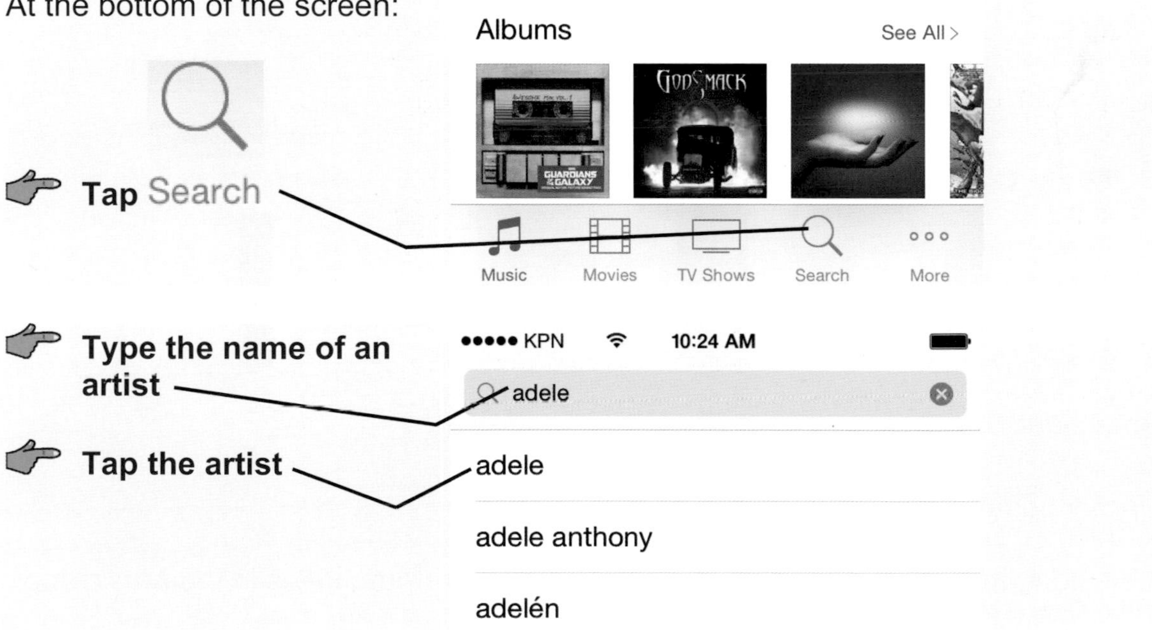

Purchasing a song works the same way as purchasing an app, as explained in *Chapter 7 Downloading and Managing Apps*. You can also use the prepaid credit on your *iTunes Gift Card* to download music.

Please note:

In the following section, we explain how to make a purchase in the *iTunes* store. To do this yourself, you need to have an *Apple ID* and some prepaid credit or a credit card that is linked to your *Apple ID*. Read *Chapter 7 Downloading and Managing Apps* for more information. We will purchase a song that costs $1.29. You can simply read the instructions so you will be able to purchase a song or an album later on when you are ready.

Tap the price by the song you want to buy

In this example, a single song costs $1.29. But these prices may change.

Tap BUY SONG

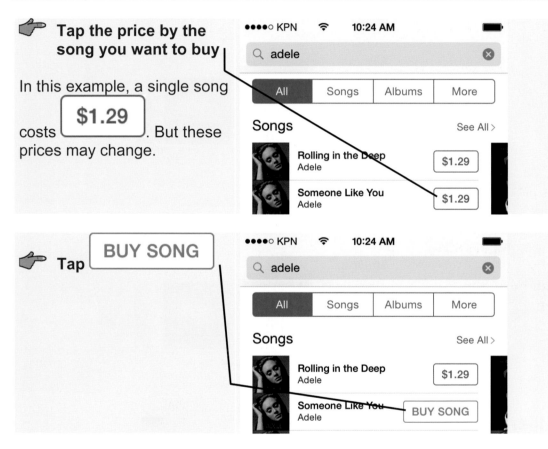

You may need to sign in with your *Apple ID*:

If necessary, sign in with your *Apple ID* 87

After the song has been downloaded, you can view your purchases in the *Music* app:

Go to the home screen 10

9.4 Playing Music with the Music App

This is how you play a song:

☞ **Open the *Music* app** [3]

At the bottom of the screen:

👉 **Tap** Songs

👉 **Tap a title, for example**
Someone Like You

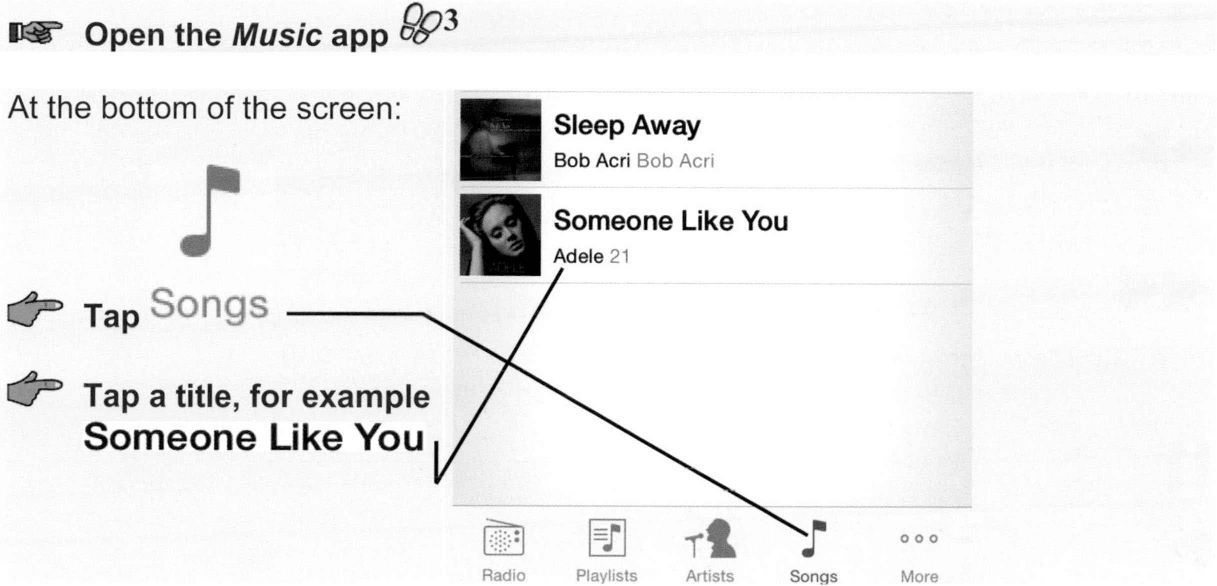

The song is played.

You will see various control buttons for playing the song:

👉 **If necessary, tap the screen**

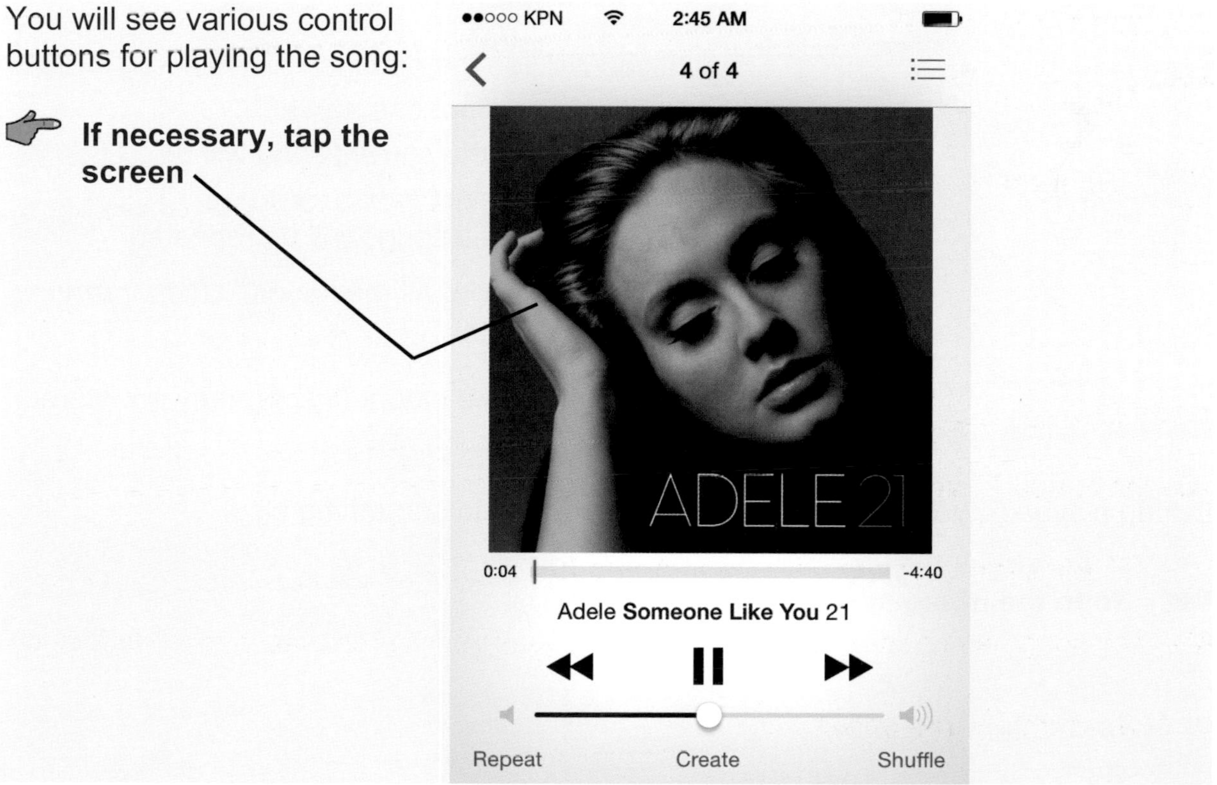

These are the functions of the control buttons:

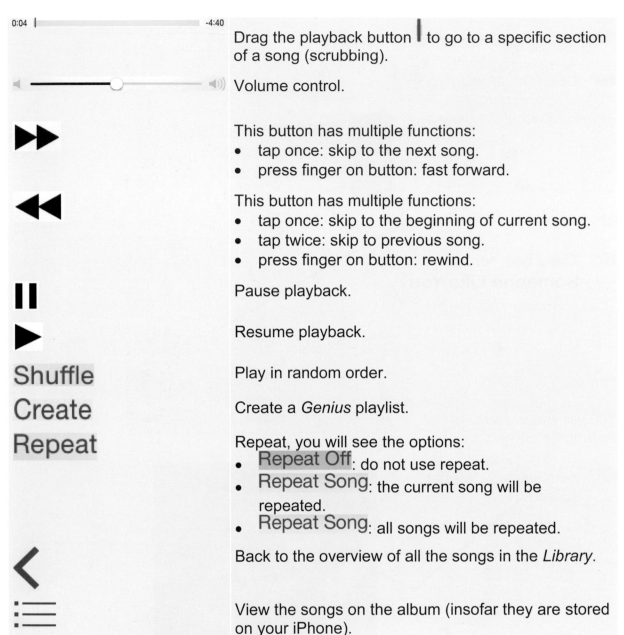

0:04 -4:40	Drag the playback button to go to a specific section of a song (scrubbing).
	Volume control.
	This button has multiple functions: • tap once: skip to the next song. • press finger on button: fast forward.
	This button has multiple functions: • tap once: skip to the beginning of current song. • tap twice: skip to previous song. • press finger on button: rewind.
	Pause playback.
	Resume playback.
Shuffle	Play in random order.
Create	Create a *Genius* playlist.
Repeat	Repeat, you will see the options: • Repeat Off: do not use repeat. • Repeat Song: the current song will be repeated. • Repeat Song: all songs will be repeated.
	Back to the overview of all the songs in the *Library*.
	View the songs on the album (insofar they are stored on your iPhone).

During playback, you can leave the *Music* app and do something else:

☞ **Go to the home screen** 10

The music is still played. You can still display the audio controls even when working with another app:

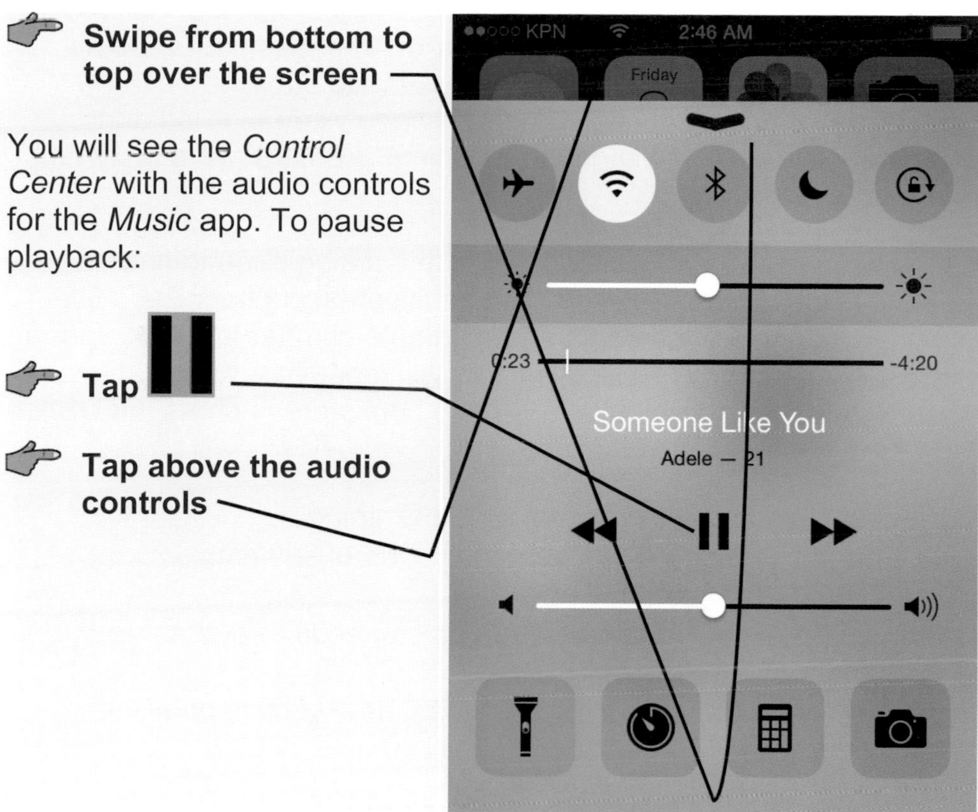

Swipe from bottom to top over the screen

You will see the *Control Center* with the audio controls for the *Music* app. To pause playback:

Tap ▮▮

Tap above the audio controls

You will see the home screen again.

If you want, you can put the iPhone into sleep mode [2]

You have reached the end of this book. In this book you have learned how to use the iPhone. Now you can start working with the apps and explore the iPhone's many other options.

On the website accompanying this book you will find a bonus chapter. You can learn how to work with *iCloud*, one of the most recent developments from Apple, with the *Bonus Chapter iCloud*. *iCloud* is a cloud storage and cloud computing service which offers you 5GB of free storage space (as of September 2014). Here you can save your photos, music, apps, contacts and calendars. This storage method allows you to keep everything up to date by managing these files from one central location and collectively syncing them to all of your devices, such as an iPod touch, iPhone, iPad, a Mac or *Windows* computer. You can read how to open these bonus chapters in *Appendix B Opening Bonus Chapters* at the end of this book.

9.5 Visual Steps

By now you will have noticed that the Visual Steps method is the quickest and most efficient way to learn more about computing and software. All books published by Visual Steps use this same method. In various series, we have published a large number of books on a wide variety of topics, including *Windows*, *Mac,* iPad and iPhone, Samsung Galaxy Tab, photo editing, video editing, (free) software programs such as *Picasa* and many other topics.

On the **www.visualsteps.com** website you can click the Catalog page to find an overview of all the Visual Steps titles, including an extensive description. Each title allows you to preview the full table of contents and a sample chapter in a PDF format. In this way, you can quickly determine if a specific title will meet your expectations. All titles can be ordered online and are also available in bookstores across the USA, Canada, United Kingdom, Australia and New Zealand.

Furthermore, this website offers these extras, among other things:

- free computer guides and booklets (PDF files) on all sorts of subjects;
- frequently asked questions and their answers;
- information on the free Computer Certificate that you can acquire at the certificate's website www.ccforseniors.com;
- a free notify-me service: receive an email as soon as a new book is published.

9.6 Exercises

To be able to quickly apply the things you have learned, you can work through these exercises. Have you forgotten how to do something? Use the numbers next to the footsteps [1] to look up the item in the appendix *How Do I Do That Again?* This appendix can be found at the end of the book.

Exercise 1: Listen to Music

In this exercise you are going to listen to music on your iPhone.

- If necessary, wake the iPhone up from sleep mode or turn it on. [2]
- Open the *Music* app. [3]
- Open the list of song titles on your iPhone. [71]
- Play the first song. [68]
- Turn the volume up. [61]
- Skip to the next song. [60]
- Repeat the current song. [48]
- Disable the repeat function. [31]
- Enable the shuffle function. [21]
- Skip to the next song. [60]
- Disable the shuffle function. [15]
- Go back to the list of song titles. [12]
- Pause playback. [6]
- Go to the home screen. [10]
- If you want, put the iPhone into sleep mode. [2]

9.7 Background Information

Dictionary

Apple ID	A combination of a user name and a password. You need an *Apple ID* to use *FaceTime* as well as for downloading music from the *iTunes Store*, or apps from the *App Store*, for example.
Genius playlist	A generated list of songs based on a specific music selection that sound good together. The *iTunes Genius* feature builds this list automatically by gathering anonymously acquired information about your own music library and other libraries from *iTunes*.
iTunes	A program with which you can manage the contents of the iPhone. You can also use *iTunes* to listen to music, view videos, and import CDs. In *iTunes* you will also find the *iTunes Store* and the *App Store*.
iTunes Store	An online store where you can purchase and download music, movies, podcasts and audio books.
Music	An app that plays music.
Playlist	A collection of songs, ordered in a certain way.

Source: User Guide iPhone

9.8 Tips

 **Tip**

Import CDs into iTunes

You can also transfer songs from a CD to your iPhone. But first, you will need to import these songs into *iTunes*. From there you can transfer the songs to your iPhone, as described in *section 9.2 Copying Music to Your iPhone*.

Open *iTunes* on your computer 11

Insert a music CD from your own collection into the CD/DVD drive on your computer

You may see a windows like this:

Click the desired cd

Click OK

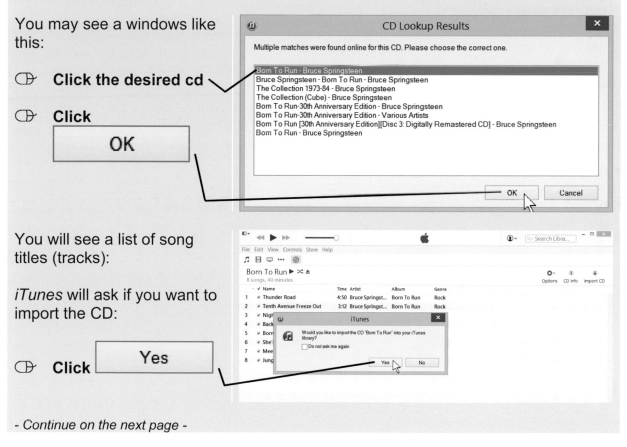

You will see a list of song titles (tracks):

iTunes will ask if you want to import the CD:

Click Yes

- Continue on the next page -

By the track that is currently imported, you will see this symbol in the list :

In the information pane you will also see which track is currently being imported and how long the operation will take:

By default, all tracks will be selected, so they will all be imported. If you want, you can uncheck the boxes next to the tracks you do not want to import.

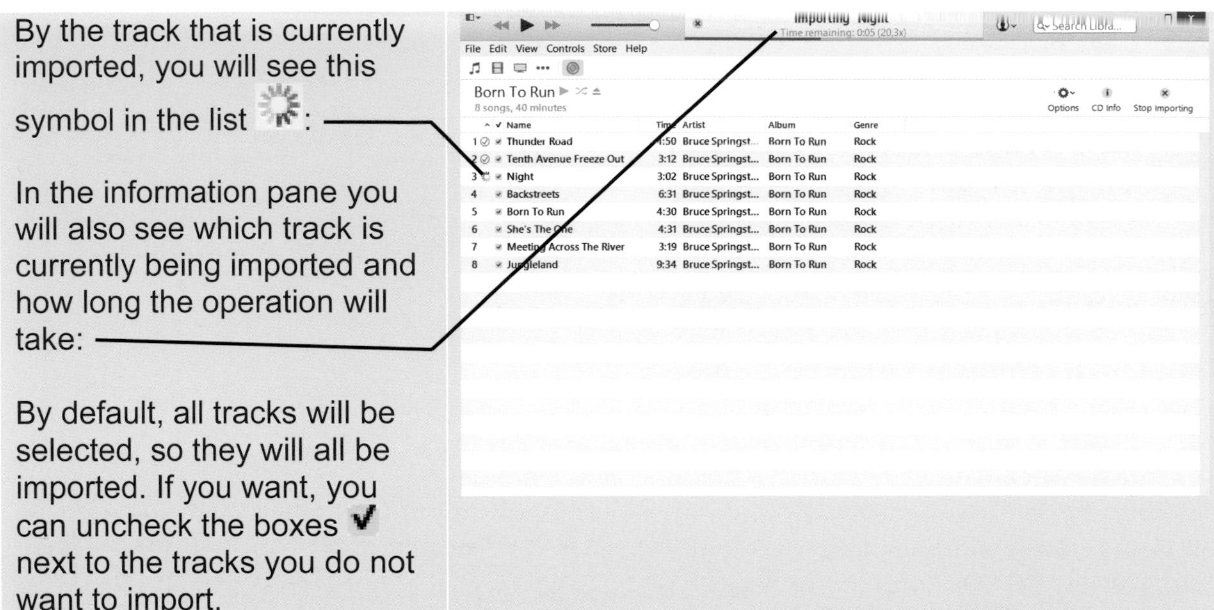

After the CD has been imported, you will hear a sound signal. All tracks are now marked with a . This means the import operation has been successfully concluded. Now the songs have been added to the *iTunes Library*.

Tip

Delete a song from the iPhone

On your iPhone you can also delete songs in the *Music* app. You can do this while in the *Songs* or *Artists* view. This is how you delete a song:

If necessary, tap

At the bottom, tap

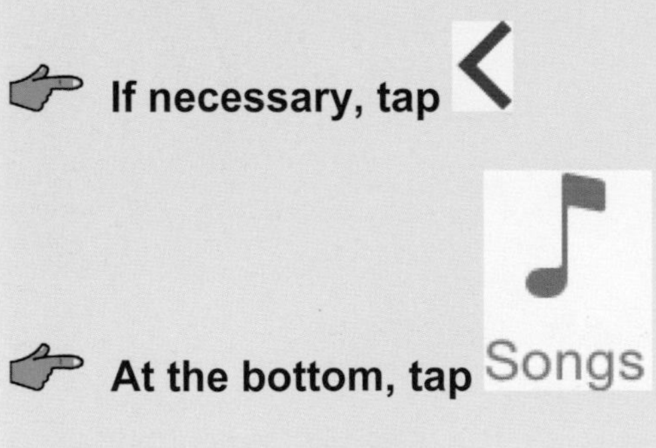

- Continue on the next page -

By the song you want to delete:

Swipe your finger across the desired song from right to left

Tap Delete

Tip

Create a playlist

A useful function in the *Music* app is the option of creating playlists. A playlist will allow you to list all your favorite songs and arrange them in any order you like. Afterwards you can play the playlist over and over again. This is how you create a new playlist in the *Music* app. At the bottom left of the screen:

Tap Playlists

To create a new playlist:

Tap New Playlist...

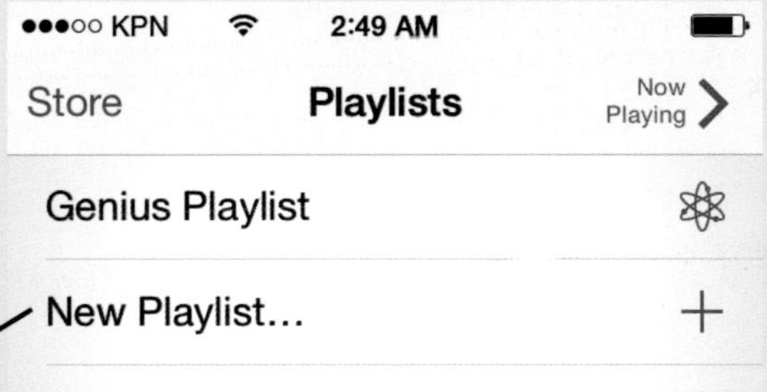

●●●○○ KPN 2:49 AM
Store Playlists Now Playing
Genius Playlist
New Playlist...

Enter a name for the new playlist:

Type a name, for example: `Favorite songs`

Tap **Save**

New Playlist
Enter a name for this playlist.
Favorite Songs
Cancel Save

- Continue on the next page -

Now you can add songs to the playlist:

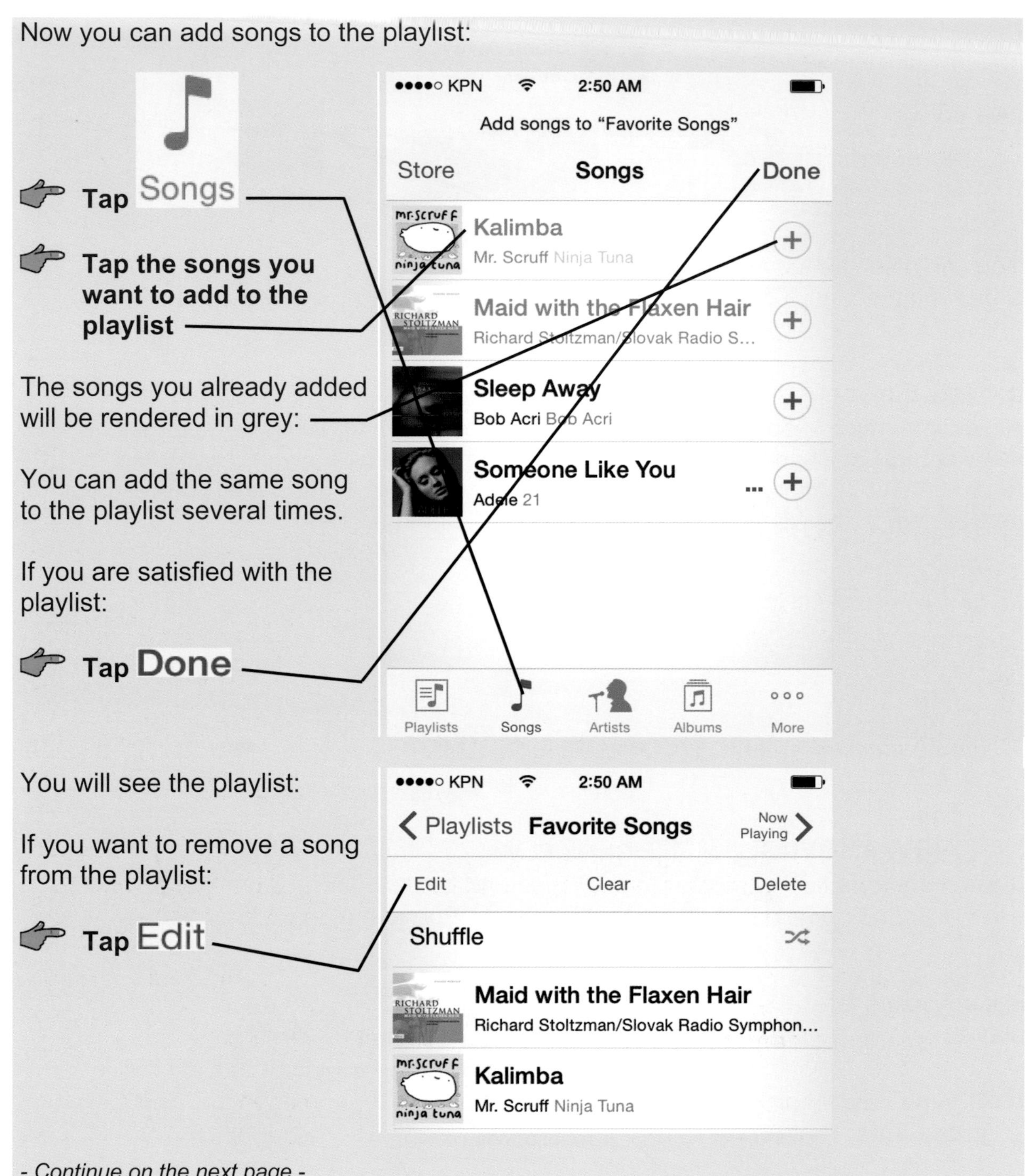
Tap Songs
Tap the songs you want to add to the playlist
The songs you already added will be rendered in grey:
You can add the same song to the playlist several times.
If you are satisfied with the playlist:
Tap Done
You will see the playlist:
If you want to remove a song from the playlist:
Tap Edit
●●●●○ KPN 2:50 AM
Add songs to "Favorite Songs"
Store
Songs
Done
Kalimba
Mr. Scruff Ninja Tuna
Maid with the Flaxen Hair
Richard Stoltzman/Slovak Radio S...
Sleep Away
Bob Acri Bob Acri
Someone Like You
Adele 21
Playlists
Songs
Artists
Albums
More
●●●●○ KPN 2:50 AM
Playlists
Favorite Songs
Now Playing
Edit
Clear
Delete
Shuffle
Maid with the Flaxen Hair
Richard Stoltzman/Slovak Radio Symphon...
Kalimba
Mr. Scruff Ninja Tuna

- Continue on the next page -

By the song, tap ⊖

You will see the remove option:

Tap Remove

You can also change the order of the songs. To move a song:

By the song, drag ═ **to the desired spot in the list**

Tap Done

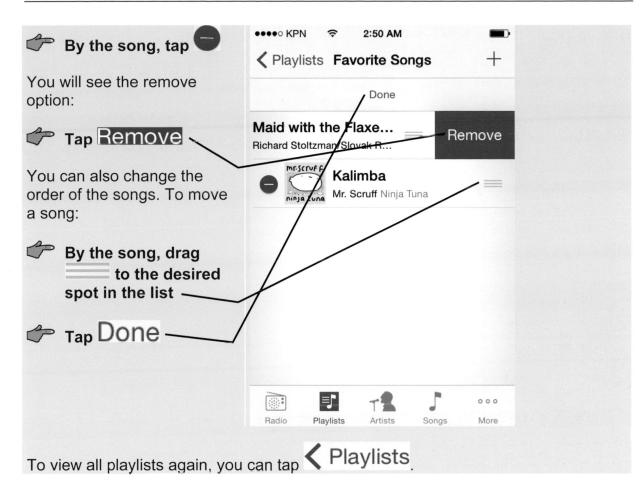

To view all playlists again, you can tap ❮ Playlists.

Tip

Automatic downloads through iCloud

You can automatically transfer music, apps and books you have purchased on your iPhone to other devices, such as an iPad or an iPod touch, and vice versa.

In the free *Bonus Chapter iCloud* you can read more about this useful function. You will find this bonus chapter on the website accompanying this book: **www.visualsteps.com/iphone8**

In *Appendix B Opening Bonus Chapters* you can read how to open this bonus chapter.

9.8 Notes

Write your notes down here.

Appendix A. How Do I Do That Again?

The actions and exercises in this book are marked with footsteps: 1
In this appendix you can look up the numbers of the footsteps and read how to carry out a certain action once more.

1 **Wake up/unlock the iPhone from sleep mode or turn it on**
Wake up from sleep mode:

- Press the Home button 

Or:

- Press the on/off button
- Swipe across the screen from left to right

If you have set up a four-digit passcode:

- Enter the code

Turn the iPhone on:

- Press and hold the on/off button pressed in until you see the Apple-logo
- Swipe across the screen from left to right

If you have set up a four-digit passcode:

- Enter the code

To unlock the SIM card:

- Tap **Unlock**
- Type the passcode
- Tap OK

2 **Put the iPhone into sleep mode/lock or turn it off**
Put into sleep mode:

- Press the on/off button

Turn the iPhone off:

- Press the on/off button until you see

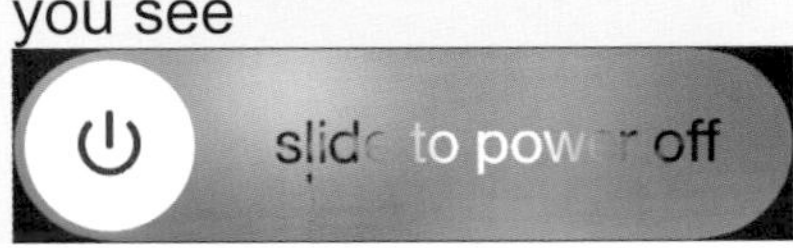

- Drag the slider to the right
- If necessary, type your passcode

3 **Open an app**

- Tap the icon and name of the app, for example, 

4 **Open a website**
On a Windows 8.1 computer, on the desktop:

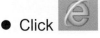

- Click

On a Windows 7 or Vista computer:

- Click 
- Click All Programs
- Click Internet Explorer

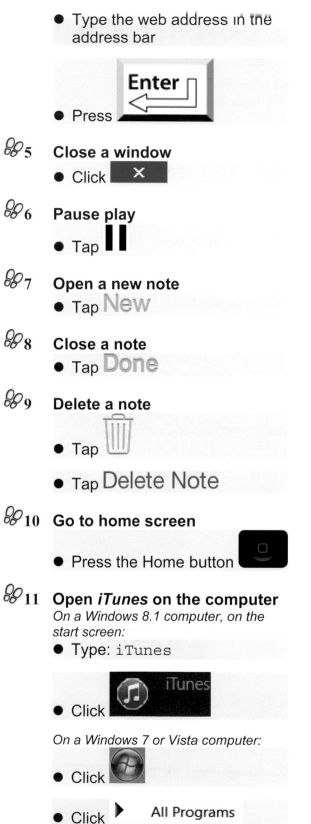

- Type the web address in the address bar
- Press 

5 **Close a window**
- Click ×

6 **Pause play**
- Tap II

7 **Open a new note**
- Tap New

8 **Close a note**
- Tap Done

9 **Delete a note**
- Tap 
- Tap Delete Note

10 **Go to home screen**
- Press the Home button 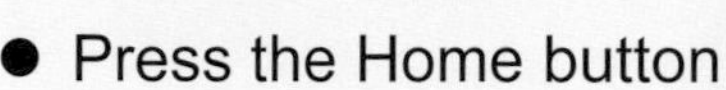 

11 **Open *iTunes* on the computer**
On a Windows 8.1 computer, on the start screen:
- Type: `iTunes`
- Click 

On a Windows 7 or Vista computer:
- Click 
- Click ▸ All Programs
- Click iTunes
- Click iTunes

12 **Return to the *Library***
- Tap 

13 **Add contact information**
- Tap the desired field, for example, Last
- Type the information

14 **Add a contact**
- Tap 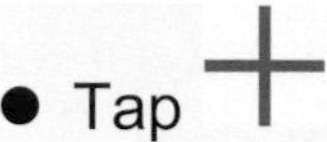
- Tap a field
- Type the information
- Repeat this action for all the fields you want to use
- Tap Done

15 **Disable shuffle function**
- Tap Shuffle All

16 **Call someone**
- If necessary, tap Keypad
- Type the phone number
- Tap 

17 Disconnect the call

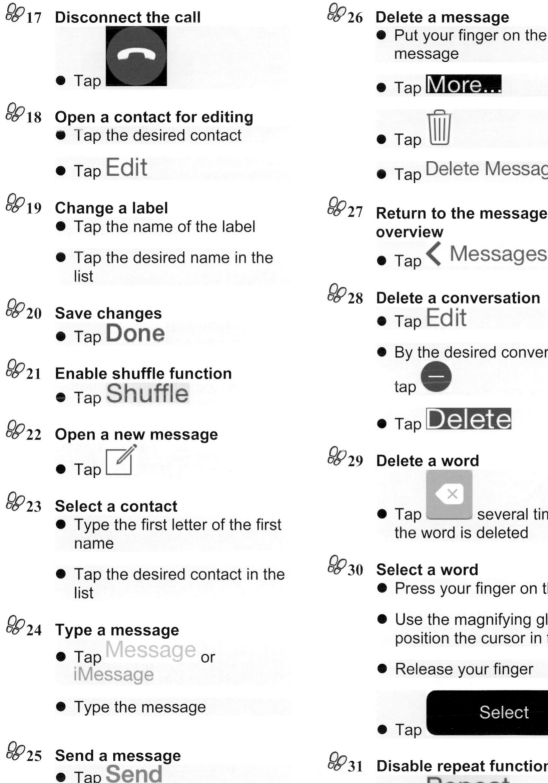

- Tap 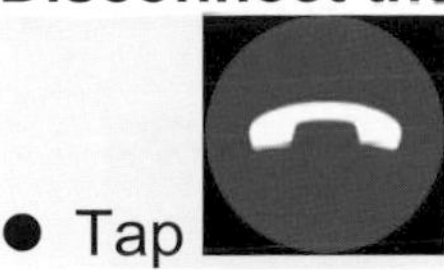

18 Open a contact for editing

- Tap the desired contact
- Tap Edit

19 Change a label

- Tap the name of the label
- Tap the desired name in the list

20 Save changes

- Tap Done

21 Enable shuffle function

- Tap Shuffle

22 Open a new message

- Tap

23 Select a contact

- Type the first letter of the first name
- Tap the desired contact in the list

24 Type a message

- Tap Message or iMessage
- Type the message

25 Send a message

- Tap Send

26 Delete a message

- Put your finger on the message
- Tap More...
- Tap
- Tap Delete Message

27 Return to the message overview

- Tap < Messages

28 Delete a conversation

- Tap Edit
- By the desired conversation, tap
- Tap Delete

29 Delete a word

- Tap several times, until the word is deleted

30 Select a word

- Press your finger on the word
- Use the magnifying glass to position the cursor in the word
- Release your finger
- Tap 

31 Disable repeat function

- Tap Repeat

- Tap Repeat Off

32 **Open a new email message**
- Tap

33 **Type an email address**
- Tap To:
- Type your email address

34 **Add a subject**
- Tap Subject:
- Type the subject

35 **Type text in an email message**
- If necessary, tap the blank area where you want to type your message
- Type the text

36 **Refuse correction**
- Tap the correction that is shown between the double quotes

37 **Go to a new line**
- Tap return

38 **Copy a selected word**
- Tap Copy

39 **Paste a copied word**
- Put your finger on the spot where you want to paste the word
- Release when you see the magnifying glass
- Tap Paste

40 **Send an email message**
- Tap Send

41 **View incoming messages**
- If necessary, tap Inbox or tap your account's name
- Tap the message

42 **Delete a message**
- Tap

43 **View *Trash* folder**
- Tap < Mailboxes
- Tap Trash

44 **Permanently delete a message**
- Tap Edit
- Tap the message
- Tap Delete

45 **Open *Inbox* folder**
- Tap < Mailboxes
- Tap Inbox

46 **Check for new email messages**
- Swipe your finger downwards over the screen

47 Safely disconnect the iPhone
- By the iPhone's name, click ⏏
- Disconnect the iPhone

48 Repeat the current song
- Tap Repeat
- Tap Repeat Song

49 Open a website
- Tap the address bar
- If necessary, tap ⊗
- Type the web address
- Tap Go

50 Scroll downwards
- Swipe your finger upwards over the screen

51 Quickly scroll downwards
- Quickly flick your finger upwards over the screen

52 Return to top of web page
- Tap the status bar twice

53 Zoom in
- Double-tap the page

Or:
- Move your thumb and index finger away from each other on the screen

54 Zoom out
- Double-tap the page

Or:
- Move your thumb and index finger to each other on the screen

55 Add a bookmark
- Tap 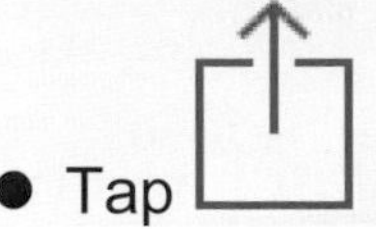
- Tap  Add Bookmark
- Tap ⊗
- Type a name for the bookmark
- Tap Save

56 Open a link
- Tap the link

57 Open a link on a new tab
- Put your finger on the link
- Tap Open in New Tab

58 View recently used apps
- Press the Home button twice, in rapid succession 

59 Switch to a recently used app
- Tap the desired app

60 Skip to the next song
- Tap ▶▶

61 Turn up the volume

- Drag the volume control slider to the right

62 Flip to current day

- Tap Today

63 Flip to day after tomorrow

- Swipe from right to left over the screen until you see the desired day

64 Open a new event

- Tap +

65 Add name and location for an event

- Tap the desired field
- Type the information

66 Change start and end time

- Tap Starts
- Turn the wheels to change the starting time
- Tap Ends
- Flick the wheels to change the end time

67 Save changes

- Tap Add

68 Play a song

- Tap the song

69 Add a task

- If necessary, tap the list
- Tap the first line
- Type a description for the task
- Tap Done

70 Set a reminder for a task

- Tap the task
- Tap ⓘ
- By Remind me on a day, drag the slider to the right
- Tap the suggested date
- Turn the wheels to change the date and time
- Tap Done

71 Open a list of songs

From the last played song:

- Tap <

From the home screen:

- Tap Songs

72 Find current location

- Tap

73 Change view

- Tap ⓘ
- Tap the desired view

74 Find a location

- Tap the search box

- If necessary, tap
- Type the desired keyword
- Tap 

75 **Stop slideshow**
- Tap the screen

76 **Start a slideshow**
- Tap 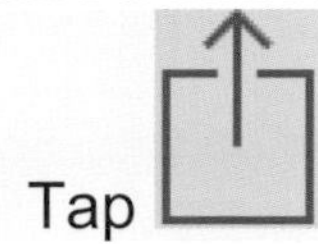
- Tap Next
- Tap 

- Tap Start Slideshow

77 **Flip to the previous photo**
- Swipe across the screen from left to right

78 **Open *Spotlight***
On the home screen:
- Swipe downwards across the screen a bit, halfway the screen

79 **Search in *Spotlight***
- If necessary, tap
- Type the desired keyword

80 **Open the *App Store***
- Tap 

81 **Flip to the second page**
- Swipe across the screen from right to left

82 **Move an app to the home screen / second page**
- Drag the app to the left or right side of the screen

When you see wanted screen:
- Release

83 **Make apps jiggle**
- Press your finger on a random app for a few seconds

84 **Remove an app from a folder**
- If necessary, tap the folder
- Drag the app out of the folder

85 **Search for an app in the *App Store***

- If necessary, tap Search
- If necessary, tap Not Now
- Tap the search box
- If necessary, tap
- Type your keyword

- Tap 

- Tap the desired search result

86 **Download a free app**
- By the desired app, tap FREE
- Tap INSTALL

87 **Sign in with *Apple ID***
- Type your password
- Tap OK

Or if you had signed off:
- Tap Use Existing Apple ID
- Type your email address
- Type your password
- Tap OK

88 **Flip to the first page**
- Swipe across the screen from left to right

89 **Move an app**
- Drag the app to the desired position

90 **Add apps to a folder**
- Drag one app over the other

91 **Close a folder**
- Tap below the folder

92 **Fix apps**
- Press

93 **Open a folder**
- Tap the folder

94 **Delete an app**
- By the app you want to delete, tap
- Tap Delete

95 **Flip to the next photo**
- Swipe across the screen from right to left

96 **Open a photo**
- Tap the desired album
- Tap the photo

97 **Switch to the camera on the front or on the back**
- Tap 

98 **Zoom in**
- Move your thumb and index finger away from each other, on the screen
- Drag the slider to the right

99 **Focus**
- Tap the object on which you want to focus

100 **Take a photo**
- Tap 

Appendix B. Opening Bonus Chapters

On the website accompanying this book you will find several bonus chapters in PDF format. You can open these files (on a pc) with *Adobe Reader,* free software that lets you open, view and print PDF files. Here is how to open these files from the website:

Go to www.visualsteps.com/iphone8 4

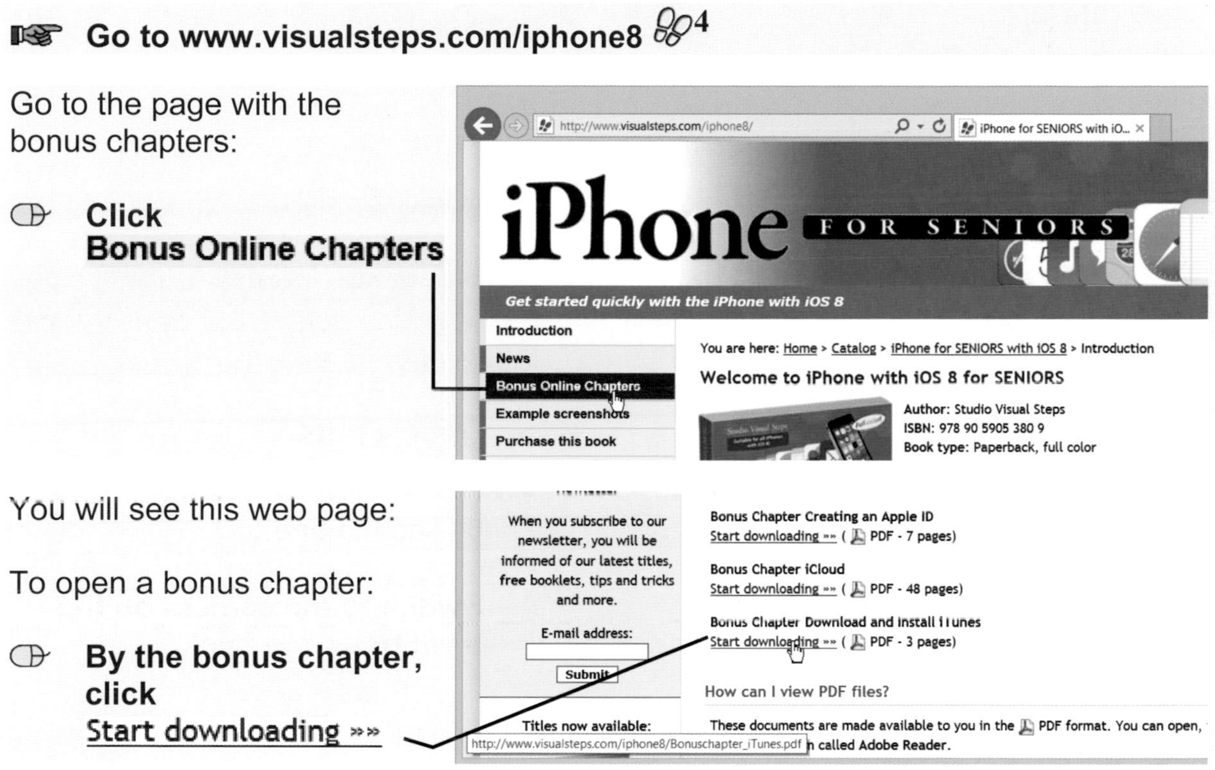

Go to the page with the bonus chapters:

Click **Bonus Online Chapters**

You will see this web page:

To open a bonus chapter:

By the bonus chapter, click Start downloading »»

The PDF files are protected with a password. To open the PDF files you will need to enter this password:

Type: `96548`

Click OK

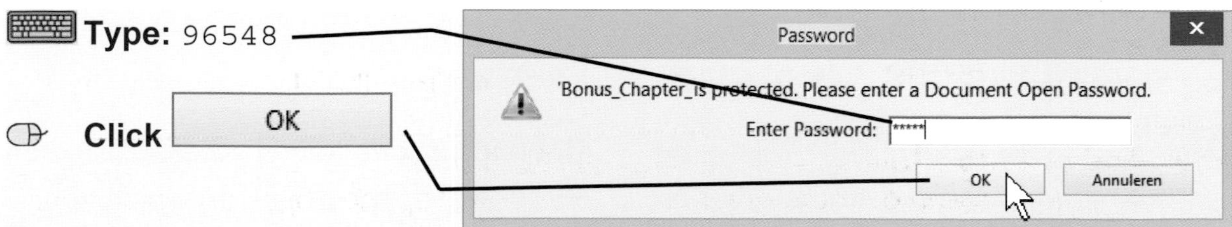

You will see the bonus chapter. You can read the chapter. Use the scroll bars to go to the previous and next page. You can also print the file by clicking the button.

Close all windows 5

Appendix C. Index